Church of England Record Society

Volume 12

EVANGELICALISM IN THE CHURCH OF ENGLAND *c.*1790–*c.*1890

A MISCELLANY

Between the end of the eighteenth century and the end of the nineteenth evangelicalism came to exercise a profound influence over British religious and social life – an influence unmatched by even the Oxford movement. The four texts published here provide different perspectives on the relationship between evangelicalism and the Church during that time, illustrating the diversity of the tradition. Hannah More's correspondence during the Blagdon controversy illuminates the struggles of evangelicals at the end of the eighteenth century, as she attempted to establish schools for poor children. The charges of Bishops Ryder and Ryle in 1816 and 1881 respectively reveal the views of evangelicals who, at either end of the nineteenth century, had a forum for expressing their views from the pinnacle of the church establishment. The major text, the undergraduate diary of Francis Chavasse (1865–8), also written by a future bishop, provides a fascinating insight into the mind of a young evangelical at Oxford, struggling with his conscience and his calling. Each text is presented with an introduction and notes.

Dr MARK SMITH is Lecturer in the Modern History of Christianity at King's College London; Dr STEPHEN TAYLOR is Reader in Eighteenth-Century History at the University of Reading.

EVANGELICALISM IN THE CHURCH OF ENGLAND *c.*1790–*c.*1890

A MISCELLANY

EDITED BY

Mark Smith and Stephen Taylor

THE BOYDELL PRESS

CHURCH OF ENGLAND RECORD SOCIETY

First published 2004

A Church of England Record Society publication
Published by The Boydell Press
an imprint of Boydell & Brewer Ltd
PO Box 9, Woodbridge, Suffolk IP12 3DF, UK
and of Boydell & Brewer Inc.
668 Mt Hope Avenue, Rochester, NY 14620, USA
website: www.boydellandbrewer.com

ISBN 1 84383 105 8

ISSN 1351–3087

Series information is printed at the back of this volume

A catalogue record for this book is available
from the British Library

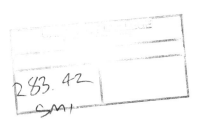

This publication is printed on acid-free paper

Printed in Great Britain by
St Edmundsbury Press Ltd, Bury St Edmunds, Suffolk

For

JOHN WALSH

Contents

Preface

In 1999 the Church of England Record Society published its first miscellany volume under the title *From Cranmer to Davidson*. The appearance of that volume reflected a decision by the Society's Council that the time was appropriate to provide a forum for the publication of shorter documents which could not form volumes by themselves. In putting it together a deliberate decision was made to include material from the reformation to the twentieth century, illuminating aspects of the Church's history across the full chronological range of the Society's remit. In the Preface to that volume I made it clear that the Society was committed to publishing further miscellany volumes, but I also stated that these need not necessarily take the form of *From Cranmer to Davidson*. The present volume is the Society's first 'themed' miscellany volume, focusing on a particular period or issue in the history of the Church. I am particularly glad that it has been possible to put together a volume on evangelicalism in the late eighteenth and nineteenth centuries, as it enables us to give some coverage to a period – the nineteenth century – and a theme – evangelicalism, which hitherto have not received the attention that they merit in the Society's publications. If this volume suggests to any of its readers ideas for further miscellany volumes, the general editor will be very pleased to discuss them.

Over the years I have often found editing to be one of the most enjoyable and rewarding aspects of academic life. This volume has been no exception. I am particularly grateful to Mark Smith – the original idea for this volume was his and it has been an enormous pleasure to co-operate with him in putting the volume together. John Walsh, without doubt the most influential historian of eighteenth-century evangelicalism over the last fifty years, was as generous as ever with advice when the project was at the planning stage and has remained supportive throughout. Mark and I have also enjoyed working with an excellent group of contributors, all of whom produced texts which were models of both scholarship and professionalism. They met often tight deadlines without complaint, have been unfailingly helpful in answering queries and kindly generated indexes to their contributions. I am once more grateful to Meg Davies for relieving me of the burden of copy editing the text. Mark Smith wishes to record his thanks to the earl of Harrowby for permission to reproduce material from the Harrowby papers at Sandon Hall and to the British Academy for making a research award which facilitated the completion of the project.

Stephen Taylor
September 2004

Introduction

The evangelical tradition has been, and in the twenty-first century continues to be, one of the most vital expressions of christianity within the Church of England. Since its rise in the eighteenth century, modern evangelical anglicanism has provoked opposition and support, applause and exasperation in almost equal measure. It has exercised a strong appeal for clerics and laypeople, men and women, adults and children. Its adherents have exhibited a wide diversity of methodologies, theologies and spiritualities. They have often disagreed fiercely among themselves while sharing sufficient in common to enable them to recognize each other as belonging within the evangelical fold. Although the Church of England has provided a home for evangelical christianity, the movement has also overflowed the boundaries of the Church. The relationship between the two has, therefore, been marked by a remarkable degree of complexity. Some late Hanoverian high churchmen, for example, opposed evangelical initiatives because they might provide a means for dissenters to subvert the establishment. Conversely, others supported them because they might provide a way for dissenters to rejoin the Church. On the other side of the fence some evangelical anglicans may have continued in the Church pragmatically because they thought it would provide the widest scope for the ministry to which they had been called – it was simply the best boat from which to fish. Others certainly supported the Church conscientiously as the primary means providentially ordained by God for the conversion and pastoral care of the English people. They supported it too because they felt it to be their natural home. Evangelicals were, after all, the heirs of its reformers and theologians, of Cranmer and Hooker. Their doctrines were its doctrines – to be read in its articles and homilies. Indeed for some, evangelicals were *the* true anglicans, exhibiting the Church's expression of the faith in its purest form. No short collection of documents can hope to do justice to a tradition of such size and diversity. Neither can it claim to be representative. What is offered here is instead a sample illustrative of some aspects of that diversity. It covers a period of almost a century from 1799 to 1881 and comprises four different kinds of texts written by rather different kinds of evangelical.

The first of these texts is a collection of manuscript correspondence relating to the 'Blagdon controversy' of 1799–1801. The controversy arose from the attempts of a leading evangelical lay woman, Hannah More, to establish, in the classic mode of later Hanoverian philanthropy, schools for the poor children of her neighbourhood in the Mendips. The correspondence illustrates the depth of suspicion that such lay evangelical initiatives could arouse, especially in a period still haunted by the threat of European revolution. It also shows the tensions that could arise as a result of the close connection between evangelical members of the establishment and nonconformist evangelicals – in this case both the recently separated methodists and the independent William Jay. However, the text is also illustrative of the firmness with which evangelicals of the school of More and Wilberforce remained attached to the Church of England and their capacity to generate support from ostensibly unlikely quarters. In this case the most prominent of these unlikely supporters was the high church bishop of Lincoln, George Pretyman Tomline, author of the *Refutation of calvinism*.

The second document is a single printed text: the primary visitation charge of Henry Ryder as bishop of Gloucester. Its most obvious significance is its status as the first formal episcopal statement by a modern exponent of the evangelical tradition. It illustrates some of the continuities in both interest and theology between the evangelical and high church schools of the later Hanoverian period – even in areas of controversy. It also reveals some striking differences. These are most apparent in the tone of the charge which took the form of a pastoral exhortation rather than that of the theological disquisition or business statement which was characteristic of most other contemporary charges. Ryder's charge is also illustrative of some of the tensions intrinsic to evangelical episcopacy in the early nineteenth century. Ryder was a man clearly identified with a controverted perspective within the Church and possibly regarded with suspicion on his entry into the diocese. In this context, he sought to deal with ecclesiastical controversy in an even-handed 'diocesan' manner while continuing firmly to maintain his own position on the issues in question.

The third and longest text in the collection is a previously unpublished manuscript: the diary of Francis Chavasse for the years 1865–8. This, in contrast to the *Charge*, is quintessentially a personal and private rather than a public document. It is significant as a record of the early spiritual development of one of the most prominent evangelical leaders of the later nineteenth- and early twentieth-century Church of England – Chavasse founded Wycliffe Hall in 1877 and became bishop of Liverpool in 1900. It is also significant for the insight it provides into the spiritual world of a particular kind of evangelical in the mid-nineteenth century – thus complementing the existing historiographical interest in tractarian-inspired high-church spirituality. The diary depicts, albeit with a particular undergraduate intensity, the earnest desire for an ever closer walk with God which characterised much of evangelical anglicanism. It shows, especially via Chavasse's practice of the disciplines of self-examination, a concern for the development of holiness conceived as a personal struggle with sin. This struggle was to be undertaken with the help of the grace of God mediated through faith in the atoning work of Christ, the sacraments of the Church and the practice of appropriate spiritual disciplines. Such a perspective places Chavasse in a long-standing anglican evangelical tradition with links both to puritan spirituality and the holy living traditions of eighteenth-century high churchmanship. It contrasts, however, with the growing contemporary evangelical enthusiasm for the possibility that holiness, like justification, might be received by faith, a view popularized by the influential

Mildmay conferences and Keswick conventions. The diary also displays the tensions inherent in the pursuit of holiness amidst the pleasures and temptations of the world and the delicacy of the judgments with which a tender conscience might be faced in the social circumstances of middle-class and undergraduate life. Finally, and perhaps most vividly, the diary portrays the intimate connexion for evangelicals like Chavasse between the development of an interior spirituality and the activism that continued to be characteristic of mid nineteenth-century evangelicalism.

The final document is a text by perhaps the most prominent anglican evangelical of the later nineteenth century – the first bishop of Liverpool, J. C. Ryle. *First words*, Ryle's address to the first Liverpool diocesan conference of 1881, in contrast to the More correspondence and to Ryder's charge, illustrates the increased security of the evangelical position within the Church of England by this time. However, the statement also dates from a period when anglo-catholic and broad church influence was growing within the Church and evangelicalism may have been felt to have passed its peak. It also concerned an issue – diocesan conferences – that had earlier proved controversial in evangelical circles. As a consequence, *First words* shares with the first two documents in the collection a sense of the tensions intrinsic to the relationship between evangelicals, no matter how firmly they adhered to the establishment principle, and the established Church. Like Ryder, John Ryle, in making a statement to his diocese, was concerned that his tone should be diocesan rather than partisan while at the same time choosing to articulate key evangelical priorities in evangelism. Perhaps most significant in this edition of Ryle's address, however, is its recognition of the potential for flexibility and pragmatism in a late nineteenth-century anglican evangelicalism which has acquired an unenviable reputation for rigidity and oppositionalism.

Individually, each of the documents in this collection provides a starting point for an exploration of a particular facet of the evangelical tradition within the Church of England. Taken together, they illustrate changes in the movement itself and in its relationship with the Church. They are also suggestive of the richness of the material that awaits future students of evangelical anglicanism.

1

HANNAH MORE AND THE BLAGDON CONTROVERSY 1799–1802

Edited by
Anne Stott

Introduction

The so-called Blagdon controversy was a pre-emptive strike by some high churchmen against the growing evangelical movement, represented by the writer and philanthropist Hannah More (1745–1833) and her friends in the Clapham sect.[1] For this reason it is a significant moment in the history of the late Georgian Church of England.

In October 1789, partly at the instigation of William Wilberforce, Hannah More and her sister Martha (Patty) (1750–1819) founded a Sunday school at Cheddar near her home at Wrington in Somerset. Other Sunday schools, adult schools and women's friendly societies soon followed.[2] Sunday schools were a newly fashionable form of philanthropy for both anglicans and dissenters. The inter-denominational Sunday School Society had been set up in 1785, and by 1789 41,000 pupils were attending its schools. Women were prominent in the venture from the start, and Sarah Trimmer's school in Brentford received the accolade of a visit from Queen Charlotte. In spite of this royal support, Sunday schools were controversial institutions. Critics believed that, by teaching reading, they gave the poor ideas above their station and unfitted them for their lowly occupations. However, their defenders, who included Hannah More's friend, Beilby Porteus, bishop of London (1731–1809), argued that the schools would produce a generation instructed in both the christian religion and the necessity of political obedience,[3] and until the loyalist panic of the late 1790s, his arguments were steadily gaining ground.

In sounding out a local parish about the possibility of setting up a school, More had first to find a suitable building. As will be shown, where the local farmers were hostile, this could cause her great difficulty. The school in Cheddar, housed in an unused ox-house, which she rented for six and a half guineas a year, was typical of the type of accommodation provided in the early days. The curriculum was worked out by trial and error. The More sisters taught selected passages from the Bible and the Prayer Book, and also used books provided by the Society for Promoting Christian Knowledge. In addition they wrote their own *Questions and answers for the Mendip and Sunday schools*, which were more explicitly evangelical than the official anglican catechism. The children started school at about the age of 6 (the sisters had to resist pressure from hard-pressed

1 See Anne Stott, 'Hannah More and the Blagdon Controversy, 1799–1802', *Journal of Ecclesiastical History*, LI (2000), 319–46; *idem*, *Hannah More. The first Victorian* (Oxford, 2003), ch. 11.

2 See Stott, *Hannah More*, ch. 5 and *passim*.

3 Beilby Porteus, *A letter to the clergy of the diocese of Chester concerning Sunday schools* (London, 1786).

mothers who wanted to offload their younger children) and most of them left for domestic service aged 12. Some teenage boys and girls went on to attend evening classes and the more promising could became under-teachers and then masters and mistresses. Although More was eager to allay conservative anxieties by stressing that she taught no writing at her schools, future teachers were almost certainly taught this skill.[4] The schools were funded by donations, most notably from the wealthy individuals such as the Clapham evangelical, Henry Thornton (1760–1815), the Kentish heiress Elizabeth Bouverie (*c.* 1726–98), and from Wilberforce himself, who regularly sent £50 per annum. Following Elizabeth Bouverie's death in 1798, Wilberforce and Thornton clubbed together to buy the sisters a chaise; previously, they travelled the tortuous roads on horseback.

The progress of the schools depended to a very great extent on the quality of the teachers. Hannah More spent the spring of every year with friends in the London area, and in the winter her frail health and the state of the roads kept her in Bath. This made it all the more important to hire the right teachers. When she appointed her first mistress for the Cheddar school in the autumn of 1789 she took Wilberforce's advice that she should send for 'a comet', someone in the mould of John Wesley, risky methodist 'enthusiasm' being preferable to the safety of cold formalism. This was controversial advice and would become even more so during the late 1790s when methodism became a separate denomination and the conservative reaction spearheaded by John Gifford's ultra-loyalist *Anti-Jacobin review and magazine* forced evangelical anglicans like More and Wilberforce on to the defensive. In practice Hannah More found it difficult to distance herself from methodism, and years later, More's friend, the Bath dissenting minister William Jay (1766–1853), remembered her saying, 'I find none [but Methodists] seem to do my poor children good beside.'[5] Her 'methodist' teachers included Sarah Baber at Cheddar, Henry Harvard at Wedmore, and Henry Young at Nailsea. Before she began to teach at Cheddar, Mrs Baber had been involved in a controversial exorcism in Bristol carried out by a group of anglican clergymen with methodist sympathies; Harvard was alleged (perhaps wrongly) to have called the bishops 'Dumb Dogs' and to have distributed methodist literature; Young, a proud quarrelsome character, was in constant dispute with the powerful farmers of his mining parish. At a time when methodism, sometimes in its most radical form, was spreading rapidly in the Mendips, and when the boundaries between methodism and evangelical anglicanism were still blurred, More increasingly ran the risk of being tainted by association with religious (and even political) radicalism.

4 Stott, *Hannah More*, p. 168.

5 Quoted in *Autobiography and reminiscences of the Rev. William Jay*, ed. G. Redford and J. Angell James (London, 1855), p. 337 n. 338.

Clerical support was always vital to the success of the schools. From the start, More voiced stinging private criticisms of many of the local clergy – the absentee John Rawbone of Cheddar, the old and incapable Henry Penny of Shipham, the eccentric Thomas Gould of Axbridge, the scandalous William Eyre of Wedmore. Using her contacts with the cathedral and chapter of Wells she secured the appointment of the evangelicals John Boak and Thomas Drewitt as successive curates of Cheddar and of James Jones as rector of Shipham. She also secured the temporary use of pulpits for visiting evangelical clergy such as John Venn (1758–1813) and John Newton (1725–1807). By the mid 1790s she had become one of the most influential lay people in the Mendips – a fact that was noted with outrage by local high churchmen such as Archdeacon Charles Daubeny (1745–1827), acutely alive to the perceived dangers of evangelical infiltration.

Anxiety about Hannah More – suspicions about the nature of her churchmanship, and fears that as a mere laywoman she was taking too much on herself – surfaced in 1799 following the publication of her most successful conduct book, *Strictures on the modern system of female education.* In September of that year, Daubeny published *A letter to Mrs Hannah More*, in which he took her to task for her description of christian duties as 'the natural and necessary' productions of the 'living root' of christian faith.[6] The September to November issues of the *Anti-Jacobin* followed this up with a review of Daubeny's *Letter*, in which the Anglo-American loyalist the Revd Jonathan Boucher (1738–1804), who had been carefully primed by Daubeny, accused her outright of 'calvinism in disguise'.[7] More's friends rushed to defend her and in doing so they opened up a theological battle that exposed the developing fault lines between the evangelical anglicans of the Clapham sect on the one hand and the type of high-church opinion represented by Daubeny and Boucher on the other.

Whatever the growing misgivings about More's activities and her theology, anecdotal evidence suggested that her schools were extremely effective in calming disorderly parishes and in increasing church attendance. It was because of her high reputation that, in the summer of 1795, the curate and churchwardens of Blagdon had begged her to open what would be her eighth school in their impoverished and violent parish. After some hesitation she accepted the request, and appointed as teacher the Nailsea master, Henry Young, in spite of the fact that he was an avowed 'disciple of John Wesley'. As his quarrel with the farmers showed no sign

6 C. Daubeny, *A letter to Mrs Hannah More on some part of her late publication entitled 'Strictures on female education'* (Bath and London, 1799).

7 *The Anti-Jacobin review and magazine*, IV (Sept.–Nov. 1799), p. 255; the reference here is to the master copy of the first six volumes of the *Anti-Jacobin* (P. P. 3596 in the British Library catalogue), which has the names of the contributors inked in. For an overview of this controversy see Stott, *Hannah More*, pp. 228–9.

of dying down, it must have seemed a good move to remove him and allow him to exert his undoubted gifts in a new missionary field. At first, the curate Thomas Bere (d. 1814) was enthusiastic about Young, but in early 1799 his wife wrote to Hannah More complaining of his unofficial evening meetings, which were conducted on lines closely resembling the class meetings of the methodists: this at a time when methodism, in its most radical form, was spreading rapidly throughout the Mendips. Hannah More did not deny Mrs Bere's accusations, and moved to suppress her master's 'excesses'. However, the curate's hostility, if anything, increased, and he continued to undermine Young's work in the parish. In the summer and autumn of 1800, he collected a series of affidavits against Young, and on 12 November he convened a meeting of fellow clergy and magistrates at the George inn at Blagdon. As a result of their deliberations, Young was forced to resign his post and the Sunday school was closed four days later.

However, this was not the end of the matter. Early in 1801, Hannah More's friends (almost certainly with her covert encouragement) began spreading rumours that Bere was theologically unorthodox, and on 17 January he was ordered by his rector, Dr George Crossman (1754–1803), to resign his living. The school re-opened, but Bere refused to step down, much to the embarrassment of his rector, as well as the octogenarian bishop of Bath and Wells, Dr Charles Moss (1711–1802) and his son, also Dr Charles Moss (1763–1811), the diocesan chancellor. After months of mounting acrimony, the ecclesiastical authorities were the first to blink. Bere was reinstated in August, and the school was closed for a second time.

The curate had not been idle during the summer of 1801; between April and September he published three pamphlets, giving his side of the story and abusing Hannah More in increasingly lurid terms.[8] Two local landowners, the Revd Sir Abraham Elton (1755–1842) and Thomas Sedgwick Whalley (1746–1828), went into print to defend her, but Bere's case was vehemently taken up in the *Anti-Jacobin*.[9] More was also attacked in further pamphlets, some of them extremely scurrilous,[10] and defended in others.[11] The controversy had become a battle for the soul of the Church of England, with neither side willing to take prisoners.

Although the Blagdon school was never re-opened, Hannah More saw off her enemies, and remaining schools continued to flourish. Her national reputation and

8 *The controversy between Mrs Hannah More and the curate of Blagdon* (London, 1801); *An appeal to the public on the controversy between Hannah More, the curate of Blagdon, and the Rev. Sir A. Elton* (Bath, 1801); *An address to Mrs Hannah More on the conclusion of the Blagdon controversy* (Bath and London, 1801).

9 For the *Anti-Jacobin* attacks on More, see especially vols. IX (1801) and XI (1802).

10 [William Shaw], *The life of Hannah More with a critical review of her writings, by the Rev. Sir Archibald MacSarcasm, Bart* (London, 1802); Edward Spencer, *Truths respecting Mrs Hannah More's meeting-houses and the conduct of her followers* (Bath, 1802).

11 See, for example, [Thomas Drewitt] *The force of contrast*... (Bath and London, 1801).

her skilful networking of potentially sympathetic bishops gained her valuable allies at her moment of greatest need. Her supporters included the high-church *British critic*, the majority of Mendip clergy, and her new diocesan, Richard Beadon (1737–1824). However, the controversy was a salutary experience, and in future she was to distance herself from the methodists, and be more cautious in the way she expressed her evangelical sympathies.

The controversy sheds much light on the nature of evangelical/high-church relations at the turn of the eighteenth and nineteenth centuries, when the French revolution and the subsequent revolutionary and Napoleonic wars inspired apocalyptic anxieties in otherwise balanced individuals. It demonstrates deep fractures within the common protestant identity that, according to Linda Colley, was fundamental to the creation of 'Britishness'. It also shows that J. C. D. Clark's picture of an undivided anglican political and theological hegemony needs considerable nuancing.[12] Hannah More survived her bruising experience because she had influential high-church allies, and because in the first decade of the nineteenth century there was no united 'orthodox' party ready to mount a coherent attack on evangelical entryism. But her enemies proved extremely vocal, and their accusation that she and her fellow evangelicals were potential schismatics – forming a church within a church – was extremely damaging. Tensions were to resurface with the foundation of the Bible Society in 1804, a development that deeply alarmed many (though not all) high churchmen. Evangelical willingness to work with dissenters showed that their ecclesiology differed very radically from that of high churchmen such as Daubeny. The sacraments and the doctrine of the apostolic succession mattered far less to them than the experience of conversion – an experience that united evangelicals and dissenters and set them apart from those who stressed the supreme importance of the ordained ministry and the visible church.

It has recently been suggested that Hannah More had no fundamental theological differences with high churchmen, that she was always an anglican first and an evangelical second.[13] However, this is not borne out by her correspondence during the Blagdon controversy, where again and again she showed her hostility to what she regarded as the 'bigoted' end of the high-church spectrum. The same sentiments cropped up in the many letters she later wrote about the debates on the Bible Society.[14] The inescapable conclusion is that though Hannah More had close

12 Linda Colley, *Britons. Forging the nation* (New Haven, 1992); J. C. D. Clark, *English society, 1688–1832. Ideology, social structure and political practice during the ancien regime* (Cambridge, 1985).

13 *Selected writings of Hannah More*, ed. Robert Hole (London, 1996), pp. xxii–xxiv.

14 For More's acerbic views on the high-church opponents of the Bible Society, see Anne Stott, 'Hannah More. Evangelicalism, cultural reformation and loyalism', unpublished Ph.D. dissertation, University of London, 1998, pp. 42–6.

friendships with eirenical high churchmen such as Alexander Knox (1757–1831) and Thomas Burgess (1756–1837), she remained firmly evangelical, and often preferred dissenters to her fellow anglicans. It is surely significant, for example, that in her will she left £100 to the baptist missionaries at Serampore and nothing at all to the Society for the Propagation of the Gospel.

More's extensive correspondence is found in a variety of repositories. Most of her letters relating to the Blagdon controversy, written between 1795 and 1802, are found in the William Wilberforce papers, Duke University, Durham, North Carolina. This correspondence is especially revealing, as, knowing she was guaranteed confidentiality and a sympathetic ear, she spoke her mind extremely freely; it is for this reason that her Blagdon correspondence with him is here printed in full for the first time. This correspondence is interspersed with letters, also found in the Wilberforce papers at Duke University, to two other close friends, Henry Thornton and his wife, Marianne. Two revealing letters from Thomas Bere are also included: one from the Duke manuscripts, showing his initial support for the school (something he later played down), and another, in the William Andrews Clark Memorial Library, University of California at Los Angeles, which demonstrates his unseemly eagerness to secure Henry Young's dismissal. Two other previously unpublished letters shed further light on the controversy. A letter to Henry Thornton, from the Thornton papers at Cambridge University Library, shows how her problems in setting up a school at Wedmore were to feed into the later Blagdon controversy. Another, to George Pretyman-Tomline, bishop of Lincoln, found in the Stanhope papers, Centre for Kentish Studies, Maidstone, shows her successful attempt to secure the support of this influential high churchman at a time when her loyalty to the Church of England was being called into question. However, an extract from an earlier letter to Wilberforce, printed in an Appendix, reveals her private mistrust of a man she believed to be fundamentally hostile to evangelicalism.[15]

More's letters – lengthy, repetitive, sometimes paranoid, often self-deceiving – reveal her growing animosity to Bere, her distrust of the local clerical hierarchy, and her sufferings, physical and mental, under a campaign of increasingly vicious abuse. They tell one side of the story. Bere's pamphlets and the *Anti-Jacobin review and magazine* tell the other.

15 This correspondence can be supplemented by reading a printed collection of letters from More to her friend and champion, the Somerset landowner, Thomas Sedgwick Whalley, who wrote one of the more effective pamphlets in her defence. *Journals and correspondence of Thomas Sedgwick Whalley*, ed. Revd. Hill Wickham (2 vols., London, 1863), II, 144–227.

Editorial note

Spelling and punctuation have been slightly modernized. Except where otherwise stated, all the letters printed below are to be found among the letters from Hannah More to William Wilberforce located in the William Wilberforce Papers, Rare Book, Manuscript and Special Collections Library, Duke University, Durham, North Carolina.

Hannah More and the Blagdon controversy 1799–1802

1. THE FOUNDING OF THE BLAGDON SCHOOL

Hannah More set up the Blagdon school at a time when the parish was in turmoil and the local *élites* felt powerless to control the situation. The school was successful from the start, and initially Bere was an enthusiastic supporter.

Hannah More to William Wilberforce, Cowslip Green,[16] 27 August 1795

Most of this letter deals with other concerns, but an extract is included here as it contains the first reference to the Blagdon school.

We are invited to a new and very laborious undertaking – the field is intensive and the object important – but my mind is in suspense – Henry[17] stimulates me and says we *must* engage in it – but my health is bad, my time and Patty's does not more than suffice to our present schemes, and our expences are already very heavy – I cannot doubt but God will furnish means for the last article as he has already done, nor ought I to doubt that he will give me as much strength as is necessary for these additional exertions, nor do I wish much to spare myself, I hope. Yet I have so far lost ground this summer as never to have lost my cough, and [I have] difficulty of breathing even in the hot weather for more than a day or two, so that I have some sinful fears of not being able to work long, counteracted, I trust, by a desire to work more earnestly and vigorously…

More to Wilberforce, 14 October 1795

An extract from this letter gives a vivid account of the opening of the Blagdon school.

... This hot weather makes me suffer terribly, yet I have now and then a good day. And on Sunday [I] was enabled to open the new School. It was an affecting sight. Several of the grown-up youths had been tried at the last assizes; 3 were the children of a person lately condemned to be hanged;[18] – many thieves! all ignorant, profane, and vicious beyond belief! Of this Banditti we have enlisted 170. And when the Clergyman [Thomas Bere], a hard man, who is also the magistrate, saw

16 More's cottage, near Wrington, Somerset, from 1786 to 1801.

17 The Clapham evangelical, Henry Thornton (1760–1815). Wilberforce, his second cousin, was at this time sharing his house at Battersea Rise.

18 The records do not reveal that anyone from Blagdon was hanged in 1795 or 1796.

these Creatures kneeling round us, whom he had seldom seen but to *commit* or to punish in some way, he burst into tears. I can do them little good I fear, but the grace of God may. Your friend Henry [Thornton] thought we ought to try...

[The next two paragraphs deal with the unpopularity of the local member of parliament, Lord Sheffield, and the failure of the Quiberon expedition.]

Have you never found your mind when it has been weak, now and then touched and raised by some trifling circumstance? So I felt on Sunday. The principal people from many Parishes came to the opening of this scheme for the instruction of this place, which is considered as a sort of Botany Bay. Some musical Gentlemen, drawn from a distance by curiosity (just as I was coming out of Church with my ragged regiment, much depressed to think how little good I could do them) quite unexpectedly struck up that beautiful and animating anthem 'Inasmuch as you do it to one of the least of these you have done it unto me'. It was well performed and had a striking effect.

More to Wilberforce, Bath, 25 January [1796]

In a letter dealing with her poor health and local politics, More gave Wilberforce an optimistic account of the progress of the Blagdon school.

... I ought thankfully to remark that our Schools and other Institutions are prosperous in a very high degree. At no period has there been such an appearance of good being done.[19] My addition of a new Parish where we have already near 200 must oblige me to accept your offered assistance.[20] Indeed I fear I have increased my expenses beyond the bounds of prudence – but 'the time is short' – I at least shall not have long to work, and I ought not to distrust Providence. A number of Farmers and their Wives as blind and ignorant as Africans come in secret for Instruction at this new School and receive it with alacrity. By what poor Fools does God work! it only humbles me the more, by showing the power is entirely his. Don't send more than £50. I wish to spare you all I can...

Thomas Bere to More, Blagdon House, 3 December 1796

As More was later to regret that she had no early letters from Bere to produce in her defence, this glowing (if eccentric) commendation of the school must have been lost. The most likely explanation is that she sent it to Wilberforce, that it lay buried for months (even years) under a pile of papers in his somewhat chaotic house, and was only recovered when it was no longer needed.

19 The 'other Institutions' were adult evening classes and women's benefit clubs.

20 In a previous letter More had stated that she needed £70 per annum. Duke, More to Wilberforce [December 1795].

In the hurry and unpleasant feeling of our taking leave we forgot the Good Bishop's books; we are very ardent to know as much of him as possible and therefore send our servant for them: I love a book, and will take care *those* shall sustain no injury.[21] *Alexander Stevens* (the unhappy person who two years since was tried for a murder) is now a pupil of Mr Young's. This is proof positive of the effects of your labors. Mrs Bere is just returned from Mr Young's readings where were about 60 auditors (farmers and labourers and women). He with great propriety expatiated on the 13th Chapter to the Romans and thence drew sound inferences of subjection to the higher Powers applying them to the present times.[22] What do you think now of this clever and useful man? I dare say he has done more essential good by informing and therefore quieting his people than their Squire-ships and Worships will effect in the whole progress of this turbulent business. I hold myself obliged to him for this very seasonable and valuable assistance. We ambled home very friskily, my wife on the light fantastic toe, her husband pacing with the caution and gravity of a huge Don, but the man has good spirits enough, only he has very feeling feet. Adieu, God bless you all and bestow on you health and happiness.

2. THE BEGINNING OF TROUBLES

Bere soon changed his mind about Henry Young. In the summer of 1798, Hannah and Patty More founded a new school at Wedmore, in the face of much opposition. Hannah More's letter to Henry Thornton shows how fears of 'methodism' were beginning to undermine her work. In this and the two subsequent letters, she accuses Bere of hostility to her schools and of heresy.

More to Henry Thornton, Cowslip Green, 12 September [1798][23]

The first part of this vivid and revealing letter deals with the winding up of the Cheap Repository Tracts.[24] *The Bath printer of the tracts was Samuel Hazard. More was persuaded, against her better judgment, to employ his nephew, Henry Harvard, as teacher at her new school at Wedmore, in spite of his known methodism.*[25]

21 Possibly a reference to the works of Bishop Porteus.

22 'Let every soul be subject to the higher powers. For there is no power but of God: the powers that be are ordained of God.' This was the classic text of anglican political theology and was much quoted during the political debates of the 1790s.

23 Cambridge University Library, Thornton MS, Add. 7674/1/E/1.

24 For the Cheap Repository Tracts, see G. H. Spinney, 'Cheap Repository Tracts: Hazard and Marshall edition', *The Library*, 4th ser., XX (1939), 295–340; Stott, *Hannah More*, chs. 8–10.

25 For Harvard's methodism, see Stott, *Hannah More*, pp. 213–14.

I own I do not feel disposed to make Hazard any compensation for what I know has been a gainful business to him. He thinks there is a deal of money and he may get a share. I will give you an instance of his covetousness. He has just recommended to me his nephew as master of my new school at Wedmore with a high character. This man has been in trade and failed for want of capital. As usual I found I must pay his debts before I could get him, but he and his wife seemed such superior people I thought it right to put up with this business. It was 30 or £40 – I proposed to Hazard to advance £15 only, which he was to be repaid but he refused to so near a relation, and has thrown the debt on my hands. I must pay £25 or lose the man. To keep at this expense I assure you I refused to have any medical assistance after my accident,[26] for being so far from Bristol I knew it would cost me a great deal.

This subject of money leads me to say (which I did not intend) that I believe I must desire you not to give away the interest of Mrs Bouverie's money any more but to let me have it; do not however tell her this just now.[27] I am now engaged in such very large expenses that humanly speaking I do not very well see how I shall get through it, and my faith, which is not over strong, is kept pretty much on the stretch. Assessed taxes and some other things have reduced my sisters' income £150 a year and they spend all before; as I shall feel it right to help towards this deficiency, I shall not be able to make that new addition towards the schools which I had hoped. I will not however distrust that Providence which has so unexpectedly carried me on hitherto, and I hope to use these little difficulties and uncertainties as an exercise of my trust in him. You will think so when I tell you that in spite of the continued opposition at Wedmore, we are building a house there. P[atty] says she thinks we tire you with our stories. I will however tell you one, which I think will be much to Mrs Clarke's taste.[28] After going on Sunday to Wedmore (30 miles there and back) on the wettest day I was ever out in, we found our poor 300 Children assembled in the half finished room without a floor, a door or a window. We taught them with great peace and content, not one of the Farmers considering to come nigh us or offering the least accommodation though the rain was so violent (but I borrowed a Cottage). At length the reason came out. The children had been trying to sing for the first time one of Watts's hymns. This brought a farmer who said now he was sure we were *Methodys*; on being asked

26 In August 1798 More, who was at the time crippled with a headache, fell down and lay unconscious on the floor until her sisters found her. For a while they believed her to be dying. Wilberforce papers, Duke University: More to Wilberforce, 15 Aug. [1798].

27 The evangelical philanthropist Elizabeth Bouverie of Teston, Kent, was a substantial contributor to the Mendip schools. She was more sick than More seems to have realized, and she died at the end of September 1798.

28 Wilberforce's sister, Sarah Clarke (later Stephen) (1758–1832), was noted for her eccentric sense of humour.

what gave the parish such a terror of Methodists, this was his answer. 'Some years ago a *Methody* preacher came and preached in our orchard under my mother's best apple tree; immediately after, the leaves withered and the tree died; we saw at once this was a *judgment*, and called a vestry to see what could be done to save our orchards. We there agreed that we should not have an apple left in the parish if we suffered a Methody to stay. So we ordered all the people to get all the stones and rotten eggs they could muster and beat the whole crew out of the Parish; they did so and have not lost an apple since.' I have told it verbatim – This is the enlightened nineteenth century![29]

But we have difficulties of a far more serious nature than this, which I would not trouble you with an account of, but that perhaps you may be able to suggest some useful hints to us. In two or three of our most established parishes where most good seems to be doing, there is risen a most violent opposition against us or rather against religion. They let P[atty] and I [*sic*] go on quietly while there was no serious Clergyman[30] in the Country,[31] but 2 or 3 of our young Oxford men having been down in the summer and preached about at our Clubs &c has excited an animosity that is dreadful. One of the worldly clergy has declared he will give himself the trouble to set up an evening Lecture at the Church as the only means he can devise to destroy our evening Reading. I should rejoice at this did I not know what stuff he will preach. If he does, however, I shall endeavour to make our people go, but as many of them seem really serious, I fear they will not. Our other great trial is at Blagdon where the Clergyman (the magistrate you saw here once) is such a hypocrite that he affected to shed tears when I was ill and said in a canting tone 'what would become of the Country' yet is doing all he can to knock up the school thro' a genuine hatred of Xtianity and a personal hatred of one of the serious young Ministers who has awakened a dying woman and several others.[32] This Blagdon Parson has been reading Socinian books and now boldly preaches against the Trinity, St Paul etc and tells the people that they need pay no attention to any part of Scripture but the Sermon on the Mount. He has so disturbed the faith of the whole parish nearly that they are afraid to attend the School where they say other doctrines are taught and if the Parson is in the right the ladies must be in the wrong. I am extremely distressed what to do having no Bishop nor Rector who cares for any of these things...

29 In spite of this comment, internal evidence shows conclusively that the letter was written in 1798. In September 1798 Thornton wrote what was clearly a reply. The letter sympathizes with More's troubles at Wedmore and refers to news of Bonaparte's capture of Cairo and Rosetta. C.U.L., Thornton MS, Add. 7674/1/N, fos. 85–6.

30 Claphamite code for evangelical.

31 In the eighteenth and early nineteenth centuries, 'country' could also mean 'county'.

32 Either James Vaughan or Thomas Fry, two young clergymen who had helped More set up the Wedmore school.

More to Wilberforce, Cowslip Green, 11 September 1799

More's letter begins with further details of what she calls 'the Wedmore Prosecution', as the farmers tried to shut down the school.[33] *She proceeds to attack Bere for unorthodoxy and to warn Wilberforce about what she sees as the malevolent intentions of the* Anti-Jacobin review and magazine.

... But the mischief lies deeper than with these vulgar Farmers. A Clergyman in my own neighbourhood where we have a flourishing School, and where you were last year [Blagdon] always a hypocritical man, has turned Socinian, and is now enraged at the doctrines *we* teach; and is doing under hand all possible injury to us and our schemes. This cause, too has a cause – And this man's malice is inflamed by the Antijacobin Magazine, which is spreading more mischief over the land than almost any other book, because it is doing it under the mask of Loyalty. It is representing all serious men as hostile to Government, and our enemies here whisper that we are abetted by you, and such as you, to hurt the Establishment.[34] This is only an episode for I must talk to you more at large and see if no means can be employed to stop this spreading poison. I hear the author is one Williams, who, having been refused some favour by the Bishop of London, exercises his malignity towards him in common with those whom he calls Methodists...

[The rest of the letter deals with the Wedmore school.]

More to Wilberforce [May 1800]

I am truly sorry you did *not* read the papers you sent me, as they all related to the transaction with Mr Bere.[35] He is gone to London ever since I came home[36] either to publish a book against us or to institute a process of law or both. He has raised a fine flame in the Country. Some of his own poor told me the stream of abuse and

33 See Stott, *Hannah More*, p. 214. A tactfully censored version of this letter is printed in W. Roberts, *Memoirs of the life and correspondence of Mrs Hannah More* (4 vols., London, 1834), III, 101–4.

34 This letter coincides with the Rev. Jonathan Boucher's review of More's *Strictures on the modern system of female education* in the September 1799 edition of the *Anti-Jacobin*. In his review, Boucher accused More of 'Calvinism in disguise', and his accusations echoed word for word a letter critical of More from the high-church clergyman, Charles Daubeny. See Stott, *Hannah More*, pp. 228–31.

35 On 5 April 1800 Bere wrote to More describing Henry Young as 'a turbulent, troublesome person', and adding that 'if this man continues here in his present character, I must infer ... that it is avowedly with intent to render my ministration in the church as little effectual as possible, and I shall be driven to seek my remedy, where and how I can.' On 11 April he wrote to his rector, Dr George Crossman, claiming that 'under the sanction of the establishment, the man [Young] has assumed and openly uses most of all the privileges of a Licensed Conventicle'. Bere, *Controversy*, pp. 17–18, 20–1.

36 Earlier in May, More had been staying with her friend, Sir Charles Middleton, at Teston, Kent.

personal invective against us and the School for some months would disgrace a common alehouse, and that they dreaded the return of Sunday. After having said in one of his Sermons that our principles gave reason to suspect we might be connected with the Attack on the King's life, he then ordered one of his people to stand at the Church Door and read the newspaper account of Hadfield's attack to the people, as they went out, by way I suppose of following up the impression.[37] I have had a very civil letter from Dr Moss, enclosing one to him from Bere's Rector, highly complimentary to me but which shows he is not aware how bad a man his Curate is. I have written by Dr Moss's desire, a long and plain statement of the whole business to the Rector offering to lay down the school if *he* and the *Bishop* desire it, but refusing to give up the master a victim to Bere's revenge. The whole story of the Affidavit is dropped, they have parted from the Servant, he was *so silly and so great a liar*; yet they will receive its oath.[38]

Luckily for us Bere has preached openly his disbelief in the Trinity several times. I have not plainly told his Rector this, but I have plainly told him that Mr Bere's dislike is not to the Schoolmaster but the Cause, and that our orthodoxy is our crime. Sir Abraham Elton[39] I believe will take it up with a high hand – Bere's having refused his mediation has hurt himself a good deal.[40]

3. THE FIRST CLOSURE OF THE SCHOOL

The following letters deal with the events leading up to and following the meeting at the George inn at Blagdon on 12 November 1800, which condemned Young for methodism and led to the closing of the school. Hannah and Patty More's letters seem to show that some of the local élites *were less concerned with Young than with the way the More sisters were conducting the school.*

37 On 15 May 1800 James Hadfield (*c.* 1772–1841) had fired a pistol into the Royal Box at the Theatre Royal, Drury Lane. For an account of the incident see the *Gentleman's magazine*, LXX (1800), 478–80.

38 This seems to be a reference to the first of the Blagdon affidavits. This was from Bere's servant, Silas Derrick, who on 4 April 1800 deposed that on 29 March Young had said to him, 'I would not advise you to go to service at Mr Bere's at all; and if you do go, I would not advise you to stay there long – *For there is no knowing what they might put into your mind, to make you sign away to [your] house and orchard.*' Bere, *Controversy*, pp. 15–16.

39 Abraham Elton (1755–1842), 5th baronet, clergyman and magistrate, head of a distinguished family of Bristol merchants, and owner of Clevedon Court in Somerset.

40 On 9 April, More, who was about to leave for Teston, suggested Sir Abraham Elton as a mediator. On 8 May, Bere turned down this offer. *Controversy*, pp. 20–1, 24–5.

More to Wilberforce, 2 September 1800

After telling Wilberforce that the great evangelical preacher Thomas Scott has sent her £50 for the schools, More proceeds to inform him of the growing Blagdon crisis.

The Storm of opposition which has beaten so heavily upon us the whole Summer is about to sink us: at least the Blagdon Bark will be soon engulfed. The list of follies and crimes transmitted by the Curate and believed by the Rector will oblige me to give up the School. The stale charge of Methodism I should have borne I hope with more temper than our friend Lord Kenyon,[41] but *blasphemy* and *sedition* are charges one is not so accustomed to repel. It is said that the Rector has let his Tithes to Bere which being an illegal transaction, he cannot easily part with him.[42] So instead of coming up, as Dr Moss desired, as examining things on the spot, where false allegations could have been refuted, he sent for Bere down to him: where as Lord North once said, 'all the reciprocity being on one side, we are tried, found guilty and condemned'. We have no chance with people who make nothing of oaths, but on the slightest subjects swear through thick and thin.

You mistake in thinking we intended to resist the law by refusing to pay the fine. That fine, it was concurred, could only be levied on unlicensed Methodist meeting houses. Now ours, being a new case, the Church Congregation assembled under the sanction of the Minister, and by his express Consent which it was, it was thought for the sake of examples, as it was a new thing, it should be tried on new ground. If you think, however, that it is more right to pay the fine than to go to prison, I readily will do it. But at present the menaces of the law seem to give way to a private blackening of reputation. – I hope I do not murmur – It is enough for the servant to be as his Master,[43] but the being obliged to *defend* ourselves (which is contrary to my avowed firm principle) not only in the neighbourhood but in voluminous correspondence was so trying to me that I believe I should have sunk under it had not Sir Abraham Elton seeing my spirits and health failing taken it in a good measure out of my hands. He has entered into it on the grounds of public justice; it being his avowed principle to resist all oppression and intolerance in his own district as Magistrate. It is a trying duty for a nervous man in bad health to bring on himself the abuse of two Clergymen both Magistrates also, but a redresser of wrongs is the character he has maintained since he set down here; and the matter in debate is that he will protect against false charges an honest, laborious pious man, the Schoolmaster, who has done no evil and much good.

41 Lloyd Kenyon, first Baron Kenyon (1732–1802), master of the rolls.

42 *The Anti-Jacobin*, IX (1801), 288 n. reported that Crossman had granted Bere his lease of tithes for ten years from Lady Day 1798.

43 Matthew x. 25.

Bere pretended at first he would be satisfied with this victim but now we are afraid tis not the Man but the cause. You need not fear that Sir A. is a raw rash man, he is one deeply versed in the obliquities and wickedness of the human heart, and an excellent Lawyer, civil and Ecclesiastical We wait for the answer to a letter to know when we are to abandon the instruction of 400 poor Creatures who did not know when we began, who made them, and who are now well versed in the Scriptures. It is the will of God and I labour much after a submissive Spirit.

P[atty] and I are poorly in health, broken up with the weather; I have a slight fever, restless nights and a cough. We are both drinking asses' milk to try to patch up for a little further service if it shall please God. My flesh and heart fail about this *new* place, as it is so distant and winter comes on 'but get thee behind me Satan'[44] is the language I try to use to the suggestions of an indolent body and a feeble faith. As to the resources for supporting it, I hope not to draw you or Mr Thornton into any fresh expense. I wrote to beg of Mr Hoare[45] who has kindly promised me £30 per annum which with my own savings will I trust suffice for the short time I shall probably be able to attend to it.

[The next paragraph deals with the death of More's friend, the bluestocking, Elizabeth Montagu.]

It makes me almost sick to tell you that the Blagdon Inquisition have driven our poor Schoolmaster to take an oath that he is not a Calvinist! 'Murderers of fathers and murderers of mothers'[46] are good people compared with those whom they accuse of Calvinism. This is a nickname. They do not at all know what it means. The poor man being a disciple of John Wesley's could do it with a safe conscience but distinguished those points in which he was and was not. I wish I could have your advice but I must be contented at this distance with your prayers.[47]

More to Wilberforce, Cowslip Green, 29 September 1800

… It is all over with us at Blagdon. I have struggled hard to keep my footing, and would have borne any obloquy on my character while the least chance of doing good remained. But when I consider the dreadful perjuries which my perseverance is every day exciting I can no longer answer it to my conscience to persevere. Among Bere's affidavits which are 'as plenty as Blackberries'[48] one is taken by a Lunatic, whom, as such, I have helped to maintain. People start up out of ditches,

44 Luke iv. 8. The 'new place' was Chew Magna, where the More sisters were considering founding a school.

45 Henry Hoare (1750–1832), banker and subscriber to evangelical causes.

46 I Timothy i. 9.

47 Wilberforce and his family were then on holiday at Bognor.

48 William Shakespeare, *Henry IV, Part I*, Act ii, Sc. 4.

or from under hedges, to listen to the talk of our poor pious labourers as they are at work, and then go and make oath and (which it seems is unexampled) Mr Bere (having doubtless set them to listen) receives Depositions in his own cause! I really did not take the pains to read them through it was such wretched stuff. Some I think go to prove that Young is a Calvinist; several that he was heard to pray extempore in *private*; no-one accuses him of the heavy sin of having done it on the public nights. Another is that he told a dying woman he thought 'she *might* go to heaven though he did not think she had faith enough'. Though I am ashamed to write such stuff, our Bishop, or rather Dr Moss as Chancellor has thought proper on such testimony to order me to dismiss the master.[49] That cheap religion which consists in crying *The Church is in danger* has completely won him over. Bere though notorious as a liar and a preacher of heretical doctrines is credited, while my reputation is treated with as much contempt as if I were Hardy or Thelwall;[50] and indeed *their* political doctrines changed to my own. Mr Whalley has done himself great honour by writing a strong and very spirited state of the case to the Bishop, expressing his strong conviction of the moral benefit to the County from all my Schools; his firm belief in the integrity of the Blagdon Master and describing at large his having witnessed together with Dr Maclaine,[51] Mrs Henry and many other equally respectable testimonies the conduct of the School for a whole Sunday and the practical and useful work of instruction, with the regularity and good order of the Parish. Now as my friend W is not *particularly religious*, I own I did think *his* testimony would have been of use. But no – he was very coolly received. *The man had prayed extempore*, he *must* be a *Calvinist*. The *Church was in danger*.

My dear friend! I have prayed and struggled earnestly not to be quite subdued in my *mind* – but I cannot commend my *nerves*, and tho I do pretty well in the bustle of the day, yet I get such disturbed and agitated nights that I cou'd not speak for my lasting if the thing were to go on much longer. This is such a specimen of the State of religion that *I* too really think the Church *is* in danger, though in another and far more awful sense.

Sir A. Elton is devoted to our cause, and only wants Bere's recovery from a fit of the Gout (as he would take no advantage of him) to re-examine these *oath-takers*; he is still sanguine that good will come out of all this evil. A volume of letters have been written. Happily for me he will not allow me [to] write any, it

49 This is confirmed by Thomas Bere's letter of 3 November. For More's defiance of this order, see the letter dated 28 October 1800.

50 The radicals Thomas Hardy (1752–1832) and John Thelwall (1764–1834) had been acquitted of treason in October-November 1794.

51 Dr Archibald Maclean (1722–1804); presbyterian divine; translator (1765) of Mosheim's *Ecclesiastical history*; settled in Bath, 1796.

affects me so much. 'How shall I give you up, O Ephraim'?[52] is my frequent exclamation as I walk in my Garden and look at the Steeple and the village of Blagdon. I know if I had a lively faith I should rejoice that I was thought worthy to suffer in the cause of Christ, but I mourn for our Jerusalem – I mourn to see that nothing is thought a crime but what *they* are pleased to call enthusiasm. I heartily wish I were a greater Enthusiast in their sense of the word.

What you suggest in your very kind and feeling letter about my taking out a license is impracticable on every ground. In the first place there would be a duplicity in it which on reflection you would disapprove for how could I acknowledge myself a Dissenter? I who am firmly attached to a Church which is behaving so ill and who abhor the doctrines of which I am suspected?

Mr Hart the Clergyman of Nailsea where Young was my Schoolmaster three years has sent a most handsome testimony to Young's moral and religious character, his firm attachment to the Church and his freedom from the doctrines and practices of which he is accused – his letter Sir A. has sent to the Bishop.

I hope you are still enjoying peace and quiet and the company of our friends at the sea; be so good as to show or to send this letter to Mr Thornton.[53]

More to Wilberforce *c.* 28 October 1800

I truly rejoice in the good accounts of Mrs W[ilberforce].[54] I deferred writing as I expected to have gone to Wedmore yesterday, and as that is a land of *great Farmers*, to have picked up better intelligence respecting *grain* than I could get at home;[55] but deluges of rain and indisposition obliged me to change Wedmore for Blagdon. Our business gets more complicated and puzzling. We have at length obtained from Dr Moss thirteen affidavits *extorted* no doubt by Bere and taken by himself in his own cause, from the lowest and most disreputable people in his Parish to blacken Young the master. Yet *such* affidavits, *such* trash, so absurd on the very face of them you never saw. How a man of Moss's sense and knowledge of the world can lend himself to such a business is inconceivable – but he has been *appealed* to! and the high Church spirit *must* protect its own. The affidavits go to prove that they heard Young say he was a Calvinist. That a Carpenter from another place passing through Blagdon called at Young's, and that this Carpenter is *reported* to be a Methodist. – That Young was heard *once* and two of his scholars to pray extempore – that when the minister was reading the Exhortation to the Sacrament at Church Young's wife elbowed one of her Scholars and lifted

52 Hosea xi. 8.

53 The Wilberforces were on holiday with the Thorntons at Bognor.

54 Barbara Wilberforce had been taken seriously ill at Bognor, an event that naturally diverted Wilberforces's attention from Hannah More's Blagdon troubles.

55 A reference to the bad harvests and food shortages of 1800.

up her eyes!!! – So far the Oaths – the private information which we cannot fully get at, goes to prove deeper crimes I fancy, Young's and even my disaffection to Church and State, Psalm singing and various other misdemeanours. When Moss (who is Chancellor of the Diocese) was first appealed to by the Rector, who will go through thick and thin to save his Curate, to whom he has let the Tythe, Moss wrote to me that he thought, as there were so many charges against the Schoolmaster, I ought to dismiss him. As I believe hardly any of the charges, and all to be greatly aggravated, I felt that on my firmness in supporting this innocent Master depended the existence of all my Schools. Sir A. Elton wrote therefore to Moss that I received his decree with becoming submission but tho I obeyed *in iure* I should disobey *in modo*, for that, as I was persuaded Bere meant it as an attack on all my Schools and that the Masters by my yielding would always be liable to the untruths of every opponent, I was resolved that, the School and the Master shou'd stand or fall together. Bere in the mean time gave out that the Chancellor had ordered the dismissal of Young and gave three triumphant dinners in one week in consequence. At one of these the Clergyman of my own Parish[56] and Mr Addington assisted!![57] Sir A[braham Elton] now sent to Bere a handsome letter desiring him 'to produce his Deponents and Sir A. himself would attend with *Young* that the accused might have the benefit allowed to the meanest Englishman of being conftonted with his accusers'. This Bere positively refused, saying the business was already settled by the Bishop and his son. This produced a large correspondence between Sir A. and Moss in which the latter said that he only gave me his opinion as a *private Man* and that it was not an *official decree*. On the strength of this I venture to go on a little longer being determined to die hard, and struggle to the last in such a cause: though I can hardly tell you what this determination of duty has cost me. Sir A. has *re*-demanded of Bere to bring forward his people, to this he can get no answer; and a violent fit of the gout in which he now lays delayed Sir Abraham's 3rd letter. A letter from Moss today however does express his astonishment at Bere's refusal, but he spoils this concession again by hinting that if the cause should finally be brought before him in the Ecclesiastical Court this *confronting* may be dispensed with. Sir A. who abhors all intolerance and of course all Ecclesiastical Courts is telling him that the law of the land is paramount, and that this oppressed Schoolmaster shall have justice. Moss's eyes are a little opened by a very strong letter from Mr Hart, Minister of Nailsea where Young taught my school 3 years representing him as a *rationally* pious man utterly exempt from any fanatical or seditious propensities, and that he brought numbers to Church and Sacrament on whom *his* public

56 The Rev. William Leeves (1756–1828), rector of Wrington from 1799.

57 Hiley Addington (1759–1818), local landowner and brother of the future prime minister, Henry Addington (1757–1844).

ministry produced no effect. Sir A. Elton conducts this trying business with great energy and zeal but with equal wisdom and moderation. He has (though a sickly man) rode 60 miles a week ever since June, and in all that heat, to console and direct me; and in more than four months has never once missed being here on a Monday morn to meet our Infirmities. His is a trying duty. Moss is his friend, but he is sacrificing this friendship to the Cause of Justice and Religion. I wish I had kept some of those flattering letters Bere used to write about the School.[58] I had a letter from Col. Scott inviting himself and two other Gentlemen to come down from Bath on Sunday morn, and go to the Schools fancying they had nothing to do but to walk about this Parish, and then return back. I was obliged to write and explain the mistakes, telling him the distance, our engagements &c and inviting them all *next* Sunday to Cheddar & to come over Saturday night in order to be ready to start.[59] I hope they will not be gone; but *their* plan was impracticable.

A full reading and School at Blagdon last night; all peace and quiet for the oppressor was confined to his bed. What a pity to break up such a scheme but it *must* come to that. I strive not to be impatient under the indignity of being suspected to connive at least at Sedition and fanaticism; and that Bere is listened to; a man whom his best friends allow to swear, lie, and drink; a known friend to heresy and a suspected Jacobin. On that work we split – it is to varnish over these cracks in his character that he lays these very charges on us. May these trials be sanctified to us, and may I submit cheerfully to any event; indeed, knowing the cause to be prejudiced it requires no spirit of divination to foretell the catastrophe... Patty's journal of our persecutions consists of several little volumes and is so interspersed with other thoughts & that she dares not let it go out of her hands – She will at more leisure copy some extracts for you.[60]

Thomas Bere to G. P. Seymour, Blagdon House, 3 November 1800[61]

It is with extreme reluctance that I am constrained under the imperious purpose of a very unpleasant controversy to solicit your kind attention to the following particulars, as it implicates everything estimable in my principle and practice.

You may have heard that Mrs More's Teacher at Blagdon so conducted himself as to have made it my Duty as Curate of that Parish to inform her of his

58 But see above for Bere's letter of December 1796.

59 Hannah More's strenuous Sunday schedules involved calling at the schools at Shipham, Cheddar and Axbridge one week, and Nailsea, Yatton and Blagdon the other.

60 This was subsequently edited by Arthur Roberts and published as *Mendip annals: or a narrative of the charitable labours of Hannah and Martha More in the Mendips* (London, 1859). The book contains many robust comments on the shortcomings of the local clergy.

61 The William Andrews Clark Memorial Library, U.C.L.A., More, Hannah More 1745–1833. Papers, 1777–1829.

extravagant irregularities. Instead of attending my complaint, this Lady wrote (without my knowledge) to the Chancellor and Dr Crossman apparently with intention to Strangle the investigation, by destroying in the minds of those Gentlemen whatever respect they might have entertained for my moral or clerical character. This ultimately brought the matter to issue before our venerable Diocesan & his most highly respected son. The result was that on the evidence before them they adjudged my complaint well founded, & the latter immediately wrote to Mrs More acquainting her 'that her Teacher was unworthy of his station: and in his opinion ought to be removed from his situation'. Dr Crossman & all who knew it (the party only excepted) deemed this perfectly conclusive. Nevertheless the Teacher is yet continued at Blagdon & the Party now impeach the Chancellor's Decision & except to the Credibility & competency of the evidence upon which he determined the Cause. I am therefore permitted in defence of the Chancellor's impartiality to swear the witnesses to their several depositions in the presence of the most respectable Gentlemen of the neighbourhood. The day fixed for this purpose is Wednesday the 12 inst at 11 o'clock, the place Blagdon. Permit me therefore Dear Sir most earnestly to entreat the honor of your presence to meet the Gentlemen that will attend upon this occasion to hear the witnesses as sworn & by so doing to suppress if possible the indecent Clamor raised against the Chancellor's judgment…

PS I hope to have the pleasure of your company to dinner – the business, I apprehend, will not require one hour's attention.

Martha (Patty) More to William Wilberforce, Cowslip Green, 14 November 1800

Following the fateful meeting at the George inn on 12 November, Hannah More became too ill to write, and it was left to Patty to communicate the bad news to friends. This letter highlights the More sisters' vulnerability. As women, unable to be clergy or magistrates, they could not be present at proceedings where their conduct was being questioned and the fate of their school decided. It was left to Sir Abraham Elton to mount their defence.

I scribbled a few incoherent lines in the midst of much bustle and hurry last night to acquaint Mrs H[enry] Thornton[62] of our complete defeat at Blagdon; but if you will permit me, I shall be more circumstantial tonight. Sir A. Elton had defied Bere to confront his accusers, to this he gave a false colouring; & summoned together the malignants of the Country, both the Laity & Clergy, that he knew were hostile to us & our schemes, & also the worldly & indifferent ones, that seemed

62 Marianne Thornton, née Sykes (1765–1815).

unfavourable to serious religion. They erected themselves, or rather Mr Bere erected them, into a Court. Sir A. Elton went entirely alone, [and] with too much nobleness & dignity perhaps, refused to solicit any body to attend him. Bere opened with a Speech endeavouring to touch their passions completely turning the tables against us, complaining that he was the persecuted man & making it appear that he was the accused. Sir A fought nobly & manfully from twelve o' clock till past five, an hour and a half at a time, with a zeal, eloquence & argument that would have been even admired in the House of Commons. They laughed & they cried, as their passions were alternately touched, just as if they had been at a well acted play; but it was not likely they should be convinced as the cause was already prejudged, as they came to carry it in favour of Bere, or as they call it the *Church.* When religion was to be attacked Herod & Pontius Pilate were to be of one mind,[63] for a Socinian Dissenter was as vehemently against Methodism, as the most intolerant Church Man. Among the Orators were the Clergyman of our own Parish,[64] Blomberg,[65] & Mr Addington's Farmer; what made it still more curious, they carried their presumption so far, as to put it to the Vote, & you may be sure all voted one way when all came prepared on one side. The Laity behaved by far the worst, the Clergy appearing to act with great moderation and professions of respect for us, while the Laymen desired, especially Mr Addington's Steward, to proceed, to detail, in what manner we were to teach. They agreed we might be permitted to read Chapters, provided we did not suffer them to be explained, this they positively forbade. When our party proceeded to overturn their affidavits, which now have been completely done, without an oath on our parts, for we have been very tender of swearing, nobody listened, no body gave us a hearing, the thing was said to be completely settled, it was not worth while to hear the other side. Among many other figures of Rhetoric, Bere accused Sir A[braham] in the most violent and menacing tone, with being a Baronet. He said he could not help it, he received it from a succession of ancestors, and he hoped it was no crime in this country that he hoped to transmit it to his posterity as pure as he received it. What concluded the business of the Day & their triumph was a master stroke of Bere's who produced an Affidavit that had not been seen before which went to prove that, after reading a Sermon, I held it high over the people's heads declaring it to be written by a Dissenter & that no Bishop would write like that. As a lie of this magnitude could not be foreseen, nobody was prepared to answer it; and I myself not being present to disprove it, it was greedily swallowed. Let me however be correct, they did not go the lengths to dismiss the *School.* Some of the Clergy did say, to be sure we have no jurisdiction here. What they pretended to

63 Luke xxiii.12.

64 William Leeves.

65 Frederick William Blomberg (1777–1847), vicar of Banwell, Somerset, 1799–1808.

was that the Man must be more subject to Mr Bere, be directed entirely by him, & never explain any thing. The voting went to this. This was the *pretence*, but that Carthage must be destroyed[66] was the real object. There was only one went the length of saying [that] all our schools should be abolished. Poor Bere was sunk deep into the most horrid perjuries. The whole Parish of any respectability was standing about the doors, & passages, all day to bear their testimony to Young's character, & not one suffered to be heard; however Bere at last was brought to confess he was a moral man, tho' he had written to his Rector that he was the most 'infuriate Fanatic' guilty of the most 'nefarious practices & delinquencies'! Sir A, came here to six o'clock dinner exhausted, further enraged, but still glorying in his cause though justly anathematizing triumphant villainy. I am afraid I may say scarcely a soul of us closed our eye; and my poor sister lying in the eleventh Day of her fever, did not gain much, but had a most dreadful night, & is very poorly today. I must not omit to mention how splendidly the evening was concluded at Blagdon, When this honourable Court was dissolved, Mr Bere stepped into the Kitchen of the public house & said Gentlemen I wish you joy, the Church has gained it. The Bells were then set ringing & such ale houses and other houses where Bere had influence were illuminated, & suitable Inscriptions signifying that the true Church was now safe. Blagdon illuminated, or Methodism defeated, we shall not be surprised to see in the news papers.

It is a solid comfort to think we have struggled to the last, through all this ignominy, in hopes to preserve the School; but this is at an end, even you would not wish us to carry on the mere form of an Institution, at a great expense, under Mr Bere's management. It will be my melancholy task on Sunday, to hear Mr Bere preach, go through the normal School duties, & then dissolve it for *ever*. It is unlucky that we lost most of Bere's panegyrical letters of the School, for he denies now having ever written any. On Sunday excessing *four hundred* Souls will be turned loose upon the world, & all to wickedness. – May God assist and direct them. It is not the voice of resentment to say that this Man lies, swears & Drinks, preaches not only nonsense but heresy, & has been off his guard, in bestowing invectives on the Government. Such is this world, that he is exalted, & we are rejected. It is a wholesome humiliation. As soon as H[annah] is able she is to write to Moss her final letter.

Be so good as to show this tedious account to Mrs T[hornton] as writing time is rather precious.

I hope Mrs Wilberforce is gaining ground daily and that your health is in some measure equal to the present nervous occasion… We had but one friend present,

66 The Roman senator, Cato the Elder (234–159 BC) ended every speech with 'Delenda est Carthago'.

a Captain Simmons, who volunteered in the Service.[67] Our friend Whalley[68] was from home.

More to Wilberforce, Cowslip Green, 2 December 1800

In Blagdon is still 'a voice heard lamentation and mourning' and at Cowslip 'Rachel is still weeping for her Children and refuses to be comforted because they are not'[69] – instructed.

This heavy blow has almost bowed me to the ground. It was only last night I began to get a little sleep. My reason and my religion know that it is permitted by that gracious being who uses sometimes bad men for his instruments, but religion and reason do not operate much upon the *nerves*. I doubt not but that He who can bring much real good out of much scorning evil will eventually turn this shocking business to his glory, and even already a *little* light seems to be springing out of the darkness, as some eyes which seemed judicially blinded seem to begin to open. Though I knew Bere and his adherents have spread abroad the most flagitious reports concerning my political and religious principles, yet I own I was inexpressibly shocked the other night at Patty's receiving from the Bishop of London[70] a most ambiguous and alarming note expressing the utmost terror on my account, yet refusing to explain himself, saying if it was true what was reported she would understand what he meant. All we can collect from this obscure giving out, and which out of tenderness he concealed is, that this *mock* trial has been fabricated by Bere's Emissaries into an *official* one and that I am found guilty of sedition and perhaps taken up and sent to Prison. – Remember this is a mere surmise. Have you had any communication with the Bishop of London, or have these strange reports reached *you*?

I have at last got a letter from Dr Moss, polite and handsome as to my motives, character and usefulness, but quite blind as to the atrocity of Bere's conduct towards me and ignorant of the general worthlessness of his character. I pity these men in high stations for not being more in the way of ascertaining the real characters of their Clergy, it might to be sure be done in one way, by employing conscientious and pious men in their inquiry. But there is a sort of Esprit de Corps which makes them support each other in public even when (as in the present case) their private language is different. Dr Moss, however, totally exculpates himself from having had any hand in this famous trial, expresses much

67 Captain Thomas Simmons of Bath, husband of the More sisters' former pupil, Frances Lintorn.

68 Thomas Sedwick Whalley (1746–1828), a local landower and magistrate, later to be Hannah More's most ruthlessly effective defender.

69 Matthew ii. 18.

70 Beilby Porteus (1731–1809), an evangelical sympathizer, was one of More's closest friends; he was much disliked by some of the *Anti-Jacobin* writers.

regret at their indecent rejoicings, and laments the loss of so many useful institutions to the Parish – thinks me obstinate but, I believe, nothing worse.

I mean to re-read for the fiftieth time your Chapter on the overvaluing of human Estimation.[71] I have perhaps been too anxious on that head – yet few people have cared less about *general* opinion except as it has attacked me in that vital vulnerable point on which one's usefulness depends.

We received a kind letter from Mrs W[ilberforce] during my illness for which pray thank her. It is a great comfort she goes on so well. I have had a return of my complaint, and am still very poorly.

Patty behaves nobly – and only works the harder for all these attacks. She has been in all this weather on a three day's mission to Wedmore where things look very smiling. Our persecutors are become our Admirers, now they say they have seen our goings on, and that we are not *Methody People*. And that rich farmer who presented us at the visitation for *teaching French Principles*, sends his own family to the School and the reading, both of which are very full. But I greatly dread that Bere's success at Blagdon will induce a second visit to Wedmore where *he* first stirred up the opposition.

My wounds are still fresh and raw, and want much wine and oil. This your kind letters never fail to administer. But I hope I strive to look for still higher and better consolations, and that these may be granted me I am persuaded I have your prayers.

Be so good as let Mr and Mrs H. Thornton see this scrawl, as I am not equal to much writing on this subject.

I have some good things to tell you as to the increase of religious clergy among us.

4. THE ATTACK ON BERE

In spite of the pessimistic tone of her letter to Wilberforce, More refused to accept defeat at Bere's hands. She looked for allies among the local clergy and on the episcopal bench and was pleased (and somewhat surprised) to receive an extremely supportive letter from an ecclesiastic she privately mistrusted, George Pretyman (later Pretyman-Tomline), bishop of Lincoln (1750–1827). Her visit to Bath at the end of 1800 gave her the opportunity to tell her side of the story to George Crossman, the rector of Blagdon. As a result of those meetings, Crossman wrote a series of letters to Bere telling him he was not satisfied of his trinitarian orthodoxy and warning him he was to be dismissed. On 25 January the Blagdon school was re-opened and Young was reinstated. However, Bere refused to stand

71 From Wilberforce's *A practical view of the prevailing religious system of professed christians in the higher and middle classes* (London, 1797).

down and in March he launched the first of his three pamphlets attacking More. In August he was restored to his curacy and the school was closed again.

More to the bishop of Lincoln, Bath, 30 December 1800[72]

This carefully worded letter to an unexpected ally shows Hannah More at her most resourceful and accommodating, putting over her case while making light of her evangelical beliefs. In giving her own version of events, she attacks Bere's political rather than his religious heterodoxy.

I know not how to express with sufficient force the comfort and support my mind has derived from the letter you have done me the honour to write me. To be absolved and even approved by your Lordship and the Bishop of London is a circumstance which ought to banish from my mind every painful feeling which the Tribunal and the Verdict of Blagdon have a tendency to excite. I feel much gratified by the goodness which led your Lordship to suggest the Plan of a kind of Counter Meeting. A few weeks ago I might have been induced to feel the propriety and even necessity of adopting it. But such a change of opinion and circumstances has taken place that I think you will agree with me that this necessity is in a good degree done away. The four neighbouring Clergymen have made their *amende honorable* and have repeatedly expressed their regret at having been drawn in by Mr Bere's artifice by which they were made to believe that they were obeying a Decree of the Chancellor. They have expressed to me and to others their detestation of Mr Bere's falsehood, and their concern that on account of my being dangerously ill at the time they could not know the true state of the case. The truth however might easily have been known if they had been very zealous about it – but I spare them. Mr Bere's character they well know, all except Mr Blomberg, who was but just come among us; they know about the taint of heresy which stuck to it; but a good natured fear of injuring a Brother Clergyman and of spoiling a good neighbourhood were the reasons assigned for their making part of the Blagdon Court. Mr Bere when he got them there gave a new turn to the meeting. Now, my Lord, I have a delicacy about calling another meeting on account of these very men, because they are Clergymen, and because they are my neighbours. I wish to practise that very delicacy which they wanted. I wish to spare *their* feelings who have so deeply, though I believe unintentionally, wounded mine.

The Affidavits were completely discredited had the Gentlemen been disposed to listen to the Evidence on the other side. But a sensible young Attorney who

72 Centre for Kentish Studies, Stanhope Papers, U1590/S5/03/S6. Quoted by kind permission of the Trustees of the Chevening Estate.

volunteered his services to poor Young without fee or reward has drawn up the Case with the testimony on both sides. Thirteen Depositions were taken by Mr Bere *in his own cause*, a large proportion of the deponents declare they were sent for by him; and that Mr Bere has tampered with almost all, and put words into their mouths there is little doubt. To this many creditable witnesses are prepared to swear, but I will not allow it. Oaths have been too sadly multiplied. Of the depositions produced all except one ought to have excited nothing but contempt. Of the credit due to that one, the character of M[argaret] Thorne in the Bishop of London's possession is a sufficient answer.[73] Ten persons offered to swear point blank against her, but I think only two were admitted. Young's character is fully cleared to all honest and unprejudiced minds. That of Mr Bere is also I think in the way to be completely laid open. As to the Laymen, who were indeed the great acting characters and Orators of the day, I feel more pleasure, I had almost said more pride, in forgiving than exposing them. They already make a very bad figure in their own neighbourhood, and they are most of them so insignificant that out of it they are not at all known.

Besides, my Lord, having borne the smart, I am trying to reap the profit of this blow, and to submit to it from the consideration that it has pleased God to employ a bad Man as an instrument for my correction and improvement; and I would not defeat the *end* for which the chastisement was permitted. It was *his* will, and for my humiliation that I should suffer just in that part where I thought myself least open to attack, and that I should be accused of the very crimes I fancied I was strenuously opposing.

I must regret with my wise friend Dr Maclaine [*sic*] (who is himself free from Enthusiasm as *any* good man is so) that these Clergymen and, as he says, too many others, should be so ready to join in the popular cry of Enthusiasm at the first suspicion of a little more than usual zeal, to which appearance they cannot but know that charge is always attached. I asked one of these very Clergymen how many persons he thought he had in his own Congregation (except two or three whom I named) who know the meaning of those words with which so many of our Church Prayers close, I mean *Advocate and Mediator*. He owned he was not sure there was one; yet he seemed to think this evil small compared with the danger of Enthusiasm. His reasoning however seemed false even on his own principles, as religious knowledge does not seem the probable cause of religious error. The truth is, as your Lordship knows, in their ideas of enthusiasm people do not always distinguish between an enlightened zeal which combats vice and irreligion, and a

73 In the autumn of 1800 Margaret Thorne, wife of the parish carpenter, had testified that Young had prayed for the French, had declared himself a calvinist, and had stated that the prayer book service 'did not exactly in his opinion agree with the Scripture'. Bere, *Controversy*, pp. 69–73. Thorne's moral character was subsequently attacked by More's defenders.

mischievous zeal which propagates error and absurdity. The consequence is, this Gentleman's Parish is now overrun with Methodists. I once planted a school there but withdrew it, as it did not meet with support where I had reasonably looked for it.

On the subject of what Mr Bere was pleased to call the *Seditious Nocturnal Meeting* – Nocturnal by the way is a strong word to designate *seven o' clock* – allow me, my Lord, to remark that Methodism on the one hand and vice and profligacy on the other *must* be triumphant if in a remote Village, in which no idea of Jacobinism ever entered (unless perhaps in that very mind which ought to guide and guard the principles of the rest), if I say half a dozen sober Church-going neighbours may not meet one hour in a week after their daily labour, for the purpose of religious readings and conversation, and to strengthen each other in their good dispositions without being harassed and tormented, tried and condemned, I leave your Lordship to judge what impressions of right and wrong must be made on the Blagdon people when they see *my* poor Schoolmaster brought to ruin merely from the above circumstance, while the *Parish* School Master, Mister Bere's confidant who assisted him in the far-famed Affidavit business, passes part of every day at the ale-house, and was described formerly to me by Mr Bere as an idle drunken fellow he should be glad to get rid of. Will their horror of enthusiasm with which their minister is inspiring them, do them much good while their regard to morality is much weakened? I have not been able to see Sir A. Elton since I had the honour of your letter. He is most laboriously occupied, not only in his ordinary duty as the most able and independent Magistrate in a very large district; but in this period of peculiar difficulty he is instructing the Overseers and others, over a space of near forty square miles, both how to *feed* their parishes and keep them in *humour*; in the admirable addresses which he delivers to them in various places he insists much on the duty of the *latter* part. His arrangements have been of vast importance to the quiet of this County. When the French were expected to land on *our* Coast 700 men were prepared to rise at the sound of his Trumpet. Yet with this load of business he did not omit one Monday morning for five months to ride twenty miles to us to direct me, in the case of an information which Mr Bere's menaces led me to expect. At the Mock Trial Mr Bere accused Sir A. Elton with being a *Baronet*; he corrected this Democratic attack with great moderation by observing that in *this* Country at least he hoped it was no crime to have a *Title*.

From my venerable Diocesan I have always been honoured with favour and commendation; and I believe that both his Lordship and Dr Moss have frequently had the goodness to repel little spiteful representations which such a scheme as mine would be likely to occasion. Through Mr Bere's misrepresentations to his Rector, I have, I fear, lost some part of Dr Moss's good opinion. It was my misfortune that I had not character enough to be credited by the Rector and my simple affirmation that I could not, like his Curate, tack an Affidavit to the tail of every assertion. But I had been so little used to this sort of work that I think I never before *saw* an Affidavit except in the Newspaper. But though I was driven to assert some things against Mr Bere they were only such as were absolutely necessary to the defence of my persecuted Schoolmaster, and in vindication of the principle of my School, and not to ruin the Curate. I am now still less anxious to expose him: I have lost the object for which I thought it so long my duty to contend at the expense of my peace, my health, and my reputation.

Having been driven to abandon my institution, I have nothing more to do with Mr Bere, except to wish him a sincere repentance; though this is one of those cases in which the repentance of the offender will be little redress to the person injured. I did not however give up my School as is supposed, from submission to the *Alehouse Tribunal* as your Lordship justly calls it, but from the fullest conviction that I could no longer continue to act under Mr Bere. A quarrel may be made up; but contending principles will continue to contend…

More to Henry Thornton, Bath, 1 January 1801

This letter and the following one, written from Bath to two of her closest friends, show More's continued distress at the loss of the Blagdon school, her gratitude to Porteus for his warm support, and her ambivalent feelings about the bishop of Lincoln.

This letter shows that More was now securing allies in the Mendips, ready to support her accusations of heterodoxy.

Your letter received a month ago would have been answered but for the very weak and precarious state of my health; we only removed hither just against Christmas.[74] I am rather better since my removal from the place where the zeal and ardent kindness of my friends oppressed my nerves almost as much as the persecution of my enemies, and they (my nerves) are so shattered that any one reading or speaking with more than usual emphasis brings on my Complaint. I am however persuaded that *all is as it should be* – my mind is not only resigned to the event but I see good arising from it. So large and complicated is the subject that I dare not enter upon it, and knowing that you and Mr W[ilberforce] had engagements of your own which more than occupied your time I should probably have spared you, even if I had been able to write – but the little strength I *have* been able to muster has been reserved for this business which seems as if it would have no end. I speak within bound when I say that Sir A. Elton and Mr Whalley

74 The Great Pulteney Street house of the three eldest More sisters.

(my neighbour at that sweet place on the Hill)[75] have written a moderate octavo volume to open Eyes which have seemed almost judicially blinded; the scales at least seem, though slowly and reluctantly, to be falling off. I enclose you the copy Dr Moss's Answer to Mr Whalley, by which you will be pleased to see that our *other* Schools are at least likely to be protected from such attacks. Bere's character is in the way to be developed completely. The Gentleman alluded to in the inclosed letter whose acquaintance Bere dropped for his heresy is a most pious and virtuous Gentleman, whom he, Bere, had traduced through our whole Country as a blasphemer and to whom he had ascribed the dreadful guilt of saying that the persons of the Holy Trinity were like three old women consulting together. The truth was, Bere in his Conversation with this Gentleman had declared that *Christ was only an angel of a superior order* – This also is the strain of his preaching – and in order to cover his own heresy cried out first. It is remarkable that this Gentlemen and another both officers in the Army, good Christians, are now in a principle of duty bringing Bere to open shame for heretical doctrines, while his own brother Clergymen have supported him through thick and thin till it is become infamous to do so, and now they too join in reprobating him.

When I spoke of some good which it would please God to educe out of this evil, I did not mean merely with reference to my own mind, but to the stirring up others in the cause of religion in general, and to the vindication of the *principle* of my Schools in particular. The Bp of London has taken up my cause with an ardour which might be expected from his affection to me, as well as a hatred to intolerance and persecution, He had written to me almost every other day for some weeks, such zealous letters as have been important in the cause; I have also sent him at his desire all the papers relative to the business which he has diligently investigated. He desired not for the conviction in his *own* mind, for *he* had no doubts, but that I might stand clear in the eyes of others, that I would send him a full and true History of my Schools, of the State in which I found the Parishes and the state in which they now are. I was too ill to do this, and indeed did not choose it, but desired the most worthy of our Clergymen to draw up a sketch each of his own Parish, which has abundantly satisfied the Bishop. I wish they may not have been too favourable in their reports, but it came better from them than from me. As to the manner of instruction and the conduct and the things taught I have described these honestly and fairly in an appendix of my own – All this is travelling about among the Episcopacy. You will be rather surprised to learn that the Bp of Lincoln acquits us of enthusiasm and irregularity. I will send you his letter and

75 Mendip Lodge.

perhaps my answer tomorrow that you may see his spirited plan and my reasons for declining it...

[The rest of the letter is taken up with good wishes to friends.]

More to Mrs Henry Thornton [?January 1801][76]

This blow has indeed very nearly demolished me. I was so completely overwhelmed by it, falling on me as it did when I had been pronounced out of danger from my fever only two days, that for several weeks the tone of my mind seemed to be quite destroyed, and this was exceeded by the force I put upon it to write so much in so worn out a state. Add to this that I had lived so long in dread how this man's machinations would terminate that I hardly had a good night's sleep without laudanum from June to November. I say this much partly to account for my seeming to bear so ill the dispensation of God, which even at the worst I was enabled to acknowledge was *most righteous*, and I every day see more and more that he will make it work for good in some way or other. I suffer extremely on the return of every Sunday from thinking of my poor scattered flock. But they are in better hands than mine. I am better since I left Cowslip Green where I constantly saw Blagdon Tower from my window. Sometimes my spasms are violent, at others my pain is but moderate and the waters are brought home to me as I have been confined to only two rooms since September.

I only sent you *one* of the Bp of Lincoln's letters, as it lets you into his views on the subjects. It was not one of the easiest things I ever did to answer it. I laboured to keep clear of religious *words* and *phrases*, and at the same time to drop *some hints* which I was not without hope might set *his Lordship a thinking*.[77]

5. BERE'S REVENGE

In spite of More's relative optimism after this demonstration of episcopal support, Bere's decision to publish his version of the affair in pamphlet warfare kept the controversy alive for the whole of 1801 and secured his re-instatement.

More to Wilberforce, Bath, 18 March 1801

I beg the favour of your sending me back by return of post the Copy of Sir A. Elton's to the Bishop of London and also as soon as you can spare Covers the Bishop's letter to me – but Sir A.'s first.

I have not troubled you for a long time knowing how much you are harassed, but have felt largely with you, and for you, in all the late changes and chances of

76 The letter is undated but it was clearly written shortly after Hannah More left Cowslip Green for Bath at the end of December 1800.

77 Presumably the heavy hints of Bere's 'Jacobin' sympathies.

this (more than usual) changeful and chanceful world. We have almost broken our hearts at the Abdication of Mr Pitt, and are very ill reconciled to his feeble and inefficient successor.[78] I have never met one person of either Party who thinks he can stand it – How dark are all our prospects, moral, political, and religious – but the Lord reigneth.[79] – It is a great comfort to me to hear that your health bears up so tolerably under all these trials.

Mr Bere's increased malignity has continued in spite of my earnest endeavours, to harass my nerves and to wear out my health. He is gone to London for the several purposes of applying to the Commons[80] to know if he cannot resist both Bishop and Rector and stay in his Curacy in spite of them; to get Counsel whether he cannot prosecute Mr Boak for defamation of his principal Evidence who has been a Thief, a common Prostitute and can be convicted of perjury;[81] and thirdly to publish a pamphlet against me – This last you have doubtless seen advertised and it is worded with his usual duplicity – He calls it '*The Controversy between Mrs H.M. and the Curate of Blagdon, with original letters by the Revd T. Bere, Vicar of Butcombe*'.[82] This implies you see that Mr Bere and the Curate of Blagdon are two persons, and people are taken in by it.

As he does not stick at perjury itself, he will make out a specious case – His infamous associate Margaret Thorne he send about the Country to get Testimonies to her Character. In order to obtain these she tells the people 'her character being cleared is of importance to the nation, as her testimony is to convict *us* of labouring for the downfall of the Country and praying for the French'. – I am sick of writing such stuff – Yet miserable as it is our whole neighbourhood is still up in arms, and Bere has a party who are all assisting in writing this precious book, among them a Clergyman, one Shaw, who has been in the King's Bench for Seditious practices.[83] The most unpleasant part of the story is that our *now* great neighbour, Mr Addington affects to consider Bere as a persecuted man, and as *his* Bayliff was one of the Judges in the Blagdon Conclave he has suffered his mind to be poisoned by the misrepresentations of this low man. – The truth is that Mr A. is extremely hostile to the religious Instruction of the poor, and is glad of showing his opposition to it. And as I believe his brother, now, alas Premier, has the same prejudices I augur ill for the Country in this point from his Election. I hope I shall bear these deep schemes for the destruction of my usefulness by this attack upon my reputation with humble patience looking at him who endured the

78 Henry Addington.

79 Psalms lxxxxvii.1; lxxxix. 1.

80 Presumably Doctors' Commons near St Paul's cathedral, which was the site of several church courts.

81 Margaret Thorne. See note 73.

82 Bere's first pamphlet; published March 1801.

83 William Shaw (1787–1831), Gaelic scholar and rector of Chelvey, Somerset, 1795–1831.

Contradictions of Sinners &c. &c.[84] but alas this frail body is neither Hero nor Christian. The School thank God is going on with the hearty encouragement of the Rector.[85]

I shall certainly not answer the book though it accuses me of all the crimes committed since the murder of Abel – but it is expected to be so mischievous that some of my friends may think it a duty.[86] – And this may detain me here a little longer than I wish – for I long to get away – I am sadly worried with Company, and I am worried with refusing as well as with seeing them – you know how that is – nothing but flight will do – I think if health and other things equally uncertain permit, to set out for Teston the beginning of April – but I am not sure of myself two days together.

More to Wilberforce, *c.* 21 July 1801

By the summer of 1801, with Bere refusing to vacate his curacy, his case had been stridently taken up by the Anti-Jacobin, *and high churchmen were lining up on either side in the controversy. Because of Mrs Wilberforce's uncertain health, the Wilberforces were still at Broomfield, their house on Clapham Common.*

It is circulated among the worldly and Socinian Clergy that I have been in the constant habit of praying for the success of the French in my schools! How I shall one day admire that infinite wisdom which has thus decreed that I should be wounded just where I am most vulnerable! My gracious Father, I doubt not, saw (though I knew it not) that I was too anxious about human opinion. You have doubtless seen the Antijacobin for June – I will give you a fresh instance of the treachery of the Editor, and you will see how every thing has concurred to injure me. Randolph[87] and G[eorge] Glasse[88] were the only respectable persons that wrote for that Review. I have often lamented they did so – The latter warm hearted and extravagant in his kindness, where he has an attachment, reviewed Randolph's Sermons in a strain of Panegyric which to own the truth justly laid him

84 Hebrews xii. 3.

85 A reflexion of the transitional situation in Blagdon by March 1801.

86 More's tactic throughout the Blagdon controversy was to refuse to write in her own defence but to encourage her friends to do so on her behalf. This has been variously interpreted as duplicity or as a realistic recognition of the gender conventions which criticized women who defended themselves as 'Amazonian'. Compare Ford K. Brown, *Fathers of the Victorians. The age of Wilberforce* (Cambridge, 1961), pp. 226–8 and Stott in *Hannah More*, p. 250.

87 The Rev. Francis Randolph (1752–1831), chaplain of the duke of York and patron of Laura chapel, Bath.

88 The Rev. George Henry Glasse (1761–1809), rector of Hanwell, Middlesex.

open to censure.[89] Randolph had written to Gifford[90] that he would undertake to review all the Blagdon Pamphlets, and obtained from G— his thanks and a promise that whatever was sent against me should not be invented. G. had undertaken services of something of a similar nature. Randolph came down a fortnight ago and preached our Club Sermon at Shipham, he had some talk with the Clergy present and a Plan was settled that they shou'd make a Statement of Bere's falsehoods and he would insert it with his Critique in the Antijac. Three days later the Antijac: came out with not only a most infamous string of false charges against me; but with a most contemptuous and abusive letter against Glasse's Review and Randolph's Sermons.[91] This has naturally enough exasperated them both to such a defiance that they have for ever ceased all connexion with Gifford and his Review. I am glad to have them both cured, & their eyes open to those worldly and deceitful friendships; still I am the victim of their Secession and I doubt not that for a twelvemonth to come this Review will be made the common rallying point for all who wish to stigmatize me. Oh for more faith and more deadness to such a world! If it does but help to purify and fit me for a better, I ought to count it a light affliction. Pray for me that it may not have been sent in vain. Bere is playing some fresh trick daily, refuses to resign and threatens an appeal to the Archhishop and to prosecute his Diocesan.

More to Wilberforce, Cowslip Green, 17 August [1801]

By the middle of August it had become clear that Bere was going to retain his curacy. However, a key text in More's defence was about to be published in September, inspired by Randolph's visit. This was A statement of facts relative to Mrs H. More's schools, occasioned by some late misrepresentations, *and consisted of statements from nine local clergy. The author was almost certainly More's friend the Rev. John Boak, now rector of Brockley.*[92] *This letter shows how closely she was involved in drawing up the statement.*

It is no Compliment to say that in almost every instance in which we thought differently that I should conclude that *I* was in the wrong. But in the actions you recommend to be made to the 'Statement of Facts' I cannot quite come into your opinion. You are clearly right in the first suggestion, that of inferring Bere's

89 Francis Randolph, *Sermons preached at Laura chapel, Bath, during the season of Advent, 1799* (London, 1800) was reviewed in the *Anti-Jacobin*, VIII (Feb., Mar. 1801), 135–7, 296–302; IX (Apr. 1801), 47–52.

90 John Gifford (1758–1818), editor of the *Anti-Jacobin*.

91 See *Anti-Jacobin*, IX (June 1801), 201–7. The suggested defence of More was published as *A statement of facts relative to Mrs H. More's schools occasioned by some late misrepresentations* (Bath and London, 1801).

92 For evidence of Boak's authorship, see Stott, *Hannah More*, p. 248.

falsehoods in some instances from his known and detected falsehoods in others. But I struggled hard with my mind to have as little Acrimony, and even as little mention of Bere as possible; leaving the reader to make that inference himself, which however you are perfectly right in supposing that the generality will not do, for if you do not reason and infer for them they will not do it for themselves.

As to the second remark, I rather think you have only the unfinished Copy of 'the Statement' which I *first* sent, as there is in the letter one *little* addition, made I believe from your suggestion. Should there be another Edition I have desired Mr Pratt[93] to add one sentence 'that they are carefully taught the principles of the Gospel', or something to that effect. But as the reader is now (Page 3) referred to 'my Publications where they will see that earnest regard to Religion which is frequently branded with the names of Methodism and Enthusiasm by those who have no other Idea of Religion than the outward form of it' – As they are so referred I say, it seems to me not proper to give here a formal Confession of my Faith, especially after having given it so much at large in the last Chapter of the Strictures. My reason for this too is that the Statement not only does not *appear* to come from me, but really that it does *not* come from me, and that I had no hand in writing it. Had not my sentiments on Christianity been already so long known and so widely extended in various Publications or had it been a matter of *doubt*, I should have felt my self bound to come forward with an explicit declaration. But I think if you will consider the thing in this view you will see that this does not seem to be the exact place for such an Exposition of my Creed. And after all who does it come from? Assuredly not from myself. I shall be glad you would look into the 2nd Edition of 'The Statement'. Look also if you happen to have my 8 volumes at hand[94] into the 94th and 95th pages of Volume 6 where there is a slight account of my opinion of that Establishment I am accused of undermining. It makes part of my answer to the Duke of Grafton.[95] A propos his Grace has just sent me a large Octavo of Whitby on Original Sin with two preparatory letters from Lady Euston[96] earnestly entreating a promise from me that I would give it a fair and candid perusal. To convert me to the faith *never* delivered to the Saints[97] has been long a serious object with the Chancellor of the University of Cambridge. Do you know this book of Whitby's?[98] – But to return, I have good reason to believe Bere

93 The Rev. Josiah Pratt (1768–1844); from 1795 the assistant minister at St John's Chapel, Bedford Row; first editor of the *Christian Observer*.

94 An eight-volume edition of More's works was published by Cadell in 1801.

95 Augustus Henry Fitzroy (1735–1810), 3rd duke of Grafton, and former prime minister; became a member of Theophilus Lindsey's Essex Street unitarian chapel.

96 The former Lady Charlotte Maria Waldegrave (1761–1808), Grafton's daughter-in-law.

97 '... earnestly contend for the faith which was once delivered to the saints'. Jude 3.

98 Daniel Whitby (1638–1726). His *Paraphrase and commentary on the New Testament* went through many editions.

is restored merely to quiet a clamour and not from the smallest change in the Bishop's mind respecting him. There was a sort of combination among the lower clergy against the Bishop in his favour. It is carried by a Jacobinical spirit of opposition to the Powers that be – it is a hard blow struck at Episcopal Authority… If the truth were known they would find it was I and not they who tremble for the Church – for I do verily believe it to be in danger. If Dr Phillott[99] &c knew they were supporting a Socinian and Jacobin, and one who is leagued with Infidels and Jacobins, but they are judicially blinded, that seeing they might not see &c and hearing &c.[100]

You ask what is to be done with that vile Antijacobin? I answer there should be a combination among honest men and Christians against them, and the first step should be that none should take their Review. I say not this now because they are assassinating me, but I have long said it. In order to keep my mind from being disqualified for duty in my nervous state I now do not read any of the trash that comes out, and of course I have not seen the last Antijacobin but I hear with deep concern of their brutal attack on Sir A. Elton.[101] We hope that as he is just returned from a Tour in Wales he may miss it. – He is so feeling and so irritable[102] that from what I hear of it, it would half destroy him. I am so long used to abuse it does not hurt me so much but as it threatens to destroy my usefulness, although at the Peter Pindars I only laugh.[103] Every one thinks something ought to be done, but no one does any one thing. Bere now gets his Pamphlets let out to read for six pence in the distant parishes where I have Schools by way of influencing the Farmers and Common people against us.

Nothing can exceed the kindness of the Bishops of London and Durham.[104]

Are you gone to Teston? We look for Sir Charles here and the two young Noels.[105] We also hope to remove late next month into a half-finished house, about which I have had nothing but vexation, loss and disappointment.[106] O for more preparedness for that house from which I shall remove no more!

99 James Phillot (d. 1815), archdeacon of Bath.

100 'Hearing ye shall hear and not understand; and seeing, ye shall see and not perceive.' Acts xxviii. 26.

101 See the *Anti-Jacobin*, IX (July 1801), 289–95. The most serious charge made against Elton was that he had 'actually preached in a *Tabernacle* before he was admitted into the pale of the Church!!!'.

102 Meaning 'prone to nervous irritation' rather than 'bad-tempered'.

103 In 1799 the former doctor John Wolcot ('Peter Pindar') had mocked More and Bishop Porteus in his *Nil admirari; or a smile at a bishop* (London, 1799).

104 Shute Barrington (1743–1826), bishop of Durham from 1791.

105 Sir Charles Middleton, who had inherited Teston from Elizabeth Bouverie, and his two eldest grandchildren, Charles-Noel Noel (1781–1866), later earl of Gainsborough, and Gerard Thomas Noel (1782–1851).

106 Hannah and Patty More moved to Barley Wood in Wrington, Somerset, at the end of September.

More to Wilberforce, Cowslip Green, 19 August [1801]

This letter shows More's dislike of the radical methodists of the new connexion. Astonishingly, she and Patty were preparing to open a new school, though this venture came to nothing.

As I do not think you and Mr H. Thornton are aware of the new Principles and practices of what are called the seceding and Dissenting Methodists I send you a letter of Mr Boak (which pray return when you have both read it) in order that you may get at *their* opinions as *I* do those of Paine and Godwin, by means of the Answers. These Methodists are more angry with me for drawing people to the church as they suppose, than the worldly Churchpeople are for my making Methodists as they in *their* turn suppose; and I have the honour to be abused by name in some of their Conventicles from the Pulpit. These contests incline me more and more to range under the Banner of good Erasmus in the golden mean. He I suppose would have been guillotined for a modéré had he lived in our days.

I know not whether you will blame or commend, when I tell you that P[atty] and I have been busily engaged for many weeks past in a bold attempt to break up some very stony ground in a fresh Country in a direction quite foreign to all our old Colonies. I am impelled to this laborious scheme, for such it proves to be, by various motives – viz: an increased conviction of the duty of turning the short term of life to speedy account; an interval more ease as to bodily sufferings, and above all a dread lest the undiminished opposition and persecuting spirit of Mr Bere might be converted by the great enemy of souls into a means of making one shrink from labour and calumny; and that not being able to stand my ground in one place might be pleaded by me as a sufficient reason for idleness and indulgence in all. It is a large populous Parish called Chew Magna above two hours drive from hence. There are several opulent and rather genteel Inhabitants but that does not prevent the lower Class which are very numerous from being in as sad a state of vice, ignorance and total neglect as I ever beheld. The people whom we have to propitiate are an old Methodist lady, a Quaker Lord of the Manor, and a Socinian Clergyman. He is nearly connected with Lindsey[107] and Disney,[108] his wife a Daughter of Archdeacon Blackburn[109] of your County. But they seem candid and tolerating, and are less prejudiced than some more orthodox folks I hope it may please. Sad to say, this Rector not only was never at any University but was bred in a Military Academy and was going into the Army when this great living, £600

107 Theophilus Lindsey (1723–1808), unitarian minister of Essex Street chapel.

108 John Disney (1746–1816), unitarian minister; in November 1782 he threw up his preferments and offered his services to his friend Lindsey.

109 Francis Blackburne (1705–87), latitudinarian clergyman, rector of Richmond, Yorkshire. His stepdaughter Sarah Elsworth married the Rev. John Hall, vicar of Chew Magna.

a year, was obtained for him. He rather seems unacquainted with religion than hostile to it. He is from Richmond, Yorkshire, his name Hall – his connexions the Mildmays. Do you know them?

There is much pioneering work to be done, Teachers to be *created* – a Malthouse to be converted into a Dwelling House; but for this latter mechanical part the minister is our right hand man. How he will be when we come to introduce doctrines so opposite I do not know. It is our part to try. – I leave the event to higher hands, desiring your prayers for our direction and success.

I hope it may please God to turn the heart of poor Bere, but at present it is exceedingly mad against us. His outrageous conduct has had the good effect of raising in our favour the torpid and silencing the hostile. Our good neighbour Mr Whalley came forward very handsomely at Blagdon Church with me voluntarily as the avowed defender of our cause, and sat the rest of the day at the School, hearing the teaching, the evening Sermon, and making a handsome present to the School. He goes about bearing his testimony in favour of the *sobriety* and *practical* turn of the whole. Had the Archbishop of Canterbury done so the surprise would have been far less to me. Having struggled alone for eleven years against the prejudices of near half a County, it was become a doubtful point whether the whole of our Institutions should not have been ruined by the calumnies and misrepresentations of this Bere, for however civil and friendly to they may be to us personally, yet not only the worldly and the negligent, but also the High-Church-Methodist-Haters would not have been sorry that we should have been knocked up. The able exertions of Sir A. Elton whose friendship for me and zeal for the cause seems quite heroic in this tame land, has given a new turn to public opinion. How it will end I leave to Providence; whether Bere will oust us, or his Rector him. The latter writes most handsomely to me, but I am afraid he is implicated with his Curate by letting the Tythes, if so he cannot get rid of him. In the mean time the school is full and we attend it though it is a painful Trial. He still threatens us with fines, and we expect an information [?] every Sunday. It is settled by Sir A. and our friends that I shall refuse to pay, and that I am even to submit to imprisonment should he push matters so far; as we think it a duty to prove what the law *can* do, in this case. I confess however I know not how I should stand it, and I am not so brave as to go without a little palpitation, and I am always glad when the Blagdon Sunday is well over. I rather think he has tried what *law* he can get and has failed. A public statement of the case in a Pamphlet is what we expect. I hear he has above 100 Charges against us. – Dr Valpy,[110] Editor of the Star, was by chance at our Cheddar Club and I find has put a most flaming Account of it in his Paper. I was ashamed of it. – The Tudways came to us from

110 Richard Valpy (1754–1836), headmaster of Reading school.

Wells. The Dean[111] sent a handsome subscription & on the day £25 was given me as a Legacy from the Lady of the Manor as a token of her dying approbation of the Schools. A propos of money – you must send some when you can spare it. Can you get Mr Gisborne[112] to give us some of his £100,000. A friend of mine, unknown to me, wrote to his Colleague Hawkins Brown to beg for us, but I suppose in vain…

More to Wilberforce, Cowslip Green, 27 August [1801]

With Bere's restoration confirmed, More realized that the Blagdon school would have to close, and that she would have to fight to keep her remaining schools.

The Storm rages with increasing violence. I had hoped that things would have mended when B— was restored to his Curacy; which had it not been for so bad a man having the care of so many Souls, I should not have been sorry for, as I believe there was no other way of quieting the Democratic violence of the lower Clergy who use it against the Bishop's Sentence with a fury which bodes no good to Church government. For this spirit I truly grieve. I wish they knew how much more I have at heart the peace of the Church than many of her own Ministers. The truth is the Chancellor reprimanded B— for his duplicity, party spirit and misconduct, but B— was so intoxicated at his restoration that he proclaimed aloud and inserted in the papers that the Bp. and Chancellor were 'perfectly pleased' with his conduct. This has injured my fame more than all the rest, as the inference is that they must perfectly *disapprove* of me. Of course the spirit of opposition and abuse runs higher than ever. – The truth [is] however that those timid people, who gave at Christmas accounts of B—'s heresy to the Bishop refused in July to come forward as public Accusers, through fear I suppose of being involved in a prosecution. I of course am made the victim and incur the odium of having tried to get him out. B's friends are united in the course of sin, more are divided and at variance. The Chancellor and Dr Crossman are very ill together, the latter loudly complaining of his wrongs; *all* indignant with the first informers against B – which informers are equally displeased with them. I do what I can to quiet all parties and to make them patient with each other, and pray to be enabled to bear my own lot with patience, and to act aright whatever I suffer. I send you enclosed a Copy of my Answer to the Chancellor's letter announcing B's restoration though you

111 George Lukin (1740–1812), dean of Wells 1799–1812.

112 Thomas Gisborne (1758–1846), evangelical clergyman and author.

probably will not like it.[113] His reply was handsome on the whole. – He expressed 'much concern at my sufferings – said the Bishop had disapproved of *his* restoration of the Schoolmaster but added that the Bishop was a friend to the general Plan of my Institutions', as to your question he says 'I can only refer you to your own superior sense and discretion as to the expediency or inexpediency of continuing or dissolving the Bl—n School as to the rest allow me to observe that your high character places you above the influence of idle reports' &c &c. These private compliments however unless he would put a line in the papers contradicting Bere's paragraphs do me no good.

Finding my difficulty not removed by his refusal, I set out ill as I was to Taunton to consult Dr Crossman. I found him much irritated against the Chancellor whose cause I pleaded, and provoked that his Curate has not made him the least concession but sets him at defiance. Not this but to determine conscientiously about the School was my object in going. He was very friendly, eager that the School should be continued if it could any how be contrived. After much discussion in which I had come to the resolution of sacrificing my ease and peace if that could accomplish the preservation of the School, so much fresh matter has come to light as makes me see it is not merely difficult but impossible to retain it. Nay it will be well if I can retain any one School. No wonder B will not endure one in his own Parish when he is resolved never to rest while I have one left. – Wedmore is next to be abolished tis the most flourishing we have and perfectly correct. The Curate who at 40 years old has never been able to obtain Priests orders on Account of having two Wives with some other flaws in his character is taken into the Confederacy.[114] He wrote to me while I was at your house asking me to write to the Dean to beg the Living of Wedmore for him assuring me the Rector (who is still living) was dead. I of course refused. Since then he is become an open enemy and joins with those who accuse me of being engaged in a Scheme to destroy Church and State. They say 'It's a smothered flame, which we shall keep back till all is ripe for our purpose'! That these low people should invent such stuff is not wonderful but that some of the more considerable Clergy should propagate it that is the marvel. The Party are going about Boak's and Drewitt's Parishes to excite suspicions in the common people against these two worthy men, and to accuse them as disaffected.

[The rest of the letter missing.]

113 In her letter to Moss, More asked him to 'favour me with your counsel & direction, whether the Blagdon School should, or should not be continued. Painful as any further connexion with that Parish must be to me, after all that has passed … if *you*, Sir, recommend the continuation of the School, your commands shall meet with implicit obedience'. Duke University: More to Dr Charles Moss, n.d.

114 William Eyre, curate of Wedmore.

More to Wilberforce, Barley Wood, 21 October 1801

Wilberforce wrote at the top of this letter 'Bere still foaming'.

I was so much better for a day or two that I had hoped every day to be able to write to you on the next, but I have had many relapses and am still very poorly. The fever has in a good measure subsided but has left something of the old complaint, and the bad nights I get keep me back. I was promised to be quite well when I got to this elevated and really beautiful situation, but have been confined to my bed or room ever since I came to it.[115] It puts me in mind of the old remark that the first spot of Earth which Abraham took possession of in the Land of Promise was a *grave*. It is a salutary reflection. It is a little trying to me to know you and Mrs W. are so near and not to be able to see you. I hope the waters strengthen and do you good, but such a short course I fear can do but little towards setting you up for a winter's labour. Blessed be God the most painful parts of that labour will be mitigated by the restoration of *Peace* and plenty![116] How utterly undeserving are we of such blessings! Not for any works of righteousness &c &c.[117] – I agree with you in deploring the dark prospect as to Religion, It is, as it is connected with the reigning temper and spirit of the times, that I chiefly lament the Blagdon business. Alas! It is not me individually. I am only a petty victim. Could such a man as B— with principles equally hostile to the Church and State be supported by men professing themselves warm friends to both, if they were not judicially blinded, and if a general hostility to serious religion were not a common rallying point to two descriptions of men opposite enough in all other respects? As to myself I bless God though broken down in nerves and health my mind is in general quiet and resigned. It is enough for the Servant if he be as his Lord. I resolve not to defend myself, let them bring what charges they will. If it pleased God to put an end to my little (how little) usefulness, I hope to be enabled to submit to His will, not only to submit because I can't help it, but to acquiesce in it because it is holy, just, and good. Bere's threatened Pamphlet is suspended by a fit of the Gout, but *Shaw* is at work with him and he has emissaries in all the villages who are sent to pick up any stories they can against me. His object is to destroy my remaining Schools. It is said he is sadly disappointed to sit down quietly on his old Curacy – Stalls and Benefices he thought awaited him for his zeal for the Church. It was my fixed resolution to answer not one of his baseless false assertions in the Papers; far from it, he has ventured ten times greater lengths from the certainty of not being contradicted. I believe the whole

115 More was to live in Barley Wood until 1828, when she moved to Clifton.

116 The peace preliminaries with France were signed in October 1801. Wilberforce was a strong supporter of these preliminaries and of the Treaty of Amiens which followed.

117 Titus iii. 5.

to be a deep Socinian and Jacobinical Plan. Randolph is very warm and zealous, and I believe fights my battles earnestly...[118] I wish you would talk to Randolph about what he saw and heard from our Clergy when he preached the Club Sermon and to Dr Maclaine [*sic*] of what he knows of Blagdon School that you may be able to tell it to the Bp of London. Nothing can exceed his kindness in this whole business.

More to Wilberforce, Barley Wood, 15 December 1801

On 11 December Wilberforce had written to More passing on his own and Bishop Porteus's advice that she should not sue Bere, but suggesting that she might publish a pamphlet in her defence.[119] *When he received the following distraught reply, he wrote on top of the letter 'Poor thing sadly wounded'.*

I wish you could have sent me the Bishop's note. I wanted to see what he says. I wish much to undeceive both you and him. *I* never dreamed of prosecuting – it came from your quarter; though I yielded to the opinion of my friends here that it might not be amiss to take a legal opinion. For one, as I wrote to Henry Thornton I am sure I should not *live* through a public trial – besides he is so poor it would ruin him which I should be sorry to do, though he has ruined me, as far as a blackened reputation is ruin. Still less do I think of *answering* him - that is all he wants. I suppose he has ten rejoinders ready. You have little notion of the depth of the man or the extent of the mischief. I endeavour to see only the hand of God in this trial and to consider these evil men as tools with which *He* is working for my purification. I hardly dare expect to preserve my Schools unless some part of this load of obloquy is removed, and to remove it do not think of stirring a step.

Wilberforce to More, London, 17 December 1801[120]

...The Bishop, the other day, warmly expressed in conversation what he may perhaps express to you in writing; and lest he should, I must anticipate him. He seemed to wish you would give up all your schools, by way of escaping from a situation which exposed you to attacks and conflicts to which your health was not equal.

But the Bishop never saw the schools; he never saw the country in its former and in its present state. He has no adequate notion of the degree in which it has

118 The next few sentences deal with the financial problems created by the move to Barley Wood.

119 Bodleian Library, MS Wilberforce d. 16, fo. 2.

120 From *The correspondence of William Wilberforce*, ed. Robert Isaac and Samuel Wilberforce (2 vols., London, 1840), I, 235–6.

pleased God to bless you and your sister's efforts; nor of the consequent hostility to be expected from those who are represented in Scripture (which does not refine away plain practical truths as we are apt to do) as opposing the establishment of the kingdom of Christ; whether evil spirits, or human beings acting under their influence... But for the relinquishment of the schools - as long as you can, continue them through evil report and good report. Quench not the Spirit...

6. THE JAY'S CHAPEL AFFAIR

After this letter, More's correspondence with Wilberforce dried up until the summer of 1802. She was ill and under doctor's orders to keep her mind as quiet as possible.[121] Meanwhile in March her friend Thomas Sedgewick Whalley published his scurrilous but effective *Animadversions on the curate of Blagdon's three publications*. However a fresh crisis blew up when the April 1802 issue of the *Anti-Jacobin* triumphantly revealed that More had taken communion at the Independent Argyll chapel, whose minister, William Jay (1769–1853), was a personal friend. Coming at a time when anglican-dissenter relations were strained, this was a deeply embarrassing fact, and More's agitation comes over in the following letter to Wilberforce.

More to Wilberforce, Barley Wood, 17 August 1802

The letter begins with comments on Wilberforce's successful election campaign in Yorkshire.[122]

From two or three attacks of sickness and other causes I have not yet sent my letter to my Diocesan,[123] but I have seen one from him to my neighbour Whalley (his relation) expressing himself sincerely enough on my subject – but I depend on nothing! My health being, on the whole, better, I bless God that I am better able to encounter such fresh trials and difficulties as continue to occur. – Mr Jay's behaviour is not the smallest – I remember you thought me uncandid and I condemn'd myself for being so – but he *has* repeatedly said that I took the Sacrament *frequently* – I sent Miss Schimmelpenninck[124] over to him to assure him in the most friendly manner how much he was mistaken – he was unluckily out – *Mrs* J— behaved very properly but in a few days I received from *him* a letter which Miss Schim will send you to morrow. You will I think agree that it is not

121 *Correspondence of Whalley*, II, 211–12.

122 On 11 July 1802 Wilberforce was re-elected MP for Yorkshire.

123 Richard Beadon succeeded the deceased Dr Charles Moss as bishop of Bath and Wells in April 1802.

124 A member of the (originally Dutch) Schimmelpenninck family of Berkeley Square, Bristol. For More's connexion with the family see Christiana C. Hankin, *Life of Mary Anne Schimmelpenninck* (London, 1860), pp. 331–2.

written in *quite* a good spirit – I enclose you my Answer. I desired Miss S— to tell him that it is not a thing of moral turpitude from which I am meanly defending myself; but it is a simple question of truth and falsehood, and that I dread the thought of being driven to vindicate my own veracity at the expense of his – and how painful it must be – and what a triumph to the ungodly to see two persons professing religion, palpably contradicting each other. It hurts me for his own sake to see him ungenerously recriminating – Were I to do the same, he would be the sufferer. But I never will. An Enemy-Clergyman declares he has seen me at Jay's within two or three years (The Object now is to Convict me of *falsehood*). I know it is *seven* years it may be eight, but I cannot be sure which. I can find nothing which proves me to have been at the Chapel since 1794, but it may have been a little later. If Mr Babington[125] is with you be so good as to ask him to set down with his name at what time he came to Bath and I told him I had totally discontinued going to Mr Jay's – that would ascertain what is a trifle indeed, & which it is shocking to be called on to prove. – I shall probably make no use of his paper, but to make assurance doubly sure to my own mind. – The Antijacobins mean to produce another letter next month, proving my communicating 'several times' – My conscience is so clear that my mind is comparatively easy but my friends may require some proof – Had I been to a *hundred* Masquerades nobody would care about it.

Pray return me Jay's letter when you have shown it Henry Thornton... Spencer is bringing out another Book to prove that I have as much influence in the Army and Navy as in the Church, and on using it to the same pernicious purposes.[126] I was loath to write to Jay, I don't know what use may be made of it. – I am not equal to the Question of the School... You heard of Shaw's producing a forged letter from me at the Clergy visitation and showing it round...

7. THE TURN OF THE TIDE

As More had half hoped, Richard Beadon's appointment as bishop of Bath and Wells marked a pronounced turn in her favour. In her letter to Beadon, dated 24 August, she set out her case and was cautiously relieved to receive a supportive reply from the new bishop.[127] However, the letter below shows how her bruising experiences had dented her self-confidence.

125 Thomas Babington (1758–1837); evangelical; M.P. for Leicestershire.

126 Edward Spencer seems to have thought better of writing this book. His caution reflects the fact that events were moving More's way.

127 The letter is now in the library of St John's College, Cambridge, MS k 34. A slightly shortened version was published by Henry Thompson in his *Life of Hannah More with notices of her sisters* (London, 1838), pp. 200–2. In the section omitted by Thompson, More describes William Eyre, curate of Wedmore, as 'one of my most active opponents' (fo. 24).

More to Wilberforce, Barley Wood, 10 September 1802

The enclosed letter from my Diocesan you will be so good as to return me, after you have shown it to Mr Henry Thornton. I think you will agree with me that I could not have expected a more handsome or more unqualified answer to my long letter. It came too the very next day. I shall however be cautious of availing myself of it. – I mean I shall not say yet that I have received it. – It may be the more prudent to wait till next month when he is to come to Wells, to see if his conduct corresponds with his professions and to let him be a Volunteer, if he be so disposed, in his good offices in that land of Enemies. I feel thankful for such an honourable support and sanction – but after what has passed I hardly depend on any body – It is from no kindness to *me* that the Antijacobin has changed their Note, but they are frighten'd for themselves now the world has found out what are the real principles, religious and political, of the party they have so zealously espoused: but even Jacobins and Infidels are to be upheld if by so doing Methodism (or what they call so) may be crushed. Peace be with them! Their repentance comes too late to do my any good. – I am sorry you did not read it, because you would have seen how I was in love with an *Actor* and *two Officers*, with my other previous Adventures.[128]...[Comments about Wilberforce's health follow.]

I observe attentively all you say about the importance of lending a little vigour and spirit to the Christian Observer.[129] But it in order to *give* a thing one must *have* it, and there is no affectation in saying I feel as it I should never be able to write again. I have been so battered daily and monthly for the last two years about the wickedness and bad tendency of my writings, that I have really lost all confidence in myself, and feel as if I never more could write what any body would read. Besides, the soil, naturally meagre, is exhausted and must lie fallow before another Crop can be hoped for. – But foolish metaphor apart – my nerves are far from being sufficiently strong for me to write – I have acquired such a dislike to it, that I hesitate and procrastinate for days when I have even a common letter to write. I used to defy mere pain and sickness and found little difference when any thing was to be written whether I was well or ill. But the late disorders of the body have introduced now diseases into my mind, listlessness and inapplication, two words of which before I hardly knew the meaning. – Yet as to health, I have gained much ground lately. – It would grieve me sadly if my want of power should prevent your want of will to take up the Observer. My inability should rather stimulate your zeal. I see how important it would be. I know what strength you

128 These scurrilous allegations are contained in William Shaw's anonymous *Life of Hannah More*. The book was an attack too far and the August issue of the *Anti-Jacobin* (XII, 444) dismissed it as 'this worthless performance'.

129 The evangelical periodical founded in 1802.

gave to the first number by a striking Essay. – It is certainly a valuable Miscellany, written in an excellent temper, sensible, judicious, and in general candid and moderate, but it wants a little *Salt*, a little sprinkling of *manners* as well as *principles*. – Good people will like it as it is, but we do not so much want books for good people as books that will make bad ones better. – Do write without once thinking of such a Pigmy associate as I should be – a Dwarf in my best Estate, and now a dwarf crippled. If I should ever feel able I shall think the Xtian Observer has a right to my first services...

8. POSTCRIPT

Nine years after the Anti-Jacobin *ended its hostilities, More published* Practical piety. *One uncharacteristically autobiographical passage gives an insight into her later reflexions on the controversy.*

By a life of activity and usefulness, you had perhaps attracted the public esteem. An animal activity had partly stimulated your exertions. The love of reputation begins to mix itself with your better motives... It is a delicious poison, which begins to infuse itself into your purest cup... He who sees your heart, as well as your works, mercifully snatches you from the perils of prosperity. Malice is awakened. Your most meritorious actions are ascribed to the most corrupt motives. You are attacked where your character is lest vulnerable. The enemies whom your success raised up, are raised up by God, less to punish than to save you... Your fame was too dear to you... It must be offered up... He makes us feel our weakness, that we may have recourse to his strength, he makes us sensible of our hitherto unperceived sins, that we may take refuge in his everlasting compassion.[130]

APPENDIX: HANNAH MORE AND THE BISHOP OF LINCOLN

Hannah More had an ambivalent relationship with George Pretyman-Tomline, bishop of Lincoln and former tutor to William Pitt. They knew each other socially, and he clearly thought highly of her, though she did not entirely return the compliment. In 1794 he sent her a copy of his charge, after which she reported to Wilberforce: 'It is sensible and, as far as it goes, good – But I wish Bishops had not got a trick of considering Christianity like Statesmen, as a good popular thing. I am however much pleased with the spirit of moderation and temperance in this Charge'.[131] In January of the following year, she wrote to enlist his support for her

130 *Practical piety; or the influence of the religion of the heart on the conduct of the life* (2 vols., London, 1811), II, 211–12.

131 Duke University, Wilberforce Papers: More to Wilberforce, 29 Nov. 1794.

Cheap Repository Tracts, her plan to counter Paineite literature with stories and ballads for the poor, and was gratified when he became one of the subscribers to the scheme.[132] Later in the year she asked Mrs Pretyman to ask her husband to recommend clergy in his diocese who were likely to support it.[133] When she was in London in the spring of 1796 she spent five hours with him, poring over Pitt's proposed Poor Law Bill, 'making pretty free use of our pencils in the margin', though her proposals came to nothing as the bill never became law.[134] But in spite of this apparent community of interests, she had considerable private reservations about Pretyman's usefulness to the evangelical cause. In the summer of 1796 she and Wilberforce were discussing the possibility of ensuring the appointment of an evangelical fellow to Lincoln College, Oxford in the face of opposition from Edward Tatham, the college head, and 'a blind and furious stickler for Aristocracy'. More added in her letter to Wilberforce, 'We dare not apply to the Bishop of Lincoln, I know full well that he would recommend precisely such a man as would mar our project.'[135] This was for private consumption, as to all outward appearances she and Pretyman remained cordial acquaintances. He wrote to congratulate her on the publication of her *Strictures*, telling her that 'no age owed more to the female pen than to yours'.[136] In the summer of 1799 she was on holiday at Christchurch with the Thorntons, and, as the Pretymans were near neighbours, she saw a good deal of them; she did her best to make the rather prickly Henry Thornton more accommodating in his manners to the bishop: 'I carried the Thorntons to the Bishop of Lincoln – Henry you know is not very coalescing, but worst of all does he mix with any thing that has a particle of the Hierarchy in it.'[137] She had no such problems of accommodation.

Her mistrust of Pretyman surfaced in the spring of 1800, just as her Blagdon troubles were beginning. In 1799 Pretyman had commissioned a report on the state of religion in a hundred parishes in his large diocese. Its alarming findings showed a growing indifference to the Church of England caused partly by the activities of itinerant radical methodists. A bill to tighten up the law on licenses for dissenting preachers was abandoned in the commons but taken up again by the government on Pretyman's advice. 'I have heard a good deal of Mr Pitt's bill',

132 Centre for Kentish Studies, Stanhope Papers, U1590/S5/03/S6: More to the bishop of Lincoln, 21 Jan. 1795.

133 Centre for Kentish Studies, Stanhope Papers, U1590/S5/03/S6: More to Mrs Pretyman, 11 June [1795].

134 *Memorials of Gambier*, I, 310.

135 Duke University, Wilberforce Papers: More to Wilberforce 3 Aug. 1796 [wrongly catalogued 1799].

136 Roberts, *Memoirs of Hannah More*, III, 94.

137 Duke University, Wilberforce Papers: More to Wilberforce, 'Priory, Monday' [July or Aug. 1799].

Hannah More told Henry Thornton; 'made in *the Lincoln School* I fear.'[138] The dissenters' case was taken up by Wilberforce, who successfully pressured his friend, the prime minister, to withdraw the bill.[139] But as has been shown, by the end of the year, when she needed all the allies she could lay her hands on, she enlisted him as an influential ally, and kept to herself her strong opposition to the bill. After this, whatever her private views of his deficiencies, there is no record of further criticisms. She could never forget that he had come to her aid in her time of need.

138 Duke University, Wilberforce Papers: More to Henry Thornton, 1800.

139 David Hempton, *Methodism and politics in British society* (London, 1984), pp. 78–9.

2

HENRY RYDER: A CHARGE DELIVERED TO THE CLERGY OF THE DIOCESE OF GLOUCESTER IN THE YEAR 1816

Edited by
Mark Smith

Introduction

Life and Career

If they are to be measured by the conventional expectations of the early nineteenth century, in which personal connexions carried significant weight, then Henry Ryder's qualifications for appointment to the episcopal bench were more than adequate. He was born on 21 July 1777 the youngest son of Nathaniel, the first baron Harrowby of Sandon in Staffordshire and his wife Elizabeth, the daughter of Richard Terrick the bishop of London.[1] His eldest brother, Dudley Ryder, from 1809 the first earl of Harrowby, although he suffered throughout his career from ill-health, was a distinguished statesman associated successively with Pitt, Addington, Perceval and Liverpool. He held a number of government positions, serving *inter alia* as vice-president of the board of trade 1790–1801, foreign secretary 1804–5, ambassador to Berlin 1805–6, minister without portfolio 1809–12 and finally as lord president of the council throughout the administration of Lord Liverpool from 1812 to 1827 after which he declined an offer of the premiership.[2] In addition to his ministerial responsibilities, Harrowby took considerable interest in the reform of the established Church, including the promotion of legislation to improve the position of curates which culminated, in 1813, in the successful passage of the Stipendiary Curates Act.[3] He subsequently also served as a member of the Church Building Commission and as an Ecclesiastical Commisioner. Henry's middle brother, Richard, despite suffering even more seriously from debilitating illness, also achieved cabinet rank – serving, with some reluctance, as home secretary between 1809 and 1812 in the Perceval administration.[4]

Henry Ryder was educated at Harrow and subsequently at St John's College, Cambridge, where he graduated M.A. in 1798. According to his obituary in the *Christian observer*, 'he passed through the University with a generally high character as a young man of literary taste, studious habits and outwardly at least of irreproachable conduct', though, 'he was leading at this time, like other young men of rank and fashion, a life of worldly pleasure.'[5] In 1800 he was ordained by the bishop of Lichfield, James Cornwallis, to the curacy of Sandon, a living in the patronage of his own family. In 1801, he succeeded through the influence of Addington to the crown rectory of Lutterworth in Leicestershire and in the

1 M. A. Smith, 'Henry Ryder', in *The Oxford dictionary of national biography* (Oxford, 2004).

2 D. R. Fisher, 'Dudley Ryder', in *The house of commons 1790–1820*, ed. R. G. Thorne (5 vols., London, 1986), V, 75–8.

3 53 Geo. 3 c.149.

4 D. R. Fisher, 'Richard Ryder', in *House of commons,* ed. Thorne, V, 78–83.

5 *Christian observer* (1836), p. 503.

following year he married Sophia, the daughter of a local gentleman Thomas March Phillipps of Garendon Park. In 1805, Ryder added to Lutterworth the neighbouring vicarage of Claybrook which he held in plurality with his first benefice and in 1808 he also became a canon of Windsor. In the first part of his career as a clergyman Ryder seems to have combined a full participation in the fashionable social life which might be expected of a gentleman of his means and connexions with a careful attention to his clerical duties. He sought to develop his own theological education beginning a course of reading in the Fathers and a critical study of the Bible with the assistance of 'approved commentaries' and took great care over the preparation of his sermons. Ryder also seems to have been an active pastor, being kind to the poor,[6] and diligent in visiting the sick and catechizing the young. At this stage of his career, according to the *Christian observer*, 'he was looked upon by the world at large as quite a model of a young parish priest.'[7] Despite the *Christian observer*'s assertion that his religion was, at this time 'rather professional than personal',[8] Ryder conducted regular devotions in his own family, which eventually grew to include thirteen children, and also paid attention to the development of a personal piety, consulting a range of works including some in the evangelical tradition like Richard Cecil's *Friendly visit to the house of mourning*, which he seems to have read in the wake of the death of his father in 1807.[9]

As a conscientious and extremely well-connected young clergyman, Ryder was bound to attract official notice, and he was chosen to preach at the visitation of George Pretyman-Tomline, the bishop of Lincoln, in 1806 and again at the visitation of the archdeacon of Leicester in the following year. Both these visitation sermons were published and they provide a good indication of Ryder's theological position at that time.[10] The episcopal visitation sermon was a straightforward attack on the characteristic calvinist doctrine of indefectible grace and the particular evangelical understanding of immediate or complete assurance

6 From December 1811 until early April 1812, for example, the Ryders provided free soup for 160 poor families every Friday and organized a subscription to bring in large quantities of bacon and rice which they sold at a further discount to the poor at Lutterworth and Claybrook in order to relieve distress during the winter. Sandon Hall, Harrowby MSS, vol. V, fos. 102–6: H. Ryder to Dudley Ryder, 15 Apr. 1812.

7 *Christian observer* (1836), p. 503.

8 *Ibid.*

9 *Ibid.*, p. 504.

10 H. Ryder, *On the doctrines of final perseverance and assurance of salvation. A sermon preached at Leicester June 6th, 1806 at the visitation of the right revd. the lord bishop of Lincoln* (London, 1806); *idem.*, *On the propriety of preaching the calvinistic doctrines, and the authorities for that practice. A sermon preached at Leicester; May 20th 1807 at the visitation of the Reverend Archdeacon Burnaby* (London, 1808).

of salvation.[11] His argument was based on a combination of scripture, the fathers of the first four centuries and the doctrine of the English reformers and also on the alleged effects of those doctrines in promoting either presumption or despondency. Ryder instead favoured a notion, based on his interpretation of the life of St Paul, of a gradual growth in assurance as the normal pattern of christian experience. On this understanding, full assurance could only be expected to appear late as the fruit of a holy life.[12] The second sermon used a similar combination of authorities to challenge the propriety of preaching on the doctrine of election or a limited atonement, arguing that speculation on the divine decrees was no more a part of gospel preaching than the reduction of christianity to mere moralism or the republication of the law of nature.[13] Here Ryder seems to stand squarely in the mainstream of a pre-tractactarian high-church theological tradition with a reverence for scripture, the fathers of the undivided church and the English reformation and a characteristic stress on the duty of cultivating holiness of life as evidence of the sanctifying presence of the holy spirit in the life of the believer.[14] This mainstream high-church position and the marked anti-calvinism of both sermons would certainly have recommended Ryder to Bishop Tomline, three of whose early nineteenth-century charges, including that of 1806, were focussed on this issue and were incorporated in his *Refutation of calvinism* published in 1811.[15] The two seem to have remained on excellent terms throughout Ryder's incumbency at Lutterworth and in 1807, for example, Henry Ryder could be found staying with the Tomlines at Buckden and acting as a go-between for his brother Dudley and the bishop in relation to schemes of ecclesiastical reform.[16] The espousal of high-church views did not imply for Ryder an automatic opposition to

11 For a view the characteristic evangelical understanding of assurance see D. W. Bebbington, *Evangelicalism in modern Britain* (London, 1989), pp. 42–50.

12 Ryder, *Final perseverance*. There was, however, a degree of variation in evangelical views on this point and some anglican evangelicals could espouse a position which approached in effect that proposed by Ryder here. See, for example, *Notes of the discussions of the Eclectic Society, London during the years 1798–1814*, ed. J. H. Pratt (2nd edn., London, 1865), pp. 220–1, 500–1.

13 Ryder, *Calvinistic doctrines*, esp. pp. 22–6.

14 The best study of pre-tractarian high churchmanship remains P. B. Nockles, *The Oxford movement in context. Anglican high churchmanship, 1760–1857* (Cambridge, 1994). See also, *idem*, 'Church parties in the pre-tractarian Church of England 1750–1833: the "Orthodox" – some problems of definition and identity', in *The Church of England* c. *1689* - c. *1833. From toleration to tractarianism*, ed. J. Walsh, C. Haydon and S. Taylor (Cambridge, 1993), pp. 334–59.

15 G. Tomline (originally Pretyman, later Pretyman-Tomline), *A charge delivered to the clergy of the diocese of Lincoln at the triennial visitation of that diocese in May, June and July1812* (2nd edn., London, 1813), p. 5.

16 Harrowby MSS, vol. IV, fos. 192–3: Henry Ryder to Dudley Ryder, 25 July 1807. See also vol. V, fos. 127–9: Henry Ryder to Dudley Ryder, 1815, for Tomline's expression of regret at losing Ryder as one of his diocesan clergy on his move to Gloucester.

the evangelical school as such. He seems to have been willing to employ evangelical curates[17] and, even the sermon at the archidiaconal visitation, in which he argued that preachers should make their congregations 'experimentally sensible of their own personal need of a Redeemer',[18] may bear some traces of evangelical influence.

Nevertheless, it is noteworthy that both the visitation sermons were preached at Leicester and must have been construed as a direct attack on the town's most prominent clergyman – the calvinist evangelical incumbent of St Mary's, Thomas Robinson.[19] Ryder seems to have been impressed that, when Robinson himself preached the visitation sermon in 1808, he did not take the opportunity to reply, instead simply urging his brethren to cultivate personal religion and to base their preaching on the Articles and Homilies.[20] Thereafter, in 1809, following a chance encounter between the two men, first an acquaintance and then a friendship began to develop.[21] Partly though his relationship with Robinson, Ryder's views seem to have been increasingly influenced by evangelicalism. He began to read more works of evangelical literature like John Newton's *Cardiphonia* and the biblical commentaries of Henry and Scott. By 1811, he was openly associating with the local evangelical clergy and could be found presiding at the annual meeting of the Leicester Auxiliary of the British and Foreign Bible Society.[22] According to the *Christian observer*, whose information originated with Robinson,

> The change produced in Mr Ryder's mind was progressive; but, being founded on conviction, was powerful and abiding in its effects ... His was not a change, as some men call conversion, from *one set of opinions to another*, but from *opinions to deeply grafted principles*, attested by the habitual evidence of a fervent zeal and a holy practice.[23]

These changes led not so much to a transformation as to an intensification of Ryder's parochial ministry. Already a conscientious clergyman, he seems to have become even more assiduous in his attention to his flock, visiting both the well and the sick on a regular basis. He also sponsored pastoral innovations including a

17 *Christian observer* (1836), p. 505.

18 Ryder, *Calvinistic doctrines*, p. 23.

19 For Robinson, see E. T. Vaughan, *Some account of the reverend Thomas Robinson. With a selection of original letters* (London, 1815).

20 T. Robinson, *Serious attention to personal holiness, and soundness of doctrine considered in a sermon preached June 1, 1808 at the visitation of the Rev. Andrew Burnaby D.D. archdeacon* (London, 1808).

21 *Christian observer* (1837), pp. 214–17. Riding past in a hurry, Robinson issued an invitation to Ryder, having mistaken him for someone else, and the acquaintance began when Robinson called to apologize for the mistake.

22 *Christian observer* (1836), p. 505.

23 *Christian observer* (1837), p. 216.

cottage lecture at Claybrook and a weekly lecture in a local factory at Lutterworth – amply demonstrating the activism which, according to Bebbington, represents a key characteristic of evangelicalism.[24] It was this sort of activity that formed the basis of Ryder's claim to authority in delivering his primary charge on the basis of 'a somewhat intimate acquaintance with the condition, the feelings and the duties of a Parochial Minister'.[25] That his new found evangelicalism also made a discernible difference to his preaching can be inferred from the farewell sermon which Ryder addressed to his parishioners at Lutterworth and Claybrook in 1815:

> Oh! That those momentous, those precious truths of the gospel, which for several years I have sought to press upon your minds, (would to God I had done so during the whole period of my ministry!) may be admitted into more hearts and evidenced in more lives! These truths have been the tests of my ministry, so far as it has been Evangelical.[26]

Initially, Henry Ryder's public identification with the evangelical school within the Church probably seemed unlikely to affect adversely his prospects of promotion since both his brothers were members of a cabinet headed by a prime minister – Spencer Perceval – who was himself known for evangelical views.[27] Indeed, these connexions probably bore fruit in Ryder's promotion to the deanery of Wells in 1812, and in the same year, Perceval seems to have told the earl of Harrowby that he also wished to advance his brother to the episcopate.[28] Nevertheless, Ryder's arrival at Wells was greeted with some suspicion by the local clergy – suspicions which were confirmed by his energetic promotion of pastoral innovations there. He introduced an evening service in the cathedral, an afternoon lecture in St Cuthbert's (the parish church in Wells) to congregations which eventually grew to 2,000 people, founded a National School in the city and exercised an active interest in the parishes of Wedmore and Mark which were peculiars of the deanery.[29] Although an attractive character and evident good intentions enabled Ryder to conciliate some of the initial opposition to his measures, his cultivation of acquaintances like Hannah More and Thomas Gisborne,[30] together with his decision to preach a commemorative sermon for Thomas Robinson in 1813 and

24 *Ibid.*, pp. 505–7; Bebbington, *Evangelicalism*, pp. 10–12.

25 See below p. 88.

26 H. Ryder, *A farewell sermon by the honourable and very reverend the dean of Wells; preached in the parish churches of Lutterworth and Claybrook, on Sunday July 2nd 1815* (Lutterworth, 1815), p. 14.

27 For Perceval, see D. Gray, *Spencer Perceval. The evangelical prime minister* (Manchester, 1963).

28 Gray, *Spencer Perceval*, p. 127; Harrowby MSS, vol. V, fos. 107–10: Henry Ryder to Dudley Ryder, 22 May 1812.

29 *Christian observer* (1836), pp. 568, 629.

30 G. C. B. Davies, *The first evangelical bishop* (London, 1958), p. 5.

anniversary sermons for the Church Missionary Society and the Jews Society in the following year, continued to mark him out as a prominent supporter of the evangelical school and thus to provoke those (especially some high churchmen) who were suspicious of its growing influence.[31] The assassination of Perceval in 1812, therefore, seemed certain to reduce Ryder's chances of further advancement and, according to his biographers, William Wilberforce, for example, noted in his diary, 'Alas! I fear that Mr Henry Ryder's being a bishop, as humanly speaking he soon would have been, will be prevented.'[32]

Perceval's successor, Lord Liverpool, did not share his evangelical principles[33] and some contemporaries believed that he relied for advice with respect to episcopal appointments largely on the opinions of Henry Hanldey Norris, the high-church rector of Hackney and a central figure in the leading group of high churchmen known as the Hackney Phalanx.[34] Dr Gibson, on the other hand, on the basis of his analysis of surviving Liverpool correspondence, has suggested that his primary ecclesiastical advisors were William Howley, bishop of London, and Charles James Blomfield, bishop of Chester – also high churchmen.[35] Nevertheless, initially at least, the earl of Harrowby, who continued to serve in the cabinet as lord president, remained sanguine about Henry's prospects for promotion. In August 1812, for example, the two brothers corresponded about the possibility

31 H. Ryder, *A sermon preached for the benefit of St Mary's School, in Leicester in pursuance of the request of the late vicar* (Lutterworth, 1813); *idem, A sermon preached in the parish church of St Bride's Fleet Street ... before the London Society for Promoting Christianity amongst the Jews* (London, 1814); *idem, A sermon preached at the parish church of St Andrew by the Wardrobe and St Ann Blackfriars... before the Church Missionary Society for Africa and the East* (London, 1814).

32 R. I. Wilberforce and Samuel Wilberforce, *The life of William Wilberforce* (5 vols., London, 1838), IV, 27. It should be noted, however, that this sentence does not appear in Wilberforce's manuscript diary at the date cited in the biography. Bodleian Library, MSS Wilberforce, d. 54, 16 May 1812.

33 Although Norman Gash has identified Liverpool as, 'at heart... a liberal evangelical', and his attitudes may display slight signs of evangelical influence, his suspicion of calvinism and ecclesiastical connexions place him firmly in the 'Orthodox' camp. N. Gash, *Lord Liverpool. The life and political career of Robert Banks Jenkinson, second earl of Liverpool, 1770–1828* (London, 1984), p. 201.

34 H. H. Norris's alleged influence on episcopal appointments earned him the informal title of the 'Bishopmaker'. See, A. B. Webster, *Joshua Watson. The story of a layman 1771–1855* (London, 1954), p. 25. For Hackney high churchmanship in general, see Nockles, *Oxford Movement*; for the Hackney Phalanx as a patronage network, see C. Dewey, *The passing of Barchester* (London, 1991).

35 W. Gibson, 'The tories and church patronage, 1812–30', *Journal of Ecclesiastical History*, XLI (1990), 266–74. Howley, who was bishop of London from 1813, was an intimate of the Phalanx and helped to promote Blomfield. However, Blomfield did not become bishop of Chester until 1824 and seems unlikely to have exercised significant influence on Liverpool earlier in his premiership. Dewey associates both men with the Hackney Phalanx. Dewey, *Barchester*, pp. 152–5.

that Henry might succeed to the bishopric of Llandaff in the second round of episcopal appointments under the new government and engaged in a detailed discussion about whether it might be possible also to hold a deanery (preferably Bristol) as a commendam in order to make viable the occupation of a see which was notoriously poorly endowed.[36] Liverpool's first appointments, for example the promotion of G. H. Law to the see of Chester in 1812 and Howley to London in 1813, were entirely orthodox, but it is possible that Henry's name was thought likely to receive serious consideration, if only because of his political connexions, because at this point he began to face the accusation that he was a calvinist. The first allegations seem to have been made in an anonymous letter to the earl of Harrowby – perhaps with a view to weakening his support for his brother. The charge was renewed two years later in the context of Henry's imminent promotion to Gloucester and on this occasion the correspondent was identified as a Mr Johnson,[37] described by Ryder as 'respectable and in his way active – especially about charitable contributions – but very High Church – very busy and forward. He is said to have been in the Law'.[38]

The charge of calvinism was a familiar one to early nineteenth-century evangelicals and was often deployed unsystematically as in the suggestion by Jonathan Boucher that the arminian Hannah More was in fact a calvinist in disguise.[39] However, when it came to episcopal appointments it was a serious matter because the prime minister, Lord Liverpool, seems to have had a particular sensitivity on this point. As late as 1820, for example, responding to a suggestion by William Wilberforce that he might appoint more evangelicals to dignities in the Church, Liverpool wrote,

> I own to you I have a great horror of the doctrines of Calvinism...I am perfectly ready to admit that some of the most learned and some of the best men have, in former times, as well as now, entertained these Opinions, and preached these Doctrines, I know that they endeavour to explain away the most obnoxious parts of them, but I have always considered these explanations much in the same light as the explanations of the Papists of the idolatrous practices of their Church... I must moreover add that I cannot regard the Doctrine of Calvinism, or Predestinarianism, as many other erroneous opinions which, however mistaken, may have little influence on the conduct and characters of Men. I have always felt them peculiarly objectionable from their tendency to give a cast to the *character* the most unamiable, and if I may say so, unchristian.

36 Harrowby MSS, vol. V, fos. 111–14: Henry Ryder to Dudley Ryder, 12 Aug. 1812.

37 *Ibid.*, fos. 115–16, 124–6: Henry Ryder to Dudley Ryder, 15 Feb. 1813; Henry Ryder to Dudley Ryder, 1813.

38 *Ibid.*, fos. 147–9: Henry Ryder to Dudley Ryder, 1815.

39 An accusation that was also laid against Wilberforce. See, for example, A. Stott, *Hannah More, the first Victorian* (Oxford, 2003), p. 229.

I am far from saying that there have not been, and are not, many amiable and most virtuous Calvinists, but I suspect these to have been men of strong Minds, and I think experience and history would warrant the conclusion which I draw as to the effect of these Opinions upon the ignorant, the disappointed and those who are not blessed by Providence with kind and affectionate tempers ... if I have not been instrumental in promoting one particular class of clergy, it has been from a sincere conviction that their opinions are erroneous.[40]

In this context, it was clearly important for Ryder to clarify his own theological position which he did in his commemorative sermon on the life of Thomas Robinson and in a series of letters to his brother. The sermon, which was published with extensive notes in 1813, celebrated the life and work of Robinson but also carefully distinguished between the views of the author and his subject. Speaking of the

really distinguishing features of the Calvinistic system and especially the doctrine of election, the only one of them upon which Mr Robinson appeared to lay much stress. The author confesses that he was one of the many, who could not agree in sentiment with his friend upon this subject, but this disagreement had no effect whatever upon their mutual regard and the harmony of their intercourse.[41]

This position was elaborated in his correspondence with his brother:

To the charge of intimacy with some Calvinistic ministers of the establishment I plead guilty, but, as that intimacy is founded not upon agreement with them in their peculiar opinions, but upon respect for their conduct and esteem for their characters, in all future trials and attacks 'I will call to mind this accusation and be comforted.' Gisborne, who is, you know, a decided anti Calvinist once said to me in a letter what I have experienced to be true that some of the best clergymen of his acquaintance held the Calvinistic opinions. I certainly know and particularly regard many excellent members of the Clerical body who are not Calvinists, but at the same time several others who are, and who are not only eminent as useful teachers of religion in general, but are, declare and prove themselves to be devotedly attached to the Church.[42]

In 1815, Ryder noted that Johnson had made two main allegations: first, that he was on intimate terms with calvinist ministers and, second, that his own preaching was marked by calvinism. With regard to the first point he reiterated his defence that intimacy with calvinists was in itself no crime – a position which, Ryder

40 B.L., Add. MS 38287, fos. 272–8, Liverpool to anon., 26 Sept. 1820. Dr Best has identified the recipient of the letter as William Wilberforce. G. F. A. Best, 'The evangelicals and the established Church in the early nineteenth century', *Journal of Theological Studies*, n.s., X (1959), 64–78.

41 Ryder, *Sermon for St Mary's school*, p. 19.

42 Harrowby MSS, vol. V, fos. 115–16: Henry Ryder to Dudley Ryder, 15 Feb. 1813.

asserted, was not his or even Gisborne's alone,[43] but was also endorsed by bishops Secker, Horne and Horsley – authorities to whom he was to return in his visitation charge.[44] With respect to his own preaching of calvinism, Ryder made it clear that the allegation was false – 'I never did preach the Calvinistic doctrines' – but then went on to assert, again citing the authority of Bishop Horsley, that both arminian and calvinist opinions were acceptable within the Church whose articles were purposely designed to accommodate both traditions.[45]

Ryder's resolute defence of his own position seems to have been convincing, if not to Mr Johnson and some other high churchmen, then at least within his own circle and, most importantly, to the prime minister for the final letter in the sequence ended, 'Thank you and Lord L. and Richard 1,000 times for the kindness and friendship with which you have stood up for me… I hope that through the blessing of God I may not gratify my adversaries or disgrace you.'[46] Certainly, when in 1815 the opportunity for a new round of episcopal appointments presented itself, Lord Liverpool had shown a determined independence of any remaining pressure in some high-church circles not to include Ryder. Among the surviving correspondence of Archbishop Manners-Sutton (a key ally of the high-church Hackney Phalanx), who expected to be consulted by the prime minister *before* episcopal nominations were made, there is a note from the prime minister inviting the archbishop to an interview. The note is endorsed in Manners-Sutton's own handwriting:

> I am this moment returned from Fife House. Lord Liverpool told me that he had requested an interview for the purpose of relating the ecclesiastical arrangements *already determined* upon, in consequence of the Bp of St Asaph's death. – The Dean of Wells is to supply a vacancy on the bench.[47]

Whether he conscientiously objected to the appointment of a known evangelical or was simply piqued by being presented by the prime minister with a *fait accompli*, it would appear that Manners Sutton was not happy at the prospect and may have sought to oppose it.[48] However, Liverpool stuck to his guns and Ryder

43 Here, Ryder was associating himself with one of the most respected contemporary evangelical ministers, a highly cultured man, most famous for his *Inquiry into the duties of men in the higher ranks and middle classes* (1794), known for his arminian theological position and, perhaps most importantly for Ryder's immediate purpose, a dignitary of the Church, having been appointed to a canonry of Durham.

44 See below pp. 100–1.

45 Harrowby MSS, vol. V, fos. 124–6, 127–9: Henry Ryder to Dudley Ryder, 1815; Henry Ryder to Dudley Ryder, 1815. Neither of these letters carries a date but on the basis of the frank and internal evidence in the letters they can be assigned to the summer of 1815.

46 *Ibid.*

47 L. P. L., MS 3274, fos. 64–5: Liverpool to Manners Sutton, 17 May 1815.

48 *Christian observer* (1836), pp. 634–5; Davies, *Evangelical bishop*, pp. 8–9.

was finally issued with letters patent appointing him to the see of Gloucester on 21 August 1815.[49]

The Visitation and the Charge

In the early nineteenth century, both the episcopal charge and the visitation of which it formed an essential part were institutions on the eve of significant reform.[50] Although bishops were required by the sixtieth canon to visit every three years, practice varied significantly according to local custom. In the large diocese of Norwich, for example, visitations seem to have been conducted on a septennial basis, while at Winchester, after the episcopate of Jonathan Trelawny at the start of the eighteenth century, it had become customary for bishops to visit only once.[51] When they did occur, visitations seem generally to have consisted in a tour of major diocesan centres at which the clergy and churchwardens of one or more deaneries would be required to attend the bishop or his representative. The clergy would produce their titles to orders and licences to officiate in the diocese, would hear a visitation sermon, like that preached by Ryder in Leicester in 1806, and also a charge delivered by the bishop. The day would be rounded off with a dinner which provided a rare opportunity for the clergy to meet socially with their diocesan. Churchwardens would be formally admitted to their offices and be issued with a set of 'articles' which were queries relating to the fabric and fittings of the church building and some other matters relating to the state of the parish.[52] In the eighteenth century, episcopal visitations seem in most dioceses also to have been combined with confirmations.

By the early nineteenth century, triennial episcopal visitations, matching the canonical requirement, seem to have been fairly well established at Gloucester. This was certainly the model observed by Ryder's predecessor G. I. Huntingford who conducted visitations in 1807, 1810 and 1813 and Ryder's primary visitation of Gloucester in 1816 seems largely to have followed an established diocesan pattern. His tour, which lasted from 28 June to 17 July, accommodated both visitation and confirmations and, like Huntingford's, comprised stops at nine centres: Gloucester (Gloucester deanery), Cirencester (Cirencester and Fairford deaneries), Stow (Stow deanery), Chipping Campden (Campden deanery),

49 Gloucestershire Record Office, GDR A14/3.

50 The best accounts of the eighteenth-century development of episcopal visitations and the subsequent process of reform in the nineteenth century can be found respectively in S. J. C. Taylor, 'Church and state in England in the mid-eighteenth century: the Newcastle years 1742–62', Ph.D. dissertation, University of Cambridge, 1987, esp. pp. 124–31, and A. Burns, *The diocesan revival in the Church of England c. 1800–70* (Oxford, 1999), ch. 2.

51 For Norwich, see Burns, *Diocesan revival*, p. 25. For Winchester see Hampshire Record Office, 21M65: B1/66/1, B1/67–140.

52 Burns, *Diocesan revival*, pp. 23–5.

Tewkesbury (Winchcomb deanery), Stroud (Stonehouse deanery), Chipping Sodbury (Hawkesbury deanery), Dursley (Dursley deanery) and Newnham (Forest deanery). In 1813 Huntingford had added to his tour three additional confirmations at Chipping Sodbury, Chipping Camden and Stow respectively, held on the day before the visitation.[53] In 1816 Ryder arranged for the confirmation to begin at 9 a.m. at each of the nine main centres, leaving most of the day for the visitation which was scheduled to begin at 11 a.m. He also, in a significant departure from the established pattern, introduced a further eight confirmation services at alternative centres on different days. He thus both provided a more convenient location for clergy and their confirmation candidates and avoided the worst of the congestion problems caused by combining visitation with confirmation. This was just as well because he had to confirm a total of 10,656 candidates in 1816.[54] The pattern established by Ryder was sufficiently durable to form the basis of his successor's primary visitation in 1825.[55]

From the early eighteenth century, following an initiative by William Wake at Lincoln, bishops, especially at their primary visitations, had begun to supplement the articles issued to churchwardens with sets of queries issued to the clergy seeking information about a range of pastoral issues.[56] By the second half of the eighteenth century, in the better run dioceses, such questionnaires were beginning to become more elaborate and, in some cases, were also issued at subsequent visitations as Ryder certainly did in 1819 and may have continued to do thereafter.[57] Nevertheless, as Dr Burns has pointed out, the clergy returns contributed little to the occasion of the visitation since they were handed out on the day itself and the information returned could not therefore be reflected in the charge. At the end of the century there were the first signs of the emergence of a new procedure in which the queries were distributed and answers returned in advance of the visitation process so that the charge could be used to reflect on the

53 Gloucester R.O., GDR 337; GDR 346; *Gloucester journal*, 3 May 1813.

54 Gloucester R.O., GDR, 346; *Gloucester journal*, 13 May 1816.

55 *Gloucester journal*, 9 May 1825.

56 R. Cole (ed.), *Speculum dioceseos Lincolniensis sub episcopis Gul: Wake et Edm. Gibson ad 1705–1723* (Lincoln, 1910).

57 H. Ryder, *Three charges delivered to the clergy of the diocese of Gloucester, at three visitations held in the years 1816, 1819 and 1822* (Gloucester, 1824), p. 57. For an example of excellent practice in designing a set of visitation queries, see those issued to the diocese of Salisbury by Bishop Barrington in 1783 in M. Ransome (ed.), *Wiltshire returns to the bishop's visitation queries, 1783* (Wiltshire Record Society, Devizes, 1971). For a striking example of poor practice in visitation, see the discussion of the diocese of Winchester in W. R. Ward (ed.), *Parson and Parish in Eighteenth Century Hampshire* (Hampshire Record Society, Winchester, 1995) and M. A. Smith (ed.), *Doing the Duty of the Parish. Surveys of the Church in Hampshire 1810* (Hampshire Record Society, Winchester, 2004).

state of the diocese and propose schemes of improvement.[58] However, this development seems to have been rare before the later 1820s and the reference in his charge to 'the queries, which I have directed to be given to you today' and the request for punctual and precise answers indicate that here the bishop was following the traditional practice.[59] Unfortunately, no copy of the queries issued by Ryder survives in the diocesan archives, but it is probable, given the issues with which he was concerned in his charge, that they would at least have covered, in addition to material relating to schools, the question of how many services were performed and how many sermons preached in each parish.[60]

Size and Shape

Dr Burns concludes that most charges of the late eighteenth and early nineteenth centuries continued to make little reference to returns and often avoided comment on topical issues. Only with the growing crisis of the later 1820s and 1830s did diocesan pastoral concerns and contemporary controversies in church and state begin to dominate the charge. The consequence was an increase in size from an average of around thirty pages in the period 1816–20 to approximately forty pages by 1840.[61] Ryder's original text, which comprised thirty-four pages in its printed edition, was a little longer than the average for its period but by no means remarkably so and must have taken approximately one hour to deliver. Burns notes some exceptions to the avoidance of controversy around the turn of the century and again in the 1820s.[62] The period between 1813 and 1818 might also be added to this list since in those years published episcopal charges frequently commented on the controversy between supporters of the S.P.C.K. and the British and Foreign Bible Society.[63] In this context, it is not surprising that reference to

58 Burns, *Diocesan revival*, p. 26. The first example cited by Burns is that of Bishop Porteus of London in 1790. For further examples, see Samuel Horsley's charge to St Asaph in 1806, in S. Horsley, *The charges of Samuel Horsley late lord bishop of St Asaph, delivered at his several visitations* (Dundee, 1813), p. 178, and H. W. Majendie, *A charge delivered to the clergy of the diocese of Bangor 1814* (Chester, 1814), p. 21.

59 See below p. 103.

60 Ryder's queries may have been identical to the list of seventeen questions which can be inferred from a volume of answers to visitation queries dating from 1825 in the diocesan records – probably the primary visitation of Ryder's successor, Bishop Bethell – a serviceable if not state of the art set of queries. Gloucester R.O., GDR 383–4.

61 Burns, *Diocesan revival*, pp. 27–32.

62 *Ibid.*, p. 27.

63 See, for example, Majendie, *Charge... 1814*, p. 28; T. Burgess, *A charge delivered to the clergy of the diocese of St David's in September 1813* (2nd edn., Durham, 1813), pp. 19–32; G. H. Law, *A charge delivered to the clergy of the diocese of Chester at the primary visitation of that diocese in July, August, and September 1814* (Chester, 1814), pp. 11–14; B. E. Sparke, *A charge delivered to the clergy of the diocese of Ely at the second quadrennial visitation of that diocese in the year MDCCCXVII* (London, 1817), pp. 15–21.

controversy occupied almost a third of Ryder's charge – a preoccupation virtually forced on the bishop by the coincidence of his elevation to the episcopate not just with the Bible Society row but also with two other significant controversies within the Church: the Western schism and the controversy over baptismal regeneration.[64]

Ryder's text seems to be unusual in the explicit reflexion that it contains on the appropriate shape of a charge: 'The grand object originally designed and properly to be pursued in these occasional addresses, appears to consist in *general* exhortation, and in *appropriate* instructions and admonitions, as suggested by the peculiar exigencies of the time; by public acts and occurrences, which affect the interests of the Church, chiefly as a spiritual body; and by the ever-varying state of opinions and manners amongst our flocks.'[65] Ryder followed his plan precisely, devoting eight and a half pages (roughly one third of the charge) to general exhortations, and a further fifteen pages to admonitions concerning the performance of the liturgy and preaching (dealing with the Western schism and the controversy over baptismal regeneration along the way). In the printed version the division of the text by a double horizontal line then indicated a transition to more specific topics, comprising the addition of a sermon to evening prayer, the promotion of National Schools, and his opinion on 'Societies for Religious Charity'[66] – specifically the respective merits of the Bible Society and the S.P.C.K. which together occupied seven pages. The charge concluded with a peroration stressing the importance of unity, activity and reliance on Christ. The pastoral focus of Ryder's text represented a significant departure from the content of the charges which the clergy of Gloucester had received from his predecessor. In 1813, for example, in his last charge before his move to his new diocese of Hereford, Huntingford had presented a thirty-five page disquisition on the errors of unitarianism with virtually no pastoral instruction or exhortation at all. Huntingford seems to have been wedded to this mode of composition – it dominated his primary charge at Hereford in 1816[67] and Burns describes his series of charges there between 1816 and 1831 as a 'leisurely and appropriately schoolmasterly essay'.[68]

64 See below pp. 94–7, 104–6.

65 See below p. 89.

66 See below p. 104.

67 *Thoughts on the trinity, charges and other theological works by the late Right Reverend G. I. Huntingford*, ed. H. Huntingford (London, 1832), pp. 183–241.

68 Burns, *Diocesan revival*, p. 27. Huntingford also served as warden of Winchester College.

Style and range of reference

It is not merely in content that Ryder's charge differed markedly from that of his predecessor but also in style. Huntingford presented his clergy with an argument, carefully constructed and well-supported but essentially an appeal to the intellect – simultaneously affirming and appealing to the self-perception of his audience as an educated elite.[69] Ryder on the other hand offered an exhortation based on the awful responsibility of christian ministry: 'The people, not warned by the watchman, may perish; but "their blood, saith the Lord God, will I require at the watchman's hand"'[70] – a challenge to cultivate the character, spirituality and pastoral activity appropriate to the 'Ministry of an Apostolical Church'.[71] The tone of spiritual exhortation marks out Ryder's charge not just from those of his predecessor but also, seemingly, from all the other charges published in the same period.[72] Two styles predominated in these charges. Like Huntingford's, many charges presented a theological, ecclesiological or political argument, including Richard Watson's at Llandaff in 1805, Shute Barrington's at Durham in 1806 and George Tomline's series of charges to the diocese of Lincoln in the first two decades of the nineteenth century.[73] The alternative style was exemplified by William Howley's charge at his primary visitation of the London diocese in 1814. It was primarily practical in intention and recommended both charity among his clergy and zeal in the discharge of their duties, but had more of the tone of a plain business statement than an exhortation.[74] This style was also characteristic of G. H. Law's primary charge at Chester in 1814, Herbert Marsh's at Peterborough in 1820 and also John Kaye's at Bristol and William Van Mildert's at Llandaff both in 1821.[75] In effect Ryder maintained throughout a tone of exhortation which other

69 See, for example, 'As the human mind has never ceased to be fertile of invention through successive periods of the Christian era have arisen different occasions, which from time to time have called on some of the clergy for mental exertions, superadded to those which they regularly employed in the discharge of congregational and parochial duties.' Huntingford, *Thoughts*, pp. 187–8.

70 See below p. 92.

71 See below p. 106.

72 This statement is based on a comparison of Ryder's charge with twenty other published charges delivered by a total of sixteen bishops between 1804 and 1825. Some bishops positively eschewed exhortation – see, e.g., Randolph, *Charge ... 1810*, p. 30; Horsley, *Charges*, pp. 1–2.

73 R. Watson, *A charge delivered to the clergy of the diocese of Llandaff in June 1805* (London, 1808); S. Barrington, *Sermons, Charges and Tracts* (London, 1811), pp. 323–43. See, e.g., G. Tomline, *A charge delivered to the clergy of the diocese of Lincoln at the triennial visitation of that diocese in May and June 1803* (London, 1803); Tomline, *Charge ... 1812*.

74 Howley, *Charge ... 1814*.

75 Law, *Charge ... 1814*; H. Marsh, *A charge delivered at the primary visitation of Herbert lord bishop of Peterborough in July 1820* (London, 1820); John Kaye, *Works of John Kaye, bishop of Lincoln. Vol. VII: Charges speeches and letters* (London, 1838), pp. 1–20; W. Van Mildert, *A charge delivered to the clergy of the diocese of Llandaff at the primary visitation in August*

bishops (if they employed it at all) reserved for a peroration at the end of the charge.[76] In consequence, Ryder's charge read more like a sermon than the usual episcopal statement and for a comparable tone it is necessary to look at some of the more earnest bishops of the 1820s like C. J. Blomfield at Chester in 1825 and to a lesser extent Ryder's successor at Gloucester, Christopher Bethell.[77]

In composing his charge, Ryder clearly had reference to three main sorts of text: official anglican formularies – particularly the Prayer Book, ordinal, articles and homilies, the Bible – especially the prophet Ezekiel and the New Testament epistles, and the works of anglican writers – notably the charges of other bishops. The use of anglican formularies, especially the exhortations in the ordination service, clearly provided both an ideal set of tools for bishops wishing to stir their clergy to greater efforts and a source to which no clergyman could readily take exception. They might have been expected, therefore, to have been deployed regularly in episcopal charges, but here too Ryder was unusual and few of his contemporaries chose to make this kind of reference.[78] Ryder's use of the Bible in his charge is particularly striking. It is by far the most significant source – of a total of seventy-two quotations or references in the text, fifty-three are from the Bible. Where he quoted, Ryder used the language of the Authorized Version, but perhaps the most notable feature of the quotations is the relative rarity with which they are found to be accurate. Of a total of forty-seven biblical quotations, only eleven gave the translation word for word, the remainder presented a wide range of variations on the text. In one case – a quotation from II Peter iii. 1 – Ryder explicitly presented a variant from the received translation and cited the German biblical scholar J. F. Schleusner in support of his reading.[79] Elsewhere the variations appear to be rather more casual. Sometimes the quotation was simply shortened by a few words, in other cases the grammar or tenses of the originals were altered or singular nouns turned into plurals in order to harmonize with the flow of Ryder's own prose. In a few cases, the impression is created that the

MCCXXI (Oxford, 1821).

76 See, e.g., Tomline, *Charge ... 1812*, pp. 34–5.

77 C. J. Blomfield, *A charge delivered to the clergy of the diocese of Chester at the primary visitation in August and September 1825* (London, 1825); C. Bethell, *Charge ... delivered at the primary visitation of the diocese of Gloucester in the months of June and July 1825* (Gloucester, 1825). For an earlier example, see B. Porteus, *A charge delivered to the clergy of the diocese of Chester at the primary visitation of that diocese in the year 1778* (Chester, 1779). In none of these examples, however, was the exhortatory tone so marked or so sustained as in the case of Ryder.

78 Such references when they occurred at all were generally brief and passing rather than extended as in Ryder's case. Howley, for example, recommended the homilies on salvation, faith and good works as a source of sound doctrine but did not quote from them. Howley, *Charge ... 1814*, p. 21. Porteus in 1778 and Blomfield in 1825 were, in this respect, again the closest to Ryder.

79 See below p. 89.

inaccuracy has arisen by pure inadvertence as in, 'lest you should "bruise the broken reed,"' as opposed to the, 'A bruised reed shall he not break', of Matthew xii. 20 in the Authorized Version.[80]

This pattern throws an interesting light on Ryder's method of composition. Clearly, for the bishop, the introduction of quotation marks did not so much signify (as in modern prose) a precise word-for-word rendering of an original, as a more general reference to the sense of a text with which his readers were expected to be familiar. It was simultaneously a disclaimer that he was simply using his own words and an invocation of an unimpeachable external authority. A reading of the charge as a whole gives the impression of an author whose mind was deeply immersed in the Bible and whose discourse was naturally coloured by a native scriptural dialect. Sometimes Ryder appears to be quoting from memory perhaps suggesting that in part at least the charge was composed in some haste or even (though rather less likely) that some sections were delivered from notes rather than a full text. However the charge was originally composed, it is apparent that Ryder made no attempt to correct the variations from the text of the Authorized Version either in the first published version of the charge or the second edition published in 1824.[81] Ryder seems to have been far more concerned to convey accurately the meaning and the tone of the biblical passages that he used than to quote the words precisely. His methodology seems therefore incompatible with a high doctrine of the plenary verbal inspiration of the scriptural text and in this respect he appears representative of an evangelical mainstream before the 1820s which located divine inspiration primarily in the sense rather than the expression of scripture.[82]

The reference to other anglican writers served a similar purpose to that of the reference to scripture, allowing Ryder to rest his views (sometimes on potentially controversial issues such as the nature of baptismal regeneration and the propriety of preaching for conversion)[83] on external authorities – in this case men of high repute among early nineteenth-century anglicans. There are ten such quotations or references in the charge the vast majority of which are to well-known writers in the high-church tradition like the Rev. Andrew Bell – the high churchmen's favourite educationalist – Archbishop Thomas Secker and Bishop George Horne and, most prominently, Bishop Samuel Horsley, perhaps the leading high-church

80 See below p. 99.
81 For a note on the editions of the charge, see below p. 86.
82 The distinction between sense and expression is usually associated with Henry Martyn. For a discussion of the early nineteenth-century evangelical view of biblical inspiration see Bebbington, *Evangelicalism*, pp. 86–91. For an example of evangelical divergence of view over the issue of inspiration see the discussion at the Eclectic Society on 19 Jan. 1800 in Pratt, *Eclectic Society*, pp.154–6.
83 See below pp. 96–101.

bishop at the turn of the century who was quoted on three occasions in the charge. By contrast there is only one reference to a work by an evangelical (John Owen's history of the Bible Society) and the only quotation from an evangelical was presented with no acknowledgment of its source either in the text or in the notes. References to writers in the latitudinarian tradition are similarly sparse. Ryder used only two, one of whom, Archbishop Tillotson, was quoted mainly for the purpose of refutation.[84] The invocation of these mainly high-church authorities may have been intended to reassure clergy fearful of evangelical innovation or enthusiasm and they certainly helped to sustain Ryder's contention at the beginning of his charge that, 'Upon the subject of general exhortation, I can have no *new* motives to offer, no *new* incentives to urge, no *new* views of responsibility to bring before your eyes.'[85] It should not, however, be assumed that the deployment of high-church writers by Ryder was purely tactical. It reflected a common evangelical conviction that theirs *was* the doctrine of the Church of England and aspects of it were naturally to be looked for in devoted churchmen of other schools.[86] It also reflected significant continuities between Ryder's earlier doctrinal position as a high churchman and his later one as an evangelical.[87] Ryder's extensive use of quotation and reference of all kinds is, nevertheless, particularly striking when his charge is set against those of his contemporaries. At most, charges by bishops like Majendie, Howley and Sparke contained a handful of quotations – usually brief phrases or sentences from the Bible.[88] Although he provided a number of scriptural references, the most prominent quotations in Huntingford's charge at his visitation of Gloucester in 1813 were from Herbert Marsh's translation of Michaelis on the New Testament and from Virgil's *Georgics*![89] Others, like Van Mildert in 1821, reserved their quotations for the peroration at the end of their charges, while G. H. Law managed to deliver his primary charge to the Chester diocese in 1814 with no references or quotations whatsoever.[90]

The Major Themes of the Charge

i. *The Character of Ministerial Obligations*

The first major theme which Ryder treated in his charge fell into the section which he described as 'general exhortation' and constituted an outline of his view of the obligations of a minister in the established church. After stressing the primary

84 The unacknowledged evangelical author was Charles Simeon. See below p. 96.
85 See below p. 89.
86 For an example of this sort of conviction see, Robinson, *Serious attention, passim.*
87 For a further discussion of this point, see below pp. 78–9.
88 Majendie, *Charge ... 1814;* Howley, *Charge ... 1814*; Sparke, *Charge ... 1817.*
89 Huntingford, *Thoughts*, pp. 183–218.
90 Van Mildert, *Charge ... 1821*; Law, *Charge ... 1814.*

accountability of ministers to God both for their talents and the charge committed to them he proceeded, by means of a series of questions based on the ordination service, to emphasize their roles as messengers, watchmen, stewards and shepherds. Of these, an emphasis on the role of the clergy as messengers was perhaps the most likely to distinguish an evangelical view of parish ministry from that of the majority of contemporary churchmen. In Ryder's charge, the idea has not yet been informed by the notion of the 'aggressive approach' to working a parish, popularized by Thomas Chalmers, which can be glimpsed in J. B. Sumner's use of the word 'messenger' in his charge to the diocese of Chester in 1835.[91] It was, however, clearly linked to the importance of preaching for conversion as opposed to a reliance on baptism and moral instruction which was stressed later in the charge[92] and to what Alan Haig has described as an evangelical re-introduction of 'a vision of clerical work based firmly on the salvation of individual souls'.[93] It is also noteworthy, given the multitude of roles commonly played by clergymen in the later Hanoverian period,[94] that Ryder here construes their obligations in exclusively spiritual terms. This was far from being a universal approach. Bowyer Sparke, for example, encouraging his clergy in his 1817 charge to resist the spread of infidelity, noted that, 'Into your hands have been committed the dearest: the most important interests. You are the guardians of religion, that bulwark of every state; that sacred pallium, to the preservation of which it must owe its happiness; its security, its very existence.'[95] Since, for Ryder, the ministerial vocation was essentially spiritual in character and orientation, the pre-requisites for its effective application were also spiritual. He thus went on to exhort his clergy to daily study of the scriptures, self-examination, private prayer and attention to personal holiness both in respect of the minister as an individual and of the conduct of his family.

The arrival of a new seriousness about the ministerial vocation, which was here set consciously against distraction by temporal concerns, has often been associated primarily with the tractarian movement of the 1830s.[96] Ryder's charge is thus an important reminder that it was earlier a characteristic of evangelicalism and was

91 J. B. Sumner, *A charge delivered to the clergy of the diocese of Chester at the triennial visitation* (1835), pp. 22–5, 44–50. See also the discussion in M. Smith, *Religion in industrial society. Oldham and Saddleworth 1740–1865* (Oxford, 1994), pp. 99–101 and A. Haig, *The Victorian clergy* (London, 1984), pp. 12–15. For Chalmers and the aggressive approach, see S. J. Brown, *Thomas Chalmers and the godly commonwealth in Scotland* (Oxford, 1982), chs. 3, 7.

92 See below p. 96–101.

93 Haig, *Victorian clergy*, p. 13.

94 See, e.g., A. Russell, *The clerical profession* (London, 1980), pp. 53–229.

95 Sparke, *Charge ... 1817*, pp. 6–9.

96 This identification began remarkably early. See, e.g., A. Trollope, *Clergymen of the Church of England* (London, 1866), ch. 2.

also making an impact on the church more widely in the generation before the tractarians. A high churchman like Thomas Burgess, for example, while he might have devoted his primary charge at St David's to stressing the privileges rather than the responsibilities of christian ministry,[97] was just as keen as Ryder that his clergy should practice appropriate spiritual disciplines. Indeed he went so far as to insert after the usual canonical oaths and subscriptions required of the parochial clergy, an additional oath for ministers serving in his diocese:

> I further solemnly promise That I will to the utmost of my power promote among my parishioners the duty of Family prayer, by my example as well as by my Instructions and that, for this purpose, I will not fail to have daily Prayer in my own family.[98]

The quickening of the pace which is observable around the turn of the century in respect of the development of a more conscientious approach to ministry may well owe much to the anxieties created by the French revolution and the wars against Napoleon, and may also have been part of an incipient process of professionalization among the clergy.[99] It would be a mistake, however, to discount the role of the renewed spiritual dynamic within the Church created by the warm high churchmanship of men like Bishops Horne, Horsley and Burgess and also the growing forces of the evangelical revival represented by men like Ryder who could challenge each of his clergy not just to do his duty by the establishment but also to ask himself, 'Have I ever been able to speak of religion with that truth and warmth peculiar to one who knows and loves it from the bottom of his heart? And have my people learnt to know and love religion too, by its visible fruits in my conduct and conversation?'[100]

97 T. Burgess, *Peculiar privileges of the christian ministry considered in a charge to the clergy of the diocese of St David's at the primary visitation of that diocese in the year 1804* (Durham, 1805). For the character of Burgess's high churchmanship, see M. A. Smith, 'Thomas Burgess, churchman and reformer', in N. Yates (ed.), *Bishop Burgess and his world*, forthcoming.

98 National Library of Wales, SD/SB/8: diocese of St David's subscription book 1810–22. I should like to thank Dr Burns who first drew my attention to this source. It seems to have been common in Welsh dioceses for bishops to add to the usual requirements for subscription – clergy in St David's, St Asaph and Llandaff, for example, were all required to take an oath to reside on their benefices – but Burgess's requirement about family prayer seems to have been unique. N.L.W., LL/SB/12: Llandaff subscription book 1802–15; SA/SB/10: St Asaph subscription book 1805–18.

99 For a discussion of the professionalization of the clergy see, Russell, *Clerical profession*, pp. 9–49; Haig, *Victorian clergy*, pp. 4–19. P. J. Corfield, *Power and the professions in Britain 1700–1850* (London, 1995), pp. 102–29, compares the clergy of the established Church as professionals with those of other denominations.

100 See below p. 92.

ii. *The public ministry of the Church*

Turning to the public ministry of the Church, Ryder was again concerned to focus the attention of his hearers not on the externals of 'the duty of the parish' but on its spiritual impact. According to stereotype, he might have been expected, in this part of his charge, to concentrate on the issue of preaching. However, in common with many other contemporary evangelicals, the bishop deeply valued the liturgy of the Church[101] and he therefore began by discussing the usual round of services. For Ryder the regular performance of Sunday duty was necessary but not sufficient – 'the punctual performance of duty will not suffice; upon the nature and spirit of its performance your ministerial character and success depend',[102] while the liturgy, 'incomparable, unalterable as it is, … is but a vehicle'.[103] For liturgical worship to be acceptable to God, 'the feelings of our hearts must correspond with the sentiments expressed; the prayers must be appropriated by each worshipper and made his own.'[104] In Ryder's view, such personal appropriation of the prayers clearly depended on the work of the grace of God in each individual. However, he also believed that it could be aided by close attention to proper performance which he therefore enjoined on his clergy in the charge, concentrating on issues of pronunciation, speed and manner of delivery. Here, Ryder seems to have been expressing a concern common to a number of bishops in the early 1800s about the dangers to the Church of a perfunctory performance of the liturgy. In his charge to Chester in 1817, for example, Henry Law warned that a lifeless delivery was likely to produce a lifeless congregation, while Thomas Burgess, at Salisbury in the 1820s, considered appointing commissioners to investigate the ability of candidates for holy orders to read the liturgy and to preach.[105] It is also significant for our understanding both of the spirituality of early nineteenth-century evangelicalism and its attitude to its place in the established Church to note that so committed a preacher as Ryder could assert that, 'The prayers used *from,* or *without* the heart, make the grand, fundamental, characteristic difference between a Minister and Congregation who are holy and happy, and those who are not.'[106]

101 See, e.g., C. Simeon, *The excellency of the liturgy in four discourses preached before the University of Cambridge* (Cambridge, 1812); T. Robinson, *A serious call to a constant and devout attendance on the stated services of the Church of England; in an address from a clergyman to his parishioners* (London, 1803).

102 See below p. 92.

103 See below p. 93.

104 See below p. 93.

105 G. H. Law, *A charge delivered to the clergy of the diocese of Chester at the visitation of that diocese in July and August 1817* (3rd edn., Chester, 1817), pp. 24–5; *Manchester Mercury*, 26 Aug. 1817; Bodl. Library, MS Eng. Letters c. 134, fos. 180–1: J. Dennis to T. Burgess, 8 Oct. 1825.

106 See below p. 94.

Having established the pre-eminence of prayer in the public ministry of the church, Ryder then moved on to emphasize the importance of instruction, stressing the importance both of 'genuine principles' and of 'the indispensible effects in a holy life'.[107] As a model not just of sound doctrine but also of exhortation, he directed his clergy to the New Testament epistles as a whole and, as a secondary authority, the articles and homilies of the Church. To some extent this recommendation is indicative of the influence of evangelicalism. It certainly represented a clear break with the argument of Ryder's 1807 archidiaconal visitation sermon where he had cautioned against preaching from Romans and Corinthians because of the particularity of their doctrinal content and favoured concentration instead on the pastoral epistles. Indeed, the recommendations of the charge bore a much closer resemblance to Thomas Robinson's visitation sermon of the following year than to Ryder's own.[108] However, it was not unusual for episcopal charges to recommend attention to the homilies. Horsley, as Ryder pointed out, had strongly endorsed their use in his primary visitation charge to the diocese of St David's in 1790 and, more recently, Howley had recommended particular attention to the homilies on salvation, faith and good works in his charge to the London diocese in 1814.[109] It is unlikely therefore that Ryder's hearers would have detected anything of a peculiarly evangelical stamp in this part of his discourse.

Concern about the quality of instruction in the diocese was also reflected in the specific recommendations Ryder included in his charge. The first of these recommendations was for the introduction of a sermon at evening prayer in addition to the one already preached in the morning and was addressed, with a rare use of irony, only to those clergy,

> who wish to attract their people to the public worship of the Church, and who have that zeal for the interests of the Establishment, that conviction of its superior excellence and usefulness, which would make them ready to exceed the prescribed line of compulsory labor, and sacrifice a little more time and thought, in order to retain the wavering, and recall the wanderer within its pale.[110]

Clearly not wishing to try such zeal too hard Ryder suggested that a catechetical lecture addressed to children and servants or the reading of one of the homilies might suffice. In recommending the homilies not merely as a model for sermons but also as a potential replacement for them, Ryder may have had in mind, as well as the experience of the clergy to whom he referred, the impact of the Prayer

107 *Ibid.*
108 Ryder, *Calvinistic doctrines*, pp. 15–20; Robinson, *Serious attention, passim.*
109 See below p. 102; Howley *Charge ... 1814*, p. 21.
110 See below p. 102.

Book and Homily Society of which he was a vice-president and which had between May 1815 and April 1816, for example, succeeded in distributing 69,283 copies of individual homilies as tracts as well as 436 bound volumes[111] – adding at least some colour to this claim that the homilies were 'affectingly interesting to the common people'.[112] The overt appeal to antiquity and tradition in the discussion of the homilies may also have been intended to counterbalance the impression of novelty implicit in the recommendation of the introduction of a second sermon – an innovation which had brought Ryder some recent notoriety at Wells.

The bishop's second specific recommendation for the improvement of the role of the Church as instructor of the people was concerned with the introduction of schools. This was a common feature of charges at this period because the National Society for Promoting the Education of the Poor in the Principles of the Established Church, which had been established in 1811, was gradually developing a national organization by means of the creation of diocesan associations. Law, Majendie and Howley, for example, all recommended the National Society to their respective clergy in 1814.[113] For Sparke at Ely, the creation of a mechanism for educating the poor as efficient as the Madras system[114] was so potentially dangerous that it called for the utmost vigilance on the part of the clergy to ensure that it was used, via the National Society, to support the establishment in Church and state rather than to subvert it. If, however, the clergy took care to supervise the teaching they would find, he concluded in characteristic fashion, 'without encroaching too much upon your other avocations, you have it in your power to render most essential services to your country.'[115] It would appear that Ryder's predecessor as bishop had lacked either the time or the energy actively to promote the National Society in his diocese.[116] Ryder, on the other hand, had himself been instrumental in the establishment of a National School while dean of Wells, and he arrived at Gloucester determined to launch a major educational initiative in his new diocese. The queries prepared at Ryder's request for the visitation were especially designed to provide information to support this initiative[117] and the

111 *Fourth annual report of the Prayer Book and Homily Society* (London, 1816), pp. 8–10.

112 See below p. 102.

113 Law, *Charge ... 1814*, pp. 15–17; Majendie, *Charge ... 1814*, p. 16; Howley, *Charge ... 1814*, pp. 22–4. See also Burgess, *Charge ... 1813*, p. 19.

114 The Madras system, developed by the Reverend Andrew Bell, used monitors rather than trained teachers to pass on much of the knowledge, thus significantly increasing the number of children who could receive a basic education from a single teacher.

115 Sparke, *Charge ... 1817*, pp. 11–13.

116 A number of other bishops set up diocesan National Societies in 1811 and 1812. See *Annual reports of the National Society for Promoting the Education of the Poor in the Principles of the Established Church* (London, 1812–16).

117 See below p. 103.

bishop contented himself with a relatively short discussion in the charge encouraging the establishment of National Schools in the parishes and trailing the launch of his diocesan National Society in the following month.[118] In addition to the focus on daily education Ryder also recommended the introduction of evening schools, especially in manufacturing centres where daily child labour made regular school attendance difficult, and the introduction of Sunday schools where they did not already exist. This close attention to the necessity for improving provision for the education of the poor was neither unusual nor controversial in charges of this date. Ryder's charge was unusual, however, in its relative neglect of the traditional method of instruction in basic christian doctrine – the catechism. Emphasis on the importance of regular catechizing was a commonplace of other bishops' charges, though again Sparke was exceptional in finding even the catechism potentially dangerous unless carefully explained by the clergy.[119] Apart from his almost casual mention of a catechetical lecture to children and servants as a possible substitute for a second Sunday sermon, Ryder left the subject untouched. This was probably an omission produced by simple shortage of space, but it is just possible that it may also represent a realistic appreciation, based on Ryder's own extensive experience in parish ministry, both of the growing difficulty in attracting a sufficient proportion of children and servants to catechism in early nineteenth-century parishes, and of the emerging potential of church schools and Sunday schools to fill that gap.[120]

iii. *Controversy*

The first of the controversies that Ryder chose to address in his charge related to 'the Ministers who, in some neighbouring dioceses, have lately seceded from the Church; and *to the few* who may remain in it, but who adopt, in some measure, their opinions and practice.'[121] This was the so called 'Western Schism', a small wave of evangelical secessions from the Church which began in Hampshire in 1815 among a group centred on a branch of the influential Baring family.[122] It gradually spread to encompass a number of other individuals in the south-western

118 Ryder seems to have launched his 'Gloucester Diocesan Society for the Education of the Poor in the Principles of the Established Church' at a two-day meeting on 20 and 21 August 1816 – a month after completing his visitation. *Gloucester journal*, 26 Aug. 1816; *Sixth annual report of the National Society for Promoting the Education of the Poor in the Principles of the Established Church* (London, 1817), pp. 166–70.

119 Sparke, *Charge ... 1817*, pp. 11–12. For examples of episcopal emphasis on catechizing, see Burgess, *Charge ... 1813*, pp. 44–5; Law, *Charge ... 1814*, p. 17.

120 If so, Ryder's successor Christopher Bethell did not agree, but the sharp reminder in his own primary visitation charge of 1825 that schools were no substitute for catechism may also provide indirect evidence of a contrary policy under Ryder. Bethell, *Charge ... 1825*, p. 23.

121 See below p. 94.

122 The Barings ran perhaps the most influential merchant bank in England in the early nineteenth century.

counties of England.[123] The lack of organization and divergent views of the seceders together with the relative paucity of their writings makes it difficult to reconstruct the precise causes of the schism. However, Carter has drawn attention to a number of leading features, including the recent controversy within the Church over baptismal regeneration, a high calvinism which, in some cases, bordered on theoretical antinomianism, concerns about some parts of the liturgy (especially the baptism and burial services) and about the lack of discipline in the Church (especially in relation to access to communion), and finally, fears about the corrupting influence of the link between church and state.[124]

Moderate evangelicals, as Carter notes, were among the most vehement critics of the seceders, both because they considered their doctrines to be unsound and because they feared that such extremism might bring into disrepute the whole evangelical movement within the Church. Although he conceded that the seceders might be 'well intentioned and pious persons', Ryder was no exception to this rule, describing their doctrine as 'a snare of the devil, and an awful wresting of Scripture, to the destruction of those who hear'.[125] His discussion of the schism centred on the issue of antinomianism, pointing out that the seceders were charging their brethren with underestimating the 'all-sufficiency of faith' and with promulgating 'an imperfect and even another gospel'. To this allegation, Ryder responded with a discussion of the proper relationship between faith and works, with reference to the epistles of St Paul and St James and to the homily on faith, stressing both the all-sufficiency of Christ's pardon and grace and 'the indispensible necessity of maintaining and the tremendous danger of neglecting, good works'.[126] Ryder's views on this point can be further amplified by consulting a three-part review of Herbert Marsh's *A comparative view of the Churches of England and Rome* which he published in the *Christian observer* between April and September 1815 under the cipher S. W. and a letter he wrote to Bishop Thomas Burgess in the following year.[127] In the review as well as the charge Ryder's prime source of reference was to the homily on faith, from which he concluded that

> Our faith is ... *without justifying* works, in opposition to the Roman Catholic opinion; but *with* works, that is, *with* the germ and root of them in the heart, in

123 This account rests mainly on the best modern analysis of the Western schism which is to be found in G. Carter, *Anglican evangelicals. Protestant secessions from the via media, c.1800–1850* (Oxford, 2001), pp. 105–51.

124 *Ibid.*, esp. pp. 132–47.

125 See below p. 95.

126 *Ibid.*

127 *Christian observer* (1815), pp. 227–31, 501–4, 581–4. Ryder revealed his authorship of the review confidentially to Burgess in the letter. Bodl. Library, MS Eng. Letters c. 138, fos. 46–7: H. Ryder to T. Burgess, 26 Oct. 1816.

> opposition to the Antinomian heresy. The doctrine of 'justification by faith only', is thus the chief characteristic of the Via Media Ecclesiae Anglicanae by which she stands of all Protestant churches confessedly the first... In such a state, while we think and humbly trust that we stand, we should take heed lest we fall. Cleaving to our principle of *true, lively, justifying faith,* we should be ever seeking and striving to *assure ourselves of its existence,* and *to manifest its productive nature to the world, by an holy life and conversation.*[128]

Similarly, in the letter to Burgess, written at roughly the same time as the charge, Ryder explained,

> I believe that we are justified (meritoriously) only by the obedience of Jesus Christ unto death, and (instrumentally) by faith only, as the instrument, whereby we become interested in this saving work of Jesus Christ.
>
> I thus differ from the Socinian who ascribes salvation to works alone, and from the Papist, who allows to them a *joint* efficacy in that transaction between the soul of each believer and his God. And I differ (no less ...) from the Antinomian both ancient and modern as to the nature of that faith which is thus the instrument of justification. This difference I must further explain.
>
> In *their view* justifying faith is not indeed like the faith of the Socinian a bare assent of the understanding, but it is little more valuable, being only the temporary rapturous feeling conviction or assurance of the heart or more probably of the imagination.
>
> In my view justifying faith is the practical permanent presiding principle of the heart and life, and, if not possessing in some good measure those qualities (which involve the only Christian motives to all zeal and virtue) it is wholly unavailing in its above mentioned instrumental property. It does not justify or give an interest in the justification wrought out by Jesus Christ.[129]

In both these passages, the first written *against* and the second *for* a high-church theologian we can perhaps discern the authentic voice of early nineteenth-century evangelicalism, confident that its doctrine was indeed the doctrine of the articles and homilies, suspicious of the enthusiasm of 'temporary rapturous feeling' and, irrespective of the doubts of its critics, holding firmly together justification by faith only and the necessity of a holy life. It was also an understanding with clear affinities to some varieties of later Hanoverian high churchmanship, which is hardly surprising given both the particular eighteenth-century origins of evangelicalism and Ryder's own religious background.[130] To this moderate evangelical vision, the extremism of the Western schism was a challenge at the heart of both

128 *Christian observer* (1815), pp. 583–4.

129 Bodl. Library, MS Eng. Letters c. 138, fos. 46–7: H. Ryder to T. Burgess, 26 Oct. 1816.

130 For a discussion of the high-church contribution to the origins of evangelicalism see, e.g., J. D. Walsh, 'Origins of the evangelical revival', in *Essays in modern English church history*, ed. G. V. Bennet and J. D. Walsh (London, 1966), pp. 132–62.

its doctrine and its spirituality and it is to the significance of the challenge rather than simply to the dangers of bad publicity that the vigour of the moderate response should probably be ascribed.[131]

After the Western schism, Ryder turned to deal, and at rather greater length, with the debate which had helped to provoke it – the controversy over baptismal regeneration. Though an almost perennial source of discussion within the Church, the issue of baptismal regeneration had been given a fresh currency first by the debate over the case of *Kemp* v. *Wickes* between 1809 and 1811[132] and then by Richard Mant's 1812 Bampton Lectures. Mant rejected the evangelical notion of conversion in favour of a doctrine that regeneration was conditional on rightly administered baptism, a position, he argued, which was the doctrine both of the Bible and of the formularies of the Church of England.[133] For Ryder, the first issue to be settled was the 'use of the *term*'[134] regeneration which, he argued, was restricted by the fathers of the first four centuries and by the Church of England to baptism and, he continued,

> I would therefore wish generally to restrict the term to the baptismal privileges; and, considering them as comprehending, not only an external admission into the visible Church – not only a covenanted title to the pardon and grace of the Gospel – but even a degree of spiritual aid vouchsafed and ready to offer itself to our acceptance or rejection at the dawn of reason.[135]

Here, Ryder accepts both the language of baptismal regeneration and a notion of the sacrament as a means of conveying grace, at least in a seminal form capable of bearing full fruit 'at the dawn of reason'.[136] He should, therefore, be ranked along with other moderate evangelicals, like J. B. Sumner, who also accepted a version of baptismal regeneration.[137] It is important to note, however, that Ryder's view that the term 'regeneration' should be regarded as synonymous with baptized was not specially developed in an attempt to moderate the evangelical position

131 For the moderate evangelical understanding of justification, see W. J. C. Ervine, 'Doctrine and diplomacy: some aspects of the life and thought of the anglican evangelical clergy, 1797–1837', Ph.D. dissertation, University of Cambridge, 1979, pp. 231–50.

132 The case concerned the eligibility of a person baptized by a dissenting minister to receive burial according to the Book of Common Prayer. For a discussion of the debate about baptismal regeneration produced by this case see Smith, 'Thomas Burgess'.

133 For a treatment of Mant and the general evangelical response see Carter, *Anglican evangelicals*, pp. 133–5, and the rather longer discussion in Ervine, 'Doctrine and diplomacy', pp. 61–86.

134 See below p. 96.

135 See below p. 96. This quotation follows the text of the second edition which makes better sense of the passage.

136 See the brief discussion in Ervine, 'Doctrine and diplomacy', pp. 71–4.

137 J. B. Sumner, *Apostolical preaching considered in an examination of St Paul's epistles* (London, 1815). See also the brief discussion in Nockles, *Oxford movement*, pp. 229–30. Further examples are given in Ervine, 'Doctrine and diplomacy', pp. 70–84.

either from principle or as a tactic to defuse high-church criticism but rather was continuous with the views that the bishop had held as a high churchman prior to his conversion. Thus in his archidiaconal visitation sermon of 1808 he noted,

> The appropriation of the term regeneration to the change effected by that sacred rite will hardly be doubted by those who have read Wall's History of Infant Baptism; since he proves, that for the first four centuries of the church, the word regenerate was used, and only used as synonymous to baptised. Much confusion and erroneous doctrine might have been avoided, if this use of the term had been adhered to, and some other less ambiguous expression agreed upon to describe that total change and renovation, which must take place in many baptized persons, after a long career of sin, in order to restore then to a state of acceptance with God.[138]

Ryder's evangelicalism emerged rather more strongly, however, in his understanding of the minister's task in relation to a baptized congregation. In 1808, his understanding of the importance of renovation was strong but relatively muted:

> With St. Peter, therefore, we call upon men to repent; but his flock were to repent of the sin of unbelief, rejection of and opposition to the Gospel; ours are to repent of faith nearly nominal or not sufficiently strong, of faith perhaps wholly unfruitful.
>
> With St Peter, we call upon men to change; but his flock were to change to a new state by baptism; ours are to return to a former state, in which they were placed by baptism already received.
>
> He, therefore exhorts them to believe; we exhort those, who profess to believe, to grow in faith, to be careful to maintain good works.[139]

By 1816, however, the post-baptismal task had become much more decisive:

> I would solemnly protest against that most serious error (which has arisen probably from exalting too highly the just view of baptismal regeneration) of contemplating all the individuals of a *baptized* congregation as *converted*, as *having* all once known the truth, and entered upon the right path, though some may have wandered from it, and others may have made little progress, as not therefore requiring (all by nature, and most, it is to be feared, through defective principle and practice,) that 'transformation' by the 'renewing of the mind', that 'putting off the old man, and putting on the new man', which is so emphatically enjoined by St Paul to his *baptized* Romans and Ephesians.[140]

Since baptismal regeneration was not to be equated with conversion and sermons based on this erroneous idea 'soothe and delude the people into a false peace',[141]

138 Ryder, *Calvinistic doctrines*, p. 13.
139 *Ibid.*, pp. 14–15.
140 See below pp. 96–7.
141 See below p. 97.

clergy were instead to encourage their flocks, whatever their outward state, to serious self-examination and were themselves to preach for conversion. In practice, Ryder recommended the characteristic evangelical form of 'discriminating preaching', expecting that different members of the congregation would be at different stages of the spiritual journey and including matter in the sermon appropriate for different levels of spiritual attainment.[142] At the same time he avoided potential accusations of enthusiasm by stressing that the congregation would be divided 'not indeed externally in the view of each other, but through the estimate which each individual will take of his own state' and that the clergy should, 'without venturing… to assign it positively to any individual, offer to each character his portion which he may apply to himself.' Sermons should concentrate on an exaltation of Christ as Saviour to spur those already converted on to sanctification and, for the rest of the congregation,

> by every alarm and encouragement, constrain or win them to come in true repentance and lively faith to the Saviour, and receive their portion in his meritorious atonement, prevailing intercession, efficacious grace, and unspotted righteousness, if peradventure they may be converted and saved.[143]

Such preaching, the bishop assured his hearers, would produce neither barren theory nor enthusiasm and, far from risking antinomian excess, it would 'require the most particular enforcement of moral duties, in all their detail and in the highest perfection'.[144] If at this point in his exhortation to his clergy, Ryder appeared at his most nakedly evangelical, so he was also at his most concerned to wrap himself in the mantle of anglican tradition. He thus took care to refer his readers to the leading martyrs of the English reformation including the sixteenth-century bishop of Gloucester John Hooper, and to the most respected contemporary latitudinarian divine, William Paley. He also provided extensive quotations from a slate of prominent eighteenth-century high churchmen: Archbishop Thomas Secker, and Bishops George Horne and Samuel Horsley.[145]

The final controversy addressed in Ryder's charge related to what he described as a 'collision, however unintentional'[146] between the two most eminent societies for religious charity, in other words the ongoing row about the respective merits of the Society for Promoting Christian Knowledge and the British and Foreign Bible Society. The Bible Society had, from its inception in 1804, been treated with

142 For 'discriminating preaching' as a characteristic of the evangelical revival, see the brief discussion in W. R. Ward, *The Protestant evangelical awakening* (Cambridge, 1992), pp. 244–6, 270–1.

143 See below p. 99.

144 See below p. 100.

145 See below pp. 100–1.

146 See below p. 104.

suspicion by some high churchmen like Thomas Sikes the vicar of Guilsborough and associate of the Hackney Phalanx.[147] The spread of local auxiliaries to the Bible Society after 1809 spawned a number of *causes célèbres* especially at Colchester in 1810, Cambridge in 1811 and Hackney in 1814 which re-ignited the controversy. A pamphlet war broke out with Thomas Sikes, Herbert Marsh and H. H. Norris leading the opposition to the Bible Society and William Otter, Thomas Burgess and William Dealtry prominent in its defence.[148] In 1812, the controversy had become particularly prominent in Gloucester when Bishop Huntingford's refusal to accept the offer of a vice-presidentship of a local Bible Society auxiliary provoked a brief flurry of pamphleteering.[149] The objectors to the Bible Society raised three main issues: an alleged diversion of resources away from the S.P.C.K. which distributed the prayer book and anglican tracts as well as the Bible and as the older society had a prior claim on the support of churchmen; the drawing of anglican supporters of the Bible Society into an association with dissenters who were clearly disaffected from the Church and might also be disaffected from the state; and the breaches of church order inherent in a society which was organized independently of the hierarchical and territorial structures of the establishment.[150]

By 1816, commentary on the relative merits of the Bible Society and the S.P.C.K. had become a common feature in episcopal charges and at the same time reflected a wide spectrum of views. Clear opposition to the Bible Society came from Bishop Samuel Goodenough in his charge to Carlisle in 1814 and G. H. Law at Chester in 1814 and in 1817. H. W. Majendie at Bangor in 1814 also criticized the Bible Society and recommended Norris's pamphlets to his clergy, but did so in rather milder tones.[151] Sparke at Ely was even more circumspect, questioning the judgment but not the zeal or the motives of Bible Society supporters and concluding,

> Although I have explained to you my sentiments on the subject of the Bible Society, I by no means expect that any implicit deference should be paid to my opinion: this

147 For Sikes, see Nockles, *Oxford movement.* The best modern account of the Bible Society controversy can be found in R. H. Martin, *Evangelicals united. Ecumenical stirrings in pre-Victorian Britain 1795–1830* (London, 1983), pp. 99–118.

148 *Ibid.*, pp. 102–5. Significantly, these examples indicate that the debate over the Bible Society did not divide on simple party lines, a subject which I intend to develop in a later project.

149 See, e.g., Clericus, *A letter to the right reverend the bishop of Gloucester in vindication of his lordship's refusal to accept a vice-presidentship of an auxiliary Bible Society at Gloucester* (Canterbury, 1813); T. Gisborne, *A letter to the right reverend the lord bishop of Gloucester on the subject of the British and Foreign Bible Society* (London, 1815).

150 Martin, *Evangelicals united*, pp. 105–18.

151 Law, *Charge ... 1814*, pp. 9–14; Law, *Charge ... 1817*, p. 6; Majendie, *Charge ... 1814*, p. 18. Goodenough's charge was summarized in *British Critic* (1816), pp. 432–7.

> is a point on which many good men have been much divided in their sentiments; and everyone must decide according to the dictates of his own conscience.[152]

At the other end of the spectrum could be found the orthodox high churchman, Thomas Burgess, who presented an extensive and resolute defence of the Bible Society to the clergy of St David's in 1813.[153]

In this atmosphere, Ryder, a well known supporter of Bible Societies, could hardly be expected to avoid the subject altogether in his primary charge. He did, however, begin cautiously, declaring that a *vehement* advocacy of either side would be both contrary to his principles and inappropriate to his position as a bishop but that it was proper for him to declare his own opinion without desiring that it should influence his hearers unduly. He indicated that there was no doubt as to the utility of the S.P.C.K. and then proceeded to defend the Bible Society by reference to the biblical command to preach the gospel to every creature and the spirit of the reformation. After vindicating the Bible Society from charges of tendencies hostile to the established Church and its liturgy by reference to its actual record over the last twelve years, the bishop went on to assert

> that the support of *both* Societies is not incompatible with the character of a cordial friend and conscientious Minister of the Established Church. And, (while I gladly repeat, what I have before publicly stated, as my deliberate conviction, that, in cases where very contracted means would appear to permit a Parochial Minister to subscribe only to one Society, he should chuse that which would enable him to provide the Liturgy as well as the Bible, for *his own* people), may I not add, *without fear of offence,* that, if by elevating his estimate of the claims of charity a little higher above the worldly towards the Christian standard, if, by a little further stretch of self-denial, he can augment his fund for charitable contribution, he may safely and joyfully cast his mite into the treasury of the British and Foreign Bible Society, enroll his name amongst a large proportion of the most justly distinguished characters in Church and State, and assume his share in the labour and delight of erecting that stupendous edifice, which is the glory of his age, his country and his Church.[154]

The apparently gentle irony of this passage, however, becomes rather more pointed when set in the context of his predecessor's published reason for not accepting a vice-presidency of the Gloucester Bible Society auxiliary, which was that the S.P.C.K. 'claimed from the clergy of the Establishment all the pecuniary and mental exertions which can possibly be contributed by them'.[155] It was perhaps just as well, therefore, that Ryder thereafter moved rapidly to conclude his charge

152 Sparke, *Charge ... 1817*, pp. 15–21.
153 Burgess, *Charge ... 1813*, pp. 19–32.
154 See below p. 105.
155 See, e.g., Clericus, *A letter*, p. 12.

with a brief peroration stressing the importance of unity within the ministry of 'an Apostolical Church', the good conduct of the clergy and ultimate reliance on Christ.

Conclusion

The Reception of the Charge

Although evidence is sparse, the initial reactions to Ryder's charge appear to have been favourable. It was reported that one group of clergy who had determined beforehand to register their disapproval of their new diocesan by declining the invitation to the visitation dinner were so impressed by the charge that they instead appeared to dine in unusually large numbers.[156] Hannah More was another supporter. She wrote to the *Christian observer*: '"I am highly pleased with it. The writer has turned some difficult points with great dexterity. The tenor and spirit of it would be good but", she added, "there is more beauty in the composition, especially of the exordium", than she had been prepared to expect.'[157] The charge does not seen to have been noticed in the main high-church periodicals like the *British critic*, but it did receive a review almost twelve pages in length in the October number of the moderate evangelical *Christian observer*.[158] Such a journal might have been expected to be supportive of the first acknowledged member of the evangelical school in the Church to sit on the episcopal bench and this support was certainly forthcoming in respect of Ryder's pastoral exhortations and practical suggestions which, the reviewer thought, gained additional force from the bishop's own record as a pastor. The review was also strongly supportive of his critique of the Western schism concluding that, 'to enter into any confutation of a creed which seems necessarily to tend to the subversion of all good morals, and to the substitution of unwarranted theories for holiness of life, will be thought superfluous by every sober man who is in possession of a Bible.'[159] The bishop's encouragement of the Bible Society also received a warm welcome, though it was felt that he had been rather too generous in his estimate of its critics.[160] Nevertheless, at the outset, readers were warned that, 'we cannot concur with him in every sentiment he has expressed',[161] and a major point of disagreement emerged over Ryder's treatment of baptismal regeneration, a discussion of which occupied almost two-thirds of the review. In the opinion of the reviewer, the bishop's position was disturbingly ambiguous because, in confining the term 'regeneration'

156 *Christian observer* (1836), p. 570.
157 *Ibid.*, p. 316.
158 *Christian observer* (1816), pp. 653–65.
159 *Ibid.*, p. 656.
160 *Ibid.*, p. 664.
161 *Ibid.*, p. 653.

to baptism, it remained unclear whether he conceived the Church as teaching that infants or adults were '*necessarily, and merely from the circumstance of being baptized*, regenerated by the Holy Spirit, and heirs of the Kingdom of Heaven'.[162] Furthermore, following an extensive consideration of a catena of quotations from the Fathers and commentaries on them, the reviewer concluded, 'We do not think ourselves authorized to confine the term Regeneration to baptism; and we know of no scriptural evidence, and no record of our church, which justifies the belief of grace *always* given in baptism either to children or adults.'[163] Clearly, both Ryder's terminological argument and seminal theory of baptismal grace could seem even to moderate evangelicals too close for comfort to the views of bishop Mant and other defenders of a high view of baptismal regeneration.

Henry Ryder and early nineteenth-century evangelicalism

It would be easy, from the evidence of the charge alone, to demonstrate that Ryder's attitudes and priorities were congruent with David Bebbington's celebrated quadrilateral of core evangelical characteristics: conversionism, activism, biblicism and crucicentrism.[164] Conversionism and crucicentrism were, notwithstanding the *Christian observer's* concern about his doctrine of baptismal regeneration, both key features of the approach to preaching commended by the bishop to his clergy. Activism is apparent not just in his practical suggestions for pastoral improvements in the diocese but also in his conception of the roles of christian pastors as 'messengers, watchmen, stewards, and shepherds'. Finally, biblicism is most prominent not just in his concern that the Bible should form the basis of preaching and his support for its widespread distribution by means of the Bible Society, but in the range of reference and the language used in the charge. Perhaps more interesting, however, are the points at which a study of the bishop suggests a divergence from the received picture of the early nineteenth-century evangelical school in the Church of England. Most obviously, his anti-calvinism is important not just as a key to his promotion to the bench, but also as an indication of the continuing importance of this stream within evangelicalism, despite the tendency of its contemporary opponents and of some historians to assume that almost all evangelicals were calvinists.[165] Other examples would include an range of appreciative reference stretching to prominent high churchmen and latitudinarians and a prominent commitment both to the establishment for its

162 *Ibid.*, p. 657.
163 *Ibid.*, p. 663.
164 Bebbington, *Evangelicalism*, pp. 2–17.
165 See, e.g., Best, *Evangelicals*, p. 73.

own sake[166] and to its liturgy as 'an affecting, inspiring, and effectual instrument of communion with … God'.[167] Perhaps most important of all, however, are the clear continuities between his earlier theology as a high churchman and his later theology as an evangelical as evidenced, for example, by his views on baptismal regeneration. This clearly points to the danger of presenting evangelicalism in the early nineteenth century in hard-edged terms as a party in the Church with firm boundaries and a clearly worked out set of doctrinal principles or as a complete package of theology, spirituality and practice to which all its exponents necessarily adhered. It might be much more accurately conceived in looser terms as a movement with a varying degree of attraction to and influence over a range of people and a set of ideas and approaches still very much in the process of evolution.[168]

166 Ryder's attachment to the establishment can be found even more starkly in the farewell sermon preached to his former parishioners in 1815 in which, for example, he admonished them, 'Forsake not then our Apostolical Church'. Ryder, *Farewell sermon*, pp. 19–20.

167 See below p. 94.

168 For an example of the relative fluidity of evangelical ideas on a wide range of issues and the continuing process of defining evangelical attitudes, see Pratt, *Eclectic Society*, *passim*.

The text

There are two editions of Henry Ryder's primary visitation charge to the diocese of Gloucester. The first was published in Gloucester in 1816, printed by Walker and Sons; and sold by Payne and Hatchard, London; Evill, Wells; Bottrill, Lutterworth; Combe, Leicester and Hough and Son, Gloucester – a range of distribution that clearly reflected Ryder's continuing interest in the location of his earlier ministry. The charge ran to thirty-five pages and included the customary dedication:

> To the Very Reverend the Dean and the Chapter of Gloucester and to the Reverend the Archdeacon and the Clergy of the Diocese, this Charge Printed in consequence of their General Request is Inscribed by their Affectionate Friend and Brother, Henry Gloucester.

It retailed, according to the review in the *Christian observer*, at 2s 6d. The second edition formed the first thirty-eight pages of a collection: *Three charges delivered to the clergy of the diocese of Gloucester at three visitations held in the years 1816, 1819, and 1822 by Henry Ryder, lord bishop of Lichfield and Coventry late lord bishop of Gloucester*. It was again published in Gloucester, in 1824, by D. Walker and Sons, but this time sold by Hough, Gloucester; Upham, Bath; Richardson, Bristol and Hatchard, Rivingtons and Seely, London. The two texts are virtually identical with only minor changes to punctuation that probably simply reflect the preferences of individual type-setters and a handful of verbal changes. The text presented here is that of the first edition with the verbal changes introduced in the second edition indicated in footnotes. The published version of the charge was itself furnished with a large number of notes, some of them very extensive. These have been reproduced in the text with alphabetical markers; editorial material is given in a separate set of notes with numerical markers.

Henry Ryder:
Charge to the clergy of Gloucester in 1816

A Charge delivered to the clergy of the Diocese of Gloucester, at the Primary Visitation of that Diocese, in the Year 1816, by Henry Ryder D.D. Bishop of Gloucester.

Gloucester, Printed by Walker and Sons (1816)

To the Very Reverend the Dean and the Chapter of Gloucester and to the Reverend the Archdeacon and the Clergy of the Diocese, this Charge Printed in consequence of their General Request is Inscribed by their Affectionate Friend and Brother, Henry Gloucester.

MY REVEREND BRETHREN,

The first opportunity of public intercourse between the Diocesan and his Clergy, cannot fail to excite emotions of a two-fold nature. It brings at once under your view, the connection which is terminated, and that which has commenced; and it is impossible to look backward to the one, or forward to the other, without considerable interest.

I cannot, therefore, hope more effectually to engage your attention, than by referring briefly, in the first instance, to considerations which must, at the present moment, be predominant in your own minds.

In the present case, the retrospective feeling must surely be affectionate regret.

If, indeed, a character distinguished by extraordinary features of self-denial and disinterested friendship – if a mind stored with sound learning, and capable of exhibiting that learning in its best dress of classical accuracy and taste – if such endowments could command respect, and conciliate regard – if an official conduct, in which a conscientious sense of his own and your awful responsibility, was ever tempered with the most earnest desire to encourage those whom he had to admonish, to win rather than force, and to please all 'to edification'[1] – if such conduct could deserve and secure attachment, my predecessor had the fairest ground for expecting what accordingly he obtained – an ample portion of your esteem and love; he retains, I well know, a proportionate share of your recollections and regret. May they be ever present to his remembrance: may they be the forerunners of similar feelings among those with whom he is now connected, and

1 Romans xv. 2.

prove, as far as any human tribute can prove, the balm and solace of his declining years![2]

But if such be the emotions with which you look back upon the past, what must be your anticipations for the future?

The qualifications of his successor are chiefly confined to a somewhat intimate acquaintance with the condition, the feeling, and the duties of a Parochial Minister; to some knowledge of the instructions and the care which the people require, and have a right to demand, at our hands.

The claims of his successor to your regard consist mainly in a hearty desire and determination, which he now solemnly professes before Almighty God, to fulfil, under the guidance of his Holy Spirit, the arduous office committed to his charge, not 'as a man-pleaser, but as unto the Lord, and as in his sight',[3] to be the counsellor and friend of those whose heart is in their work, while he is the firm reprover of open offences and obstinate negligence; 'to be so merciful that he be not too remiss, and so minister discipline that he forget not mercy';[a] esteeming it his highest privilege to send forth well qualified labourers into the vineyard of his Lord, and not only to direct, but as far as in him lies, to share their labors, their trials, and 'their joy'.[5]

May your indulgence to his many defects, your prayers for his support and success, and you cordial co-operation in his efforts to promote the usefulness of the Ministry, ever animate, sustain, and carry him forward in his course! May He, whom, I trust, we mutually desire to serve – the 'High Priest, who can be touched with a feeling of our infirmities',[6] and 'without whom we can do nothing'[7] – vouchsafe to us all such a hope of his pardon, and such a measure of his grace, that we may fulfil each his portion in the great work appointed to us, with *one*

a *Vide* Form for the Consecration of Bishops.[4]

2 Ryder's predecessor was George Isaac Huntingford (1748–1832), a traditional tory protestant churchman. He owed his advancement primarily to his friendship with Henry Addington, who had been his pupil at Winchester College. Addington secured his appointment to the see of Gloucester in 1802. In 1815, at the age of 67, Huntingford was translated to the rather more wealthy see of Hereford, which he held for a further seventeen years.

3 Ephesians vi. 6: 'Not with eye service, as men pleasers; but as the servants of Christ, doing the will of God from the heart.'

4 The quotation is from an exhortation by the archbishop on delivering the Bible to the elected bishop in the form of ordaining or consecrating of an archbishop or bishop in the Book of Common Prayer. The original reads, 'Be so merciful, that ye be not too remiss; so minister discipline, that you forget not mercy.'

5 II Corinthians viii. 2.

6 Hebrews iv. 15: 'For we have not an high priest which cannot be touched with our infirmities.'

7 John xv. 5: 'He that abideth in me, and I in him, the same bringeth forth much fruit: for without me ye can do nothing.'

heart and *one* voice; and then may He re-unite us all in one 'House eternal in the Heavens',[8] the house of rest and peace, and love and praise to the common 'shepherd and bishop of our souls!'[9]

The grand object originally designed, and properly to be pursued in these occasional addresses, appears to consist in *general* exhortation, and in *appropriate* instructions and admonitions, as suggested by the peculiar exigencies of the time; by public acts and occurrences, which affect the interests of the Church, chiefly as a spiritual body; and by the ever-varying state of opinions and manners amongst our flocks.

Upon the subject of general exhortation, I can have no *new* motives to offer, no *new* incentives to urge, no *new* views of responsibility to bring before your eyes. I can only, in the emphatic language of St. Peter, 'Stir up your sincere[a] minds by way of remembrance'.[11]

Such, however, is the weak and naturally corrupt constitution of our souls; such is the debasing tendency and entangling influence even of necessary intercourse with the world, that the strongest and deepest impression engraven on the tablets of the heart, soon begins to be effaced, and requires to be retraced and revived: the brightest polish on the inward mirror is soon tarnished or becomes dull, and requires to be refreshed and brought back to its first clearness and original lustre.

'To the law then, and to the testimony';[12] – in this my office of remembrancer, I *would refer you* to the general record of your obligations, and to the particular abstract of them, by which you have most solemnly acknowledged yourselves to be individually and personally bound.

To the Scriptures, especially to the prophet Ezekiel,[b] and the Apostle Paul; to the Ordination Service, in its exhortations, and its questions and replies, I would most earnestly and affectionately entreat you to look, for the standard of your Clerical Character, and the test of your state, as, above all men, responsible to Almighty God.

I *would thus refer you,* according to the direction of St Paul to his first Bishops, Timothy and Titus; mindful of my solemn office, 'exhorting and rebuking

a Vide Schleusner ad locum. 2 Peter iii. 1.[10]

b Chapters iii. xxxiii. and xxxiv.

8 II Corinthians v. 1: 'an house not made with hands, eternal in the heavens'.

9 I Peter ii. 25: 'the Shepherd and Bishop of your souls'.

10 Cf. J. F. Schleusner, *Lexicon Graeco-Latinum in Novum Testamentum* (London, 1826), p. 117.

11 II Peter iii. 1: 'stir up your pure minds by way of remembrance'.

12 Isaiah viii. 20: 'To the law and to the testimony'.

with all authority';[a] but at the same time mindful of our mutual infirmities, and of that brotherly-kindness, which I feel, and wish to excite, in return, 'entreating the elder as fathers, and the younger men as brethren'.[b]

I would refer you to this standard and this test – in anticipation of that far more awful trial, which is coming on apace to all, and to which several of the Clergy have been summoned, even since I entered upon my office.

I would thus refer you, under a conviction that such a comparison, frequently and seriously instituted, will be the best preparation for 'that day', when every servant will have to answer for each talent entrusted, and each charge assigned; and when he, above all, who had to distribute to his brethren their 'meat in due season', will have to give account for any that may have suffered hunger, for any that may have perished through his neglect.[15]

Let the following questions, then, be often recurring to each of your minds, and press your consciences for a full and correct answer:

Am I the very 'Messenger, Watchman, and Steward of my Lord',[c] which I was exhorted, and which I promised to be, in my ordination vows? As a *Messenger*, 'instant in season and out of season',[17] in sounding the message and call of my God in every ear that will hear: As a *Watchman* on my post, on the alert, endeavouring to ward off every danger, to seize every opportunity of duty: As a *Steward*, wisely and faithfully dispensing the blessed mysteries committed to me, so that 'He that gathereth little shall have no lack?'[d]

Am I the good *Shepherd,* guiding, feeding, guarding, rearing when young, directing when at riper years, supporting and cherishing when old, the flock over which I am appointed Overseer – regarding their souls, not as worthless or insignificant, but as 'a treasure' of infinite and eternal value entrusted to my charge, even 'the purchase of Christ's death, and the price of his blood, his spouse and his body?'[e]

a Ep. to Titus ii. 15.[13]

b 1 Ep. to Timothy v. 1.[14]

c *Vide* Exhortation in the Service for the Ordination of Priests.[16]

d Exodus xvi. 18.[18]

e *Vide* Ordination Service.

13 Titus ii. 15: 'These things speak, and exhort, and rebuke with all authority.'

14 I Timothy v. 1: 'Rebuke not an elder, but intreat *him* as a father; *and* the younger men as brethren.'

15 This passage draws on Matthew xxiv. 36 – xxv. 30.

16 Book of Common Prayer, The form and manner of ordering of priests: 'messengers, watchmen, and stewards of the Lord'.

17 II Timothy iv. 2: 'be instant in season, out of season'.

18 Exodus xvi. 18: 'he that gathered little had no lack.'

Is this my office the most valued, the chief object of my life? Am I applying myself, as appointed, 'wholly to this very thing', drawing all my cares and studies this way; laying aside as much as possible 'the study of the world and the flesh,' and never suffering any temporal avocations, however specious in their pretensions, habitually to usurp the time and thought which are mainly due to the immortal interests under my superintendance, and each moment at stake?

Has 'that *daily* reading and weighing the Scriptures' so emphatically and repeatedly inculcated, been my serious and unceasing practice? And have its effects been manifest in the Scriptural tenor of my doctrinal instructions, and the Scriptural tone of my moral exhortation?[19]

Has the *whole counsel of God* been always fully declared by me, *nothing added, nothing diminished?*[a]

Has the foundation been always deeply laid in faith in a crucified Redeemer and a sanctifying Spirit, and the superstructure uniformly exhibited in my discourses, carried on and built up in all the graces and duties of a sober, righteous and godly life?

Has the genuine, deep, and awful conviction of my personal and ministerial unworthiness laid me low in penitence and desire of pardon at the foot of the Cross?

And has 'the earnest prayer for the heavenly assistance of the Holy Spirit' been 'continually'[b] springing up in my heart and poured forth from my lips?

Have my private supplications for myself, and for my people, anticipated and cooperated with my public labours?

And, lastly, has my life, and that of my family, been 'the wholesome and godly example and pattern for my people to follow',[22] so that they might not only do

a *Vide* Revelations xxii. 18, 19.[20]

b *Vide* Ordination Service.[21]

19 The material in the four paragraphs above is drawn largely from the exhortation of the bishop in the Book of Common Prayer, The form and manner of ordering of priests.

20 Revelation xxii. 18, 19: 'For I testify unto every man that heareth the words of the prophecy of this book, If any man shall add unto these things, God shall add unto him the plagues that are written in this book: And if any man shall take away from the words of the book of this prophecy, God shall take away his part out of the book of life, and out of the holy city, and *from the* things which are written in this book.'

21 Book of Common Prayer, The form and manner of ordering of priests: 'continually pray to God the Father, by the mediation of our only saviour Jesus Christ, for the heavenly assistance of the Holy Ghost.'

22 Book of Common Prayer, The form and manner of ordering of priests: 'Will you be diligent to frame and fashion your own selves, and your families, according to the doctrine of Christ; and to make both yourselves and them, as much as in you lieth, wholesome examples and patterns to the flock of Christ?'

what I *say*, but what I *do*? Have I ever been able to speak of religion with that truth and warmth peculiar to one who knows and loves it from the bottom of his heart? And have my people learnt to know and love religion too, by its visible fruits in my conduct and conversation? Can I say, in any measure with St Paul, 'Follow me, as I have followed Christ?'[23]

SUCH my Reverend Brethren, is the series of solemn questions which form the subject of my general exhortation, and which I venture to recommend for individual use. Trite, and tedious, and even irrelevant to the present assembly, they may possibly appear; but I dare not apologize for the repetition of truths upon which our common eternity depends; nor could I venture to leave unsaid, what might charge me with the blood of any man. I feel convinced, that those to whom they are really most familiar, will be still the best disposed to welcome them with renewed interest, and to apply them with increasing profit: and such a state of mind, which I would willingly impute to all, will best incline you to appreciate the importance, and perhaps consent to the adoption, of the additional suggestions which I shall now lay before you, distrustful of my own judgement, but confident of my motive, and persuaded that you will listen without prejudice, and consider, not without a desire to approve.

The first subject, which ever presses itself upon our attention, is the nature of our public ministrations. We have the same ministry with St Paul; and he saith to the Corinthians, 'Necessity is laid upon me, yea woe is unto me, if I preach not the Gospel.'[a]

A Minister, endowed with health of body and mind, whom even the Sabbath-bell ineffectually summons to his public labours, is indeed forfeiting all claim to his title, while he is ensuring punishment for his neglect. The people, not warned by the watchman, may perish; but 'their blood, saith the Lord God, will I require at the watchman's hand.'[b] But the punctual performance of duty will not suffice; upon the nature and spirit of its performance your ministerial character and success depend.

Chief among the distinguished privileges of our Ministry are the Form of Prayer and series of Public Services. It has been admirably said, 'That, if we were to compare the prayers used in the 10,000 Churches of the country during each Sabbath of the year, with the contemporary prayers in the other places of worship,

[a] 1 Corinthians ix. 16.

[b] Ezekiel iii. 18, 20.[24]

23 I Corinthians xi. 1: 'Be ye followers of me, even as I also *am* of Christ.'

24 Ezekiel iii. 18, 20: 'his blood will I require at thine hand.'

we should be constrained to fall down on our knees, and bless God for the Liturgy of the Church of England.'[25]

Testimonies of its superior excellence abound in dead and living authors of communions differing among themselves, and all different from our own, and the well merited weight of whose opinion is therefore doubly enhanced by this undeniable proof of their impartiality.

But all its excellencies, upon which I need not here expatiate, are crowned by its incapability of change through the interference of private authority. The censers of Dathan and Abiram, those sinners against their own souls, though once filled with strange fire, and used by unworthy worshippers, yet remained the same, hallowed as before, unperverted and unpolluted:[26] so is our Liturgy unaffected by the weakness or corruption, the false opinions or even the evil motives of those to whose hands it may possibly at any time be intrusted. It ever remains unchanged, ready to become the vehicle for the purest incense, for the most genuine and the liveliest devotion. But we must never forget, that, after all, incomparable, unalterable as it is, it is but a vehicle. The feelings of our hearts must correspond with the sentiments expressed; the prayers must be appropriated by each worshipper, and made his own; the fair and exactly proportioned image must be kindled unto life by the breath of the soul; the offering on the altar must be set on fire, and its savour ascend, or it will never reach Heaven, and be acceptable to Him who is a Spirit, and must be worshipped with the spirit and with the understanding.

Whatever human aid can perform towards promoting this only effectual use of the Liturgy, must be performed by him who reads the prayers. It is his part, by clear, distinct pronunciation, by decent slowness of delivery, by unquestionable marks in his voice and countenance of deep attention, of reverential awe, and affectionate earnestness, to give to the Liturgy all its force, and draw forth all its beauties. It is his part thus to shew, that he not only reads *over*, but prays *in*, the form of soundest words. Thus might he hope to find, through the influence of divine grace, the hearts of his congregation, by imperceptible attraction, drawn into the same current, bent into the same direction, and the incense of their devotions ascending from one common censer in an united wreath, to the throne of the Most High.

Thus might he hope to experience the *sure* effect of *such* petitions, in the growth and progress of religious light and truth – of religious principle and practice amongst his people; and in an increasing love to one another, to himself, and especially to that Church which has afforded them such an endearing band of

25 This is a paraphrase of a passage in C. Simeon, *The excellency of the liturgy in four discourses preached before the University of Cambridge in November 1811* (Cambridge, 1812), pp. 78–9.

26 Cf. Numbers xvi. 1–39.

union, such an affecting, inspiring, and effectual instrument of communion with their God.

Can I offer more forcible, more persuasive arguments for peculiar attention in the public use of our Liturgy, and all our Sacred Offices? And need I add the contrast? The service, a toilsome ceremony – the worshippers, a formal few – the utter inefficacy of the prayers manifested by the extinction of the power of godliness amongst them – and, above all, the God who heareth prayer grievously offended by such lip-service and solemn mockery. The prayers used *from,* or *without* the heart, make the grand, fundamental, characteristic difference between a Minister and Congregation who are holy and happy, and those who are not.

But though the devotional part justly claim the first place and pre-eminent importance in our consideration of the public service; though the main object of all religious *instruction* be to enable us to *pray* aright, yet the instructive part must not be undervalued or neglected. From him who preaches the truth as it is in Jesus, not handling the word ignorantly or partially, but ever giving their due importance to the only genuine principles on the one hand, and to the indispensable effects in an holy life on the other; from such a preacher will, under the divine blessing, proceed a people endowed with a spirit of supplication, and *thence* abundant in every good word and work.

In the Epistles of St. Paul and his brethren, you have complete and unerring standards of doctrine, and perfect models of exhortation, derived from it, and conformable to it. And, as grounded upon such authority, the Articles and Homilies of our Church are our safest guides and our best patterns.

But, as it ever was, so in our time it will be, that 'offences must come',[27] fresh errors arise, or exploded errors are revived, calculated to deceive and mislead many, and to corrupt them from the simplicity that is in Christ, and in the authentic records of our Church, the pillar and ground of his truth.

I would allude, in the first place, to the Ministers who, in some neighbouring dioceses, have lately seceded from the Church;[28] and *to the few* who may remain in it, but who adopt, in some measure, their opinions and practice.

Their charge against their brethren is, that we do not preach Christ freely and fully; that we detract from the all-sufficiency of faith, and promulgate an imperfect, and even another gospel.

What are the grounds of this charge? That we urge the necessity of looking for the *fruit* and *evidence* of faith in a truly Christian life, before we venture to hope for the permanence, or even decide upon the utility and soundness, of the *principle* within. Against such charges, let us set the example of St. Paul, whose

27 Matthew xviii. 7: 'Woe unto the world because of offences! For it must needs be that offences come'. Cf. Luke xvii. 7.

28 The 'Western schism'. See above p. 65.

Epistles, commencing with doctrine, generally end in the most forcible and even minute exhortation to duties, as the only genuine result of the doctrine. Against such charges, let us set the positive declaration of St. James, who is generally thought to have written expressly in opposition to similar perversions in his time, and who imperatively demands evangelical obedience, as the proof of evangelical faith. 'Shew me thy faith by thy works.'[29] 'Faith without works is dead.'[30] And in this very spirit does the Homily of Faith, as it were, prophetically conclude.

'As you profess the name of Christ, let no such fantasy and imagination of faith at any time beguile you; but be sure of your faith; try it by your living, look upon the fruits that come of it, mark the increase of love and charity by it towards God and your neighbour, and *so* shall you perceive it to be a true and lively faith. And, if you perceive such a faith in you, rejoice in it, and be diligent to maintain it and keep it still in you; let it be daily increasing, and more and more by well-working; and *so* shall you be sure that you shall please God by this faith: and at length, as other faithful men have done before, so shall you, when his will is, come to him, and receive the end and final reward of your faith, as St. Peter nameth it, the salvation of your souls.'[31]

Beware, then, let me beseech you, of this error, which, however it may have sprung up upon this occasion, in well-intentioned and pious persons, is, we must fear, but a snare of the devil, and an awful wresting of Scripture, to the destruction of those who hear. While, in every discourse, you exalt the Lord Jesus Christ, leading your people to him, as the needful, the only Saviour of their souls, all-sufficient to procure them pardon, and to give them grace, never fail to press the indispensable necessity of maintaining, and the tremendous danger of neglecting, good works; the *necessity* of 'living unto Him who died for us'.[32]

The second error, against which I think it my duty to warn you, though not perhaps so obviously dangerous, is little less injurious to the real objects of the Ministry, and, without doubt, much more likely to attract and mislead. It is intimately connected with the recent controversy upon the subject of regeneration, and will ground itself upon the line of argument and tone of remark which have been adopted upon that occasion.

29 James ii. 18: 'Yea a man may say, Thou hast faith and I have works: shew me thy faith without thy works, and I will shew thee my faith by my works.'

30 James ii. 26.

31 This quotation, which is accurate with the exception of minor grammatical alterations, is from the fourth homily, 'A short declaration of the true and lively christian faith', in the *First book of homilies* (1562). The doctrine of the homilies was a common point of reference for evangelicals in the nineteenth century. From 1812, the homilies were reprinted in single numbers and cheap editions by the Prayer Book and Homily Society of which Ryder was a patron. *Proceedings of the Prayer Book and Homily Society during its eighth year* (London, 1820), p. v.

32 II Corinthians v. 15: 'he died for all, that they which live should not henceforth live unto themselves, but unto him which died for them and rose again.'

The question, so far as it regards the use of the *term*, is in my opinion satisfactorily determined by the Articles and Offices of our Church, and by the meaning uniformly annexed to it in the four first centuries of the Christian Aera.[a]

The number of eminent and justly revered writers (some of exalted station in the Church, amongst whom we must reckon Archbishop Tillotson,)[34] who have spoken at times of a *regeneration* distinct from the baptismal, though amply sufficient to excuse, and perhaps justify, is not, I conceive, sufficient to recommend such an application of the term.

It may naturally excite confusion in the minds of those hearers, whose capacity and reading may be limited, and lead them to hesitate about the propriety of our baptismal service. It is by no means indispensably necessary, in order to convey a full idea of that radical, fundamental change of views, desires, and pursuits, so generally requisite in those who, having been baptized in infancy, have reached the age, in which they can commit actual sin.

I would therefore wish generally to restrict the term to the baptismal privileges; and, considering them as comprehending, not only an external admission into the visible Church – not only a covenanted title to the pardon and grace of the Gospel – but even a degree of spiritual aid vouchsafed and ready to offer itself to our acceptance or rejection. At the dawn of reason,[35] I would recommend a reference to these privileges in our discourses, as talents which the hearer should have so improved as to bear interest, as seed which should have sprung up and produced fruit.

But, at the same time, I would solemnly protest against that most serious error (which has arisen probably from exalting too highly the just view of baptismal regeneration) of contemplating all the individuals of a *baptized* congregation as *converted,* as *having* all once known the truth, and entered upon the right path, though some may have wandered from it, and others may have made little progress, as not therefore requiring (all by nature, and most, it is to be feared,

[a] *Vide* Wall on Infant Baptism.[33]

33 W. Wall, *The history of infant baptism* (London, 1705), *passim.* William Wall (1647–1728), the vicar of Shoreham in Kent, was probably the leading anglican writer in defence of the practice of infant baptism and his works continued to be published into the second half of the nineteenth century.

34 John Tillotson (1630–94) was archbishop of Canterbury from 1691 to 1694, in place of the ejected Sancroft, but was chiefly famous for his preaching. It is noteworthy that the only divine from whom Ryder chose publicly to differ in his *Charge* was one generally regarded as representing a moderate latitudinarian position in the spectrum of anglican churchmanship.

35 In the second edition of the *Charge* the phrase 'at the dawn of reason' appears at the end of the preceding sentence, which makes rather better sense of the text.

through defective principle and practice,) that 'transformation'[a] by the 'renewing of the mind',[36] that 'putting off the old man, and putting on the new man',[b] which is so emphatically enjoined by St Paul to his *baptized*[c] Romans and Ephesians.

This erroneous view, in my opinion, strikes at the root of all useful and effectual preaching. Ministerial addresses founded upon it soothe and delude the people into a false peace; they do but half open the wound in the conscience of the sinner; they act as a dull and clouded mirror, and exhibit to him a most imperfect representation of what he is, and what he ought to be – of what must be done for him, and in him; they lull to sleep any conscientious misgivings in the man of worldly decency and reputation; they may make many a Pharisee, and produce on many a death-bed a vain self-righteous ease, which must soon be changed to self-condemnation and death eternal. But they will never be the spiritual 'weapons, mighty through God, to the pulling down of strongholds',[d] and 'bringing the servant of Satan into captivity to the obedience of Jesus Christ'.[e] They will never be instrumental in drawing forth, from practical unbelievers, the question of the gaoler – 'What must I do to be saved?'[40] nor in leading them as humbled penitents to the Cross of Christ, and 'binding them to the horns of the altar',[41] as devoted disciples of his word, and willing dependants on his grace. They will never be the means of opening the heart of a Lydia,[f] nor of building up a Philippian congregation in true Christian holiness and brotherly kindness, through a sense of their own unworthiness, and the undeserved mercies of God in Jesus Christ. They will never fulfil your promise at ordination of 'seeking for Christ's sheep, that are dispersed abroad, and for his children, who are in the midst of this naughty world, that they may be saved through Christ for ever'.[42] No – rather permit me to urge, suffer me

a Romans xii. 2.

b Ephesians iv. 22.[37]

c Romans vi. and Ephesians iv. 5.

d 2 Cor. x. 4.[38]

e 2 Cor. x. 5.[39]

f Acts xvi. 14.

36 Romans xii. 2: 'be not conformed to the image of this world: but be ye transformed by the renewing of your mind.'

37 Ephesians iv. 22–4: 'That ye put off concerning the former conversation the old man, which is corrupt according to the deceitful lusts; and be renewed in the spirit of your mind; and that ye put on the new man.'

38 II Corinthians x. 4: 'For the weapons of our warfare are not carnal, but mighty through God to the pulling down of strongholds.'

39 II Corinthians x. 5: 'bringing into captivity every thought to the obedience of Christ'.

40 Acts xvi. 30.

41 Psalms cxvii. 27: 'bind the sacrifice with cords, even unto the horns of the altar.'

42 Book of Common Prayer, The form and manner of ordering of priests.

to beseech *you*, by these very unspeakable mercies, to address *your* people with a far different feeling, and in far different language. Exhort them with parental authority, but with parental affection – exhort them, one and all, seriously to examine themselves by the tests and marks of the 'new creature',[43] of the death unto sin, and the new birth unto righteousness, which are so repeatedly and so emphatically required in the Scriptures.[a]

Recommend to them enquiries of the following nature and purport. 'What is your general course of conduct? Is it agreeable only to your natural inclinations, and to the fashion and opinions of the world; or is it your endeavour to regulate it by the rule of divine law? What is your prevailing principle and motive? Is it humble fear and fervent love of God, and desire to live in the service of Christ, whom you feel to be all in all to you; or is it self-love, and the fear and love of the world? What is your main object and hope? Is it to secure an interest in the atonement and righteousness of Christ, and a place, even the lowest in his kingdom; or is it rather worldly honour or wealth – success in earthly projects, or at best the union, if possible, of all the good things in *both* worlds, the recompense of a divided service between God and Mammon?'

Suffer none to exempt themselves from such an examination, whatever be their outward privileges and specious appearance; and the result, if they seek a right knowledge of themselves in hearty prayer, will, under the influence of the Holy Spirit, divide, as it were, the congregation, not indeed externally in the view of each other, but through the estimate which each individual will take of his own state.[b]

It is your part, then, 'rightly to divide the word of truth',[45] and, without venturing yourself to assign it positively to any individual, offer to each character his portion, which he may apply to himself, according as, thus instructed, he shall perceive his state to be in the sight of God. Exalt the Saviour before the eyes of him, whose conscience bears humble witness that he has chosen the better part, as his own God, in whom he has believed and found his soul required. Entreat

a Romans vi. Ephesians ii. 10. and iv. 22–32. 1 John iii. 3–10.

b *Vide* Paley's Sermons on Conversion – 'I think that there are two topics of exhortation, which, together, comprise the whole Christian life, and one or other of which belongs to EVERY MAN LIVING; and these two topics are, conversion and improvement: when conversion is not wanted, improvement is,' &c. &c. &c.[44]

43 I Corinthians v. 17 or Galatians vi. 15.

44 W. Paley, *Sermons on several subjects* (Sunderland, 1806), pp. 116–17. William Paley (1743–1805), archdeacon of Carlisle, was a latitudinarian theologian who was most significant by the early nineteenth century as an apologist. His *A view of the evidences of christianity* (1794) was reprinted throughout the nineteenth century.

45 II Timothy ii. 15: 'rightly dividing the word of truth'.

such a man to reply with more entire dependance upon *His* ever-faithful love, to watch more scrupulously, lest he prove ungrateful to so much mercy, and do despite to the Spirit so freely given, and to labor more assiduously in all the means of spiritual benefit, and in all the duties of private and social life, in order that he may adorn his profession, and shew that he has not received this grace in vain.

Exalt also the Saviour before those, whose consciences must bear a contrary testimony, as the God, whom they have hitherto rejected, grieved and provoked from day to day, but who has borne with them so long, and still waits to be gracious; as the God, however, whose mercy may have a limit, and whose countenance may be about to change.

Exalt him in all his offices of Prophet, Priest, and King – in all his manifestations of love – in all his exhibitions of power. Compel them to perceive and acknowledge what they are now *without Him,* and to anticipate what they will[46] be *with Him now*, in all the comforts and joys of a life of faith and duty; and admit them to a glimpse, as far as revelation warrants, of what they might then enjoy *with Him* for ever and ever. Thus, by every alarm and every encouragement, constrain or win them to come in true repentance and lively faith to the Saviour, and receive their portion in his meritorious atonement, prevailing intercession, efficacious grace, and unspotted righteousness, if peradventure they may be converted and saved. 'Turn ye, turn ye; why will ye die? Why will ye not come unto Him that ye might have life?'[47]

Thus, after the model of St. Paul, 'determine not to know any thing among your people, save Jesus Christ, and him crucified.'[a]

Let this be the general matter and strain of your addresses. It will produce no crude unqualified statement, no dry barren theory, no visionary conceits, no enthusiastic impulses. It will admit, nay demand, a deep and accurate developement of the foldings of the human heart, and its inmost motives. It will allow of the nicest adaptation of warning and encouragement to each varying shade of human character. It will accord with the tenderest and most discriminating care, lest you should wound the weak and needlessly desponding conscience; lest you should 'bruise the broken reed',[49] and make 'the heart of the righteous sad, whom

[a] 1 Cor. ii. 2.[48]

46 In the second edition of the *Charge* 'will' is replaced by 'might'.

47 Ezekiel xxxiii. 11: 'turn ye, turn ye from your evil ways; for why will ye die, O house of Israel'; John v. 40: 'And ye will not come to me that ye might have life.'

48 I Corinthians ii. 2: 'I determined not to know anything among you, save Jesus Christ, and him crucified.'

49 Matthew xii. 20: 'A bruised reed shall he not break.'

the Lord hath not made sad'.[50] It will require the most particular enforcement of moral duties, in all their detail, and in the highest perfection. 'Do we make void the law through faith? God forbid! yea, we establish the law.'[51] The whole of Scripture, its didactic, historical, and prophetical portions; its articles of belief, its practical precepts, its models of devotion, will all readily find their place in such a system, and perform their respective offices. It will be indeed the 'declaration of the whole counsel of God',[52] 'the preaching of the Cross',[53] 'the ministration of the Spirit',[54] the preaching that will be 'a savour of life unto life, or of death unto death'.[55]

It was such preaching, which, proceeding from the lips of Cranmer, Latimer, Ridley, and our own Hooper, dispelled the darkness of Popery, and erected our Church on its ruins. It is such preaching, which has ever since maintained its purity and its power of doing good. It is preaching of this general nature and tendency which Archbishop Secker,[a] and Bishops Horne[b] and

a *Vide* First and Third Archiepiscopal Charges, edition 1769, pages 1, 235–8, 298–300. For instance, 'ere lay your foundation. Set before your people the lamentable condition of fallen man – the numerous actual sins by which they have made it worse – the redemption wrought out for them by Jesus Christ – the nature and importance of true faith in him – their absolute need of the grace of the Divine Spirit, in order to obey his precepts. This will be addressing yourselves to them, as Christian Ministers ought to Christian hearers,' &c.[56]

b *Vide* Charge to the Clergy of Norwich, in Bishop Horne's Works, 6th vol. 'We can never introduce the doctrines of redemption and atonement, salvation by Jesus Christ can never be understood, nor wanted, except it be allowed that man *is* such as the Saviour found him – lame and blind, and deaf, and dumb, and even dead in sin.

'Let us endeavour, for the time to come, to speak and labour in our proper character, as embassadors who have a message from Heaven, which they are bound to deliver at the peril of their own souls; trusting that the Gospel, where it is genuine, will be followed by that grace and power, which never yet failed to attend it. "In the name of Jesus Christ of Nazareth, rise up, and walk." This was the Gospel, energetic and effective: it gave the ability with the command; the lame man felt through all his powers: "He arose – he walked – he leaped – he praised God." So

50 Ezekiel xiii. 22: 'Because with lies you have made the heart of the righteous sad, whom I have not made sad.'

51 Romans iii. 31: 'Do we then make void the law through faith? God forbid: yea we establish the law.'

52 Acts xx. 27: 'For I have not shunned to declare unto you all the counsel of God.'

53 I Corinthians i. 18.

54 II Corinthians iii. 8.

55 II Corinthians ii. 16: 'To the one we are the savour of death unto death; and to the other the savour of life unto life.'

56 *Eight charges delivered to the clergy of the dioceses of Oxford and Canterbury... by Thomas Secker LL.D. late archbishop of Canterbury*, ed. B. Porteus and G. Stinton (London, 1769).

Horsely,[c] so forcibly recommended in their Charges, and to which the humblest of their followers must now set to his seal, and bear his unequivocal and decided testimony. It is by such preaching that our incomparable Church will prove incontestably, in every part of her public Ministry, no less than in her doctrines and services, the sanctuary and dispenser of true religion and virtue, and may best hope, with the assistance of the Divine Spirit, to present to that God from whom she derives her origin, the most acceptable sacrifice of gratitude for great and peculiar blessings – a people zealous in his faith and walking in his ways.

Such, my Reverend Brethren, are my views respecting the Public Ministrations of the Church; and such are the errors against which I have thought it expedient and seasonable to admonish and warn you thus fully and in detail. The paramount importance of the subject must excuse the apparent prolixity, and perhaps unusual warmth, with which I have discussed it; and its peculiar suitableness to an introductory Charge will justify the little space which it has left to other not unimportant topics.

The propriety, where possible, of adding a second Sermon to the Evening Service; the necessity of extending the Education of the Poor in the principles of

will the people be edified; and we shall be able to give a good account of our charge at that time, when the fashion of this world, and all that is human in religion and learning, shall vanish away.'[57]

c *Vide* Primary Charge to the Clergy of St David's. 'Our proper office is to publish the word of reconciliation, to propound the terms of peace and pardon to the penitent,' &c. &c.[58]

Vide Primary Charge to the Clergy of St Asaph. 'Faith and repentance – Christ's atonement – justification – grace – the new birth – good works, as the *necessary* fruits of that faith which justifies, and the symptoms of the believer's sanctification – the merit of Christ's obedience, and the want of merit in our own. Upon these subjects you cannot preach too often.

'Apply yourselves with the whole strength and power of your minds to do the work of Evangelists. Proclaim to those who are at enmity with God, and children of his wrath, the glad tidings of Christ's pacification; sound the alarm to awaken to a life of righteousness a world lost and dead in trespasses and sins; lift aloft the blazing torch of revelation, to scatter its rays over them that sit in darkness and the shadow of death, and to guide the footsteps of the benighted wanderer into the paths of life and peace.'[59]

57 *The Works of the Right Reverend George Horne D.D., late Bishop of Norwich*, ed. William Jones (6 vols., London 1809), VI, 539, 545–6.

58 S. Horsley, *The charge of Samuel, lord bishop of St David's to the clergy of his diocese delivered at his primary visitation, in the year 1790* (London, 1791), p. 9.

59 S. Horsley, *The charges of Samuel Horsley late lord bishop of St Asaph delivered at his several visitations of the dioceses of St David's, Rochester, and St Asaph* (Dundee, 1813), pp. 223–4, 231–2.

the Established Church by the formation of a Diocesan Society, and the promotion of its objects in your respective parishes; and a statement of my opinion respecting Societies for Religious Charity, are the points, to which I wish briefly in conclusion to draw your attention.

The *first* I would only suggest for the serious consideration of those who wish to attract their people to the public worship of the Church, and who have that zeal for the interests of the Establishment, that conviction of its superior excellence and usefulness, which would make them ready to exceed the prescribed line of compulsory labor, and sacrifice a little more time and thought, in order to retain the wavering, and recall the wanderer within its pale.

A Catechetical Lecture to the children and servants, or the reading of a Homily, would suffice; and I feel convinced, by much observation and experience, that the increased attendance and probable improvement of the congregation would be an ample compensation to *such men,* for the additional exertion of body and mind.

The Homilies, as an admirable compendium of sound doctrine and of 'godly and wholesome counsel', can require no other sanction than that of the Thirty-fifth Article, to which we have all declared our unfeigned consent; and, as suitable and even 'necessary for *these* times',[60] and affectingly interesting to the common people, they have received the testimony of several highly respectable Clergymen, who have made the experiment which I recommend.[a] A very few would of course be omitted, as referring chiefly to customs now grown obsolete, and to dangers, to which, thanks be to God, we are now little exposed; and the rest should be used in their original form, with only a few verbal alterations, without addition or rather injury by professed improvements. The language is but a little more antiquated than that of our Bible; and the expressions most remote from present use are yet generally intelligible to all, and derive from their very antiquity an air of patriarchal authority and affection, which conciliates the respect and attention of the poor, far more than the most studied correctness, or even the chastest elegance of modern times.

[a] *Vide* Bishop Horsley's First Charge, published by the Society for Promoting Christian Knowledge – 'These doctrines' (viz. *Justification by lively faith, &c. &c.)* are delivered with admirable perspicuity and precision in the Homilies of our Church upon these subjects: "The misery of all mankind"; "the salvation of mankind by Christ"; "the true, lively, and Christian faith"; and "good works annexed to faith". These discourses I would earnestly recommend to your frequent study, as an unexceptionable summary of doctrine upon these important points, and an excellent model of composition for popular instruction.'[61]

60 Article XXXV: ' The second book of homilies … doth contain a godly and wholesome doctrine, and necessary for these times, as doth the former book of homilies…'

61 Horsley, *Charge*, p. 36.

The *second* point for our consideration, was the extension of the Education of the Poor in the principles of the Established Church, by the formation of a Diocesan Society, and the promotion of its object in your respective parishes.

I trust, in the course of a few weeks, to have a more express opportunity of generally recommending this mean of improvement; and may therefore content myself, on this occasion, with briefly pressing the institution of daily, or at least, Sunday Schools, where they may not already exist; the establishment of Evening Schools, for two or three nights in the week, where *manufactories*[a] and other avocations do not permit the attendance of the children during the day; and the introduction of the National System into all, where the numbers exceed twenty or thirty. The diminished expence, the increased attention and progress of the children, and their remarkable improvement in religious knowledge and moral habits, are its pre-eminent *excellencies*; and the substitution of literal for syllabic spelling, and the teaching by means of the pupils, are its characteristic *features*.[b] Several of the queries, which I have directed to be given to you to-day, relate, as you will observe, to this subject; and I will request the favour of you to return a punctual and precise answer.

I may now conclude this branch of my Address, with recalling to your recollection these words of the blessed Jesus, which give to it, in my mind, an irresistible force and sanction: 'Lovest thou me? Feed my Lambs';[64] and accommodating that verse of the Sacred Preacher, which may well apply to

a *Vide* the case of Dale's Manufactory, as recorded in the Reports of the Society for bettering the Condition of the Poor.[62]

b *Vide* Reports of the National Society, and Dr. Bell's Instructions for conducting Schools in the Madras System.[63]

62 Thomas Bernard, 'Extract from an account of Mr Dale's cotton mills at New Lanerk, in Scotland', in *The reports of the Society for Bettering the Condition and Increasing the Comforts of the Poor. Vol. II* (London, 1800), no. lxix, 'Seven o'clock is the hour of supper; soon after which (*for that pernicious practice called night-work, is entirely excluded from these mills*) the schools commence, and continue till nine o'clock. Mr Dale has engaged three regular masters, who instruct the lesser children during the day. In the evening they are assisted by seven others, one of whom teaches writing. There is likewise a woman to teach the girls sewing, and another person who occasionally gives lessons in church music. The masters preside over the boys' dinner table. On Sundays they conduct them to the place of divine worship; and in the evening of Sunday, attend to assist and improve them, by religious and moral information.'

63 *Annual report of the National Society for Promoting the Education of the Poor in the Principles of the Established Church* (London, 1812–16). Rev. Andrew Bell, *Instructions for conducting a school through the agency of the scholars themselves: comprising the analysis of an experiment in education made at the male asylum, Madras, 1789–1796. Extracted from Elements of tuition, Part 2, the English School* (4th edn., London, 1813).

64 John xxi. 15: 'Jesus saith to Simon Peter, Simon, son of Jonas, lovest thou me more than these? He saith unto him, Yea, Lord thou knowest that I love thee. He saith unto him, Feed my lambs.'

Ministerial labors in the Education of the Poor. 'In the morning, sow thy seed, and in the evening withhold not thine hand; for thou knowest not whether shall prosper, either this or that, or whether they both shall be alike good.'[a]

The *last* subject, to which I propose to allude, relates to the Societies for Religious Charity, so familiar now to every town, and almost to every village of the country. The increased disposition to promote *such* objects cannot but be in general a consoling circumstance amid so much depravity and irreligion, as the luxurious and military habits of the last twenty or thirty years have produced. But the collision, however unintentional, between the two most eminent Societies has given birth to volumes of controversy, to much alienation and dissension, to many unjustifiable misrepresentations of motives on both sides, to many retorts not very courteous. To advocate either side of the question *vehemently* would neither become my station, nor accord with my principles; and I would gladly pay sincere deference to the characters, attainments, and intentions of those, from whom I must venture to differ.

But as, from various circumstances, I may fairly be expected, so I would not decline, to deliver my deliberate and decided opinion, neither shrinking from what I may consider as my duty to God, nor expecting or desiring that this declaration should have any undue bias upon your minds. It would be dissimulation to deny that it would give me pleasure, should any one who may be 'in a strait between two opinions',[65] be induced to reconsider the subject.

My view and recommendation is, peace and union, between the two Societies, as far as the differences of their *constitutions* permit. The Societies have[66] no *differing*, no *opposing objects* in view. They have one *common* object, so vast, so undeniably, so incomparably good, that surely they need not dispute, but rather provoke one another unto love and good works, even unto tenfold exertions to supply that hunger and thirst for the Word of God, which begins to be excited throughout the world.

The Society for Promoting Christian Knowledge has afforded for a century, and still affords, an opening to so many channels of benevolence, such various and extensive good within its sphere, that no member of our Communion can doubt of its claims to his support.

The Bible Society has not indeed, in the exact and definite form in which we now view it, the same plea of prescription to urge; but its principle, 'the universal

[a] Ecclesiastes xi. 6.

65 Philippians i. 23: 'I am in a strait betwixt two.' 1 Kings xviii. 21: 'How long halt ye between two opinions.'

66 In the second edition of the *Charge* 'have' is replaced by 'aim'.

diffusion of the Scriptures', may be referred directly to Scriptural authority. 'Go ye into all the world, and preach the Gospel to every creature.'[a] And the revival of this principle was coaeval with the period, and contains the very spirit and essence, of the Reformation, when the Bible, almost for one thousand years a sealed book, was professedly unclosed, and thrown open to every eye that would see, and to every heart that would understand.

The arguments *against* the Society in its present form, which admits all Christians to promote its *simple object*, (and only, while it adheres strictly to that *simple object,* can it deserve the support of any Member of the Established Church,) may all, in my opinion, without exception, be resolved into the assumption of *tendencies* hostile to the Established Church, hostile to the circulation of the Liturgy; which assumption of tendencies the experience of twelve years has now proved to be utterly erroneous.

The argument *for* the Society is its history for those twelve years, and the declaration of a *fact*, which no one can invalidate, or would surely wish to depreciate. It has been the instrument of distributing above[67] 1,500,000 copies of the Scriptures, and circulated, or aided in circulating them, in sixty-three different languages;[b] and its opening prospects far exceed its recorded benefits. May I not then *without presumption,* assert, that the support of *both* Societies is not incompatible with the character of a cordial friend and conscientious Minister of the Established Church? And, (while I gladly repeat, what I have before publicly stated, as my deliberate conviction, that, in cases where very contracted means would appear to permit a Parochial Minister to subscribe only to one Society, he should chuse that which would enable him to provide the Liturgy as well as the Bible, for *his own* people,) may I not add, *without fear of offence,* that, if by elevating his estimate of the claims of charity a little higher above the worldly towards the Christian standard, if, by a little further stretch of self-denial, he can augment his fund for charitable contribution, he may safely and joyfully cast his mite into the treasury of the British and Foreign Bible Society, enroll his name amongst a large proportion of the most justly distinguished characters in Church and State, and assume his share in the labour and delight of erecting that stupen-

a Mark xvi. 15.

b *Vide* The History of the Origin and First Ten Years of the British and Foreign Bible Society, by the Rev. John Owen; and the Annual Reports of the Society, with their Appendixes.[68]

67 In the second edition of the *Charge* 'above' is replaced by 'about'.

68 J. Owen, *The History of the Origin and First Ten Years of the British and Foreign Bible Society. Vol. II* (London, 1816), p. 591; *Annual reports of the British and Foreign Bible Society* (London, 1805–16).

dous edifice, which is the glory of his age, his country and his Church; which is so prosperously begun, and which must surely continue, till the Word of God shall have not only 'mightily grown', but 'prevailed'[69] to the enlightening and the trial of every people; and till all 'the kingdoms of the world shall have become the kingdoms of our Lord and his Christ'.[70]

Having thus brought the observations with which I purposed, on this occasion, to trouble you, to a close, I must take my leave, with an assurance of my hearty regard and desire to promote whatever may be justly desirable, and really beneficial to yourselves and to your people.

May *we*, my Reverend Brethren, ever recollect, that we are bound together by no common tie, not only, as members of one body, but as fellow workers in one Ministry, even the Ministry of an Apostolical Church. May we from this time ever seek to look at one another with an aspect of genuine kindness, correspondent with the nature of the work in which we are jointly engaged, and congenial to the mind, that was in the Master, whom we serve, 'bearing with each other's infirmities',[71] making allowance for difference of opinion upon non-essential points, striving chiefly to be fellow-helpers in the same service, and hoping thus to be fellow-heirs in the same joy.

May *we* ever look at our common Church in full sympathy of respect and affection; and, the loftier the views we entertain of her claims to preference, (and too lofty we hardly can entertain,) the higher may we raise our estimate of the character and duties, which become those who minister at her altars; the more anxious may we be to act up to *our* privileges and obligations; lest her sacred name should be prophaned through the inconsistency of our private life, or her usefulness impeded through the remissness of our official conduct!

May *we* ever look at ourselves, as unworthy and helpless in the sight of God, but capable of 'doing all things through Christ that strengtheneth us';[72] and then look *up* in the prayer of faith, and in the conscientious exercise of every duty, to Him, who has been with His Church, and will be with it to the end of the world, and who is pledged and ready to make each of us an instrument in edifying that Church, in converting many an inanimate into a lively stone, and in building up her believing people in their holy faith!

Thus *only* shall we all, whether now in higher or lower places, 'taking heed unto ourselves and unto the doctrine, save both ourselves and those that hear

69 Acts xix. 20: 'So mightily grew the word of God and prevailed.'

70 Revelation xi. 15: 'The kingdoms of this world are become the kingdoms of our Lord and of his Christ.'

71 Romans xv. 1: 'We then that are strong ought to bear the infirmities of the weak, and not to please ourselves.'

72 Philippians iv. 13: 'I can do all things through Christ which strengtheneth me.'

us';[73] and when, 'the Chief Shepherd shall appear, receive' each, as exactly proportioned to his service, but wholly and exclusively due to the merits of his Saviour, 'a Crown of Glory which fadeth not away'.[74]

FINIS.

73 1 Timothy iv. 16: 'Take heed unto thyself, and unto the doctrine; continue in them: for in doing this thou shalt both save thyself, and them that hear thee.'

74 1 Peter v. 4: 'And when the chief Shepherd shall appear, ye shall receive a crown of glory that fadeth not away.'

3

THE UNDERGRADUATE DIARY OF FRANCIS CHAVASSE 1865–1868

Edited by
Andrew Atherstone

Introduction*

Bishop Francis Chavasse was one of the leading evangelicals on the episcopal bench during the first quarter of the twentieth century.[1] In 1900 he was chosen to succeed J. C. Ryle as bishop of Liverpool, where he consolidated the evangelical priorities that Ryle had set for this new urban diocese. To his first diocesan conference Chavasse announced that his evangelical views were 'deeply rooted', 'mine by inheritance and education, by conviction and by experience'.[2] Nevertheless, in a city dominated by protestant versus catholic tensions, Chavasse's episcopate was noted for its eirenic and conciliatory tone. His indefatigable pastoral care and widespread popularity amongst the inhabitants of Liverpool won him the epithet, 'the People's Bishop'. One of his more permanent legacies to the diocese was its massive cathedral, the foundation stone for which was laid by the king in 1904.

It was in Oxford, however, that Chavasse's reputation as an evangelical leader was first established. In 1877, aged just thirty, he was appointed rector of St Peter-le-Bailey, Oxford, one of the 'quadrilateral' of large evangelical churches in the centre of the city. Here he developed an influential ministry amongst undergraduates, just as his friend and mentor, Canon Christopher, had done at St Aldate's. Although not known for his oratory, Chavasse's practical preaching drew crowds.[3] His favour amongst students was such that Christopher often quipped, 'Brother, mind you don't enlarge your church, for if you do I shall have no congregation left.'[4]

In 1889 Chavasse was invited to be principal of Wycliffe Hall in north Oxford. This evangelical theological college had been founded a dozen years before, but under Robert Girdlestone it struggled to survive. Chavasse had not Girdlestone's reputation for biblical scholarship, yet his personal popularity and preaching ministry were a strong attraction to ordinands. The Hall was soon put on a sure

* Thanks are due to the master and fellows of St Peter's College, Oxford, and to John Chavasse (the diarist's grandson) for permission to publish the diary. I am grateful to numerous archivists, librarians, genealogists, parish clergy and others who have helped with the footnotes.

1 The standard biography is J. B. Lancelot, *Francis James Chavasse, bishop of Liverpool* (London, 1928).

2 *Guardian*, 31 Oct. 1900, p. 1538.

3 Chavasse's sermon outlines survive at the Bodleian Library, MSS Chavasse dep. 45–73. Selections have been published as F. J. Chavasse, *Plains words on some present day questions* (London, 1898); *Parochial sermons of Bishop Chavasse*, ed. H. D. S. Sweetapple (2 vols., London, 1938–48).

4 *Oxford Journal Illustrated*, 11 Feb. 1914, p. 6.

footing and went through one of the most vibrant periods of its varied history.[5] One of Chavasse's many initiatives was to help establish the Oxford Pastorate in 1893 as an evangelical chaplaincy for the university, which in turn encouraged men towards Wycliffe Hall.[6] Although offered preferment as suffragan bishop of Crediton and dean of Chichester, Chavasse believed he was of greater usefulness in Oxford.[7] There he remained until the invitation from Lord Salisbury to succeed Ryle at Liverpool.

On his retirement in October 1923, aged 77, Chavasse settled back in Oxford, renewing his involvement with student ministry and wider evangelical initiatives in the city. One of his bolder proposals was for the establishment of an evangelical undergraduate college, to parallel the anglo-catholic influence of Keble College. This finally became a reality after Chavasse's death in 1928. St Peter-le-Bailey church and rectory, together with Hannington Hall, formed the nucleus of St Peter's Hall, of which his son, Christopher Chavasse, was the first master.[8]

Sixty-four years before the first undergraduates arrived at St Peter's Hall, Francis Chavasse had himself entered upon an undergraduate career in Oxford. For the first half of his student life, from October 1865 to January 1868, he kept a diary, now published here. It is valuable as a personal record of the early spiritual development of one of the Church of England's evangelical leaders. Chavasse's diary provides insights into both his multitudinous activities and devotional life as a mid-Victorian undergraduate. It reveals not just the extent of his evangelistic labours, attendance at missionary meetings or disapprobation of cards and dancing, which were evident for all to see, but also his motivations in approaching these issues as he did. His thoughts on subjects like the Sabbath, the Lord's Supper, affliction and death are disclosed. In particular, Chavasse uses his diary to record honestly his spiritual state before God and his battle with sin, committing to paper the private results of his self-examination and heart-searching. His daily reflexions demonstrate that his life as an undergraduate was a significant training

5 Andrew C. Atherstone, 'The founding of Wycliffe Hall, Oxford', *Anglican and Episcopal History,* LXXIII (2004), 78–102; *idem*, 'Robert Baker Girdlestone and "God's own book"', *Evangelical Quarterly*, LXXIV (2002), 313–32.

6 G. Ian F. Thomson, *The Oxford Pastorate. The first half century* (London, 1946); Mark A. Smith, 'A foundation of influence: the Oxford Pastorate and *élite* recruitment in early twentieth-century anglican evangelicalism' in *The rise of the laity in evangelical protestantism*, ed. Deryck W. Lovegrove (London, 2002), pp. 202–13.

7 Bodl., MS Chavasse dep. 1, fos. 19–25, 28–30: E. H. Bickersteth to F. J. Chavasse, 26 and 27 Oct. 1890; Lord Salisbury to F. J. Chavasse, 9 and 10 Nov. 1891.

8 Eric H. F. Smith, *St Peter's. The founding of an Oxford college* (Gerrards Cross, 1978); William A. Evershed, 'Party and patronage in the Church of England 1800–1945: a study of patronage trusts and patronage reform', unpublished D.Phil. dissertation, University of Oxford, 1985, pp. 230–82; Selwyn Gummer, *The Chavasse twins* (London, 1963), pp. 112–28.

ground for the formation of Chavasse's christian character, ministerial gifts and evangelical convictions.

Spiritual Awakening

Chavasse began his diary on his sixteenth birthday, 27 September 1862, in a blank notebook received as a present from his younger brother. It was not originally intended as a 'spiritual' journal, but merely as 'The story of my life from day to day'.[9] Many of his entries over the next three years (which are not reproduced in this edition) focus on Chavasse's teenage preoccupations, such as his guinea pigs and rabbits, fishing and sparrow-shooting, cricket, croquet and ice-skating, dinner parties, visits to Birmingham and the state of the weather. He spent happy hours writing essays for competitions in the *Boy's Own Magazine* and the *Boy's Penny Magazine* or trying to solve Bible puzzles in the *Band of Hope Review*.[10]

With hindsight, however, Chavasse looked back on these last years in the family home at Wylde Green, near Sutton Coldfield, as the beginning of his spiritual awakening. Although he was not able to see it clearly at the time, he could later discern the guiding hand of 'Providence'. At the age of ten Chavasse had been sent to Chesterfield Grammar School,[11] but as a teenager complications following an attack of measles resulted in acute health problems and permanent curvature of the spine. Taken to Torquay to recuperate, he then succumbed to pneumonia and was not expected to survive.[12] Although he had been 'Born of old-fashioned Evangelical parents, whose lives beautified and illuminated their teaching',[13] Chavasse came to the realization on his sick-bed that his religion had so far been 'mere formalism & lip service'.[14] He was brought home to read under the guidance of William Felton at nearby Walmley and then sent to gain business experience in the firm of his cousin, Horace Chavasse, an iron and steel merchant in Birmingham. As an undergraduate looking back on this period, Chavasse recalled that the new sparks of spiritual life kindled on his sick-bed had almost again gone out and he had become reconciled to the worldly career of a wealthy merchant, when suddenly he was 'snatched' from commerce by 'a hand from heaven'. This divine rescue came in the form of further deteriorating health, it being advised in March 1863 that he retire from work altogether. The patient records his doctor's prescription with a certain resignation:

9 Chavasse Diary [CD], 27 Sept. 1862.

10 Bodl. MSS Chavasse dep. 23–4: Chavasse's boyhood essays 1860–3.

11 Derbyshire Record Office, D3661/3/1: Chesterfield Grammar School register of scholars 1846–83.

12 Lancelot, *Chavasse*, pp. 7–8.

13 *Guardian*, 31 Oct. 1900, p. 1538.

14 CD, 27 Sept. 1866.

That I should give up business for two years.
That I should lie down 5 or 6 hours every day.
That I should go into Mr Ridgeway & be drilled &c [in exercises].
That I should take quinine, steel, bark, & cod liver oil.
That I should have beer for my dinner, & new milk instead of tea & coffee.
That I should hang by the arms for a quarter of an hour twice a day.
That I should go walks every day.
Not very delightful directions.[15]

It is striking that throughout his diary, Chavasse attributes affliction to the work of God. For instance, when three members of his family were near death, he noted: 'Affliction is hard to bear, but necessary for man. He who inflicts it is holy, wise, & merciful & into his hands only must we commend ourselves & those dear to us. Let him do as seemeth best to his godly wisdom.'[16] Similarly, when Chavasse's brother and sister-in-law lost their small baby to 'convulsions' aged six weeks, he prayed that God would 'mercifully bind up the wounds he has given in his infinite love'.[17] His own severe illness throughout 1863, which at times appeared terminal, was to change the course of his future life and he viewed it as, ultimately, a blessing.

During his convalescence, Chavasse came increasingly under the influence of Gilbert Robinson, vicar of Walmley. Walmley was a new district created in the 1840s out of the burgeoning parish of Sutton Coldfield and had an evangelical ministry. Robinson organized an annual Walmley Missionary Meeting[18] and his congregation was regularly treated to sermons preached for evangelical societies such as the Colonial and Continental Church Society, the Church Pastoral Aid Society, the Society for Irish Church Missions, the Church Missionary Society and the London Society for Promoting Christianity Amongst the Jews.[19] Chavasse was prepared by Robinson for confirmation and was eager to imbibe his teaching:

> Mr Robinson explains Scripture so nicely & is so earnest & yet affectionate, that he cannot help but impress you. I pray that this may be a season of penitence & prayer to me, from which I may take as it were a new start in life enrolling myself under the banner of my Saviour.[20]

15 CD, 4 Mar. 1863.
16 CD, 24 Dec. 1862. Cf. 31 Dec. 1863.
17 CD, 26 Mar. 1867.
18 CD, 2 June 1863, 9 June 1864, 23 May 1865.
19 CD, 30 Nov. 1862, 8 Mar., 10 May 1863, 28 Feb., 11 Sept. 1864, and *passim*. Cf. Gilbert W. Robinson, *Natural greatness, a call to missionary exertion. A sermon* (London,1852).
20 CD, 5 Mar. 1864.

> Mr Robinson gave us a beautiful lesson. God grant that I may profit by his instructions.[21]
>
> Oh! may his teaching take deep root in my soul.[22]

One of the books Chavasse read as a teenager was *The pathway of safety* by Ashton Oxenden (later bishop of Montreal and metropolitan of Canada), which declares:

> Besides receiving thankfully the truths which your Minister proclaims to you in public, you should look upon him as your counsellor in all spiritual matters … go to him in all your difficulties. Fly to him for advice. Open your heart to him. Tell him of all that perplexes you. … Regard him, in short, as God's minister to *you*, and also as *your* spiritual physician.[23]

Chavasse regarded the vicar of Walmley in this exalted light, calling him his 'spiritual Father' to whom he owed 'what worlds cannot repay'.[24] A portrait of Robinson was to hang above his desk for many years.[25]

After eight months of enforced and frustrating recuperation, Chavasse had recovered sufficiently for his father (a local surgeon) to propose that he enter University and then become a physician.[26] The diarist records: 'How mysterious are the ways of Providence! I should have laughed in derision, if any one had told me that I should ever go to the university, & yet how marvellously has the Almighty brought it to pass.'[27] Nevertheless by June 1864 he had again changed his career plans and was resolved to follow his mentor's example in becoming a clergyman[28] – 'the holiest & best of earthly professions'.[29] Soon Chavasse was reading Samuel Wilberforce's *Addresses to candidates for ordination*,[30] and Robinson offered encouragement, recruiting him to teach in the Walmley Sunday School and to visit elderly and poor parishioners.

During his illness, Chavasse received private tuition from Albert Smith (the new headmaster of Sutton Coldfield Grammar School) in English and Classics and from Michael de Lattre in French and Spanish.[31] In preparation for Oxford he went

21 CD, 4 Apr. 1864.
22 CD, 17 Apr. 1864.
23 Ashton Oxenden, *The pathway of safety; or, counsel to the awakened* (London, 1856), p. 34.
24 CD, 3, 12 Sept. 1866.
25 Lancelot, *Chavasse*, p. 6.
26 CD, 15 Nov. 1863 et seq.
27 CD, 6 Dec. 1863.
28 CD, 30 June 1864.
29 CD, 27 Sept. 1866.
30 CD, 11 Sept. 1864.
31 CD, 17 Aug. 1863. On Smith, see Kerry Osbourne, *A history of Bishop Vesey's grammar school. The first 375 years (1572–1902)* (Sutton Coldfield, 1990), pp. 176–341.

to live under Smith's roof for six months of studious reading,[32] but his changing religious perspective meant that he viewed his teacher with increasing discontent: 'I wish A. S. was a godly man. My heart is like a tender plant which needs assiduous care, but alas his house is very uncongenial to the growth of faith.'[33] When he arrived at University, Chavasse was glad to find wise guides who shared Robinson's evangelical viewpoint and who would promote the new undergraduate's spiritual development.

Activities in Oxford

John Reynolds has shown that by the mid-1860s the influence of evangelicals within the University of Oxford was on the wane.[34] Those heads of houses best known for their evangelicalism were in their last years: Benjamin Symons (warden of Wadham College) and John Macbride (principal of Magdalen Hall) were both octogenarians, with Richard Cotton (provost of Worcester College) not far behind. Only two of the divinity professors – Robert Payne Smith and Charles Heurtley – were known to be sympathetic to the cause, along with Monier Monier-Williams (Boden professor of Sanskrit). The earlier reputation of the University as a Tractarian hotbed had given way in part to an anti-clerical reaction, and according to Mandell Creighton (an undergraduate at Merton College in the 1860s) in some quarters anyone who wanted to be ordained was assumed to be 'either a fool or a knave'.[35] The 'high-church' circle around E. B. Pusey remained influential, but was in frequent conflict with those who promoted 'free thinking' or the secularization of the University. Benjamin Jowett and Mark Pattison led the liberal anglican cause and the controversy over *Essays and Reviews* was still smouldering when Chavasse arrived.[36]

Corpus Christi College, which Chavasse joined in October 1865, was one of the smaller colleges, with about fifty-five undergraduates.[37] His first impression was of 'a very shabby looking place',[38] but in academic prowess Corpus rivalled

32 CD, 25–6 Oct. 1864.

33 CD, 14 Apr. 1865.

34 John S. Reynolds, *The evangelicals at Oxford 1735–1871. A record of an unchronicled movement with the record extended to 1905* (Oxford, 1975), pp. 119–53.

35 Louise Creighton, *Life and letters of Mandell Creighton* (2 vols., London, 1904), I, 75.

36 For the changing nature of the university in the Victorian period, see *The history of the university of Oxford. Vols. VI and VII*, ed. Michael G. Brock and Mark C. Curthoys (Oxford, 1997, 2000); W. R. Ward, *Victorian Oxford* (London, 1965); A. J. Engel, *From clergyman to don: the rise of the academic profession in nineteenth-century Oxford* (Oxford, 1983).

37 For reflexions on life at Corpus in the 1860s, see Corpus Christi College Archives, MS 498/1–6: Samuel Brooke's diary 1860–5; Edmund A. Knox, 'Memories of Corpus Christi College, 1865–8', *Pelican Record*, XX (Dec. 1931 – June 1932), 86–92, 106–15, 136–42; *The life and letters of Edward Lee Hicks*, ed. J. H. Fowler (London, 1922), pp. 18–46.

38 CD, 9 Jan. 1864.

even Balliol College itself. Nor was it left behind in sporting achievement – the college eight won through to 'head of the river' in Chavasse's time. However, amongst the twenty fellows at Corpus only two were known for their evangelicalism: William Ranken (later vicar of Christ Church, Surbiton) and John Conington (Corpus professor of Latin). Conington, one of Chavasse's tutors, had famously undergone a conversion experience in his late twenties, a change 'as sudden as it was complete and enduring', but which some of his old friends found 'unwelcome' and even 'unintelligible'.[39] In religious outlook, such men were outnumbered by their academic colleagues. An undergraduate who began with Chavasse wrote home to explain that Corpus was sometimes considered 'a low-church college … but the Dons are Jowettites and free-thinkers, while the undergraduates are of decidedly high-church tendencies'.[40] Edmund Knox (an evangelical and later bishop of Manchester), one of Chavasse's close college friends, recalled that the scripture lectures at Corpus 'taught me more of the extravagances of Higher Criticism than of the words of Eternal Life.'[41] Meanwhile he and Chavasse caused offence in college chapel by refusing to turn east to recite the creed.[42]

As Reynolds observes, evangelical initiative had largely passed from the university to the parish clergy in Oxford, most notably to Alfred Christopher (rector of St Aldate's) and Henry Linton (rector of St Peter-le-Bailey), both of whom had an extensive undergraduate following. Joseph West laboured at Holy Trinity and in 1868 Edward Hathaway was to arrive at St Ebbe's and re-establish an evangelical ministry there, but they had less contact with the student populace. These men were not scholars and published little – Linton, for instance, described himself as 'a plain man, preaching to plain people'.[43] However, they exerted considerable personal influence, as outlined by another of Chavasse's friends, Arthur Downer:

> These clergy were not authors, but men of prayer and action. They live for us, not in their written works, which were few and of little weight, but in their saintly lives, their spirit of prayer, their constant zeal, their untiring efforts for the spiritual welfare of the undergraduates, their generous hospitality, their fervent support of foreign missions, their constant maintenance of the simplicity of worship, and the

39 *Miscellaneous writings of John Conington with a memoir by H. J. S. Smith*, ed. J. A. Symonds (2 vols., London, 1872), I, xxxii–xxxiv.

40 Charles P. Scott to Russell Scott, 24 Apr. 1866, in J. L. Hammond, *C. P. Scott of the Manchester Guardian* (London, 1934), p. 16.

41 Edmund A. Knox, *Reminiscences of an octogenarian, 1847–1934* (London, 1934), p. 71.

42 *Frances James Chavasse. Impressions by five of his friends on the occasion of his death* (Oxford, 1928), p. 10.

43 Henry Linton, *Sermons preached in the parish church of St Peter-le-Bailey, Oxford* (Oxford, 1878), p. vi.

> brightness and loving warmth of their teaching and of the Gospel which they proclaimed.[44]

From the time he first arrived in Oxford, Chavasse was often to be found at St Aldate's and to some extent Christopher stepped into the role which had been fulfilled in Walmley by Robinson. After his initial encounter with Christopher, Chavasse felt that he had 'met with one who was a true father in God, and one to whom he could look for strength and counsel in the vicissitudes of University life'.[45] Fifty years later Chavasse tried to explain why he and other undergraduates had been so strongly attached to the St Aldate's rector:

> It was not the wisdom of his word that attracted them; it was not the depth of his thoughts which he put before them, but it was the atmosphere of prayer. It was the feeling of the presence of God, and the sincere and lovable character of the man himself. Today there were scattered throughout the towns and villages of the country and in many parts of the world men who looked back with thankfulness on those all-too-short hours spent week by week with him in prayer, and who thanked God that when at Oxford they had the unspeakable advantage of his friendship and his help.[46]

Chavasse regularly attended Christopher's meeting on Saturday evenings for prayer and Bible exposition, at which visiting speakers would enthuse the gathered undergraduates and where Downer witnessed 'such powerful influences of the Spirit of God, that it seemed like heaven'.[47] Chavasse also frequently participated in Linton's meeting on Friday afternoons for missionary intercession and the Greek Testament class held on Sunday evenings by George Tonge, Linton's curate. At the start of his second year he began to teach in the Sunday school at St Peter-le-Bailey. He later rejoiced that this contact with Christopher and Linton 'helped to crystallize good impressions already made, and to keep me steadfast in "the old paths".'[48]

Chavasse was involved in numerous other christian initiatives in Oxford, mainly spear headed by undergraduates. Edwin Orr has gone so far as to argue that he was a 'product' of the evangelical revivals of 1859–60 which had swept through Ulster, Scotland, Wales and Cornwall and whose effect was felt even in Oxford.[49] William Hay Aitken of Wadham (later founder of the Parochial Missions

44 Arthur C. Downer, 'Evangelical religion at Oxford in the later sixties', *Churchman*, XXIV (Sept. 1910), 682–3.

45 *Oxford Journal Illustrated*, 11 Feb. 1914, p. 6.

46 *Ibid.*

47 A. C. Downer to A. M. W. Christopher, 23 Nov. 1904, quoted in John S. Reynolds, *Canon Christopher of St Aldate's, Oxford* (Abingdon, 1967), p. 331.

48 Quoted in Reynolds, *Christopher*, p. 197.

49 J. Edwin Orr, *The second evangelical awakening in Britain* (London, 1949), pp. 118–20.

Society) was involved in revivalist activity with his father, Robert Aitken, at Pendeen in Cornwall and with his uncle, Hay Macdowall Grant of Arndilly, in the highlands of Scotland. After one long vacation engaged in such work, he and Frederic Freeman returned to Oxford with a determination to talk to every man in college about his soul, a policy which had noticeable effect. However, it is difficult to find any link between their activities and those of Chavasse and his friends in the next student generation. Indeed Downer claims that by their time the influence of Aitken and Freeman had 'spent its force'.[50]

In his second term at Oxford, Chavasse joined the Oxford University Tract Distribution Society and often walked out to South Hinksey, a nearby hamlet, to lend pamphlets to villagers and to evangelise them. The O.U.T.D.S. was not specifically evangelical, and failed to impress Downer who was also a member:

> In the Tract Distribution Society there was a fair amount of activity, but a morbid fear seemed to obsess some of the members lest their tracts should be of too Evangelistic and stimulating a character. A strong element in it voted consistently at the general meeting for confining the tracts circulated to the publications of the S.P.C.K.[51]

Nevertheless Chavasse's visits, sometimes several times a week, began to have an impact upon South Hinksey and he recruited other undergraduate friends to join him in the task. He admits that the 'poor pastorless village' had 'wound itself round my heart'.[52] In March 1867 he opened a Sunday school at New Hinksey, which soon was thriving with almost eighty children on the books and ten men teaching classes in rooms borrowed from various cottagers. Chavasse also instituted a cottage lecture at South Hinksey and helped to lead a weekly meeting at Cold Harbour, another hamlet south of Oxford. He was one of the mission workers in 1867 at the regular addresses in Oxford Town Hall, delivered by Lord Radstock and other evangelists, at which 1,500 townspeople gathered and numerous tracts were distributed.[53] In addition Chavasse frequently attended the undergraduate prayer meeting and was on the committee of the Oxford Missionary Union, although this was comparatively inactive. At the start of his third year, realizing that he had spent much of his energy outside college, he began a Sunday evening Bible reading for Corpus undergraduates. Similar initiatives took place elsewhere in Oxford and the surrounding district. Noting the ceaseless activity of these young evangelicals, Edward Hicks, another of Chavasse's tutors at Corpus, described them as 'the spiritual descendants of the Oxford Methodists of Wesley's

50 Downer, 'Evangelical religion', p. 683; Charlotte E. Woods, *Memoirs and letters of Canon Hay Aitken* (London, 1928), pp. 88–92.

51 Downer, 'Evangelical religion', pp. 683–4.

52 CD, 17 June 1867.

53 Downer, 'Evangelical religion', p. 687.

early days'.[54] Even when on a reading party near the Lake District in the summer of 1869, ostensibly preparing for Finals, Chavasse and his friends conducted impromptu evangelistic meetings. Archibald Sayce (later professor of Assyriology), who was leading the group, recalled:

> I had some difficulty in keeping them to their work for the examinations instead of spending their time in open-air preaching to the benighted natives of the neighbouring parishes or attending revivalist meetings. At the breakfast table I was obliged to start acrostics and anagrams by way of preventing conversations about the conversion of souls.[55]

Philanthropy and 'social action', often allied to political reform, were well known features of nineteenth-century evangelicalism, exemplified by the work of Lord Shaftesbury.[56] Yet Chavasse shows little interest in such issues. Even when visiting the Oxford workhouse or a pauper's cottage, his one stated aim was gospel proclamation.

When hearing passionate appeals for more young men to offer themselves for missionary service, Chavasse sometimes wondered if he was being called overseas, perhaps to India. Instead he was ordained in May 1870, five months after graduation, to the curacy of St Paul's, Preston where he worked under William Miles Myres, Linton's son-in-law. For a few months as curate Chavasse returned to diary keeping, in a much abbreviated form compared to his undergraduate journal. Yet his notes (not reproduced in this edition) reveal a constant round of pastoral visiting, cottage lectures, confirmation and Bible classes, sermon preparation and occasional offices.[57] His student experiences in Oxford stood him in good stead for this evangelical parish ministry, which was further developed as his career progressed.

Chavasse's evangelistic efforts as an undergraduate, although often at his own initiative, were undertaken with deference to higher authority. The fact that he was happy to run meetings in cottages does not mean that he had a low view of church order. For instance, he believed that tract distributors ought only to operate with permission of the local clergyman. He was likewise uneasy that his friends Downer, Courthope Bontein (later a Plymouth brother) and Henry Bazely (later a Scottish presbyterian) continued to hold evangelistic meetings at Sutton Courtenay despite opposition from the vicar. They moved from a nonconformist chapel to a farmer's barn so as not to give the impression they were working 'under dissenting auspices', but Bontein was still forbidden from taking part by

54 Edward L. Hicks, *Henry Bazely, the Oxford evangelist. A memoir* (London, 1886), p. 159.

55 Archibald H. Sayce, *Reminiscences* (London, 1923), pp. 46–7; Lancelot, *Chavasse*, pp. 44–5.

56 Kathleen J. Heasman, *Evangelicals in action. An appraisal of their social work in the Victorian era* (London, 1962).

57 Bodl., MS Chavasse dep. 22: Chavasse diary, Jan. – Aug. 1873.

Provost Hawkins, a prohibition to which Chavasse advised him to submit.[58] Chavasse's desire for orderliness is further seen in his request that there be less spontaneity and more preparation for the daily prayer meeting (he was overruled), while his cottage lectures at South Hinksey and Cold Harbour often included written prayers. In this he followed the example of Linton who tended to avoid extempore prayer in public and used to read from a special liturgy at his weekly meeting for missionary intercession.[59]

Although much of Chavasse's time as an undergraduate was spent with fellow evangelicals, his friendships were not limited to this circle. Amongst his close colleagues at Corpus were Walter Lock (later warden of Keble College), who became a life-long friend, and Charles Scott (later editor of the *Manchester Guardian*), whose unitarian views were already evident. Surprisingly Chavasse took Lock to visit Oscott College and the Birmingham Oratory, although he also invited him to evangelistic meetings in the hope that he would find 'the narrow way'.[60] Further links with non-evangelicals were fostered at the 'New Vitality', an undergraduate essay society where men from a wide range of theological opinion read papers to each other and debated them. Alongside evangelical members were others such as Edmund Geldart (later a unitarian minister), Vincent 'Stuckey' Coles (later principal of Pusey House) and Herbert Russell, who flirted with Roman Catholicism and almost seceded with Gerard Manley Hopkins in October 1866. Chavasse also intermittently attended the university sermons or Lenten lectures, where preachers from a variety of theological perspectives could be heard. He considered Roman Catholics to be 'Satan's emissaries',[61] yet when visiting Cambridge one summer he dined with Gerard Cobb, a Tractarian who publicly campaigned for the reunion of the Church of England and the Church of Rome.[62] This wide interaction with non-evangelicals was to become a noted feature of Chavasse's later ministry. He recalled that during his years in Oxford 'contact with the finest examples of other schools of thought won my reverence and admiration, but not my allegiance'.[63] Bishop Edward H. Bickersteth, amongst others, remarked on his friend's 'staunch adherence to Evangelical truth with wide sympathies to true men of other schools.'[64] Chavasse's preaching in Oxford

58 Arthur C. Downer, *A century of evangelical religion in Oxford* (London, 1938), pp. 43–4.

59 Downer, 'Evangelical religion', p. 688.

60 CD, 19 May 1866.

61 CD, 20 Oct. 1866.

62 Gerard F. Cobb, *The kiss of peace: or, England and Rome at one on the doctrine of the holy eucharist* (London, 1867); *idem*, *A few words on reunion and the coming council at Rome* (London, 1869); *idem*, *"Separation", not "schism". A plea for the position of anglican reunionists* (London, 1869).

63 *Guardian*, 31 Oct. 1900, p. 1538.

64 Bodl., MS Chavasse dep. 1, fo. 20: E. H. Bickersteth to F. J. Chavasse, 26 Oct. 1890.

attracted listeners from diverse theological backgrounds and his episcopal leadership in Liverpool was characterized by an ability to build good relationships with people from a wide spectrum of opinion.[65]

Self-examination

'Conversionism' (the belief that lives need to be changed by the Christian gospel) and 'activism' (the expression of that gospel in energetic endeavour) both form part of David Bebbington's well-known quadrilateral of attributes which characterize evangelicalism.[66] These themes have been extensively investigated by historians and both can be seen clearly in Chavasse's ceaseless evangelistic activities in and around Oxford. Less often examined is the attitude of evangelicals to their private devotional lives, yet Chavasse's undergraduate diary reveals significant insights into this domain. Indeed the honesty and detail with which he writes about his spiritual state before God is one of its most striking features. He often commits to paper the results of his regular 'self-examination' or scrutiny of his inner soul, with increasing length as the diary progresses.

During the middle decades of the nineteenth century there was a rash of publications giving guidance on this subject.[67] It was probably a theme about which Gilbert Robinson had taught in the confirmation classes which Chavasse so enjoyed, and was the focus of Robinson's chief publication, *Aids to self-examination*:

> Nothing, perhaps, more strikes us in the contemplation of the present state of the religious world, than the absence of a habit of strict self-examination. Public meetings abound for the dissemination of the gospel; many other laudable endeavours are made to promote man's welfare; the preaching of the gospel is

65 Lancelot, *Chavasse*, pp. 156–7.

66 David W. Bebbington, *Evangelicalism in modern Britain: a history from the 1730s to the 1980s* (London, 1989), pp. 1–19.

67 For example, Hugh Stowell, *Hints on self-examination* (London, 1840); *Help to self-examination* (Durham, 1841); [Frederick Oakeley?], *Questions for self-examination* (London, 1843); Walter F. Hook, *Helps to self-examination* (Leeds, 1846); George Prevost, *Officia Anglicana; or, a manual of daily devotion* (London, 1847), pp. 40–60; Thomas H. Ashhurst, *The duty and importance of frequent self-examination* (Oxford, 1848); John Hughes, *The self-searcher; or, brief remarks on self-examination* (London, 1848); Helen S. Herschell, *The child's help to self-examination and prayer* (3rd edn., London, 1848); John Foy, *Motives and helps to self-examination* (London, 1851); James G. Darling, *An address from a clergyman to his parishioners, on the duty of self-examination* (London, 1854); Elizabeth Sewell, *Self-examination before confirmation* (London, 1859); George H. Wilkinson, *Break up your fallow ground. A help to self-examination* (London, 1871); Edgar D. Whitmarsh, *Forms of sin or a manual of self-examination* (London, 1871); *Questions for self-examination, for Lent and other seasons* (London, 1871); *The churchman's manual of daily private devotion* (4th edn., London, 1872), pp. 292–340; Joseph Deharbe, *Questions for self-examination for use of the clergy* (London, 1872); *A few remarks on self-examination* (London, 1874).

> attended – *visible activity* is the striking feature of the day. The closet! the closet! here is the infirmity. This is the weak point.[68]

Oxenden agreed: 'It is much easier to sit down and read a book, or to walk two or three miles to see a sick neighbour, than to spend ten minutes before God in searching our hearts. We do not like to lay open the secret working of our minds.'[69] In their discussion of 'means of grace' – prayer, public worship, Bible reading and the sacraments – many authors added self-examination. One writer even proclaimed that this practice, because closely linked to repentance, was 'generally indispensable to salvation'.[70] Robinson explained why it was vital for spiritual growth:

> what can be more apparently necessary, as a means to promote increase of grace, than self-examination? For who can know his wants, when he searches not for them? who can know his besetting sin that inquires not after it? who can exercise gratitude, joy, and hope, that never cares to mark the cause for either one or the other?[71]

Similar passionate appeals were made by others:

> O, fellow-Christians! let us cease to wonder why our heads are so full, and our hearts so cold – why our doctrine is so correct, and our experience so low – why our privileges are so highly estimated in words, and so little enjoyed in the heart – why our code of Christian morality is so good, and our tempers so unmortified – why the way to heaven is so clearly known, but our growth in the divine life so low – why Christian benevolence is so well defined, and Christian self-denial so little practised. Let us cease to wonder, while we search not, probe not, sift not, and penetrate not more into the quick of our selfish, back-sliding, and unhumbled hearts.[72]

After his study of Victorian pastoral theology manuals, Brian Heeney concluded that the advice they offered was 'strikingly unaffected by the peculiarities of party opinion ... ordinary Englishmen in ordinary parishes received pastoral care which was little touched by the disputes of churchmanship'.[73] The same is true of publications on self-examination, which were issued by clergymen from a wide theological spectrum. Although some ritualists recommended that auricular confession follow self-scrutiny, their advice on the process of examination itself is indistinguishable from that of their evangelical colleagues. Some publications

68 Gilbert W. Robinson, *Aids offered to a young Christian in the consideration of some heads of self-examination* (London, 1843), pp. ix–x.

69 Ashton Oxenden, *The Lord's Supper, simply explained* (5th edn., London, 1861), p. 64.

70 John C. Boyce, *The ground of hope: or, self-examination the christian's safeguard* (London, 1859), p. 207.

71 Robinson, *Aids*, p. xi.

72 William B. Hayne, *Self-examination; or, 365 questions, being one for every day in the year* (7th edn., London, 1862), pp. iv–v.

73 W. Brian D. Heeney, *A different kind of gentleman. Parish clergy as professional men in early and mid-Victorian England* (Hamden, Conn., 1976), p. 117.

recommended a specific technique ('self-examination is a science, and must be learnt just like any other science'[74]), while most just offered general principles ('nothing is worse than being enslaved to cut and dried Rules'[75]). Typically, self-examination should take place every day (perhaps for ten minutes), with more time given to it on Sundays and at other key moments such as birthdays or new year's eve. Edward Bickersteth of Watton expected everyone to commit at least an hour to the practice before the Lord's Supper, while those with more leisure should spend 'several hours'. He explained that this was to be viewed 'not as a task but as a blessing: not merely as a requirement, but as a privilege and advantage'. The more diligent the self-examination, the more benefit would be derived.[76] Many devotional manuals included detailed questions to ask about the state of one's soul, perhaps based on the ten commandments, the beatitudes, or the seven deadly sins. Edward Prest (master of Sherburn Hospital) produced a tabulated booklet in which penitents could calculate the total number of their various sins each day, and so keep track of whether they were making progress in the christian life or backsliding.[77] Another author went further and encouraged the earnest christian constantly to carry around a notebook in which he could stop to record each sin (signified by an initial) with the time at which it occurred.[78] Some advised fasting before lengthy self-examination,[79] a form of asceticism not seen in Chavasse's undergraduate diary, although he did begin to fast occasionally as a curate.[80] Others encouraged the self-examiner to end by making specific resolutions, a practice which Chavasse occasionally followed.

According to Robinson, self-examination involved allowing the Holy Spirit and the Bible to reveal anything that was 'noxious and disgusting' in one's character, 'every wrinkle, blot, stain … every deformity'.[81] He encouraged readers to keep nothing back from God, 'not even struggling corruptions, and besetting sins: drag them all out – lay them before Him, faithfully desire their extinction'.[82] Likewise Oxenden commanded, 'The heart … must be searched – searched to the very core. The deepest recesses of it must be sounded.'[83] Such investigation was to be

74 *Questions for self-examination on the Ten Commandments* (London, 1853), p. [2].
75 George H. Wilkinson, *Instructions in the devotional life* (London, 1871), p. 34.
76 Edward Bickersteth, *A treatise on the Lord's Supper: designed as a guide and companion to the holy communion* (11th edn., London, 1841), p. 174.
77 Edward Prest, *Book of self-examination, arranged for daily use* (London, 1861).
78 Boyce, *Ground of hope*, p. 85.
79 *Ibid.*, pp. 218–21.
80 CD, 13 Feb., 11 Apr. 1873.
81 Robinson, *Aids*, p. xvii.
82 *Ibid.*, p. 42.
83 Oxenden, *Pathway of safety*, pp. 88–9.

conducted 'under the All-seeing Eye of the Searcher of all hearts!'[84] Oxenden's writing about the depravity and pervasiveness of sin is stark:

> Think of past sin – lost days, that cannot be gathered up – idle words, that cannot be recalled – wasted opportunities – sabbaths unimproved! Think what grace you have rejected; how often you have resisted convictions; how carelessly you have felt towards Him who has so much loved you; what an earthly life you have led, and how little you have thought of that better world before you! Think, too, how much has been wrong in you, *even since you fairly set your face Zionward*; how slowly you have opened your heart to Christ; how coldly and feebly you have served him! Oh, are there not ten thousand thoughts that make your very heart bleed – ten thousand reasons why you should be humbled in the dust? You are still a sinner before God, and undeserving in His sight... Be not so anxious then to ask God to heal up your wound, as to probe it to the very bottom, even though it should give you much pain. Ask Him, to grant you brokenness of heart, so that you may mourn over your sins with 'godly sorrow'... Think often of your sins, to humble you, and to keep you low.[85]

Chavasse's acute awareness of the grip of sin in his life characterizes many of his diary entries. He terms himself a 'vile wretch' and a 'sinful worm'.[86] His heart is labelled with epithets such as 'cold', 'dead', 'evil', 'deceitful', 'desperately wicked', 'frozen in sin' and 'blacker every day'.[87] One of his recurring fears is that he might be back-sliding, 'drifting back again into the ocean of Sin',[88] and he longs for more of the Holy Spirit. The following lengthy reflection, penned on the eve of 1865, is typical of passages which are found more frequently in the undergraduate portion of his diary:

> Who as he looks back upon the past never to be recalled can refrain from feeling solemn & very sad. Hasty words, hasty actions, all recorded in a book on High, stand up to witness against us. Lost opportunities sadly meet my eye on every side. Broken Resolutions, made with a firm & hopeful spirit, but alas not sufficiently grounded & founded & resting on the Rock of Ages, & consequently swept away by the opposing tide, lift up only their sad ruins to remind us of man's weakness & God's strength. In what state am I the professing follower of Xt, who if God grant me health hope to enroll myself beneath the banner of his labourers. Lord I am in very truth but filth & rotten rags. Stripped of sanctity, of the righteousness wherein I trusted, & imposed upon men, a poor, shivering naked sinner I feel. O praise be to God for it my utter complete unworthiness & the completeness of my most precious Saviour. Ah, when I sit alone at night when the whirling excitement of the

84 Boyce, *Ground of hope*, p. 16.
85 Oxenden, *Pathway of safety*, pp. 192–5.
86 CD, 3 Feb., 25 Aug. 1867.
87 CD, 19, 26 Aug., 8 Sept. 1866.
88 CD, 16 Oct. 1864.

day is past & the busy turmoil of life's duties is for a while stilled, when I am no longer enchained by the fascinations of my books, nor lulled by the praises & flattery of this most deceitful world to a state of fancied security, then indeed I feel how miserable & vile I am, & how unworthy of a Saviour's love. Where are the fruits of a holy love to God displaying themselves in all my actions, subdueing [*sic*] self, restraining temper, breathing a spirit of meekness, lowliness, gentleness, & filling me with a yearning love for lost & wandering Souls? – where indeed. Pride, Envy, Malice, Ill temper, Covetousness, Indolence, Selfishness & hypocrisy, terrible foes lie hid in the citadel of my heart. Hurried prayers, careless reading of God's own Holy Word, a disregard of religious Services, wandering thoughts & a feeling of distaste & weariness for holy things press me & well nigh overcome me. May God help me to subdue them. Implicitly relying on his gracious aid & humbly asking his gracious assistance in earnest prayer, I hereby make the following solemn resolutions, & may he to whom all hearts are open grant me strength to fulfil them:

1) To subdue my Spiritual Pride.
2) To deny myself, & give way to others.
3) To take a more lively interest & share in the spreading of the Gospel.
4) To be more fervent in Prayer & more diligent & devout in all religious duties & ceremonies.
5) To be kind & brotherly to all men.
6) To pray more constantly for the outpouring of God's spirit in my heart.

And may God be with me in life & in death. *Amen.*[89]

In using his diary in this way to record his spiritual state and his battle with sin, Chavasse stood in a long evangelical tradition. Many puritans of the seventeenth century and Wesleyans of the eighteenth century used their journals as an aid to self-examination.[90] Indeed the journals of John Wesley and his circle have been described by Richard Heitzenrater as 'a Methodist's constant companion and conscience … a ledger of the soul and a mirror for the spirit, recording and reflecting the progress and pitfalls of his struggle to advance along the path of holy living.'[91] The diary of David Brainerd, first published by Jonathan Edwards in 1749, went through numerous editions on both sides of the Atlantic and became a devotional classic amongst nineteenth-century evangelicals, inspiring many to self-denying christian enterprise. It was soon an archetype, both for the missionary

89 CD, 31 Dec. 1864.

90 Charles E. Hambrick-Stowe, *The practice of piety. Puritan devotional disciplines in seventeenth-century New England* (Chapel Hill, North Carolina, 1982); Owen C. Watkins, *The Puritan experience* (London, 1972); Tom Webster, 'Writing to redundancy: approaches to spiritual journals and early modern spirituality', *Historical Journal*, XXXIX (1996), 33–56; Effie Botonaki, 'Seventeenth-century Englishwomen's spiritual diaries: self-examination, covenanting, and account keeping', *Sixteenth-Century Journal*, XXX (1999), 3–21.

91 *Diary of an Oxford Methodist. Benjamin Ingham, 1733–1734*, ed. Richard P. Heitzenrater (Durham, North Carolina, 1985), p. 2.

biography and for the journal writing of those who would imitate Brainerd's quest for holiness.[92] A similar style is evident in the diaries of later evangelical leaders, such as Henry Martyn, William Wilberforce, Robert Morrison and Edward Bickersteth, with their combined emphasis on personal self-sacrifice and public christian activism.[93] These writings were recommended by Gilbert Robinson as evidence for his bold claim that all eminent christians have practised self-examination.[94] Chavasse's diary bears a close resemblance to theirs.

Besetting Sins

One of the recommended components of self-examination was to identify one's habitual or 'besetting' sins. Thomas Bund warned that to turn a blind eye to these areas of major weakness was to leave 'the canker worm in the very heart to work its destruction'.[95] The three spheres in which Chavasse battled most frequently were pride, timidity and wandering thoughts.

i. Pride

Chavasse was aware that he took part in almost everything, even evangelistic endeavours, with mixed motives – perhaps with one eye on impressing his friends or hoping to gain a 'reputation for sanctity'.[96] For instance, he noticed the growth of his spiritual pride when appointed to the committee in charge of the undergraduate prayer meeting. On another occasion he was humbled when demoted to teach a more junior class in the Walmley Sunday School. Wanting to show off to Lock his well-organized Sunday school at New Hinksey, he was again humbled when it turned out to be 'a perfect rabble'.[97] Even praise for a speech at his brother's wedding reception was temptation for a swelled head and he prayed for salvation from the 'snare of flattery'.[98] With curvature of the spine and standing only five feet three inches tall, Chavasse battled with his natural desire to be taller and better looking, but his 'uncouth ungainly diminutive form' reminded him that he had no

92 Jonathan Edwards, *The life of David Brainerd (1749)*, ed. Norman Pettit (The Works of Jonathan Edwards,.7, New Haven, 1985); Joseph Conforti, 'Jonathan Edwards's most popular work: "The life of David Brainerd" and nineteenth-century evangelical culture', *Church History*, LIV (1985), 188–201.

93 John Sargent, *Memoir of the Rev. Henry Martyn* (London, 1819); Robert I. Wilberforce & Samuel Wilberforce, *The life of William Wilberforce* (5 vols., London, 1838); Eliza Morrison, *Memoirs of the life and labours of Robert Morrison* (2 vols., London, 1839); T. R. Birks, *Memoir of the Rev. Edward Bickersteth* (2 vols., London, 1851).

94 Robinson, *Aids*, p. xii.

95 Thomas H. B. Bund, *Aids to a holy life, in forms for self-examination* (London, 1846), p. 13.

96 CD, 25 Aug. 1867.

97 CD, 14 Apr. 1867.

98 CD, 14 Sept. 1865.

reason to be proud in his physical appearance.[99] He further struggled with a stammer which afflicted him when he was tired or over-worked, which he declared 'painful for flesh: good for Spirit'.[100] Knox could describe his friend as 'a little man, rather deformed, a stammerer, but alive with the fire of divine love, and full to the brim of quiet, mischievous humour'.[101]

Failure was often the means by which Chavasse was humbled, particularly in his academic studies. When struggling to prepare for Oxford, he observed: 'If I were clever, I should probably be conceited, as it is I have nothing to be conceited of.'[102] Nevertheless, he maintained the ambition of carrying off university honours. When he failed to gain a scholarship at Corpus in March 1865, he reflected:

> In this rebellious heart of mine there have at times arisen feelings of envy at those whom my Father has endued with talents so far superior to mine own, & my wicked heart would often murmur & wonder why. But then comes the sweet, soft, soothing thought, that an omniscient God knows best.[103]

The following year he failed to gain a scholarship at Oriel College, and the ultimate humiliation occurred when he was placed in the third class in Moderations. This he considered a 'disgrace' upon himself, but was grateful to God that the 'idol' of study had been broken.[104]

ii. Timidity

Chavasse often prays for greater 'moral courage' or 'holy boldness'.[105] This did not come naturally, however. Indeed he describes himself as 'sinfully shy' and 'bashful to a painful degree, easily silenced, cowardly, reserved'.[106] For instance, he rebuked himself for not challenging someone who swore at breakfast or not refusing an invitation to a Sunday wine party. When he gave in to walking with friends on a Sunday, against his conscience, he lamented, 'Alas! what a weak, fickle wavering mortal I am'[107] and pleaded, 'Oh thou Captain of my Salvation endue me with the fearless spirit of a true soldier.'[108] Likewise, when he failed to speak out in defence of the truth of the Bible, he termed himself 'a miserable craven-hearted coward'.[109] In particular, Chavasse often wanted courage to invite

99 CD, 13 Apr. 1866.
100 CD, 10 Aug. 1873; Lancelot, *Chavasse*, p. 42.
101 Knox, *Reminiscences*, p. 73.
102 CD, 7 Oct. 1864.
103 CD, 24 Mar. 1865.
104 CD, 1 July 1867.
105 CD, 10 Feb. 1867.
106 CD, 15 Sept. & 18 Oct. 1867.
107 CD, 19 Mar. 1865.
108 CD, 30 July 1865.
109 CD, 1 Nov. 1865.

more men to evangelistic meetings and to speak to them about Jesus. His natural timidity sometimes held him back, and he observed: 'My lips seemed sealed when I wd talk on spiritual things. Oh Lord loose my tongue.'[110] At the same time he wanted to avoid destructive religious controversy and tried to remain silent when his friends would embroil him in heated doctrinal argument.

iii. Wandering Thoughts

One of the repetitive refrains in Chavasse's diary is his despair at his 'wandering thoughts', particularly when he attempted to pray or read a spiritual book or listen to lengthy sermons. Oxenden warned his readers:

> you are in danger in God's sanctuary, as well as elsewhere. Satan will endeavour to draw away your eyes, and make them wander, and to steal away your heart, and fix it on some trifling object... Ask God, then, to fix his truth in your heart, and to rivet it there by the power of his grace.[111]

Another of the authors Chavasse read, Charles Vaughan (later dean of Llandaff), explained that to sing or repeat responses in church in an absentminded manner, with one's thoughts elsewhere, was to break the third commandment: 'How profane! this is indeed *taking God's name in vain.* Let us hear and fear.'[112] Many examples could be given of Chavasse's struggle in this area:

> My thoughts still very wandering, but I must pray for more strength to resist the insidious attempts of Satan to call off my attention from what pertains to my eternal welfare.[113]

> My thoughts still wander in my prayers, oh so terribly. Even in my own private prayers I seem to be getting far more heedless. Lord am I drifting back? Snatch me I pray you from destruction.[114]

> My thoughts so wandering in Church. Hardly heard anything of the Sermons. God grant me an attentive mind... Felt listless & indifferent to all religion throughout the day. Father! let me not slip back into sin.[115]

> My thoughts *so* wandering, sometimes I almost seem to despair of ever subduing them. Of myself I certainly cannot. I must pray more to my Father for he *can.*[116]

110 CD, 22 Mar. 1866.

111 Oxenden, *Pathway of safety*, pp. 24–5.

112 Charles J. Vaughan, *Notes for lectures on confirmation, with suitable prayers* (Cambridge, 1859), p. 28.

113 CD, 24 July 1864.

114 CD, 28 Aug. 1864.

115 CD, 20 Nov. 1864.

116 CD, 13 Aug. 1865.

Oxenden instructed, 'Listen *with deep attention* to every sermon you hear; for it concerns your very life.'[117] Chavasse was often distressed that he was unable to do this, and wished that he had a greater love of hearing the word of God preached. On one occasion he found it easy to concentrate when Robinson spoke about Allen Gardiner and the formation of the South American Missionary Society, which only brought home to him his lack of focus during the usual doctrinal sermons.[118]

During his self-examination, Chavasse identified several other recurring sins. One was irritability, and he prayed that God would curb his 'vile temper'.[119] He also lamented his slothfulness, especially if he overslept in the mornings and so lost time for private devotions. Eventually the diary itself was sacrificed, in January 1868, with a resolution to economize on time. Despite his extensive missionary activities, Chavasse often looked back with regret on how little he had attempted for the cause of Jesus Christ. There is a surprising absence in the diary, however, of any struggles with sexual temptation, unless these are included under 'wandering thoughts'. Probably Chavasse considered this subject too personal to commit to paper. It is true that some passages have been censored, torn or cut out of the diary at a later date, and these appear to refer to the mysterious 'Euphrosyne' to whom Chavasse was romantically attracted.[120] They had met briefly in June 1864 and she tragically died in Chavasse's second term at Oxford, but his lengthy reflexions on her death were probably expunged because of their intimate, rather than their sexual, nature.

During the 1870s British evangelicalism became increasingly influenced by the 'holiness movement', with its emphasis on victory over sin and the belief that christian perfection (or 'entire consecration') was attainable on earth. Some taught that sanctification could be received immediately 'by faith', rather than via a slow process of spiritual conflict and hard grind. The annual conventions held at Keswick from 1875 onwards were a focal point for this new spirituality, although they were anticipated by some of the holiness teaching at William Pennefather's Mildmay Conferences in the previous decade.[121] Alfred Christopher was an early supporter of this movement and organised the 1874 Oxford Conference for Robert Pearsall and Hannah Whitall Smith, the American publicists of the new doctrine.[122]

117 Oxenden, *Pathway of safety*, p. 29.

118 CD, 18 Dec. 1864.

119 CD, 19 Apr. 1864.

120 The name 'Euphrosyne' twice escapes the censor's scissors. CD, 30 June, 9 July 1864.

121 Melvin E. Dieter, *The holiness revival of the nineteenth century* (2nd edn., Lanham, Maryland, 1996), pp. 129–69; John H. S. Kent, *Holding the fort. Studies in Victorian revivalism* (London, 1978), pp. 295–355; Bebbington, *Evangelicalism*, pp. 151–80.

122 Reynolds, *Christopher*, pp. 178–85.

A number of the evangelical leaders who Chavasse heard as an undergraduate, invited to Oxford by Christopher, became sponsors of the Smiths – such as William Haslam, Lord Radstock, Stevenson Blackwood and Edmund Fishbourne. Nevertheless, those who adhered more firmly to the calvinist tradition, like J. C. Ryle, Henry Bazely and Horatius Bonar, were highly critical of their holiness teaching.[123] Bonar's *God's way of holiness*, gifted to Chavasse by Christopher when they first met, explains that ongoing warfare against sin is necessary even for the regenerate believer.

Chavasse's diary shows that he was convinced personal holiness could only be achieved as a result of lengthy spiritual struggle. He identified easily with the Apostle Paul's description of his battle with sin in Romans vii (a classic text about which interpreters argued during the holiness controversy) and reflects, 'is Sin then conquered? ... The fight seems getting harder every day'.[124] Although Chavasse records occasional periods of exhilarating joy in his christian life and a feeling of closeness to God, it is more common to read of his deep depression at his spiritual state. In this he follows the example of his predecessors in the puritan tradition. Brainerd was notoriously melancholic.[125] Martyn's self-loathing was so intense that the editor of his journal had to reassure the public that his subject did not have a 'gloomy temperament' but was actually 'cheerful' and 'warm-hearted'.[126] Chavasse's first biographer concludes that a 'tendency to melancholia dogged him through life ... yet resolutely faced and nobly overcome.'[127] Indeed Chavasse admits that he was inclined to be 'morose'[128] and was sometimes too 'absorbed in contemplating my own vile heart' instead of 'looking wholly to Jesus'.[129] Dejected introspection was the obvious danger for a regular self-examiner and a number of devotional writers had to remind their readers that there was joy and peace in the christian life. As John Boyce explained, it was right to submit to the chastisement of God, but not to put oneself 'under the scorpion-lash of Satan': 'Clouds and gloom, without intermission, on the face of one born to the heavenly inheritance! Unceasing fears and mental agony for those who are travelling Zionward! ... No, these things cannot be.'[130]

123 Hicks, *Bazely*, pp. 211–17; Eric Russell, *That man of granite with the heart of a child* (Fearn, Ross-shire, 2001), pp. 111–22.

124 CD, 25 Aug. 1867.

125 David L. Weddle, 'The melancholy saint: Jonathan Edwards's interpretation of David Brainerd as a model of evangelical spirituality', *Harvard Theological Review*, LXXXI (1988), 297–318.

126 Sargent, *Martyn* (10th edn.), preface.

127 Lancelot, *Chavasse*, p. 55.

128 CD, 28 Dec. 1866.

129 CD, 19 Nov. 1866.

130 Boyce, *Ground of hope*, pp. 128–9.

One of Chavasse's responses to his sin was to throw himself with renewed vigour into evangelistic activity. Sometimes, however, this could be from suspect motives. On one occasion he was struck by a chapter in George Sargent's *Story of a pocket Bible* which he was reading to a poor parishioner in Sutton Coldfield. The book tells of a university undergraduate who is convicted of his sin and so tries to earn the mercy of God by numerous religious observances, such as giving alms to the destitute, visiting the sick and dying, and avoiding wine parties and billiards. The man will not renounce 'self-dependence and self-atonement' and so becomes 'weary, heavy-laden, and agonizing for rest and peace' until a dying christian tells him that justification comes by faith.[131] Chavasse reflected: 'Was much struck & astonished, aye almost awed by what I heard & read... No news probably, & yet a startling truth. It set me thinking. Have I been living this life, trusting to Good works? Oh Father give me this justifying faith.'[132] Often in the face of his sin he explicitly reminds himself of the mercy of Christ. Statements such as 'I have nothing, nothing to plead save Jesus & his death' appear frequently.[133]

Worldly Distractions

The 1850s and 1860s have been described by David Bebbington as the period when the 'cult of duty, self-discipline and high seriousness was at its peak', largely as a result of the cultural ascendancy of evangelicalism.[134] Chavasse was certainly a serious young man and often prayed to be more 'earnest'. He frequently worried that he was 'getting too much absorbed by worldly things'.[135] For instance, after a relaxing month's holiday on the Isle of Man he asks: 'Have I not been careless in my religious duties? Have I not been too much engrossed in pleasure?'[136]

The pervasive social influence of evangelicalism was seen particularly in mid-Victorian attitudes to recreation. The boundary line separating the acceptable from the unacceptable was constantly changing, but the list of taboos was perhaps at its longest at the period when Chavasse was writing his diary.[137] He found it difficult to determine what the right attitude should be towards various forms of leisure, and indeed changed his views as time went on. Some activities were

131 George E. Sargent, *The story of a pocket Bible* (London, 1860), pp. 82–99.

132 CD, 29 June 1865.

133 CD, 31 Dec. 1865.

134 Bebbington, *Evangelicalism*, p. 105.

135 CD, 24 Sept. 1865.

136 CD, 3 Aug. 1865.

137 Doreen M. Rosman, *Evangelicals and culture* (London, 1984); Michael M. Hennell, 'Evangelicalism and worldliness 1770–1870' in *Popular belief and practice*, ed. G. J. Cuming and Derek Baker (Studies in Church History, 8, Cambridge, 1972), pp. 229–36; Brian H. Harrison, 'Religion and recreation in nineteenth-century England', *Past and Present*, XXXVIII (1967), 98–125.

obviously inappropriate for a christian, such as horse racing. Steeplechases took place in and around Sutton Coldfield each spring, against the evils of which Gilbert Robinson boldly preached.[138] Chavasse agreed that racing was 'folly' and was shocked to find that the local grammar school boys were taken along to watch by Albert Smith and had even placed bets.[139] Likewise smoking he rejected as 'an idle expensive habit'.[140] He found it less straightforward, however, to decide what approach should be taken to other recreational activities, such as dancing, acting and playing cards. All were popular pastimes amongst Chavasse's family and Sutton Coldfield friends, but as an undergraduate he decided to give them up, on principle. However, his theological objections to these pursuits only developed on the top of his natural disinclination towards them.

As a sixteen-year-old, Chavasse admitted to being 'bashful in company'.[141] He was not confident at the regular balls organized by Sutton Coldfield neighbours, although sometimes did enjoy the dancing. After one evening he records proudly: 'Danced with *10* different young ladies.'[142] This pleasure did not last, however, and it is more usual to read exclamations like 'I hate dancing'[143] or 'Dancing is not in my way… I am an egregious muff.'[144] Perhaps lack of co-ordination was added to lack of confidence, for on one occasion he fell down with his partner and determined never to waltz again.[145] Likewise Chavasse felt 'foolish' when forced to join in charades, which were a frequent part of evening entertainment at home.[146] Each Christmas there was also the serious matter of a play organised between local families, but Chavasse found it difficult to learn his lines and was a nervous performer. He was press-ganged into the production for 1863, *Sleeping Beauty*, but considered it 'wretched' and 'rather childish & stupid'.[147] Even having to watch professional productions he considered unpleasant and declares, 'I do *not* like the theatre'.[148] When Robinson suggested, on religious principle, that Chavasse give up both dancing and acting, he was not slow to comply. His mother continued to organize such parties, so he was forced to contrive different strategies to avoid damaging his new religious scruples.

138 CD, 14 Feb. 1864.
139 CD, 16 Mar., 31 May 1865.
140 CD, 4 Sept. 1863.
141 CD, 3 Dec. 1862.
142 CD, 30 Dec. 1862.
143 CD, 5 Jan. 1865.
144 CD, 11 Oct. 1864.
145 CD, 1 Feb. 1865.
146 CD, 4 Oct. 1865.
147 CD, 26 Dec. 1863, 5–6 Jan. 1864.
148 CD, 27 Dec. 1863.

Similarly, as a teenager Chavasse and his family often played card games such as whist, vingt-et-un, cribbage, 'Pope Joan' and 'Happy Families'.[149] However, in April 1866, following Robinson's example, he resolved to give up cards and never again mentions them in his diary in anything but a reproachful manner. Nevertheless, Chavasse did not go as far as the small circle of evangelical undergraduates around William Hay Aitken who in the early 1860s refused, on principle, to drink wine or row in the college boats.[150] Chavasse is often to be found coxing a Corpus four down the Isis. Not until he was a curate did he take 'the pledge' of total abstinence from alcohol and begin to lend his support to the temperance movement.[151] Other innocent pastimes such as bagatelle, chess, squails and billiards escaped censure,[152] although croquet was dismissed as a wearisome game which seemed 'to benefit neither soul or body'.[153]

When it came to literature, Chavasse's approach was similarly mixed. Novels were banned in many evangelical households and Robinson quoted approvingly Hannah More's warning against reading them:

> Many works of fiction may be read with safety, some even with profit; but the constant familiarity, even with such as are not exceptionable in themselves, relaxes the mind that wants hardening, dissolves the heart that wants fortifying, stirs the imagination that wants quieting, irritates the passions which want calming, and, above all, disinclines and disqualifies for active virtues and for spiritual exercises. The habitual indulgence in such reading, is a silent, mining mischief.[154]

It is therefore a surprise to find that in his leisure time Chavasse was not averse to reading novels such as Ellen Wood's *Verner's pride* and Sir Walter Scott's *Peveril of the peak*, or the latest tales by Henry Kingsley and Charles Dickens.[155] However, most of the books he records in his diary are of a 'spiritual' nature, often christian biography, such as Richard Cecil's *Memoirs of John Newton*, T. S. Grimshawe's *Memoir of Legh Richmond* and Norman MacLeod's *Earnest student*.[156] For birthdays his sisters gave him classic religious works such as John Keble's *Christian year*, William Wilberforce's *Practical view of christianity* and Oxenden's *Pathway of safety*.[157]

149 CD, 3 Feb., 8, 16 Sept., 16 Oct. 1863, 12 Jan. 1864, and *passim*.
150 Woods, *Aitken*, pp. 91–2.
151 Lancelot, *Chavasse*, pp. 52–3.
152 CD, 10 Oct. 1863, 9, 12 Jan., 30 June 1864, and *passim*.
153 CD, 27 June 1866.
154 Quoted in Robinson, *Aids*, pp. 103–4.
155 CD, 29 Dec. 1862, 29 Oct., 3 Dec. 1863, 18 July 1865.
156 CD, 1 Jan., 23 Apr., 15 June 1865.
157 CD, 27 Sept. 1864, 27 Sept. 1865.

The Sabbath

The middle decades of the nineteenth century witnessed an intensification of agitation on the Sunday question. Evangelicals were at the forefront of those campaigning for the restriction on Sunday not only of labour but of amusements such as drinking, train travel and newspapers, the opening of museums, parks and libraries, or the playing of brass bands. New sabbatarian organizations were founded in the late 1850s, like the Working Men's Lord's Day Rest Association and the Sunday Rest Association, which collaborated with the longer established Lord's Day Observance Society but were opposed by the secularists of the National Sunday League. The battle raged across the floor of the house of commons and spilled out on to urban streets, sometimes with physical injury, such as in July 1855 when police forcibly broke up a large demonstration at Hyde Park against the introduction of further Sunday trading regulations.[158]

Under Gilbert Robinson, the congregation at Walmley were treated to sermons on behalf of the L.D.O.S.,[159] and Chavasse carried such opinions with him to Oxford. For instance, he voted against Sunday opening of the Oxford Union and objected when friends travelled by train on Sunday. He distributed copies of *The Sunday at Home*, a magazine which was intended to provide wholesome Sabbath reading for all the family, though his beneficiaries asked for something 'rather livelier'.[160] Victorian sabbatarianism has been caricatured as 'a perverse reluctance to enjoy oneself on Sundays and a determination to stop other people enjoying themselves too.'[161] However, this was not Chavasse's motivation nor his personal experience. Instead he spoke of loving the word 'Sabbath' and of 'longing for Sunday'.[162] According to Oxenden, 'the great secret of a happy week is a holy Sabbath',[163] and Chavasse agreed. He describes his enjoyment of the day listening to Robinson's preaching at Walmley:

> I am beginning, thanks be to God, to look forward to my Sundays. They come to revive my soul, as stages on life's way, at which I may gain sustenance to bear me along for six more days. Blessed Sabbaths, in that sweet quiet church. Where the loving tone of that ringing voice is heard invoking the weary Sinner to his Saviour. With what calm delight shall I look back upon you, when I too am battling with the world.[164]

158 John Wigley, *The rise and fall of the Victorian Sunday* (Manchester, 1980); Brian H. Harrison, 'The Sunday trading riots of 1855', *Historical Journal*, VIII (1965), 219–45.
159 CD, 29 Nov. 1863.
160 CD, 4 Aug. 1865.
161 Wigley, *Rise and fall*, pp. 2–3.
162 CD, 6 May 1865, 16 Mar. 1867.
163 Oxenden, *Pathway of safety*, p. 20.
164 CD, 22 May 1864.

In contrast, a Sunday which lacked such spiritual refreshment was especially painful:

> Was late for prayers. A bad beginning for God's Day. Wandering, very wandering in prayer both at home & at Church. Is this terrible sin growing on me? God help me. Could not talk to my boys [at Sunday school] as I would have done. So cold was my heart... Examined part of the 1st chapter of Romans in the afternoon, but could not, could not pray. The stream soon disappears when its source is dry. Lord give me a prayerful spirit. Alas what a Lord's Day have I spent. Father I am a miserable sinner, but Jesus alone can cleanse me.[165]

Sundays were to be spent primarily in reflecting on the sermons and in spiritual reading. Vaughan warned, 'Much worship, many Sermons are *talked away* before we get home from Church. Who is the better for them two days afterwards? Who treasures up the lessons learnt, and carries them into life, into thought, into prayer, through the week?'[166] When at high table with the dons of University College on a Sunday, Chavasse was amazed that the conversation seemed to cover every subject except religion.[167] He refused to go walking with friends on Sundays because in 'worldly, secular conversation, spiritual things are lost & forgotten'.[168] Likewise he tried to prevent boisterous or argumentative undergraduates from visiting him on a Sunday night, so that his peaceful meditations were not disturbed.

The Lord's Supper

E. J. G. Rogers, Christopher Cocksworth and others have argued that holy communion had a central place within the public ministry and the private devotions of many early nineteenth-century evangelicals. Only in reaction against later tractarian eucharistic theology did they begin to adopt 'a non-sacramental spirituality', encouraged by the writings of scholars like William Goode and Nathaniel Dimock.[169] Chavasse's diary reveals that the Lord's Supper played a significant role in his devotional life. He looked back to his confirmation classes as a seventeen-year-old as a key moment in his spiritual awakening, and perhaps

165 CD, 21 May 1865.

166 Vaughan, *Notes on confirmation*, p. 54.

167 CD, 19 Mar. 1865.

168 CD, 30 July 1865.

169 E. J. G. Rogers, 'The evangelical fathers and the liturgy', *Churchman*, LX (1946), 177-83; *idem*, 'The holy communion in the evangelical tradition', *Churchman*, LXVII (1953), 11–18; Christopher J. Cocksworth, *Evangelical eucharistic thought in the Church of England* (Cambridge, 1993), pp. 72–94; Peter Toon, *Evangelical theology 1833–56. A response to tractarianism* (London, 1979), pp. 195–202.

for this reason the sacrament took on an extra significance. He describes his feelings on passing through that gateway to communion:

> A solemn day for me… The bishop gave us a very nice address, but I am sorry to say, that many of the candidates seemed more disposed to treat the whole matter as a joke. I felt serious, but oh not half as serious, as devout, as unworldly minded [as] I should like to have done. O my heavenly Father grant for Jesus' sake that I may indeed be brought to thee, & be taught to learn of thee… I am far oh very far from what I ought to be. Proud, wilful, disobedient, selfish & black with sin, I need indeed to be cleansed with a Saviour's blood, & to be redeemed by a Saviour's sufferings. Shall I become as thoughtless as I was before? Will the slight religious convictions, that have been hurrying like light & shade through my soul, be quenched by the pleasures & pursuits of the world? Father grant that it may not be so. Grant that each day they may become stronger & more firmly rooted in my heart.[170]

Chavasse's first reception of holy communion two weeks later made a further impact on him:

> A very solemn day for me. I first received the Sacrament. God grant that I may be refreshed & cheered by it. The service was so devout, so quiet & so beautiful that I felt very much impressed by it. Oh may I truly take my stand beneath the Lord's banner… I am still very far from being what I ought to be. Oh how hard a thing it is to be a Xtian. Lord vouchsafe to me thy guiding hand. Lead me in the narrow way.[171]

In later life, Chavasse recalled how 'Sacrament Sunday' used to make a deep impression on his whole family. His father, for instance, would be 'extra quiet all day' and could sometimes be observed returning from the Lord's Table with tears in his eyes.[172] Holy communion was frequently associated by Chavasse with designations such as 'peaceful', 'comfortable', 'refreshing'.

If Sunday was a day for extended self-examination, how much more so 'Sacrament Sunday'. Numerous communion manuals included advice on this practice, with suggested questions.[173] Before his confirmation, Chavasse read a collection of lectures by Charles Vaughan which warned against approaching the

170 CD, 18 Apr. 1864.

171 CD, 1 May 1864.

172 Lancelot, *Chavasse*, p. 6.

173 Bickersteth, *Treatise on the Lord's Supper*, pp. 149–95; Ashton Oxenden, *The earnest communicant. A course of preparation for the Lord's Table* (London, 1856); Oxenden, *The Lord's Supper*, pp. 87–93; Henry Ainslie, *Self-examination and devotions preparatory to the holy communion* (Oxford, 1861); Michael F. Sadler, *The communicant's manual* (London, 1873), pp. 1–19; *The pilgrim's bread. A manual for the holy communion* (London, 1876), pp. 38–9.

Lord's Table unprepared, 'in hurry and disorder'. Vaughan explained: 'To be really fit, is, to feel ourselves unfit. Want, and the sense of want, is our real and only passport to Christ's presence. Preparation should awaken that sense, not relieve it.'[174] Chavasse prayed to be preserved from 'eating or drinking unworthily'[175] and on occasion lamented that his self-examination had been 'very irregular & passionless'.[176] When Robinson gave only twenty-four hours' notice before a Christmas communion, he refused to attend because it did not allow enough time for preparation. However, he was pleased if he was enabled to partake in the Lord's Supper keenly aware of his sin:

> Received the Sacrament. God grant that it may be a blessing to me. I humbly believe that thro' the grace of the Holy Spirit, the examination which I have gone thro', imperfect as it is, has shewn me how sinful I am. May my prayer be 'Lord shew me *myself*'.[177]

Death

One of the purposes of self-examination was to prepare for death, which might strike at any moment. How much better to discover one's sins now, than have God reveal them on the day of judgment, at 'the Last Great Assize'.[178] Indeed George Wilkinson (bishop of St Andrews) encouraged self-examiners to imagine themselves standing before 'that great White Throne'.[179] One devotional manual for the bereaved included detailed questions for self-scrutiny, such as

> Have you reflected during your present bereavement, that God might have taken *you* instead of your friend? If so, should you have been ready for the summons? Have you understood that your friend's death is a warning to you, – a message from God, – to prepare for your own? Are you acting on that warning? *How* are you preparing yourself?[180]

Perhaps because he had almost died as a teenager, Chavasse frequently reflects on the imminence of death. The sudden removal of young men who seemed in fullness of health was particularly striking: 'Is it not the voice of my God speaking to me, warning me of the uncertainty of life, & the nearness of death & eternity?';[181] 'Surely it is a warning to me "prepare to meet thy God". Oh my

174 CD, 8 Mar. 1864; Vaughan, *Notes on confirmation*, pp. 66–7.
175 CD, 2 Dec. 1864.
176 CD, 4 July 1864, 1 Oct. 1865.
177 CD, 4 Sept. 1864.
178 Boyce, *Ground of hope*, p. 22.
179 Wilkinson, *Instructions*, p. 37.
180 *A manual of spiritual direction for mourners* (London, 1853), pp. 70–1.
181 CD, 13 Oct. 1865.

God fit me to die.'[182] The demise of parishioners in South Hinksey to whom Chavasse delivered tracts was a spur to him to speak more boldly about eternal matters, and after one death-bed visit he notes: 'Oh how awful to put off till one's dying hour, coming to Jesus.'[183] To die unprepared, without coming to Jesus, was terrible. Chavasse was shocked, for instance, when a neighbour had a fit at the card table – what if she had died engaged in such a worldly pursuit? Likewise the death of Sir William Hartopp of Four Oaks Park, Sutton Coldfield was chastening: 'Such a household too, everybody almost frantic. No religion, no God, to fall back upon. Dreadful state, what must be the life, & what the death & what the hereafter of such people.'[184]

In contrast, Chavasse considered the deathbed of a christian to be a glorious scene. He prayed for his grandmother to have 'a happy & triumphant death'.[185] This emphasis is seen at greater length in Chavasse's reflexions upon the final hours of his sister, Jenny, who died aged thirty in February 1863:

> Poor Jenny still alive but getting weaker & weaker. Gleams of consciousness. She says she is quite happy & going to Jesus. Blessed thought. May that sure hope be mine when I lie on my death bed, when the world is fading from my view & heaven's portals arise to greet my joyous view.[186]
>
> Poor Jenny died. My God thou art indeed chastening us but do as seemeth best to thy Godly wisdom. Thou doest all thing well, and everything for the best, may our hearts bow down beneath thy rod & murmur 'thy will be done'. I saw her alive in the morning for the last before I went to town. She did not know me. Death had already marked her not for his own for she was Christ's... By a quarter past three all was over. Gently she sank. Papa sat at her head & held her hands & him she knew till the last. A slight shiver, a few weary deep breaths and her unfettered soul returned to God who gave it. Happy at last. Repaid for all her suffering & woe, gone to that place 'where the wicked cease from troubling & the weary are at rest'. At peace now with her Saviour. Henry came home with us & we went up to see her with papa as she lay in her last long sleep. No sign of pain lingered on her face, all was as calm as could be.[187]
>
> How merciful has God been to us. If poor dear Jenny had lived much longer she would have had typhus fever, but he in his sovereign mercy took her, ere it should. Surely all his dealings are mingled largely with mercy. The following are a few incidents connected with dear Jenny's last

182 CD, 27 Aug. 1865.
183 CD, 7 Feb. 1867.
184 CD, 16 Oct. 1864.
185 CD, 4 Mar. 1865.
186 CD, 15 Feb. 1863.
187 CD, 16 Feb. 1863.

> moments. Every thing she saw seemed lined with gold, & over her she saw a sword, verily the sword of the spirit. She kept continually looking up and smiling, and just before she went, she turned her face to Papa actually joyously laughing. Heaven perchance she had seen angels to bear her up. May such things greet my eyes when I die, & may my death be as joyous as hers.[188]

Only five weeks later the family was again gathered around the deathbed of Howard Chavasse, aged twenty-seven. His young brother once more paints a triumphant picture:

> It was a heartrending scene. One by one we kissed him, & wished him good-bye. While all were crying bitterly, he was the calmest person in the room... how happy he was ... he trusted in his Saviour & in his Saviour alone. Blessed trust! if thy soul be anchored to such a rock in vain may the pitiless billows dash & foam, & the lowering storm roar & thunder! ... at 1 o'clock he gave one deep drawn sigh, & without a struggle or a pang, his unfettered soul returned to God who gave it... Never was there a greater example of the presence of the Saviour at the hour of death. Lord Jesus when I die, so be with me, support me through the dark valley.[189]

Such exclamations and heartfelt prayers punctuate Chavasse's diary at frequent intervals. His longing for a close relationship with Christ is a central motif which recurs throughout this personal and revealing record of his undergraduate life.

188 CD, 17 Feb. 1863.
189 CD, 21 Mar. 1863.

The text

Francis Chavasse's diary fills six octavo notebooks which were given by his family to St Peter's College, Oxford and are now on deposit in the Bodleian Library (MSS Chavasse dep. 16–21). The following transcription maintains his capitalization, spelling, abbreviations and slips of the pen, although his own corrections of his text are reproduced without comment. In a few instances the punctuation has been silently amended to aid readability. The date of each entry is given in full and the day of the week (only occasionally noted by Chavasse) is supplied.

The Undergraduate Diary of Francis Chavasse 1865–1868

Friday, 13 October 1865
... Did not get to bed until nearly 2 a.m.. How much now do I need the prayer of everyone. I am on the point of entering upon a new & important epoch of life, one which will either materially injure or benefit me. May a Father's hand guide me; may a Saviour's love overshadow me; may a blessed Spirit's sanctifying influence be shed abroad upon me; then I shall indeed be blessed & happy.

Saturday, 14 October 1865
Started at 9 o'clock in the carriage from home. Left Birmingham at 10 a.m.. My father & Mother went with me.[1] Arrived Oxford at 12.20. Took the omnibus to Corpus. My rooms on on [*sic*] the third floor. They far exceeded my expectations. The bedroom is certainly small. I am to have a new carpet & fresh paper. We had some dinner, & then went into the town & made several purchases. Soon after we came back who should make his appearance but Albert.[2] It was very kind of him to come. Father & Mother left at 6.20 by the omnibus to meet the 6.40 train. Felt a little lonely when they were gone, & my heart did ache a little. I did not think it would, but when it came to the point, I found out my mistake. How hard my Mother worked to be sure & how willingly did my Father pay sovereign after sovereign to purchase anything that might add to my comfort. Thank God for such parents. And now that I am safely lodged here, I humbly commit myself to my Father's hands. May he keep me in all temptations & bless to my Spiritual Welfare my College career. Ludovic wrote to me very kindly & gave me some excellent advice.[3] I feel my own utter impotence but the weakest child becomes endued with a giant's strength when resting on Jesus. Oh Jesus, adorable Redeemer, be with me.

Sunday, 15 October 1865
Got up about 7.20 & went to Chapel at 8 a.m.. It was quite full. There are in all about 56 men up, of whom 36 are in college. Had breakfast by myself & went to the University Sermon at Christ Church. Canon Heurtley preached a capital Sermon.[4] He gave the Freshmen some very good advice, & was so earnest.

1 Thomas Chavasse (1800–84), surgeon, and Miriam S. Chavasse née Wyld (1817–84).
2 Chavasse's cousin, Albert S. Chavasse (1840–1930), fellow of University College 1864–1902.
3 Chavasse's half-brother, Ludovic T. Chavasse (1829–92), vicar of Rushall, Staffs., 1861–7, of St Saviour's, Camberwell, 1867–91.
4 Charles A. Heurtley (1806–95), Lady Margaret professor of divinity 1853–95.

Lunched with Albert at University & then went a walk with him. Alas! alas, my conscience reproached me, but the 'fear of men brought a snare',[5] & I heeded it not. Oh Lord give me moral courage. I shall get hardened in sin unless thou help me. Chapel again at 5 & Hall at 6 p.m.. Formed an acquaintance with Jacobson son of the new B. of Chester.[6] He seems a very decent fellow. In the evening went to St Aldate's & heard Mr Christopher.[7] He was very impressive & earnest, & Christ was the Alpha & Omega of his discourse. I think under God his remarks were profitable to me. He exhorted young men just entering on their University career to take their stand boldly on the side of Jesus. Oh that I may do so, but bitterly did I reflect that I had that very morning proved myself a craven soldier & gone for a walk although my conscience forbad it. May I be endued with the unfaltering spirit of a true Xtian. Jacobson came into my rooms & talked in the evening.

Monday, 16 October 1865

Up at 7.10. Still did not have a sufficient time to myself to pray & read. I must get up earlier, for it is certain that if I do not read &c before breakfast, I shall not be able to do so afterwards. At 10 a.m. all the freshmen went to the President.[8] Paid my caution money & the valuation of my rooms to the Bursar.[9] I like his face. I do think that he is a true Xtian. Loitered about the quad waiting to see if Ilbert would come from Balliol to lecture, but he never appeared.[10] Got to know several of the freshmen. Went with Jacobson to the Museum. At 4.40 went to be matriculated. We simply had to write our names in two books, once in English, the second time in Latin. The pen was bad, & I blurred my writing in two places. Fifteen matriculated. Two of the Scholars, Maitland & Knox had come into residence immediately after the Scholarship exam.[11] Sat next to Bickersteth in Hall.[12] He is the son of the B. of Ripon. God grant that he may be as good a fellow as those holy men whose name he bears. Went to the Union & wrote home. Ford came to

5 Proverbs xxix. 25.

6 Walter H. A. Jacobson (1847–1924), matriculated [m.] Corpus 1865, surgeon, consultant to Guy's Hospital; son of William Jacobson (1803–84), bishop of Chester 1865–84.

7 Alfred M. W. Christopher (1820–1913), rector of St Aldate's, Oxford, 1859–1905.

8 James Norris (1796–1872), president of Corpus 1843–72.

9 Charles Fort (*c.*1827–68), fellow of Corpus 1852–67, senior bursar.

10 Courtenay P. Ilbert (1841–1924), fellow of Balliol 1864–74, parliamentary counsel to treasury, clerk of house of commons 1902–21.

11 Alexander C. R. Maitland (1845-1929), m. Corpus 1865, barrister. Edmund A. Knox (1847–1937), m. Corpus 1865, fellow of Merton 1868–84, bishop of Coventry 1894–1903, of Manchester 1903–21.

12 Robert Bickersteth (1847–1916), m. Corpus 1865, inspector of factories 1873–80, M.P. for Shropshire (Newport division) 1885–6; son of Robert Bickersteth (1816–84), bishop of Ripon 1857–84.

tea.[13] He is a quiet fellow. Did not feel well. Dissatisfied with myself, & with the manner in which I have spent the day. 'God has not been in all thoughts.' I have been seeking the favour of men. Oh that I may grow in grace. I fear that I am sliding back. Help me thou helper of Israel.

Tuesday, 17 October 1865

Honey & Horton from Pembroke called on me.[14] Worked a greater part of the morning but did not get through much work. Had letters from my Father & Mother. Charlie Black called at 2 p.m..[15] He is very much changed. Went to Mr Christopher's & took Mr R.'s letter:[16] he received me most kindly & gave me Bonar's 'God's Way of Holiness'.[17] Several of his protégés dropped in while I was there, & he introduced me to one Durnford whom I feel sure that I shall like.[18] He prayed with us before we went. Thank God that I enjoy the privilege of such a Xtian's supervision. Went to Furneaux & he settled with us about composition.[19]

Wednesday, 18 October 1865

St Luke's Day. Had a different service in chapel. Worked in the morning. In the afternoon the men came to paper my room. Went for a walk with Albert to Godstow. Enjoyed it exceedingly. Met Barton in the street.[20] He said he should come & call upon me. My room was not finished. It is in a state of confusion & discomfort.

Thursday, 19 October 1865

Felt out of sorts. Wrote my prose in the morning & took it to Furneaux with the others. It was badly done. Felt low, & dispirited. Stayed at the Union part of the afternoon as it proved a cold dreary day. Called on Charlie Black. Horton & Durnford of Pembroke, & James Hall called upon me.[21] Went to a debate at the

13 William W. Ford (1846–1901), m. Corpus 1865, barrister.

14 Charles Robertson Honey (*c.*1835–1918), master at Sutton Coldfield Grammar School 1857–62, m. Magdalen Hall 1862, vicar of St Bartholomew's, Earley, Berks., 1877–90, chaplain to Lord Eustace Cecil 1900–12. Alfred W. Horton (1844–1930), m. Pembroke 1863, rector of Dewsall, Hereford, 1876–1908.

15 Charles A. H. Black (1847–1928), pupil at Chesterfield Grammar School, m. Exeter 1865, barrister.

16 Gilbert W. Robinson (*c.*1810–84), vicar of Walmley 1845–84.

17 Horatius Bonar, *God's way of holiness* (London, 1864).

18 Henry F. Durnford (1844–78), m. Pembroke 1863, rector of St Clement's, Oxford, 1878.

19 Henry Furneaux (1829–1900), fellow of Corpus 1854–69, rector of Lower Heyford, Oxon., 1868–92.

20 Alfred T. Barton (1840–1912), fellow of Pembroke 1865–1912.

21 James R. Hall (*c.*1843–1927), m. Merton 1862, solicitor.

Union.[22] Heard Simcox of Queen's open the debate.[23] He certainly does not shine as an orator. Stayed about an hour & then came away. Brookes came to my rooms to tea, & we did some Sophocles together.[24] Mr Christopher called & left his card. I was out. It was very vexing.

Friday, 20 October 1865

The men came to finish my rooms. I was consequently turned out, & took refuge with Brookes. Went to Ilbert's lecture at 11. It was really splendid. He put me on to translate second, but I don't think I acquitted myself very well. In the afternoon Charlie Black came & we went a walk together. Then I went to the Union. Worked in the Evening.

Saturday, 21 October 1865

I have been at Oxford a week today – it seems like a month. Went to Furneaux to a Greek Testament lecture at 12. Scott came into my room to lunch.[25] Went a long walk with Albert. Wrote two letters home. One to my Father, & one to Kittie, the latter asked me to stand as Godfather to her baby & I have consented.[26] May God grant that I may bear in mind the importance of this office. In the evening after Hall Tovey walked in.[27] He seemed very well & stayed tea. Went at 8.30 to Durnford's rooms & thence to Mr Christopher's.[28] We had a very nice prayer meeting. About 15 men were present. The subject was 'the righteousness of God'. It is my earnest prayer that these meetings may prove a blessing to my soul. Alas how cold & inanimate is that soul. How 'the natural man' shrinks from spiritual things. What doubts, what fears, what conflicts seem in & all round me. As Mr C. said tonight I must look out of that soul up to Jesus. His perfect righteousness is mine. Oh that I may feel this great truth. May I cast myself without reserve, solely & entirely upon Jesus. He can supply what the world never can; he can silence these storms of doubts & waverings, he can whisper to the troubled waves that assault my soul 'Peace be still.'

22 Union Society debate on whether 'Fenianism is as discreditable to England as it is to Ireland'.

23 George A. Simcox (*c.* 1841–1905), fellow of Queen's 1863–1905.

24 William J. Brooks (1846–1919), m. Corpus 1865, barrister.

25 Charles P. Scott (1846–1932), m. Corpus 1865, editor of *Manchester Guardian* 1872–1929, M.P. for Lancashire (Leigh division) 1895–1905.

26 Chavasse's half-sister, Catherine H. Whitehouse née Chavasse (1833–1915), wife of Henry B. Whitehouse (1827–67), iron and coal master, of Townsend House, Sedgley. Their sixth child, Henrietta Ellen G. Whitehouse, was born on 5 October 1865.

27 Joseph D. Tovey (*c.* 1841–*c.* 1899), m. St Edmund Hall 1861, assistant minister of St James, Westminster 1878–85, chaplain at Malaga, Spain 1891–3.

28 On Saturday evenings, Alfred Christopher held a regular meeting for prayer and Bible exposition, often with a visiting speaker.

Sunday, 22 October 1865

Went to the University Sermon in the Morning. Dr Kay of Lincoln preached.[29] Intended to have read all afternoon, but Brookes dropt in & stayed a considerable time talking. After Hall went & had a glass of wine with a man named Sparks.[30] Did not feel at all comfortable in doing so. I think the principle is wrong but I was so weak & so cowardly that I had not the courage to say 'No'. Brooks went with me to St Aldate's. Mr C. preached but alas my thoughts wandered much & I kept pondering about going out on a Sunday Evening. May the Lord direct me.

Monday, 23 October 1865

Attended Ilbert's lecture. Charlie Black came to breakfast.

Tuesday, 24 October 1865

Went to Lunch with Horton. Durnford was there. About 2.45 we walked down to Port Meadow & took boats up to Godstow. I had my first lessons in sculling. In the morning went with Mackenzie to breakfast at Mr Christopher's.[31] I do so like to hear him talk.

Thursday, 26 October 1865

Put down my name at the Gymnasium & was measured &c. Height 5.3 weight 8.8. Rather ignominious figures. I should certainly like to be taller but God knows best what is good for me. Went to the Union & wrote to Tom.[32] Did not go to the debate as I wanted to work.[33] I don't think I missed much by staying away.

Friday, 27 October 1865

Went to breakfast in Rawnsley's rooms.[34] There were 10 there. Went to the Gymnasium & saw Honey & Colmore there.[35] The former came & spoke to me. Brooks came to tea in my rooms.

29 William Kay (1820–86), fellow of Lincoln 1840–67, rector of Great Leighs, Essex 1866–86.

30 Edward I. Sparks (1843–80), m. Corpus 1862, physician.

31 Donald Mackenzie (b. *c.* 1844), m. Corpus 1864.

32 Chavasse's brother, Thomas F. Chavasse (1854–1913), surgeon, consultant to Birmingham General Hospital.

33 Union Society debate on whether there was 'reason to regret the introduction of the Great Western Company's Works into Oxford'.

34 Willingham F. Rawnsley (1845–1927), at Corpus 1864–9, headmaster of Park Hill, Lyndhurst 1885–1902.

35 Thomas M. Colmore (1845–1916), m. Brasenose 1863, barrister, recorder of Warwick 1882–1916.

Saturday, 28 October 1865

Went to the Gymnasium & met Honey again. He asked me to come to dinner tomorrow. When however I got back to college I recollected Afternoon Chapel. After Hall I walked out to the Crescent & called upon him & got off.[36] At 8.45 went to the usual prayer meeting. The room was quite full [:] as many as 40 were present. Mr Greaves from Weymouth[37] gave us a most beautiful address 'on speaking the truth in love'[38] enforcing the plain Xtian duty of speaking seriously & affectionately to one's companions of eternal matters. I did so enjoy it.

Sunday, 29 October 1865

Rained all the morning. Went to Furneaux' to breakfast. About 10 of the men were there. It seemed to me a curious day to give a breakfast. Attended the University Sermon at Christ Church. Dr Shirley preached,[39] & I have no doubt it was a good sermon, but I could not hear it. Read most of the day, but my mind alas very languid & very restless. Oh when shall I feel that deep & incessant craving after things spiritual, which God's children feel. I fear there must be some thing wrong somewhere. Lord Jesus give me faith. Pearson dropped in to see me.[40] Such a nice fellow, so quiet, so unassuming, & so gentle in his ways. In the evening he took me to St Aldate's. Mr Greaves preached a most eloquent sermon on 'the two voices', the voice of God & the voice of Satan. His language was exquisite, & he was most impressive.

Monday, 30 October 1865

Went to the Gymnasium. Scot did not go[:] he was unwell. Oxford getting very muggy & cold. Felt rather lonely & down hearted. The men don't seem to care to associate with me; I yearn for some to love. But have I not Jesus? Let me then love him more, let me feel more assured of his love to me, of his continual presence, his guardian care.

Tuesday, 31 October 1865

Went & called on James Hall. Walked down to the River with him. He ran alongside a Merton boat, & so did I for a time, but stopped short as the tow path was in parts covered with water. Wrote home to my Father.

36 The Honeys were living at 19 Park Crescent, Park Town, Oxford.

37 Talbot A. L. Greaves (1826–99), rector of Melcombe Regis (part of Weymouth) 1856–81, vicar of Clifton, Bristol 1881–91, minister of Holy Trinity, Torquay 1891–6.

38 Ephesians iv. 15.

39 Walter W. Shirley (1828–66), regius professor of ecclesiastical history 1864–6.

40 Charles J. Pearson (1843–1910), at Corpus 1862–6, procurator for the Church of Scotland 1886–90, M.P. for Edinburgh and St Andrew's universities 1890–6, judge of supreme court of Scotland 1896–1909.

Wednesday, 1 November 1865

Went to a wine at Molyneux' lodgings.[41] He is stroke of the Corpus Boat & seems a very nice fellow. There was a man named Athorpe there.[42] I did not like him. With very specious, but frivolous arguments he alleged that many of the holy scriptures' characters sadly wanted veracity. Alas I had not the courage to speak in defence of my Bible. I am indeed a miserable craven-hearted coward. May the Captain of our Salvation given [*sic*] me true moral courage.

Thursday, 2 November 1865

Albert dropped in to see [me] & Alfred Horton. Had a very bad 'howler' in my prose. I am so abominably careless. I must really be more on my guard. I could see that Furneaux was vexed. It was the more annoying, as I had taken pains with the piece & thought it free from errors. Molyneux came & asked me to row or steer in the 'Scratch fours' & I consented. I went down to the river at 3 p.m. & he coached Ilbert,[43] Knox & myself. We did not acquit ourselves very creditably. At 7 p.m. went to the meeting of the Bible Society in the Town Hall.[44] The room was well filled. The Regius Professor moved the first resolution but though a very learned Oriental scholar, he does not shine as an orator.[45] His speech was however earnest & practical. Mr Birks author of 'the Bible & Modern Thought', seconded the resolution.[46] His speech was a splendid one, but unfortunately his voice is very weak. It was really grand to hear the simple & yet striking way in which he proved from the Saviour's own words the inspiration of the whole Scriptures.[47] The second resolution was moved by Dr Reece [Leask] who I think was a Dissenter[48] & seconded by Mr Linton [Litton] a former Fellow of Oriel.[49] The third resolution was moved by Lieut. Verney R. N. who gave a very simple & interesting account of British Columbia.[50] He was followed by the Rev. T. Day [Derry] who spoke

41 Henry W. M. Molyneux (1843–71), m. Corpus 1862, clergyman.

42 Marmaduke Athorpe (1843–72), m. Corpus 1861.

43 Owen Ilbert (1846–96), m. Corpus 1865, headmaster of Crediton Grammar School 1884–92.

44 Annual meeting of the Oxford auxiliary of the British and Foreign Bible Society.

45 Robert Payne Smith (1819–95), regius professor of divinity 1865–70, dean of Canterbury 1870–95.

46 Thomas R. Birks (1810–83), rector of Kelshall 1844–66, vicar of Holy Trinity, Cambridge 1866–77, Knightsbridge professor of moral philosophy 1872–83.

47 The first resolution stated that the Bible is 'the Divine rule of faith, the standard of sound doctrine, the storehouse of pure morality, the inspired record of God's own messages, and next to the Lord Jesus Christ and the Holy Spirit, God's best and highest gift to a sinful world'.

48 William Leask (1812–84), congregational minister at Ware, Herts. 1857–65, at Maberly Chapel, Hackney 1865–84.

49 Edward A. Litton (1813–97), fellow of Oriel 1836–44, rector of Naunton, Glos. 1860–97.

50 Edmund H. Verney (1838–1910), naval officer, M.P. for North Bucks. 1885–6, 1889–91, 3rd baronet Verney of Claydon House from 1894.

certainly most quaintly & well.[51] He made some very witty [remarks]. Talking of Bunyan & his book he said that Bunyan though a Baptist himself did not baptize his Pilgrim, for he knew full well that if he did he would *drown* him.[52] Again in touching upon those who deem it right to read no other book but the Bible he said that such persons set themselves on a pinnacle of pride, aye even placing themselves above St Paul who we read *sent for the parchment*.[53] Got back to college about 10.30. Felt very tired, & in saying my prayers kept half dozing. Oh Lord the spirit is indeed willing but the flesh is weak. Give me thy strength, & forgive me this sin. May my prayers be more heartfelt & earnest.

Friday, 3 November 1865

Went to the Gymnasium. Wrote home thanking my Father for the £20 he had so kindly sent me. I ought to have written yesterday. Went down the river & had a lesson in steering. I am to be the cox. of Bridges' four in the 'Scratch Fours', & they say his boat will win.[54] Scot came to tea.

Saturday, 4 November 1865

Furneaux did not lecture on the Greek Testament, as he was obliged to attend some meeting. Walked down to the river but did not go in a boat. In the evening had a short note from my Father, enquiring whether I had received the money. My letter had not reached him when he wrote (Saturday morning) at which I am much surprized. Of course I wrote back word immediately. Went to Mr C.'s meeting, only about 15 were present. He gave us a very nice exposition of Rom IV 1–8 on justification by faith. He reconciled St Paul's arguments with St James by saying that in the former Man was viewed from God's point of view, utterly unable to do anything of himself. In the latter however man was shewn from man's point of view, displaying good works as the fruit of faith. There was some fear of a disturbance in the streets, & this accounted for the scanty attendance.[55] We met the Junior Proctor on our way home & he told us to go as fast as we could to our respective colleges.[56] He seemed a very courteous, gentlemanly fellow, I thought.

51 Thomas Derry (1822–96), Wesleyan minister at Oxford 1864–6, at various stations in Lancashire, Yorkshire and elsewhere.

52 John Bunyan, *The pilgrim's progress* (1684).

53 2 Timothy iv. 13.

54 Robert S. Bridges (1844–1930), m. Corpus 1863, poet laureate 1912–30.

55 Bonfire Night (5 November) was a traditional occasion for skirmishes between local young men and undergraduates.

56 William W. Capes (1834–1914), junior proctor, fellow of Queen's 1856–70, of Hertford 1876–86, rector of Bramshott, Hants. 1869–1901.

Sunday, 5 November 1865

Went to the University Sermon with Scott. Dr Scott of Balliol preached.[57] There was a large attendance of undergraduates. Went in the afternoon & heard Mr Thorold preach at St Mary's.[58] In the midst of his Sermon an undergraduate came in who before he sat down devoutly crossed. He had not remained three minutes before Mr T. pointed out very forcibly the errors of Rome. This fellow immediately got up & walked out; it was certainly curious. In the evening went to St Aldate's. Mr C. preached, but I felt so weary that I could not listen very much. I have done too much today. His sermon was on faith, & I did indeed feel sorry I could not give my whole attention up to it. Scott came to tea in my rooms but I was glad to get to bed early.

Monday, 6 November 1865

Went to dine with James Hall at Merton. At night there was a slight edition of the town & gown rows. I heard the most awful yelling I ever listened to from the rabble. Proctors & pro-proctors were so numerous that little harm was done. Several of the colleges were gated & among them Merton for an illegal bonfire. The junior proctor it is said had a basin of cold water thrown on his head from some at St Edmund's Hall. It was really too bad. The chief damage consisted in a number of broken windows, which are decidedly to be preferred to broken heads.

Tuesday, 7 November 1865

Went to a musical party at the Halls.[59] Two other undergraduates were there. Did not get back to college until 11.30 & then left my umbrella behind.

Thursday, 9 November 1865

Went to breakfast with Digby.[60] Rowed down the river with Knox & Locke.[61] In the evening had tea with Scott & went with him to the debate at the Union on 'Church & State'.[62] Stayed about 1½ hours & then came away[:] the speeches

57 Robert Scott (1811–87), master of Balliol 1854–70, dean of Rochester 1870–87.

58 Anthony W. Thorold (1825–95), rector of St Giles-in-the-Fields 1857–67, vicar of St Pancras 1869–77, bishop of Rochester 1877–90, of Winchester 1890–5.

59 Edward Pickard Hall (1808–86), partner of Clarendon Press 1853–84, and his wife Anne Hall. They were the parents of James Hall.

60 Charles T. Digby (1845–1923), m. Corpus 1864, rector of Warham, Norfolk, 1874–1923.

61 Walter Lock (1846–1933), m. Corpus 1865, fellow of Magdalen 1869–92, warden of Keble 1897–1920, Lady Margaret professor of divinity 1919–27.

62 Union Society debate on whether 'the Union of Church and State is unsatisfactory to both parties'.

were as a general rule very poor. Sat up very late working. A row was expected but none came off.

Saturday, 11 November 1865

James Hall brought back my umbrella. Knox & Locke & myself rowed to Iffley & back. Went to Mr C.'s meeting: about 16 were present. The subject was 'Holding forth the word of God'.[63] I enjoyed it much, but alas my thoughts wandered very much during the final prayer. I have plenty of attention to give to worldly matters, but little, so very little to spiritual. Had tea with Knox when I came back.

Sunday, 12 November 1865

Commonized with Locke. Went with him & Knox to hear Archdeacon Churton Churton [*sic*] at St Mary's.[64] It was a very argumentative Sermon. Read all afternoon. In the evening Knox & myself walked down to Mr Linton's church.[65] We thought the service commenced at 7 o'clock whereas 6.30 was the time. We therefore got in at the creed. The church was quite full & we had a very useful sermon on 'The light of the world.' In the evening Brookes came into my rooms & would not go. I had to ask him to stay tea in hopes he would go directly afterwards, but he stayed until 10.30, completely stopping me in my reading. I felt angry & irritable about it. Alas what a trifle upsets me!

Monday, 13 November 1865

Steered Bridges' four once down the river and afterwards rowed down with Knox & Locke. Went to breakfast at Maitland's. There were a good many there. Although he has a second floor, I do not much like his rooms. Was glad to see from the Papers that Pearson (J. B.) had been elected Fellow of St John's Camb.[66]

Tuesday, 14 November 1865

A damp gloomy morning which ultimately turned to rain. Did not go down the river but went to the Gymnasium. Knox breakfasted with me. Colmore & Weatherley Phipson of Balliol left their cards on me yesterday.[67]

63 Philippians ii. 16.

64 Edward Churton (1800–74), rector of Crayke 1836–74, archdeacon of Cleveland 1846–74.

65 Henry Linton (1803–87), rector of St Peter-le-Bailey, Oxford 1856–77.

66 Josiah B. Pearson (1841–95), pupil at Chesterfield Grammar School, fellow of St John's, Cambridge 1865–80, bishop of Newcastle, New South Wales 1880–9.

67 Weatherley Phipson (1845–1909), m. Balliol 1864, barrister.

Wednesday, 15 November 1865

The first day of the 'Varsity four oared boats races. Exeter & Brazen-nose rowed in the first heat, & the latter won, & the Merton & Wadham in the second heat & the former won. I went to breakfast with Charlie Black at Exeter, & the Exeter men seemed rather sure of winning. C. B.'s rooms are certainly very small. Mine are regal in comparison with them. I should not like Exeter.

Thursday, 16 November 1865

Furneaux was summoned to Convocation & could not take my prose. This is the second time I have missed. Brazennose beat Merton in their heat, but it was a very hard race. The reports of the pistols were almost simultaneous. Went & had a glass of wine with Morris.[68] He is very High Church, what a pity. Poor fellow he was once he said Evangelical.

Friday, 17 November 1865

In the deciding heat for the Silver Medal & Oars, University beat Brazen-nose by several seconds. Our Challenge fours came off & our boat was beaten. Bridges was vexed. He rowed magnificently himself but he was not backed up well. It was only lost by half a length. Bussell's boat beat Ridley's easily.[69] After Hall went with Crawford[70] to Ilbert to be examined in the Antigone.[71] I don't think we acquitted ourselves very well.

Saturday, 18 November 1865

Evans' crew won the deciding heat by several lengths.[72] Went in the evening to Mr C.'s prayer meeting. Mr Langstone gave us an address.[73] He said he had been 50 years in the ministry. He was selected by William Wilberforce as tutor to his Sons.[74] He spoke to us so earnestly & impressively. The room was quite full. Knox came to my rooms to tea after I returned. I do not think I must have people on a Saturday Night. I found it banished from my mind almost all I had heard. How skilful is the enemy to abstract the good seed out of our hearts.

68 Charles Morris (1844–99), m. Corpus 1862, vicar of Marston, Oxon. 1887–99.

69 Frederick V. Bussell (1846–92), m. Corpus 1865, vicar of Balderton, Notts. 1878–92. Edward Ridley (1843–1928), m. Corpus 1862, fellow of All Souls' 1866–82, M.P. for South Northumberland 1878–80, judge of the high court 1897–1917.

70 John H. Crawford (1846–1925), m. Corpus 1865, barrister.

71 Sophocles, *Antigone*.

72 Henry Farrington Evans (1845–1931), m. Corpus 1864, Indian civil service.

73 Stephen H. Langston (1792–1878), vicar of Southborough, Kent 1847–72.

74 William Wilberforce (1759–1833), evangelical philanthropist, advocate for abolition of slavery.

Sunday, 19 November 1865

Heard the Dean at the Cathedral.[75] In the afternoon went to a meeting of undergraduates at Kitson's rooms in Queen's.[76] Some subject is taken, & discussed. This Sunday it was the 'Lord's Supper'. I wish it was not so controversial. In the evening went with Miller to St Aldate's[77] & heard Mr Langstone who preached on 'the precious blood of Christ'. I liked the Sermon extremely. It was so simple & evangelical. After Church went with Durnford & Horton to Mr Tonge's.[78] We read & examined a portion of the 1st chapter of Romans. I got back to college about 10.30. I fear that I am not so well up in my Bible as I ought to be.

Monday, 20 November 1865

Our 'Grinds' came off.[79] The ground was very heavy. I ran 2nd for my heat in the 100 yds beaten by Bridges a few inches. In the final heat which came directly afterwards I was so knocked up that I could not run half the distance. This comes of keeping late hours. I had the good fortune to win the Consolation Stakes, & the ill fortune to have my stockings stolen. Went with Richardson[80] in the evening to Ilbert with the Oedipus Rex.[81]

Tuesday, 21 November 1865

The Schools began. Corpus has 12 men in for honours. Went & called upon Black, Colmore & Phipson. Thence on to Mr Christopher's. He received me very kindly, & before I left knelt down & prayed with me. Ah! I need these prayers indeed.

Thursday, 23 November 1865

Went & dined at Mr Honey's. Hilbers there, my old school fellow.[82] I had not seen him for five or six years to speak to. I think the rest from work did me good.

75 Henry G. Liddell (1811–98), dean of Christ Church 1855–91.

76 Benjamin M. Kitson (*c.*1843–1923), m. Queen's 1864, vicar of All Saints, Clapton, 1880–92, rector of Barnes 1892–1923.

77 Henry W. Miller (1843–*c.*1890), m. Corpus 1862, vicar of St John's, Richmond 1879–85, emigrated to Tasmania.

78 George Tonge (1838–1910), curate of St Peter-le-Bailey, Oxford 1864–7, vicar of Christ Church, Sparkbrook, Birmingham 1867–89, secretary of Church of England Zenana Missionary Society 1889–1908. On Sunday evenings, Tonge held a regular Greek Testament class.

79 Corpus athletics.

80 Henry Richardson (1845–1914), m. Corpus 1865, master at Marlborough College 1870–1905.

81 Sophocles, *Oedipus Rex*.

82 George C. Hilbers (1844–1918), m. Exeter 1863, rector of St Thomas, Haverfordwest 1874–1918, archdeacon of St David's 1888–1900.

Friday, 24 November 1865

Sent in our names for 'Smalls'.[83] The floods out very high. It is a curious sight to me. Knox, Lock & myself have been up the river several times lately.

Saturday, 25 November 1865

Went to Mr Christopher's meeting. There was only a small gathering. It was very delightful[:] would that I could join more heartily in the prayers.

Sunday, 26 November 1865

Went with Lock & heard Meyrick of Trinity preached [*sic*] the University Sermon.[84] It was very clever, but I think too caustic. Went to Queen's in the afternoon & in the evening went with Durnford, Horton & Lechmere to Trinity Church.[85] We heard a very nice Sermon. Had tea with Durnford, & then off to Mr Tonge. We had a delightful hour. May these meetings promote my growth in grace.

Monday, 27 November 1865

Went a walk with Albert. The Rain cut it short. We saw the finish of a trotting match on our way home. Kitson kindly called on me.

Wednesday, 29 November 1865

Went to Furneaux with our Georgics.[86] I acquitted myself very badly. Ah! I sometimes feel disheartened, after grinding hard to come to such grief, but it is good train[in]g for me. *Perseverance.*

Friday, 1 December 1865

Honey called & asked me to dine with him at No.19 on Tuesday. Went a walk with Albert, & saw part of the Balliol 'Grinds'. Lord Jersey won the 2 mile race in beautiful style.[87]

83 Responsions (or 'smalls'), the first of the three university examinations, followed by Moderations and Finals.

84 Frederick Meyrick (1827–1906), fellow of Trinity 1847–60, an inspector of schools 1859–69, rector of Blickling, Norfolk 1868–1906. See Meyrick, *Jehovah or Baal? A sermon* (London, 1865) against the conclusions of the 'Higher Critics'.

85 William O. M. Lechmere (1845–1915), m. St Mary Hall 1863, barrister and clergyman.

86 Virgil, *The Georgics*.

87 Victor A. G. Child-Villiers, 7th earl of Jersey (1845–1915), m. Balliol 1864.

Saturday, 2 December 1865

Went to Mr Christopher's meeting. There was a very good attendance. He has asked me to go to his house next Saturday to hear Dr Miller's address.[88]

Sunday, 3 December 1865

Went in the morning with Lock to St Peter's in the East. The Church was crammed. He gave us a very grand Sermon on the Advent.[89] In the afternoon went to Queen's as usual. In the Evening went to St Aldate's. Mr C. preached the finest Sermon I ever heard from him. After Service had tea with Durnford & went to Tonge.

Monday, 4 December 1865

Last day of work. Attended Ilbert's lecture though I grudged the time. Went to bed in good time to prepare myself for tomorrow's examination. May God guide me safely through it. The heat for second place was rowed off between our boat & Bussell's. The other boat foulled [*sic*] us[:] consequently we won.

Tuesday, 5 December 1865

Got up at Seven. Very few of the freshmen in Chapel. Went to the Schools at Nine. First paper Euclid much to our consternation. Every body expected Grammar. However I did more than ¾ of the paper. In the afternoon had Prose. I did mine badly. Felt very wretched about it. Came out about 2.45 & went a long walk with Albert. He laughed me out of my fears. Dined with Mr Honey. Returned to the College at 9 p.m..

Friday, 8 December 1865

Went with Durnford & several others in the evening to a meeting of the 'New Vitality'.[90] Geldart read a paper on the 'Philosophy of Protestantism'.[91] It was decidedly good. Came back to my rooms about 9 & ground till 12. J. passed.[92] He had a narrow escape. The Examiners gave him a second & third Euclid Paper & a second Arithmetic Paper. Then he was set on in the Antigone at a hard Chorus which he construed through. He then translated 40 lines of the Georgics correctly. The examiners bothered him next about 'Partitive Genitives' &c but he floored

88 John C. Miller (1814–80), rector of St Martin's, Birmingham 1846–66, vicar of Greenwich 1866–80.

89 Edward Capel Cure (1828–90), vicar of St Peter-in-the-East, Oxford 1858–67, rector of St George's, Bloomsbury 1867–76, of St George's, Hanover Square 1876–90.

90 An undergraduate essay society.

91 Edmund M. Geldart (1844–85), m. Balliol 1863, unitarian minister in Liverpool and Croydon 1873–85.

92 ? Walter Jacobson.

their questions. Lastly they quoted two words in one the Georgics & asked him to give the context. He gave it & they passed him. Poor fellow, he was pleased.

[Thursday, 7 December 1865]
In the morning we had a Grammar Paper, & in the afternoon Arithmetic. I think I did them tolerably well.

Saturday, 9 December 1865
Bickersteth & Lock got safely through & both went home. In the evening went with Pearson, Mylne & Knox to Mr C.'s house.[93] Dr Miller addressed the undergraduates assembled, & there were some 200, on the subject of Ritualism. He spoke for about 45 minutes & very grandly. He was very tolerant of other people's opinions but still very firm in those which he believed to be right[:] got back to College about 10 p.m..

Sunday, 10 December 1865
Went to the University Sermon with Knox. Dr Cotton of Worcester preached but he was inaudible.[94] In the afternoon went to Queen's as usual. In the evening heard Dr Miller at St Aldate's. The church was crammed & people were sitting up the aisles. The sermon was 70 minutes long & was really magnificent. There was so much that could be carried away, & he again made some excellent remarks on Ritualism. After church we had our meeting at Tonge's. M. of Worcester was there, & he rather drew us away from our main subject by his irrelevant remarks & queries.[95]

Monday, 11 December 1865
Collier came into my room & we finished the Georgics.[96] Walked down to the Crescent to say goodbye to Mrs Honey but she was out.[97] In the evening went into Churchill's Room & we ran through the 'Georgics' together.[98]

93 Louis G. Mylne (1843–1921), m. Corpus 1862, bishop of Bombay 1876–97, rector of Alvechurch, Worcs. 1905–17; or John E. Mylne (1844–82), m. Corpus 1863, barrister.

94 Richard L. Cotton (1794–1880), provost of Worcester 1839–80.

95 Charles T. Moor (1843–77), m. Worcester 1862, vicar of Holy Trinity, the Sarn, Newtown 1868–72.

96 D'Arcy B. Collyer (1846–1924), m. Corpus 1865, solicitor.

97 Emma Honey née Pimm, wife of Charles Honey.

98 Charles J. S. Churchill (1844–1918), m. Corpus 1865, master at Shrewsbury School 1870–1910, vicar of Ford, near Shrewsbury 1910–17.

Tuesday, 12 December 1865

Went to the Schools with Churchill. We were kept waiting nearly half an hour in the cold. We had two pieces to translate on paper both very easy. I went out when I had given in my papers, & came in for viva voce at 12. It lasted about half an hour. Finished my packing. Robert brought me my Testamur at 2.30.[99] I was very glad to see it. Went with Albert to the Crescent & brought away the parcel for Miriam.[100] Saw the Law & History Class List as we came back. W. & L. have both seconds.[101] Went down to the Station in a cab with Knox. Left Oxford at 5.20 & reached Birmingham at 6.55. Took a cab across across [*sic*] town. Called at Cornish's & ordered a book.[102] Gave my luggage into the charge of the Porter. Went to the wrong platform & missed the Sutton Train. W[h]iled away the time at the 'Free Library' until 9.10. Got home at 9.40. Papa & Mamma out at a party at Mr J. Green's. Felt very glad to get home again. Thank God for all his goodness.

Wednesday, 13 December 1865

Went round with the Governor in the morning in the pony gig.[103] The new animal went very well. In the afternoon called on A. S.[104] He did not think I had done sufficient Composition.

Friday, 15 December 1865

Went down to see Galliers.[105] The poor old fellow was in bed with erysipelus, & seemed very sadly. His leg however seems much better. Saw Miss Catherine & Miss Jane Holbeche.[106]

Sunday, 17 December 1865

Went to the Sunday School. My boys somewhat unruly. Mr R. seemed glad to see me. Alas felt little inclined to pray, my thoughts worldly & wandering, my heart cold & unattentive. Tom who came home yesterday seems very well.

99 Chavasse's scout.

100 Chavasse's sister, Miriam T. Chavasse (later Wilson) (1848–1935).

101 Frederick W. Willis (1842–1930), m. Corpus 1861, vicar of All Saints, Wellingborough 1872–88, rector of Warrington 1888–1920. Frederick F. Lambert (1843–1920), m. Corpus 1861, rector of Clothall, Herts. 1879–91, vicar of Cheshunt 1891–1911.

102 William Cornish, Birmingham bookseller and printer.

103 'The Governor' was Chavasse's occasional epithet for his father.

104 Albert Smith (1833–1918), headmaster of Sutton Coldfield Grammar School 1863–1902, vicar of Duns Tew, Oxon. 1902–18.

105 Edward Galliers (b. *c.* 1801), wheelwright.

106 The five Holbeche sisters lived together in Sutton Coldfield: Sarah (1803–82), Jane (1812–91), Catherine (1817–87), Helen (1821–95) and Frances (1823–1902).

Monday, 18 December 1865

Walked into Birmingham & did a few errands. Came home to dinner at 5. Getting on slowly with my Virgil. I am doing it carefully. At night went to tea at T. V. H.'s.[107]

Tuesday, 19 December 1865

Went in the afternoon & read to Galliers. He seemed very much better, & I was glad to see him down stairs. Poor cheerful old man what a lesson of contentment does he teach me.

Wednesday, 20 December 1865

Went & dined with Charlie & Fanny at Mt Pleasant;[108] came home at 5 p.m..

Thursday, 21 December 1865

Walked into Birmingham at 2 p.m.. Bought Bullinger's Decades.[109] Came home in the carriage with the Governour [*sic*].

Friday, 22 December 1865

Worked little all day. Albert came by the 5.0 train. Walked down to the Grammar School & saw the prizes given away. Mr Adderley spoke a few words.[110] Called to see G.. The Lloyds came to dinner at 6.0 p.m.. Mr & Mrs Eyre & Mr & Mrs Robinson were also there.[111] Walter Chinnery came at 10.15.[112] The London train had as usual missed the Sutton & he had to cab over here.

Saturday, 23 December 1865

We all three went a long walk. First we looked over Sutton Church & then on to Weeford. I called & enquired after Ted Kendrick. His hand is not well yet.[113] Got home about 3. Enjoyed the ramble very much. Albert went at 8 p.m. I saw him off.

107 Thomas Vincent Holbeche (1846–1904), solicitor, town clerk of Sutton Coldfield.

108 Chavasse's half-brother, Charles E. Chavasse (1840–93), wine merchant, and his wife Frances née Evans (1839–1905). They lived at Mount Pleasant, Birmingham.

109 *The decades of Henry Bullinger*, edited by Thomas Harding (Parker Society, 4 vols., Cambridge, 1849–52).

110 Charles B. Adderley, 1st Baron Norton (1814–1905), M.P. for North Staffs. 1841–78, governor of Sutton Coldfield Grammar School 1839–1901.

111 Gilbert Robinson and his wife, Frances S. Robinson née Russell (*c.*1820–97).

112 Chavasse's cousin, Walter M. Chinnery (1843–1903), member of London stock exchange, deputy lieutenant and high sheriff for Surrey.

113 Edward Kendrick (1851–1920), pupil at Sutton Coldfield Grammar School 1864–6, farmer at Weeford, near Lichfield. In June 1865 Kendrick injured his hand in a gun accident.

Sunday, 24 December 1865

Went to the School. Succeeded in interesting my boys for a little, but their interest soon seemed to flag. I must spend more time in preparation & prayer. Mr R. gave notice of the Communion tomorrow. I wish he had given it out last Sunday. Walter went a walk in the afternoon. I did not go with me [*sic*], for I did not feel justified in doing so. But alas my thoughts were grievously wandering during the service & I felt very irritable & sleepy. Oh am I slipping back, slipping back? Oh Lord help me. In the evening went to Sutton with Walter. Mr Meredith preached.[114] Vincent Holbeche walked home with us from Sutton.

Monday, 25 December 1865

Christmas Day. Went to Church in the morning feeling rather poorly. Did not stay Sacrament as Mr Robinson had only given us notice of it yesterday. Nevertheless felt very sorry to turn my back on the table. Felt peevish & irritable all day. Alas how little joy filled my breast at the thought of my blessed Saviour's birth. Oh my God help me to believe. Nicholas, Mary & little Tom came.[115]

Tuesday, 26 December 1865

A very wet day which confined us to the house. In the evening went with Walter to Miss Holbeche. We had some very good fun. R. Holbeche & his sister were there.[116]

Wednesday, 27 December 1865

Got up at five a.m. & walked to Birmingham to catch the 7.30 train to London. We walked very fast & reached the Station 10 minutes before the arrival of the train. His luggage went yesterday so we had only to get it out of the Cloak Room. I came home again by the 8.40 train. In the afternoon walked down to see Bee but he was out.[117] Nicholas & Mary left.

Friday, 29 December 1865

Went & read to old Galliers. He is certainly wonderfully better.

114 Robert F. Meredith (*c.*1816–93), vicar of Halstock, Dorset 1843–93, curate of Sutton Coldfield 1864–6. On Meredith, Chavasse notes: 'I certainly do not like him in the pulpit', 30 Oct. 1864.

115 Chavasse's half-brother, Nicholas H. Chavasse (1830–1918), brick manufacturer, his wife Mary née Brown (1836–1905) and their son Thomas (b. 1860). They lived at Rowley Hall, Rowley Regis.

116 Robert N. Holbeche (1846–1911), pupil at Chesterfield Grammar School, land agent and surveyor; Sarah G. Holbeche (1849–1936).

117 Thomas H. F. Bee (1844–88), master at Sutton Coldfield Grammar School, m. Cambridge (non-collegiate) 1869, various curacies.

Sunday, 31 December 1865

The last day in the old year. Went to the Sunday School with Miriam. Tried to talk to my boys about the rapid flight of time & the approach of eternity, but alas my own heart was very cold & how could I expect to warm theirs. Oh dear Lord stir up my slumbering soul. The year has gone & what have I done for thee. I have nothing, nothing to plead save Jesus & his death.

Monday, 1 January 1866

Ring it in the happy new year's day! 1865 has gone & with a new year let me strive to lead a new life by the help of God. There was a service at Walmley in the afternoon but Bob H. & his sister came to dinner & we could not go. In the evening Miss Holbeche, Miss Jane, Dick,[118] Charlie & Fanny all came. I feel in a deep spiritual torpor neither hungering nor thirsting for heavenly things. Oh heavenly Father more light, more light.

Tuesday, 2 January 1866

Went to See the R.C. Chapel at Erdington. It is, I suppose very handsome but very taudry. I felt rather ashamed going into it. Bob & his sister went back by the 2.20 train. We are to go to them next week.

Thursday, 4 January 1866

The Rawlins & Bodkin a college friend of Willie's came & called.[119] They want me to act in an extravaganza written by W.R. & Bodkin. I consented.

Friday, 5 January 1866

Mr Smallwood's party.[120] As the carriage was full & Frank Rawlins rode on the box,[121] & as I had had no exercise all day, I walked leaving my boots to come on by carriage. They overtook me a little beyond Hodge Hill, but my boots were left behind. I had to have my walking boots brushed up & to manage as well as I could. We had tableaux which were very good though not worth the trouble. I did

118 Richard Holbeche (1850–1914), army officer.

119 The family of Samuel Rawlins (*c.*1800–85) and his wife Catherine A. Rawlins née Donaldson (*c.*1819–95). William D. Rawlins (1846–1920), m. Trinity, Cambridge 1864, fellow 1869–79, barrister, mayor of Holborn 1906–7. William D. Bodkin (1844–1919), m. King's, Cambridge 1863, chaplain at Highgate School 1869–84, rector of Harbridge, Hants 1884–1916; or Alfred A. Bodkin (1847–1930), m. King's, Cambridge 1865, professor of mathematics at the Diocesan College, Rondebosch, Cape Town 1881–1901.

120 Joseph Smallwood (1821–1911) of Stechford Hall, Castle Bromwich, wine merchant.

121 Francis H. Rawlins (1850–1920), m. King's, Cambridge 1871, fellow 1875–1920, vice-provost of Eton 1916–20.

not dance much. We came away at 12 o'clock. Frank Rawlins slept the night at Wylde Green. He is a very nice fellow.

Saturday, 6 January 1866
Frank Rawlins went home about 10 a.m.. In the afternoon I walked down to Penns[122] & rehearsed my part which I did *not* know. Went home & returned after tea to rehearsal No.2. James Lloyd came. The play is a very good one. It was acted in London at Bodkin's & much applauded.

Sunday, 7 January 1866
Sunday came & found me in a frame of mind little suitable for it. Thoughts of 'Theseus & Ariadne' were consequently running thro' my brain.[123] What wonder then if I had hard work to keep my boys in order. Oh for a graver more loving spirit. Oh for a heart that would soar far above the frivolous trifles of this fleeting world, & rest itself calmly & delightful[ly] on the solid joys of heaven!

Monday, 8 January 1866
Went into town at 2.24. Bob H. met me at the Library. Called on Sophy[124] & did various errands. Walked up to the extremity of the Hagley Road. Felt very annoyed that I should have caused Bob the trouble to have come to meet me. Had dinner at 6. Miriam & Ada were there.[125] Mr H. came in about 9.[126] I slept in Bob's room – I must have turned him out.

Tuesday, 9 January 1866
Rode in the omnibus down to the Station. But the face of nature had changed. The ground was covered with a thin coating of snow, & the streets were very slippery – consequently missed my train. Stayed until 10.30 & then went to Aston & walked home. In the afternoon had another rehearsal (No.3).

Wednesday, 10 January 1866
Had two rehearsals at Penns the last dress. Consequently I could not do much work. Frazer who is to take the part of Pente came. He seems a very nice fellow but looks ill.

122 Penns Hall, home of the Rawlins family.

123 In Greek mythology, Theseus killed the Minotaur with the help of Ariadne, daughter of King Minos of Crete. They escaped together, but Ariadne was abandoned on the island of Naxos and rescued by Dionysus. Theseus later married Ariadne's sister, Phaedra.

124 Chavasse's cousin, Sophia S. Bourne née Chavasse (1835–1900), wife of Francis C. Bourne (1821–1902), manager of Lloyd's Bank, Birmingham.

125 Chavasse's sister, Ada M. Chavasse (later Squires) (1850–1922).

126 John Holbeche (1816–76) of Birmingham, land agent and estate auctioneer.

Thursday, 11 January 1866

Went into town by the 2.20 train. Came back with Bertie at 4.20.[127] He would not go with us to Sparkbrook. We started from home a little after 6 & reached Mr Lloyd's about 7.30. I was obliged to break thro' my resolution & dance. Alas, alas how vain & fleeting are all my determinations.

Friday, 12 January 1866

Went with Bertie to call on Mr Robinson & Mr Felton.[128] The former was out. Got thro' some work in the Morning. Went to Penns at 5. Had tea & afterwards dressed. Felt tired when all was over.

Saturday, 13 January 1866

Got up feeling tired & irritable, my prayers wandering, my mind unsettled. Went again with Bertie to see Mr R.. Found him at home. Then called on Mrs Felton.[129]

Sunday, 14 January 1866

Went to the Sunday School with Bertie. My boys, thank God rather better. Poor B. not there at all. Could not get my mind into a prayerful mood – there is something wrong somewhere. Oh Lord shew it to me.

Monday, 15 January 1866

Bertie & myself drove into town in the pony carriage & did some shopping. Pony rather fagged. Rather cold work driving. I am not much of a Jehu.[130]

Tuesday, 16 January 1866

Went in the Evening to Mrs Holbeche's.[131] Of course there was dancing. Enjoyed myself as much as I generally do on these occasions.

Wednesday, 17 January 1866

Called & wished Miss Holbeche goodbye.

127 Robert A. Squires (1846–1912), m. St John's, Cambridge 1865, C.M.S. missionary in India 1870–92, vicar of St Peter's, St Albans 1895–1910.

128 William Felton (1830–70), schoolmaster at Russell House, Walmley.

129 Mary Felton née Spettigue (1827–70).

130 Jehu, king of Israel, drove his chariot 'furiously', 2 Kings ix. 20.

131 Emma Holbeche (1824–91), wife of Vincent Holbeche (1806–67), solicitor.

Thursday, 18 January 1866

Went with Bertie, Miss Bracken,[132] my Mother, Miriam & Maggie[133] to a C.M. Meeting in the Ch. Ch. School Rooms in Pinfold St.[134] There was a good attendance, & the proceedings most interesting. Dr Miller took the chair & Mr Venn of Hereford spoke.[135] I thoroughly enjoyed it. I was very sorry to hear that the funds of the Society were not increasing as they ought to do. No young men too were now offering themselves either from Oxford or Cambridge. May God stir up the hearts of his people. We came home by the 9.10 train.

Friday, 19 January 1866

Went with Bertie to see Mr R.. He spoke to me about 'private theatricals'. The words seem to startle me out of some sleep. I seemed to see all now. I have fallen. Oh Lord raise. I have erred. I was not watching & lo! I have been ensnared. Felt very miserable about it but dear Mr R. was so kind. I asked him at the same time about dancing & he recommended me to give it up, but told me to ask Mr C.'s opinion. Paid a farewell visit to Mr Felton & in the afternoon to Miss Holbeche & old Galliers. Dined at 5.30 with Charlie. Tom Bartleet there. Went to bed feeling unable to pray or to read my Bible but those affectionate words of Mr R. were ringing in my ears 'Do not let it come between you & the Lord.' Oh my Father wash & cleanse me in Jesus's blood. Alas how I have wasted this vacation. How little have I done for God. Self has been the ruling object of my thoughts, religion has been made secondary. I have been daily growing more worldly minded, daily been drifting farther from my God. Oh Lord have mercy on me.

Saturday, 20 January 1866

Packed up in the Morning. Left home by the 2.20 train. Crossed the town in a cab. Bertie going with me. When we reached Snow Hill I found there was no train until 7 o'clock, but one was just about to start. I thought it best not to wait. Reached Oxford at 5.20 took the omnibus to Corpus. My rooms looking very nice now that the doors are painted. Churchill & Knox came in. At 8.30 went & saw Albert & arranged about going to him. Wrote home. Felt rather queer at finding myself away from home again.

132 Agnes A. Bracken (1800–77), painter and local historian.
133 Chavasse's half-sister, Margaret E. Chavasse (1836–1927).
134 Meeting of the Birmingham auxiliary of C.M.S.
135 John Venn (1802–90), vicar of St Peter's, Hereford 1833–70.

Sunday, 21 January 1866
Went to the University Sermon in the Morning.[136] Horton came in after Hall. Went to Christopher's at Night. Afterward with Durnford & Horton to Tonge's.

Monday, 22 January 1866
No lectures. Called on Furneaux with Lock. Paid Mac at the Gymnasium.[137] Was much annoyed to find he brought me in a bill for £4.1. Went to Albert. It was very jolly. We had tea while we were working. Came away about 10.30.

Tuesday, 23 January 1866
Went down the river in a pair oar with L. & K.. Felt rather awkward at first. Streeten kindly came & called on me.[138]

Wednesday, 24 January 1866
Called on Mr C.. He was just going out so I promised to come some other time. Left my card on Streeten. Felt lonely & unwell. Did not get to bed until late.

Thursday, 25 January 1866
Went down the River in a dingy, & rowed over the meadows. It was very delightful. Every thing seemed so calm. And the water flashed & rippled in the sunshine until it looked as though the river were set with brilliants. Felt happier in myself. Breakfasted with Mackenzie in the morning & wined with Ing[h]am in the evening.[139] He is a very nice fellow.

Friday, 26 January 1866
Rowed down the river with Lock & Knox & went hedging i.e. charging the gaps. When about 20 yds from the hole, Knox who was steering would shout 'Quick'. We rowed as hard as we could. Then at the word 'ship' we tossed our oars into the boat, & we glided through. Spoke to George about my cake &c.[140] I hope I was not too hard on him. Went to bed late. I must really try & improve.

136 Preached by Henry A. Woodgate (1801–74), rector of Belbroughton 1837–74.
137 Archibald MacLaren (1819–84), pioneer of physical education and gymnasia. His Oxford gymnasium opened in 1859.
138 Frederick L. Streeten (1843–1907), m. Queen's 1863, various curacies.
139 Robert W. Ingham (1846–1928), m. Corpus 1865, judge of county court 1892–1928.
140 Chavasse's scout.

Saturday, 27 January 1866

Went with Albert & Called on the Halls. Wined with Bridges. Knox & myself went to hear Mr Goodhearts in the evening.[141] The room was quite full. He spoke so earnestly of the nearness of Xt to his church, his perfect knowledge of the deeds & sufferings of his people. He declared Xt to be the great Captain under whom we must array & not any earthly reader [*sic*, leader]. Very feelingly did he speak of those 'who had forsaken their first love'[142] & brought disgrace on the Xtian name. Alas his words came home with power to my conscious soul. Oh Lord wash me, tho' I have forsaken thee, draw me nearer to thee yet again & binder [*sic*] me still closer with the bands of thy everlasting love.

Sunday, 28 January 1866

Dr Pusey preached at the Cathedral.[143] The place was crammed & I had to stand. His sermon was a very fine one on the Miracles of Prayer. He has a wonderful face. Deeply furrowed cheeks & a noble forehead & eyes that seemed to light up his whole countenance. Went to Tonge's in the evening.

Wednesday, 31 January 1866

Wrote to Bertie. Went to Albert in the evening. He is very kind.

Thursday, 1 February 1866

Heard from Bertie. Bob Holbeche came by the 2 train. I was not able to meet him as I was in with Conington.[144] After lunch I took him down to the river, & shewed him several of the Colleges. He was obliged to leave at 5. I went with him down to the Station. He seemed, poor fellow, rather low & depressed.

Friday, 2 February 1866

Went a walk with Streeten; he took me to Iffley & Littlemore Churches. The former has a very fine Norman Porch. The latter interested me as being the Church that J. H. Newman was to have had.[145] The service is evidently conducted there in a florid style. Enjoyed my walk … [one line cut out here].

141 Charles J. Goodhart (*c.*1803–92), minister of Park Chapel, Chelsea 1852–68, rector of Wetherden, Suffolk 1868–92.

142 Revelation ii. 4.

143 Edward B. Pusey (1800–82), regius professor of Hebrew 1828–82. See Pusey, *The miracles of prayer. A sermon* (Oxford, 1866).

144 John Conington (1825–69), fellow of Corpus 1856–69, Corpus professor of Latin literature 1854–69.

145 John Henry Newman (1801–90), vicar of St Mary's, Oxford 1828–43, built Littlemore church in 1836. He lived at Littlemore from 1842 until his secession to the Church of Rome in 1845.

Sunday, 4 February 1866
The Archbishop of York preached in the morning & Dr Goulbourn in the afternoon.[146] Both were good sermons. The latter was rather argumentative at first, but when he came to the practical part he was grand. Durnford & Horton came to tea. The night was so wet that we did not go to Tonge's.

[Saturday, 3 February 1866]
I find I omitted Saturday. We had a very full & a very delightful prayer meeting. Mr Christopher spoke very beautifully & I never enjoyed him more. We had that lovely hymn, 'When I survey'.[147]

Tuesday, 6 February 1866
Went with Lock to the University Grinds.[148] Saw Walter Chinnery's friend Thornton win the Strangers' Race in fine style[149] … [one line cut out here].
… & we arranged about our meetings.

Thursday, 8 February 1866
Rowed down the River. I am very weak & soon get done. Nevertheless I enjoyed it.

Friday, 9 February 1866
Went a walk with Durnford towards Bagley Wood. He is so kind. In the evening I joined him at Pembroke & he took me to the New Vitality Meeting. Moor of Worcester read the Essay on Prayer. I could not quite understand all his arguments, but the whole Paper seemed good. It did not excite very much discussion. Geldart was present & so was Coles.[150] I hope I shant have to read until after the Long. It must be very nervous work. I really feel very much obliged to Durnford for getting me elected. But I must mind that controversy does not absorb too much of my attention.

Saturday, 10 February 1866
Went & dined with Streeten at Queen's. Was to have gone to Chapel to hear their organ but I was just too late. Punctuality! Afterwards went to Mr Christopher's.

146 William Thomson (1819–90), archbishop of York 1862–90. Edward M. Goulburn (1818–97), vicar of St John's, Paddington, 1859–66, dean of Norwich 1866–89.

147 Isaac Watts, 'When I survey the wondrous cross'.

148 University College athletics.

149 Percy M. Thornton (1841–1918), of Jesus, Cambridge, first secretary of Inter-University sports, M.P. for Battersea (Clapham division) 1892–1910.

150 Vincent Stuckey S. Coles (1845–1929), m. Balliol 1864, librarian of Pusey House, Oxford 1884–97, principal 1897–1909, warden of Community of the Epiphany, Truro 1910–20.

About 100 men were there. General Brown spoke & I liked him extremely.[151] Very practical & very earnest, & very soldierlike were his words. Then we had Mr Fenn[152] & last of all Dr Miller. Of course the great subject was the scarcity of Missionaries. The Speakers were very urgent, & very impressive. Men must be found somewhere. May God direct me what I ought to do. Ought not my prayer to be 'Lord send me'. It is a serious question demanding much thought & much prayers[:] truly a wide door has been opened.

Sunday, 11 February 1866

Went with Lock & heard Dr Miller at Carfax. He preached an excellent Sermon on the 'foolishness of preaching'. He shewed us how God in his wisdom left man to his own intellect for religion & how grievously did the experiment fail. Then concluded with an eloquent discourse on the utility & blessedness of preachness [*sic*]. One remark struck me. 'We must not preach Christianity but Christ.' Charlie Black came in the evening to Corpus. He could not after all come to St Aldate's. Heard Dr M. again in the evening. There was a large congregation & very many University men. He preached from Titus II 11,12,13. He drew the distinction between & the necessity of justification & sanctification very clearly & forcibly.

Monday, 12 February 1866

Gave my breakfast. Knox in for the Boden.[153] Went in the evening to the C.M.S. Meeting at the Town Hall.[154] The room was crowded. The Vice Chancellor took the chair[155] & the Regius Professor of Divinity Payne Smith, Dr Miller, Dr Kay, Dr Cotton, Mr Fenn &c all spoke. The report was read by Mr Litton. The want of missionaries was again pressed upon the earnest consideration of undergraduates. If God would have me to go, oh may I be willing cheerfully to make any sacrifice for his sake. Went to Albert afterwards. Did not get back to College until 11.20.

Tuesday, 13 February 1866

Went a walk with Lock. In the evening we gave our wine. I was glad when it was over. I like L.. Some how I feel drawn to him.

151 Charles A. Browne (*c.*1801–66), army officer in India 1821–64, a leading member of C.M.S.
152 Christopher C. Fenn (*c.*1823–1913), C.M.S. missionary in Ceylon 1851–63, general secretary of C.M.S. 1864–94.
153 The Boden scholarship 'for proficiency in the Sanskrit language and literature'.
154 Annual meeting of the Oxford auxiliary of C.M.S.
155 John P. Lightfoot (1803–87), rector of Exeter 1854–87, vice-chancellor 1862–6.

Wednesday, 14 February 1866

Ash Wednesday. Knox & Lock commonized with me. K. proxime accessit for the Boden. Poor fellow he was rather disappointed. Received a long letter from Bertie.

Friday, 16 February 1866

Rained again. Went with Mylne & Knox to the Magdalen Grinds.[156] We had to cross several fields & the mud was appalling. Phelps came into my room at 11 p.m. & stayed talking until 1.[157]

Saturday, 17 February 1866

Felt somewhat loathe to get up. Consequently had little time for my Devotions. Oh Lord help me to be more earnest & prayerful. Breakfasted at Exeter with Black. P. kept swearing but alas I had not the moral courage to speak to him openly & directly. In the afternoon went down the Cherwell in a dingy. Knox in another accompanied me. Was very much startled & awed in the evening at Mr C.'s meeting to hear that General Brown had dropped down dead. He fell in harness returning from a meeting of the C.M.S.. Devoted soldier the summons, I doubt not found thee ready. Thy words, spoken but a week ago, words of earnest, loving, thrilling import come back to my mind. I cannot realize it, his voice seems even now to be ringing in my ears. And now he has gone. Oh Lord teach me to prepare to die. Mr C. also mentioned a Worcester man named Barnes who had died this week.[158] He had been a regular attendant at the prayer meeting. Our gathering was indeed a solemn one. I could not listen as I would … [two pages torn out here].[159]

… to see it. Let me thank God that I have still so many, many dear ones left.

Friday, 23 February 1866

Felt lonely & weary at times & often my heart would ache as I thought of what had happened. Went on the Pembroke barge again. Corpus kept its place. In the evening went to the N. V.. Duggan of Lincoln read a paper on 'the want of a cheap Church literature'.[160] Went afterwards to hear Dean Alford.[161] The church

156 Magdalen College athletics.

157 Edward R. Phelps (1846–1909), m. Corpus 1865, various curacies.

158 Robert Barnes (1841–66), m. Worcester 1861.

159 Chavasse was romantically attracted to 'Euphrosyne', who died in February 1866 (see Introduction). His various reflections on her death have been torn or cut out of the diary.

160 William B. Duggan (1844–1904), m. Lincoln 1864, vicar of St Paul's, Oxford 1871–1904.

161 Henry Alford (1810–71), dean of Canterbury 1857–71. See Alford, 'The coming in of the Son of Man – his conflict and victory', in Samuel Wilberforce *et al.*, *The conflict of Christ in his church with spiritual wickedness in high places. Sermons preached during the season of Lent,*

was crowded. It was inexpressibly solemn to hear that lovely hymn Rock of Ages sung.[162] We had a very fine Sermon. One sentence struck me. 'The cross of Christ is the centre of the world's history[:] to it all before converge, & all that happened afterwards radiate.' Went to Albert at 9 p.m.

Saturday, 24 February 1866

Got up with a heavy heart & throughout the whole morning felt more or less depressed. Dear Miri sent me a short letter of comfort. How hard it is to keep one's grief locked up in the heart & not to pour it into some friendly bosom. Durnford & Horton came to Lunch. Corpus was bumped by Ch. Ch. in the Torpids – a sad day's sport. Wrote to Tom. In the evening went to Christopher's meeting. The room was crowded. Mr Hathaway gave us a beautiful address from St John XV 1–8 chiefly on the Union with Xt.[163]

Sunday, 25 February 1866

Blessed day of rest. Went to hear Mr Hathaway at St Aldate's. I think I like his address better than his Sermon. Lunched with Poole & Moore.[164] Barker of B.N.C. was there.[165] Came away about 3.45. Returned to them again at 6 & started for Hinksey – four of us in all. Poole, Barker, Elsmere of Ch. Ch. & myself.[166] Only two or three people were present at the little School Room & about 8 children. Barker read some of the Church Prayers. I read 1 Peter II & Poole gave the address. I don't think he was quite enough illustrative to interest his hearers. Left my Bible behind. Met Durnford & Horton at St Aldate's, & we went to Tonge's. I enjoyed the meeting more … [seven lines cut out here].

Monday, 26 February 1866

My alarum will not awake me. I must try some other means. Ran down with the Torpid. The path was tolerably dry going up but as we rushed back the wave from the passing boats flooded it, & we were obliged to run thro' mud & water. I got very wet & splashed. No bumps were made. Pembroke ran us close but we succeeded in escaping. Wrote to my Mother. Went to Albert & did not get back

1866, in Oxford (Oxford, 1866).

162 Augustus Toplady, 'Rock of ages, cleft for me'.

163 Edward P. Hathaway (1818–97), barrister, founder in 1864 of the Oxford Churches Trust, rector of St Ebbe's, Oxford 1868–73, of Holbrook, Suffolk, 1885–92.

164 John Poole (*c.* 1845–66), m. Christ Church 1862. Charles R. Moore (1844–1920), m. Corpus 1863, master at Radley College 1868–78, land agent.

165 Peter Barker (*c.* 1847–1937), m. Brasenose 1865, curate of South Hinksey 1870–2, vicar of St John's, Bromley 1881–1931.

166 Clement Elsmere (1847–1908), m. Christ Church 1865, vicar of St John's, Spitalgate, Grantham 1879–1908.

to college until 11.40. He advises me to go in for the C.C.C. Scholarships ... [seven lines cut out here, one page torn out].

...[167] [one page torn out].

... to the prayer meeting. Poor Mary has lost her baby.[168] And thus death seems on every side. Oh Lord let me dedicate myself to thee more fully. Let me not seek my own pleasure but thy glory. Sanctify my heart by affliction.

Sunday, 4 March 1866

Went to hear Liddon in the morning[:] the church was crowded.[169] His sermon occupied an hour & a half. It was very eloquent & learned, but many parts I could not quite understand. In the evening went with Moore & Poole to Hincksey. Moore gave the address. It was very plain & practical. The audience was somewhat small. Went to Tonge's on my return. Durnford was there & I wished him good-bye as he goes down tomorrow. Dear fellow I could not help thanking him for all his kindness to me. He has been more like a brother.

Tuesday, 6 March 1866

James came by the 5.10 train.[170] I went to meet the 3.10 but he had missed it. He dined with Albert at University, & afterwards they both came to tea with me. The Ireland began.[171] Lock & Knox in. James slept at a house in the Turle where I got him a bed.

Wednesday, 7 March 1866

James breakfasted with me. Albert was to have come, but did not. Lunched at University. Albert then shewed us the Chapel & Library. Afterwards we went to Magdalene & New Chapels; I had never seen the latter & it delighted me. James called on the Vicechancellor, & dined with me in the evening. Afterwards [*sic*] dinner he slept while I worked.

167 Here Chavasse begins a new notebook.

168 Herbert N. Chavasse, son of Nicholas and Mary Chavasse, died on 24 February 1866, aged 4 months.

169 Henry P. Liddon (1829–90), prebendary of Salisbury 1864–70, Dean Ireland professor of exegesis 1870–82, canon of St Paul's 1870–90. He delivered the Bampton Lectures for 1866, published as *The divinity of our lord and saviour Jesus Christ* (London, 1867).

170 Chavasse's cousin, James J. C. Wyld (1845–1907), barrister, deputy judge of county court. He graduated from Trinity Hall, Cambridge, but was admitted at Oxford 'comitatis causa' on 8 March 1866.

171 Examination for the Dean Ireland scholarship 'for the promotion of classical learning and taste'.

Thursday, 8 March 1866

James breakfasted at C.C.C. Our Scratch fours came off in the afternoon. I coxed Mylne, Weitbretcht [*sic*], Hilton & Collier.[172] We were on the in-side. Woodward steered the boat in the middle[173] & Molyneux was stroke of the third. We kept second the whole way until within about 150 yds from the post Woodward who was leading finding his crew exhausted, fouled us purposely & so Molyneux rowed in as he liked. It was very provoking as Molyneux won the final heat beating both Evans (2) & Bridges.

Friday, 9 March 1866

Breakfasted with Albert & James at University. Medd was there.[174] Went to the New Vitality. Ward read a portion of an Essay against the Eternity of Future Punishment.[175] I was surprised to hear it from him. Afterwards went & heard Carter, & was much disappointed.[176] Then on to Albert & then down to the Station to meet Walter Chinnery. I was obliged to get him a bed at the Randolph for one night. Introduced the two cousins who had never seen one another before. Strange!

Saturday, 10 March 1866

Gave a small breakfast in the morning. Went to meet the Cambridge train at 1. Bertie did not come. The Sports passed off very well.[177] Colmore & Vidal were equal for the 100 yds.[178] Laing beat Lawes for the mile, & afterwards amidst frantic excitement ran a dead heat with Long for the 2 miles.[179] James left by the 8.40 train. A great row at the Station. Lamps smashed & so on. Voted for

172 John H. M. Weitbrecht (later Weitbrecht-Edwardes) (b. 1843), m. Corpus 1862, barrister. Walter K. Hilton (1845–1913), m. Corpus 1865, registrar of Durham University, bursar of University College, Durham.

173 Herbert H. Woodward (1847–1909), m. Corpus 1865, musical composer, precentor of Worcester cathedral 1890–1909.

174 Peter G. Medd (1829–1908), fellow of University 1852–77, rector of North Cerney, Cirencester 1876–1908.

175 Charles H. C. Ward (1844–1926), m. Exeter 1863, private tutor.

176 Thomas T. Carter (1808–1901), rector of Clewer 1844–80, founder of Clewer sisterhood. See Carter, 'Aids in the conflict – God's heavenly host' in Wilberforce, *Conflict of Christ*.

177 Annual Oxford versus Cambridge athletics.

178 Robert W. Vidal (1843–1911), m. St John's 1862, vicar of Bayford, Herts. 1881–1902.

179 John W. Laing (b. *c.* 1846), m. Christ Church 1865. Charles B. Lawes (later Lawes-Wittewronge) (1843–1911), m. Trinity, Cambridge, 1862, athlete and sculptor, first president of the Incorporated Society of British Sculptors 1904. Charles H. K. Long (1845–1910), m. Trinity, Cambridge, 1864, vicar of Swinderby, Lincs. 1876–1910.

MacKinnon at the Union.[180] Gent of Trinity got the Ireland.[181] Could not go to Mr C.'s meeting.

Sunday, 11 March 1866

Breakfasted with Albert. Faulkner there.[182] Then heard Liddon.[183] The Church was crammed & we got very indifferent places. It was a very eloquent & learned Sermon. In the afternoon walked off to the service at Littlemore Church. Walter went by the Evening train. I did not like it [at] all. He said he could not get into town sufficiently early on Monday. Went to the meeting at Tonge's.

Tuesday, 13 March 1866

Scholarship Examination began. Cunningham & Collier in.[184] Went down the river with Lock. All lectures knocked off for this week.

Wednesday, 14 March 1866

Lunched with Mrs Honey & went for a short walk with Mr H. afterwards. Wrote several letters at the Union. In the evening went to Albert.

Thursday, 15 March 1866

Streeten dined with me. Afterwards attended a meeting at Wadham respecting the Tract Distribution Society.[185] The attendance was not large. I am [sorry?] its affairs are in some confusion – the effect of having a careless secretary. I am to have a district with an older man named Smith.[186] Praised be God that he thus opens these paths for me.

Friday, 16 March 1866

Went to the New Vitality. Russell of Wadham read a paper on St Bernard.[187] It shewed a great amount of reading & was evidently the production of a deeply

180 Campbell Mackinnon (b. *c.* 1843), m. Queen's 1862, incumbent of Port Royal, Jamaica, seceded to Church of Rome 1879. In March 1866 Mackinnon was a candidate for presidency of the Oxford Union Society, but polled third with 144 votes, behind George Simcox (261 votes) and George E. Gardiner of Brasenose (189 votes).

181 John Gent (1844–1927), m. Trinity 1863, fellow 1869–86, barrister, judge of county court in Halifax and Cornwall.

182 Charles J. Faulkner (1834–92), fellow of University 1856–92, mathematician.

183 Liddon's second Bampton.

184 Edward J. Cunningham (1846–1921), m. Corpus 1865, headmaster of King's School, Peterborough 1882–97, vicar of St Paul's, Worthing 1902–21.

185 Oxford University Tract Distribution Society (O.U.T.D.S.).

186 Charles D. Smith (1844–1923), m. Wadham 1863, rector of Didsbury, Lancs. 1881–93.

187 Herbert D. Russell (1844–67), m. Wadham 1862.

earnest mind carried away by the apparent romance of a monkish life in the Middle Ages.

Saturday, 17 March 1866

Jeudwine, Lindsell, Tupper, Channing & Russell elected scholars.[188] Coxed a four down the river. In the evening went with Knox to Mr C.'s meeting. But alas my mind was wandering, & I lost much of the address & prayer.

Sunday, 18 March 1866

Breakfasted with Moor; Eagleson [*sic*] there.[189] Heard Goulburn in the morning on the distinction between 'Imagination & Faith' & French in the afternoon;[190] both were beautiful Sermons. Went to New Hincksey – attendance again small. Attended Tonge's class. Barker brought Bazley [*sic*] who I think will attend regularly next term.[191] Moor came as well. I wish they wd keep more to the subject & not argue on extraneous subjects.

Monday, 19 March 1866

Collections began.[192] Called on Mrs Honey & at the Press. Knox came to tea. Glad to get home. Oh how merciful God is to enrich me with so many blessings. Would that my heart were more grateful.

Tuesday, 20 March 1866

In for viva voce. My paper tolerable – not so well as I expected. A timely warning. Came away by the 5.20 train & reached Wylde Green a little after 8 p.m. Papa & Hodgson met me at the Station.[193] How kind of them to turn out on so cold a night. Safely anchored at home again. What must it be to have reached one's eternal home in heaven. Oh to look forward to that day with more joy & hope. Felt distressed when I thought that one dearest one was gone since I last left Sutton. My sorrow recurs to me from time to time & I cannot but grieve inwardly. Miriam still at Rushall. Thank God for another term safely passed.

188 George W. Jeudwine (1849–1933), fellow of Queen's 1870–6, rector of Harlaxton 1889–1913, archdeacon of Lincoln 1913–25. William H. B. Lindsell (1848–96), barrister and journalist. Charles L. Tupper (1848–1910), civil servant in the Punjab. Francis C. Channing (1848–1925), civil servant and judge in the Punjab 1870–95. Spencer C. Russell (1847–73), fellow of Corpus 1870–3.

189 Thomas A. Eaglesim (1840–94), at Worcester 1864–7, curate of St Paul's, Oxford 1871–7, seceded to Church of Rome 1878, priest of Birmingham Oratory.

190 Thomas V. French (1825–91), C.M.S. missionary in India, rector of St Ebbe's, Oxford 1874–7, bishop of Lahore 1877–87.

191 Henry C. B. Bazely (1842–83), m. Brasenose 1861, evangelist.

192 'Collections' were the end of term college examinations.

193 Chavasse's brother, J. Hodgson Chavasse (1856–1906).

Wednesday, 21 March 1866

Walked up to Sutton to see A. S; he was out. Mrs S. in.[194] Saw Bee. He walked home part of the way with me. Called on G. but no one was at home. Met Sarah afterwards.[195] Was very pleased to hear that Galliers was much better & had been at work for the last fortnight.

Thursday, 22 March 1866

Bob Colmore came to spend a few days.[196] He has been very ill, & looks very sadly indeed. He has been sent to me for some object. But I am so great a coward. My lips seemed sealed when I wd talk on spiritual things. Oh Lord loose my tongue.

Saturday, 24 March 1866

Walked up & saw Albert Smith. Had a short talk with him. He wants me to go in for a scholarship. Is it advisable to unsettle myself? May God direct me. Saw Cull.[197] He looks unwell. I am sure he has been working too hard.

Sunday, 25 March 1866

Went to the Sunday School with Miss Ray.[198] Saw Mr Robinson. Boys tolerably quiet. Had two very nice Sermons. Walked in the afternoon.

Monday, 26 March 1866

Oxford won the boat race.[199] I thought we should. In the afternoon walked down to the Green Lanes School & took a class. I never feel my own ignorance so fully, as when I sit down to teach others. Wrote to Knox & Bertie.

Tuesday, 27 March 1866

Maggie, Fanny & Manny came to dinner.[200] T. V. H. & Charlie dropped in to tea. Had music & squails.[201] Walked part of the way home with Vincent.

194 Frances E. Smith née Taylor, wife of Albert Smith.

195 Sarah Galliers, wife of Edward Galliers.

196 Robert L. Colmore (b. 1849), pupil at Sutton Coldfield Grammar School 1861–7, emigrated to U.S.A.

197 John B. Cull (1850–1902), pupil at Sutton Coldfield Grammar School 1862–8, at Balliol 1870–3.

198 Elizabeth Ray (later Goode) (b. *c.* 1844).

199 Annual Oxford versus Cambridge boat race, on Saturday, 24 March.

200 G. Mainwaring Robinson (1850–1920), son of Rev. Gilbert Robinson, m. Christ's, Cambridge 1869, solicitor, emigrated in 1893 to Rondebosch, Cape Town.

201 Squails was a table game which involved propelling discs with the palm of the hand towards a central mark.

Wednesday, 28 March 1866

Went into B'ham by the 2.20 train & out by the 4.20. Met Miss Holbeche & Mr Eddowes.[202] Felt irritable, & gave way to a miserable attack of discontent. Alas how wicked is my heart & how deceitful. May God forgive me, for my sins are indeed many.

Thursday, 29 March 1866

Walked over to Rushall. Mamma brought Ada in the carriage. Fanny seemed pretty tolerable & was cheerful.[203] Saw Miriam. I seemed to remember everything again. But oh! it is wicked to brood over sorrow. If Jesus be mine what need I more. Ludovic very well. I borrowed Spencer Thornton's Life & he gave me a copy of 'Kemble's Hymns' which are used at St Aldate's.[204] Came over in the carriage. Had a nice talk with Mamma.

Friday, 30 March 1866

Good Friday. A solemn day indeed. Went to church in the morning & evening. My thoughts wandering. Alas my heart must be worldly indeed when not even the remembrance of my Blessed Lord's Passion & Death could rivet my attention. Dedicated myself anew to God. Oh may he help to devote myself to his service. Read part of Spencer Thornton's Life. What a good man he was, & how young was he when he enrolled himself under Xt's banner. Would that I had a tithe of his faith, or love, or zeal. Felt more interested in his life than usual because he was a man of but *ordinary* abilities, & consequently his example seemed to speak more forcibly, & seemed more real. The subjects of Xtian biographies are generally so clever, that we of moderate talent must look & wonder & admire from a distance – per transennam pretereuntes strictim aspiciendi sumus.[205]

Sunday, 1 April 1866

Easter Sunday. Went to the School. Did not interest my boys as I shd like to have done. Such a glorious theme & oh so coldly treated. Received the Sacrament after the Morning Service. May God help me to fulfil the resolutions I made at his holy Table. May he help me to stedfastly purpose to lead a new life. Bob Colmore left yesterday so that I had my evening to myself.

202 Thomas S. Eddowes (*c.*1826–1903), solicitor.

203 Frances M. Chavasse née Bartlett (*c.*1837–1920), wife of Ludovic Chavasse.

204 William R. Fremantle, *Memoir of the Rev. Spencer Thornton* (London, 1850); Charles Kemble, *A selection of psalms and hymns, arranged for the public services of the Church of England* (London, 1853).

205 'We, passing by, should be looked at briefly through the lattice window'. Cf. 'per transennam praetereuntes strictim aspeximus'. Cicero, *De Oratore* 1.35.162.

Monday, 2 April 1866

Walked over to Witton & called on Mrs Shyrte.[206] She seemed very glad to see me. She was not much changed. I thought she looked a shade more sorrowful than when I was at School. Tiger went with me & I left him at the gate. When I came out he had gone & was nowhere to be seen. All Enquiries were fruitless & when I reached home I found he was not there. When I had almost given up the idea of seeing him again, he quietly trotted into the yard. Keble dead.[207]

Tuesday, 3 April 1866

Weatherley Phipson & Binney Smallwood came over from Stechford in the morning in time for dinner.[208] In the afternoon we went for a walk in the Park. They returned home after tea. I walked with them as far as Passe Hayes.

Wednesday, 4 April 1866

Albert came by the 4.20 train. I went down to meet the 2.50 but he had missed it.

Thursday, 5 April 1866

Went over the Hotel with Albert. It closes on Saturday. After Lunch walked to the Witton Cemetary [*sic*] & called on Fanny on our way home, to get out of the rain. Vincent Holbeche dropped in during the evening & played a rubber. I have made up my mind by God's help to give up cards. Maggie, Miri & Ada came home.

Friday, 6 April 1866

Albert went by the 10.45 train. He is a very kind fellow, & I shall miss him much when he goes down after the Long.

Saturday, 7 April 1866

Went & dined at Mr Smallwood's. Afterwards wandered thro' the fields & had some fun. Played quoits. I am a wretched player. My Father brought me in the carriage & I walked home leaving Stechford about 7.35.

Sunday, 8 April 1866

Felt calm & peaceful. Blessed by God. My heart seemed to warm towards my boys. Praised be the Lord. Oh that I may speak to them with more fervour & love, as a dying soul to dying souls. Mr Thwaite [*sic*] a curate from Birmingham read

206 Mary Shyrte (*c.*1793–1886), principal of boys' preparatory school at Witton Hall, Witton, near Sutton Coldfield. Chavasse studied there before being sent to Chesterfield Grammar School.

207 John Keble (1792–1866), vicar of Hursley, Hants. 1836–66, figurehead of the 'Catholic Revival'.

208 The nickname, probably, of Henry W. Smallwood (1851–1934), m. Trinity, Cambridge 1870, solicitor. Phipson and Smallwood were cousins.

the service & preached in the morning.[209] Mr Robinson was laid up with influenza. In the afternoon we had Mr Milward from Nechells.[210] His sermon was a beautiful one on 'an abundant entrance into Heaven'. After service called & saw John Brown & Charlie Izon. Walked home with Miriam. Talked to her about the subject that was nearest my heart. It somewhat grieved me. I thought my grief had almost passed away, but still it is there, & strongly too.

Monday, 9 April 1866
Went into Birmingham & had my photograph taken. It was a gloomy day & I fear they will not be very good.

Tuesday, 10 April 1866
My Father poorly. I went to Mr Dixon's in his place. Only the Lloyds were there. Cards were produced after dinner. It was hard work to say no, but God helped me. Poor Miss Dixon had a fit. The thought struck me suppose she had died at the card table. Terrible, terrible.

Wednesday, 11 April 1866
Went to Charlie's & dined. T. V. H. came in to tea. Cards again proposed but I lodged my objections. May God aid me in taking a decided course. Walked with Vincent down to the Chester Road Station, & then made the best of my way home.

Thursday, 12 April 1866
Negligent & cold in my morning devotions & late for Prayers. Felt consequently languid for much of the morning. Oh that I may pray more earnestly & may read my Bible with more love, more faith, more attention. Went down to Vincent H.'s in the evening. Saw Yates in the train. Mr H. not well. Went after tea to the Reading Room & then up to Miss Holbeche's. Came home about 10.

Friday, 13 April 1866
My last day at home. Went to see Mr R. in the morning. He asked me several questions about Mr C. & Oxford. Dear man, may God preserve him. I do indeed owe him much. In the afternoon Papa & Mamma started for Worcester. My Father looked poorly. After tea called on Lakin & Galliers. The latter looked wonderfully

209 Henry G. Thwaites (*c.* 1840–1914), curate of St Clement's, Nechells, Birmingham 1863–7, vicar of St Mark's, Birmingham 1867–77, of St John's, Carisbrooke 1880–91, of Christ Church, Harrow Road 1891–1903, of Limber Magna, Lincs. 1903–14.

210 Henry C. Milward (1831–96), vicar of St Clement's, Nechells, Birmingham 1862–79.

well. Dined with Albert Smith. Dear Bal & Brown there.[211] It was very kind of him having them in. Had a long talk with him. He said I ought to get a first in Mods. But I feel that I am not up to the mark. Alas I am at times assailed with discontented thoughts. I shd like in my own vain, foolish, short-sighted mind, to be clever, & tall & better looking. My uncouth ungainly diminutive form actually troubles me. Oh Lord is not thy name Love! Hast thou not made all things well? Give oh give me a contented submissive spirit. Despicable though I may be in the eyes of men, grant that my sole object may be to seek to glorify thee. Though I am not cut out for society, does not this seem to point to my future lot in life? Nay! was it not said of my Master 'when ye shall see him, there shall be no beauty that ye shall desire in him.'[212] Is the servant above his Lord? Came over in the carriage which came up to Sutton to fetch Maggie & Miriam from Miss Bracken's. And so ends my Easter Vac. Another term is before me. May God be my guide & keeper.

Saturday, 14 April 1866

Drove into town in the carriage with Maggie & Miriam. Met Bussell at the Snow Hill Station. Reached Oxford at 5.20 in time for Hall. Went to the Union & wrote home & to Worcester. Went to Mr C.'s meeting. Thirteen were present. Among them Durnford & Moor. Called at Albert's rooms but he was engaged. Knox came in to tea afterwards. Went to Bed about 12.30.

Sunday, 15 April 1866

Got up about 7 a.m.. I awoke quite naturally notwithstanding my laziness during the Vac. Went & Heard Liddon in the morning.[213] Read by myself during the afternoon. In the evening went with Knox to St Aldate's. Mr Christopher preached. His subject was St Paul's preaching at Corinth. Went to Tonge's afterwards. Bazley & Barker there & Stewart.[214] Durnford & Horton did not come. Came away about 10 p.m.

211 William Ballenden (b. 1851) and Robert Brown (b. 1849), pupils at Sutton Coldfield Grammar School. On Ballenden, Chavasse writes: 'I quite consider him as my younger brother. May God help me to bring him into the right way. He talks about being a soldier. God grant that he be a soldier of the cross' (20 May 1865). Elsewhere he comments: 'Oh! that he may be brought to a knowledge of his precious Redeemer', 'Oh that he knew where true happiness can only be found' (22 Aug., 8 Sept. 1865).

212 Isaiah liii. 2.

213 Liddon's third Bampton.

214 ? Robert M. Stewart (*c.* 1844–76), m. Worcester 1862, principal of Bishop's College, Calcutta 1873–6.

Monday, 16 April 1866

Lunched with Albert & made arrangements for going to him during the term. He advises me to go in for Oriel. Ground hard.

Tuesday, 17 April 1866

Felt for the first time rather lonely when I got up. Heard from Mag. Went down the river in a dingy. The weather very beautiful. Took some work to Albert in the afternoon, but felt low & unwell.

Wednesday, 18 April 1866

Felt so well. Thank God for it. The magnificent weather made me feel quite buoyant. Oh how can I thank my heavenly Father sufficiently.

Thursday, 19 April 1866

Still felt well; got up about 6 & so got an hour's work before chapel. Went to the meeting of the Tract Distribution Society at Caulfield's [*sic*] rooms.[215] Smith came up & spoke to me after it was over. He promised to take me to my district on Monday.

Saturday, 21 April 1866

Went in the evening to Mr Christopher's meeting. Asked several of the men to go with me. They all refused. Alas does not the fault lie with me. Oh for more earnestness. Mr Knott spoke & gave us a very pleasant address.[216]

Sunday, 22 April 1866

Liddon preached the Fourth Bampton. The church was crowded as usual. In the afternoon went to the meeting at Queen's[:] they were held in Kitson's rooms. He has changed since I last saw him. Horton read an essay & acquitted himself very well. In the evening went to St Aldate's. Did not go to Tonge's for I felt too tired. Collier came into my room late & had some tea.

Monday, 23 April 1866

A delightful day. Went with Brookes in the evening & put down our names for the Oriel Scholarship. The Provost was a kind old man, but somewhat particular.[217]

215 Francis W. Caulfeild (1843–1934), at Wadham 1863–6, school manager in London.

216 John W. Knott (1822–70), vicar of St Saviour's, Leeds 1851–9, of Roxeth 1862–6, of East Ham 1866–8. Originally a tractarian sympathizer, he went to India with C.M.S. in 1869.

217 Edward Hawkins (1789–1882), provost of Oriel 1828–82.

Tuesday, 24 April 1866

Scholarship Exam began at 9.20. There are 19 candidates. In the Morning had Essays. Did the Paper tolerably. In the afternoon from 2 until 5 Latin Prose. My production very poor. In the evening Divinity which was easy. Thank God that he has helped thro' one day.

Wednesday, 25 April 1866

Had three papers again. Latin Verse (I had two false quantities in my copy), Greek Translation & Iambics. Breakfasted with Streeten at his new lodgings. As it is a Saint's day[218] he is going with a friend to Burford & Witney. The Lifeboat was launched with great eclat. Mrs Lightfoot named it 'The Isis'.[219] God speed it, I say for its work is a most noble & glorious one. The heat very oppressive.

Thursday, 26 April 1866

Brooks in for viva voce. I was not. God knows what is best for me. Although Albert had told me that my chance was very poor, I had still entertained some lingering hopes that I might be elected. I had done better than I expected & I certainly thought that I should be in for viva voce. The blow was sharp for the time. My pride rebelled. Lord I would bow. It is all in thy good pleasure. There is some wise reason for it; let that thought comfort me. Thank God. I think I can now look up to him with a love less bound to earth than before. He has taken from me that wherein I trusted. Blessed be his name. I must throw myself wholly on him.

Friday, 27 April 1866

The last day of the Scholarship. I went & did the Greek Prose, & hurried away again in time for Furneaux' lecture. In the afternoon rowed down the Cherwell. It was capital fun.

Saturday, 28 April 1866

Munro & Weidman elected.[220] Wrote home to my Father & told him the result, & dropped a line to Albert Smith. Went to the prayer meeting in the evening but I felt so weary that I could scarcely keep awake. Oh Lord do help me to watch & pray.

218 St Mark's day.

219 The lifeboat 'Isis', a gift by Oxford University to the National Lifeboat Institution, was to be stationed at Hayle on the coast of Cornwall. It was named by Louisa Lightfoot, wife of the vice chancellor.

220 Alexander Monro (1847–1916), m. Oriel 1866, Indian civil service, fellow of Madras University, mayor of Godalming 1909–11. George L. Weidemann (*c.* 1848–1907), m. Oriel 1866, Indian civil service.

Sunday, 29 April 1866

Did not go to the University Sermon.[221] In the afternoon read my paper on 'Baptism' at Queen's. I was obliged to hurry thro' it & I was not satisfied with the production. Durnford afterwards read a portion of his. In the evening went to St Aldate's but I felt drowsy. I must really have my dinner in the middle of the day. At 9 went to Tonge's. Barker & Stewart were there. Had a delightful meeting. Felt troubled at what occurred in the morning. At J.'s request I accompanied him to the early Communion at St Mary's.[222] I found however that it was frequented by men of the Highest Church Principles & I was quite uncomfortable throughout the whole service. Alas I derived but little comfort from it. I seemed to be compromising myself. I told J. plainly afterwards that I could not come again & he seemed rather hurt.

Monday, 30 April 1866

Breakfasted with Ward. He is an extremely nice fellow. Went a long walk with Sc. to Shotover.[223] We talked on religious subjects. Alas he is an Unitarian & holds views which I knew were wrong but which I could not prove to be such. How ignorant I feel, how small seems my knowledge of Scripture when I come to argue with earnest men who are so sadly mistaken. Oh that God may make me love & search my Bible more & more daily.

Tuesday, 1 May 1866

May day. But so cold & dreary. I resumed my winter clothing, & had a fire again. Breakfasted with Elsmere. He has a very good room. We had lectures as usual.

Wednesday, 2 May 1866

Breakfasted with Scholefield.[224] A cold raw day again.

Thursday, 3 May 1866

Went with Smith of Wadham to our District. He kindly took me round to my houses. I have about 30 in all. May God grant that I may be of some use in this neglected hamlet. In the evening went to the debate.[225] Lord Hervey was the first

221 Liddon's fifth Bampton.

222 ? Walter Jacobson.

223 Charles Scott.

224 Stuart C. Scholefield (1842–94), m. Worcester 1861, various curacies, emigrated to British Columbia in 1887.

225 Union Society debate on whether 'the Ministry has unwisely introduced and unscrupulously forwarded a measure which threatens to change the form of our Government', concerning the Reform Bill for extending the franchise.

speaker.[226] He succeeded pretty well but the beginning & end of his speech were better than the middle. Some day I shd think he wd take a distinguished place in Parliament.

Friday, 4 May 1866
Went for a walk with Ward. He is an exceedingly nice fellow. The more I know of him, the more I like him.

Wednesday, 9 May 1866
First day of the Boat races.[227] I went to the start. Corpus caught Trinity in the Gut in splendid style. Our boat has improved wonderfully. The weather delightful, & the banks & barges crowded with spectators.

Thursday, 10 May 1866
Another delightful day. Rowed down to Iffley with Knox. Ascension Day but alas my heart felt so little joyful at the thought of my ascended Redeemer. Am I not getting formal & dull in my devotions? is not my zeal flagging, my love growing cold? Quicken me with thy spirit, Holy Father. Yesterday went with Smith to Hincksey. Left tracts at several of the houses[:] in fact at most. A few were closed. Went in & prayed with one. Never do I feel my own ignorance, weakness & want of faith & love more than when I am speaking to or praying with others. Without Xt I can do nothing – oh may he strengthen me. In the evening Corpus contrary to our exspectation [*sic*] bumped Exeter at the Cherwell. The race was well contested, & the cheering great.

Friday, 11 May 1866
Corpus bumped Brazenose & so we are head of the river. The excitement was tremendous. Bridges was carried along on the shoulders of the men. Went to Albert at 9 p.m..

Saturday, 12 May 1866
Our triumph was of short duration. Our men nervous & flurried got off badly & were bumped again with comparative ease. Rather provoking to go down so soon. Went to Mr C.'s meeting. There was a good attendance. Went a walk with Albert.

226 Francis Hervey (1846–1931), son of marquess of Bristol, m. Balliol 1865, M.P. for Bury St Edmunds 1874–80, 1885–92.

227 'Eights Week'.

Sunday, 13 May 1866

Liddon preached in the morning;[228] the Church was as usual crowded. Read Magee's Sermon on the Atonement.[229] It is very fine. Charlie B. & a friend dropped in during the afternoon & remained talking for nearly an hour. I wish he wd choose some other day for his calls. In the evening went to St Aldate's. At 9 went to Tonge's. Bazeley there. His remarks were very good.

Monday, 14 May 1866

Poor Miss Ray has lost her father & young Smith is dead.[230] Death has been busy about Sutton. Oh that I may be prepared. Steered a four down to Sandford. In the races University did not succeed in catching Corpus, but Corpus amid great cheers got within a few feet of Brazenose. I hope we shall catch them tomorrow.

Tuesday, 15 May 1866

Another lovely day. Went with Smith to Hincksey. Had to hurry back to go to Albert's at 4. Boat races continued – but still no change.

Wednesday, 16 May 1866

Went down to Sandford with Scott, Jacobson, Ilbert & Hilton. Intended to have gone to the Prayer meeting but got back too late.[231] I must really try to manage better. Corpus not so near to Brazenose at the finish.

Thursday, 17 May 1866

Rowed down the river in a dingy. Went to Albert at 4 p.m.. Put Pearson in the Boat instead of B.. A very hard race between the first three boats. Corpus got nearer to Brazenose, & University pressed Corpus very hard. Bridges wd not have a bump supper; he deserves the thanks of the college.

Friday, 18 May 1866

Went for a walk with Scott. There is very much I like in him. Again intended to have gone to the Prayer Meeting & again was too late.[232] If I had been going to a coach could I not have got back in time? I think so. At 7 p.m. went to the New Vitality meeting in Ward's rooms. Bazeley read an Essay of Durnford's on the meaning of the word Regeneration. Wrote to Bertie.

228 Liddon's seventh Bampton.

229 William C. Magee, 'The relation of the atonement to the divine justice', *The sermons and addresses delivered at a conference of clergy of the diocese of Oxford* (London, 1861), pp. 33–52. See Bodleian MS Chavasse dep. 30, pp. 1–8: Chavasse's sermon notes 1866–9.

230 John Ray (*c.* 1800–66), farmer; William Smith (*c.* 1833–66), chemist and grocer.

231 An undergraduate prayer meeting was held twice a week.

232 On Friday afternoons, Henry Linton held a regular meeting for missionary intercession.

Saturday, 19 May 1866

Heard Woodward's Exercise called 'the Light of the World'. The Music School was full, & I thought the music itself very good. At 5.30 went a delightful walk with Lock thro' Bagley Wood & home by Kennington. I enjoyed it thoroughly. L. is a dear fellow. Oh that I could open my heart more to him & strive to lead him in the narrow way. Went to Mr C.'s meeting. It was delightful. I did indeed enjoy it. Next Saturday we are to meet at his house. Mr Dallas is to deliver the address.[233] 'Be resolute', said dear Mr C.. Ah! that is what I want to be – more earnestness more love.

Sunday, 20 May 1866

Heard the Bishop in the morning[234] on the sin against the Holy Ghost & Dr Pusey in the afternoon. The latter has rather a monotonous delivery which mars what is in reality a very good Sermon. Went with Knox to the Sacrament at St Aldate's. How the High Church men do put me to shame by their zeal. J. had induced three or four men to accompany him to the early Communion at St Mary's. Went in the evening to Tonge. Bazley there again. Had a very pleasant meeting. Came away about 10.15. May God indeed pour down upon me his blessed Spirit, for I do indeed long & thirst for a nearer walk with him.

Monday, 21 May 1866

Called on the Halls but they were at dinner. Read pretty hard.

Tuesday, 22 May 1866

Gave a small out-college breakfast. In the afternoon went with Smith to Hincksey. Was very shocked to learn that poor Mrs Dingle had died suddenly.[235] How my conscience reproached me. It was only last Wednesday that I had seen her apparently in perfect health & now she was a corpse. Alas I had let slip the opportunity of speaking a word in season, or of even praying with her. May God grant that I may profit by this lesson. Endeavoured to impress upon some of my people, the uncertainty of life, the nearness of death. How weak & worthless & ignorant I feel when talking to another concerning the things which concern his eternal welfare. May God strengthen me with his Holy Spirit for Christ's sake.

233 Alexander R. C. Dallas (1791–1869), rector of Wonston, Hants. 1828–69, founder in 1843 of the Society for Irish Church Missions.

234 Samuel Wilberforce (1805–73), bishop of Oxford 1845–69, of Winchester 1869–73.

235 Martha Dingle (*c.* 1792–1866).

Wednesday, 23 May 1866

Walked with S. to Heddington.[236] Had some talk with me. Alas his views are very erroneous on religious matters.

Thursday, 24 May 1866

Was very grieved & alarmed to hear from Miriam that Papa had been very poorly. Coming back from Sedgley on Monday, he had been placed in a carriage crowded with 9 people. The heat had so overpowered him that he had fainted. Oh may God spare him to us. May he bless & preserve such a Father. Distance makes my anxiety the greater.

Friday, 25 May 1866

Bazley & Barker called upon me. In the evening heard the latter read his essay on 'the Monastic System' at Russell's rooms. It was very clearly written. The Schools began. Heard from my Mother. My Father thank God getting better – but he has been very ill & is still weak.

Saturday, 26 May 1866

Went a delightful walk with Albert to Horsepath. Dined at Brazenose with Bazley. Their Hall is very comfortable. Afterwards went to Mr Christopher's & heard Mr Dallas. His address was most interesting. God grant that it may be profitable also. He must be a man of undaunted courage. I shall take more interest than ever in the Irish Ch. Missions for the future.

Sunday, 27 May 1866

Stewart came & breakfasted with me & we walked over to Islip & heard Trench preach.[237] Our way led us through a delightful country, & I enjoyed it much. We had a very good Sermon on the doctrine of the Trinity.[238] Got back to Oxford at 2.15. In the evening went to St Aldate's & heard Mr Dallas. I liked him very much. Went to Tonge & spent a very pleasant & I hope profitable hour.

Monday, 28 May 1866

Went & lunched with Smith. He took me into Wadham Chapel. I had no idea of its size & elegance. We then went to our district. I gave Mrs H. back some of her tracts which she had lent me,[239] & told her that I thought that there was not

236 ? Charles Scott.

237 Francis Trench (1805–86), rector of Islip 1857–75.

238 It was Trinity Sunday.

239 Anne E. Herbert (*c.*1815–95), author of religious tracts, librarian of the Mission Library, New Hinksey.

enough of Jesus in them. I hope she did not feel hurt. She merely replied, 'You see, Sir, I am no Scholar'. But thank God the poorest 'scholar' can cling to Jesus. Went to the Prayer meeting; about 6 were there. Had very cheering accounts again from home. My Father is progressing very favourably. Praised be God.

Tuesday, 29 May 1866

Started at 1.15 for Claydon. About 25 University men went & Tonge & Mr Christopher. The Rectory lies about a mile from the Station. It is situate[d] on the top of a hill which gradually slopes down to a delightful river beyond which stretches an expanse of park. It is a lovely spot. Mr Fremantle himself met us at the gate & gave us a hearty welcome.[240] We then went on to the lawn & had some ginger beer & biscuits. This done we all gathered in Mr F.'s study; some dozen clergymen had meanwhile joined us so that we were a goodly party. After a beautiful prayer had been offered up by an unknown clergyman, & a hymn sung, Mr Goodhart came forward & delivered an address 'on the study of Prophecy'.[241] It was most interesting; and for some forty minutes he rivetted all our attentions. What was most wonderful, it was quite impromptu. It appeared that he had misunderstood Mr F. & thought that he had only to take part in a discussion. A brief conversation ensued after the address in which Mr Fremantle, Christopher, Girdlestone of Magdalene, McNeile of St John's & some others took part.[242] I shd have mentioned that before Mr G. spoke Tonge read the report of the Oxford Prayer Union written by Mr Linton.[243] It was exceedingly well done. I shd like to have joined, but I really knew nothing about it.[244] The Meeting was concluded by Mr Goodhart praying. Such a prayer too! It seemed to thrill me. So fervent, earnest, simple, trustful, it seemed indeed like talking with God. We had dinner at 4.15 & at 6 o'clock about half of us left to catch the 6.20 train. The remainder stopped to the Jews' Society Meeting.[245] Got back to my rooms about 7. So ended the most enjoyable day I ever spent at or near Oxford. Thank God that he has raised up such devoted men in our beloved Church.

240 William R. Fremantle (1807–95), rector of Claydon, Bucks. 1841–76, dean of Ripon 1876–95.

241 See Bodleian MS Chavasse dep. 30, pp. 19–20: Chavasse's sermon notes 1866–9.

242 Arthur G. Girdlestone (1842–1908), at Magdalen 1861–6, curate of St Peter-le-Bailey, Oxford 1867–9, vicar of All Saints, Brixton 1877–1908. Hector McNeile (1842–1922), fellow of St John's 1865–71, vicar of Bredbury, Cheshire 1893–1900, of Bishop's Sutton, Hants. 1907–22.

243 The Oxford Union for Private Prayer, founded in 1850, met annually at Fremantle's rectory. Members agreed to pray each Friday for various aspects of church life, such as clergy, ordinands, missionaries, the Universities and those in secular callings.

244 Chavasse was elected a member of O.U.P.P. in 1869.

245 Meeting of the Oxford auxiliary of the London Society for Promoting Christianity amongst the Jews. Goodhart was secretary of the parent society.

Saturday, 2 June 1866

Went in the evening with L. to Mr C.'s meeting.[246] There was a good attendance. The Bishop of Carlisle addressed us, & most earnest & practical he was.[247] He drew a very powerful comparison between spiritual life & natural life, & affectionately urged on us the necessity of being decided. 'Shew your colours' was his advice. L. did not seem to like him altogether. I am afraid that the High Church Party are getting him into their hands. Would that I could speak to him as I long to do. Alas! my heart is so cold & timid the words seem to freeze on my very lips.

Sunday, 3 June 1866

The Sacrament administered in our chapel. Thanks be to God, it was more refreshing to me than any of the previous College celebrations. Oh may this blessed ordinance be to me an ever increasing means of grace. Liddon delivered the last Bampton to a crowded congregation. Took a short turn with Lock round the Magdalen grounds. Felt somewhat fagged. In the evening went with Channing to St Aldate's. The Bishop preached from the verse 'God forbid that I shd glory save in the cross of our Lord Jesus Xt.'[248] It was a most able sermon. Not eloquent, but so clear, earnest & Scriptural. How thankful we ought to feel that we have such a Bishop on the bench. Went to Tonge's after Church. Ward came with Barker & Bazley, so that we had a nice little meeting.

Tuesday, 5 June 1866

Went with Smith to Hinksey. Read to Mrs Herbert, Farbrother &c.[249] Called at two new houses. I intended to have taken several more but my tracts failed. My people are beginning to ask me more frequently into their houses.

Wednesday, 6 June 1866

Had a Paper on Tac. Ann. Books IV, V & VI.[250] Ludovic & Fanny came down from London by the 1.36 & changed at Oxford for Campden. I met them at the Station, & induced them to come to Corpus & Lunch. They liked my rooms. They only stayed about an hour. L. told me how ill my Father had been. Oh Lord spare him to us yet awhile. How much, very much, have we to be thankful for in God's dealings with us. Yea they are all 'very good'.

246 Walter Lock.

247 Samuel Waldegrave (1817–69), bishop of Carlisle 1860–9.

248 Galatians vi. 14. See Bodleian MS Chavasse dep. 30, pp. 14–18: Chavasse's sermon notes 1866–9.

249 Edmund Farbrother (*c.*1790–1869), brewer.

250 Tacitus, *The Annals*.

Thursday, 7 June 1866

The greater part of the college went to Nuneham & pic-nicked. I shd like much to have gone but was unable. Moor & Poole came to dinner. Went to the O.T.D.S. Meeting in Caulfield's rooms. About six reports were read. The tone of the Meeting was certainly encouraging. The Majority of the Distributors seem so thoroughly in earnest, & new men are coming forward to take the places of those who are going down: still several vacant places remain unfilled. We must leave it to the Lord of the Vineyard.

Friday, 8 June 1866

Collections. Paper work lasted from 10 until 1 p.m.. The men are fast going down. Went to the Prayer Meeting in the afternoon. It was the last in the term. By God's help I will try to attend more regularly next term if my life is spared.

Saturday, 9 June 1866

Ryle took the address in the evening at Mr C.'s.[251] There was a very good attendance of undergraduates. His subject was 'Decision' & he enforced very strongly upon the necessity of taking a firm stand for Xt & of manfully shewing our colours. Blessed Lord, endue me with moral courage. Let me never be ashamed of thee & of thy word.

Sunday, 10 June 1866

Walked over to Islip with Knox. I enjoyed it much, but felt tired on reaching College. Mr Trench gave us a very useful Sermon, touching very forcibly on submitting patiently to opprobrious names for the sake of Jesus. Heard Ryle in the evening. His sermon was very beautiful from Rom X 1,2.[252] Went to Tonge's for the last time this term. Asked him to give me a class. I have not been very happy lately. I have been oppressed with doubts; save me my Saviour; give me faith; take not from me thy Holy Spirit.[253]

Monday, 11 June 1866

Went with Lock for a walk. Lay down in a field & read the Newdigate wh certainly is not good.[254] At 7 walked down to the river to see the procession of the boats. A very slow sight.

251 John C. Ryle (1816–1900), vicar of Stradbroke, Suffolk 1861–80, bishop of Liverpool 1880–1900.

252 See Bodleian MS Chavasse dep. 30, pp. 9–13: Chavasse's sermon notes 1866–9.

253 Psalm li. 11.

254 The Newdigate Prize for English Verse was awarded in 1866 to George Yeld of Brasenose for his poem on 'Virgil reading his Aeneid to Augustus and Octavia'.

Tuesday, 12 June 1866

A rainy, lowering day clearing up however towards noon. Worked all morning & at 2.30 started with L. & K. to walk to Dorchester; at Nuneham however we got tired, & my boots gave away so that we had to return. We whiled away the latter half of our walk by capping lines. The class list out. Ridley a first. Fitzgerald a second.[255] Molyneux a third. I feel very sorry for the two last.

Wednesday, 13 June 1866

Commemoration.[256] Breakfasted in Hall. A dark, showery morning. Went to the Sheldonian about 10.15. The gallery was already filled with men & the area was fast filling with strangers & M.A.s.[257] The ladies' seats were all occupied & the different colours of their light summer dresses formed the prettiest part of the whole scene. Alas I thought of one, who had she lived, might perhaps someday have sat there. But she is sleeping far away across the sea, & her redeemed soul is singing praises to the Lord who bought her. The usual cheers were given for the Queen, Lord Derby &c.[258] Gladstone was cheered & hissed.[259] The same fate befell Disraeli.[260] Austria was cheered. Prussia, groaned. Italy & Garibaldi received doubtfully.[261] Meanwhile the attention of Undergraduates was drawn to a stranger in the area who wore a light coat. Immediately he was requested to withdraw. In spite of groans, hissing, & indescribable howls he maintained his ground, & it was not until the long train of D.D.s had entered & the Vice-chancellor wished to begin that he was persuaded by the Proctors to retire. As he left the theatre he bowed, waved his handkerchief, & wave[d] his hand. He appeared about 10 minutes afterwards in a black coat. Degrees were conferred upon 8 or 9 men. Gathorne Hardy was the hero of the day, & next to him Dr Merivale & Sir James Simpson were the most loudly applauded.[262] The jokes on the whole were very poor. The best was an answer to the query put by some undergraduate when Mr Joule was introduced,[263] as to who he was & what he had done – a wag replied he

255 Gerald A. R. Fitzgerald (1844–1925), m. Corpus 1862, fellow of St John's 1867–75, barrister, parliamentary draftsman.

256 The annual commemoration of founders and benefactors of the university, or 'Encaenia'.

257 'The area' is a particular section of the Sheldonian Theatre.

258 Edward G. S. Stanley, 14th earl of Derby (1799–1869), prime minister 1852, 1858–9, 1866–8, chancellor of Oxford University 1852–69.

259 William E. Gladstone (1809–98), prime minister 1868–74, 1880–5, 1886, 1892–4.

260 Benjamin Disraeli, earl of Beaconsfield (1804–81), prime minister 1868, 1874–80.

261 Giuseppe Garibaldi (1807–82), Italian soldier and politician. Shouts such as 'Austria', 'Prussia', 'Denmark', 'John Bright' or 'Italy' were variously met with cheers and groans.

262 Gathorne Hardy, 1st earl of Cranbrook (1814–1906), M.P. for Oxford University 1865–78. Charles Merivale (1808–93), rector of Lawford, Essex 1848–69, chaplain to speaker of house of commons 1863–9, dean of Ely 1869–93. James Y. Simpson (1811–70), obstetrician and pioneer of anaesthesia. These men were amongst those receiving the honorary degree of D.C.L.

263 James P. Joule (1818–89), physicist.

was the author of 'Cheek by Jowl'. Scarcely a word of the Prize Poems could be heard for the men defrauded of their cheers by the obstinate resistance of the man in the Light coat, cheered the ladies &c while the Latin Prose &c was being read. I was glad when all was over, for the noise was deafening. Went a short walk with Ward in the afternoon. Got into bed early: my head was acheing [*sic*], & I could not work.

Thursday, 14 June 1866

Worked at intervals during the day. Began to pack. Called on the Halls, Honey & on Mr Christopher. The last was so kind. He would insist on my taking a copy of Mozley's 'Review of the Baptismal Controversy'.[264] I do enjoy my visits to him. Such a holy calm seems always to pervade his features. At 6 paid a last trip to my district. Lock went with me. I was so glad. Left a tract at a new house. I was very much moved at what happened. I knocked & heard a voice say 'Please come in, for I cannot get up to open the door'. We went in & found a poor blind cripple sitting on a chair near the fire. Her face was white, worn, & haggard as if with consumption, & her sightless eye balls seemed starting from her head. I laid a tract on the table & asked her if she would like me to read her a few verses from the Bible. She answered in the affirmative, & I open[ed] at that exquisite chapter St John XIV. Tears rolled down her pale wasted cheeks, as the tender loving words of a compassionate Jesus fell on her ears. I then knelt down & prayed, forgetful that any one was with us, thinking only of that poor girl & her immortal soul. God gave me courage, & taught me how to pray. Praised be his holy name for guiding my footsteps to that cottage. Never, never did I feel more forcibly the sweetness of that blessed name of Jesus than I did then. Dear Lord may that touching scene be blessed to all … [two pages torn out here].[265]

[? Sunday, 17 June 1866]

… against such a foe were it not for the all powerful aid of an ever present God. His wife (Arthur Vandeleur's) was left a widow after four years of married life.[266] Ah! what is my loss when compared to hers?

264 J. B. Mozley, *A review of the baptismal controversy* (London, 1862).

265 Further reflections on the death of 'Euphrosyne'?

266 Arthur Vandeleur (1829–60), army officer from Ralahine, Co. Clare, Ireland, who married Mary Molony in 1856. Perhaps Chavasse had been reading Catherine Marsh's hagiography, *The life of Arthur Vandeleur* (London, 1862).

Monday, 18 June 1866

Went into Birmingham by the 2.24 train. Saw by the 'Times' that Owen & Streatfeild had both gained firsts.[267] Came out with my Father in the carriage at 4. Worked all evening. Finished the Philippics.[268] Still feeling low & dispirited; & indulged in vain & unprofitable thoughts. By God's help I must break myself of this habit. I must no longer brood over sorrow. *She* wd not wish it. She is happy. To wish her back is selfishness. Let me rather be up & doing; striving to live more closely to Xt that at last by his merits I may see her one day in heaven.

Tuesday, 19 June 1866

Drove with my father to Acock's Green. Saw Edward Holbeche.[269] Still feeling languid & moody. Grose took his double first in Mods.[270]

Wednesday, 20 June 1866

Went to call on A. S.. Stayed talking to him for about ¾ of an hour. Dropped in to see Sarah on my way home. Galliers wonderfully well & at work. Gave way to a fit of irritability at night. Alas. How much harm might I do to my Master's cause by some hasty word or some outburst of temper. O dear Lord help me to keep a bridle on my tongue & to guard the doors of my lips. Ludovic came.

Thursday, 21 June 1866

A close, cloudy day. Went & bathed with Tom & Hodgson. Mamma with Miriam & Ada went to Mr Wright's concert in Birmingham.[271] My Father seemed better. Felt happier in myself & my thoughts not wandering to & brooding over my sorrows much. At times a sickening feeling of loneliness would come over me, but the God 'that comforteth them that are cast down'[272] is in his infinite mercy comforting me. Praised be his Holy Name.

Saturday, 23 June 1866

Started at 4.20 to walk over to Rushall. The heat was very great, but towards the end of my journey, it became cooler. Reached the Vicarage very late at 6.35.

267 Henry Owen (1844–1919), m. Corpus 1862, treasurer of National Library of Wales, high sheriff of Pembrokeshire. George S. Streatfeild (1844–1921), m. Corpus 1862, vicar of Immanuel, Streatham 1883–98, rector of Fenny Compton 1901–11.

268 Demosthenes, *The Philippics*.

269 Edward A. Holbeche (1847–87), captain of New Zealand Shipping Company.

270 Thomas H. Grose (1845–1906), m. Balliol 1864, fellow of Queen's 1870–1906, university registrar 1897–1906.

271 Wright and Pickard's 'drawing-room entertainment' was on the billing at Holder's Concert Hall alongside a comic ballet, *The jolly millers of Brum*, and Don Ferreyra 'the astounding Spanish musical phenomenon'.

272 2 Corinthians vii. 6.

Ludovic seemed very glad to see me. After tea read Garbett's address on Extreme Ritual.[273] It is simply grand.

Sunday, 24 June 1866

Went down to the Church with Ludovic at 10 p.m.. He had a wedding before the Service. The congregation was large & remarkably attentive. The singing much improved, but still the people do not join in as a body. In the evening, the congregation was again large. The sermons were both extempore, & very good & earnest. In the morning the subject was the fellowship of suffering with Christ, and in the evening the lessons taught by the life of John the Baptist. Ludovic is certainly doing a great work here, & God will surely prosper him. His delivery in the pulpit is very impressive. True he has many trials to battle with, but he has much, very much to be thankful for.

Monday, 25 June 1866

Started from Rushall at 9.10 & reached home at 11.25. The heat was not oppressive. In the evening walked down to Mount Pleasant to see Fanny's brother who had come down to take her to Stanley.[274] Walked home with Miriam & Ada. Did not do very much work. I hope I am not getting lazy. Certainly I have not the chance of taking a high class – still I must look beyond examinations.

Tuesday, 26 June 1866

Worked almost continuously until 4 p.m. but the heat was great & I felt languid, so my Homer suffered. At 5 went to Mrs Holbeche's croquet party. After dusk dancing was commenced; as I have given it up I walked round the garden with Mill & some one whose name I did not know. The very sight of the room brilliantly lighted, & filled with whirling dancers seemed to sicken my heart. Can one's guardian angel enter a ball room? *She* never danced & I thought of her – ah when I shall [*sic*] forget her? True, I saw her but for a week, but that week was a crisis in my life. 'God has touched her & she has fallen asleep' & God is love. Felt somewhat low for as I was glancing thro' the 'Post' I was startled & horrified to light upon a passage describing 'the melancholy drowning of a young collegian named Poole.' It was John Poole of Ch. Ch.. And he, so dear a friend of mine is gone too. Oh! Lord give me faith that I may pierce thro' this dark cloud. His college career done, a career of usefulness (as it seemed to man) opening to him, a bright future lying before him – & God has snatched him away. He went to bathe yesterday morning in the river at 6 a.m. with his Father & brothers. As he was

273 Edward Garbett, *Extreme ritualism. An address* (London, 1866).

274 The Evans family lived at Stanley Lodge, Stanley, near Derby.

swimming across he was seen suddenly to throw up his arms & sink. A brother went to his assistance, but so convulsively did he clasp him that to save his own life, the brother had to loose his hold, & so he sank. Cramp had seized his leg, they found. Poor dear fellow how many little acts of unostentatious kindness done by him do I now seem to remember. The sad news haunted me all day long. I cannot doubt that he is safe at home, that the vail [*sic*] is entered. An easy death & sudden glory. Lord when my time comes, may I be ready. How could I then join in these frivolous festivities? How could I laugh & joke, when I thought of a beloved friend lying cold & dead not a hundred miles away? His early death seemed to recall *her* early death. But, blessed thought, God is love. Father, thou hast done it, & it must be well.

Wednesday, 27 June 1866

Had a croquet party at home. I am afraid that I am pedantic but they weary me. They appear to benefit neither soul or body. Mamma was persuaded to have a little dancing so I followed my former tactics & walked round the garden with R.N.H..[275] We talked on religious subjects. He appears to me to have been disgusted at godliness thro' the well-intended but excessive zeal of one or two excellent clergymen. He thinks, I am sure more deeply than people give him credit for; but he holds some very erroneous but prevalent views. May the all wise Spirit of God enlighten him. I felt so powerless & ignorant in combating with his peculiar tenets. But God gave me strength.

Thursday, 28 June 1866

Another croquet party. It was a very quiet affair at Mr Smallwood's; we got home in good time. In the morning Distributed books to some of the men in the Park.[276] They seemed very grateful. Several are new to the work.

Friday, 29 June 1866

Did not go to play croquet at Penns. Next Sunday is Sacrament Sunday & I did not feel justified in going out so shortly before; especially as it was to conclude with a dance. Not that I should have joined, but leaving such a wild excited scene disturbs the mind. I find it so difficult to collect & tranquillize [*sic*] my thoughts on returning home. I feel even the parties that I have been to previously this week have unfitted me for my evening devotions. I have either been so wearied out that I have almost fallen asleep on my knees, or so unsettled, as to be almost entirely unable to send my heart with my prayers. I am but a poor stumbling infant. I need

275 Robert Neville Holbeche.

276 Chavasse occasionally went tract distributing in Sutton Park.

to be fed on milk. Meat is too strong for me.[277] Oh thou compassionate Father that dost not despise the day of small things[278] fan the flickering spark of grace that thou hast mercifully kindled in my breast. I feel in great doubt whether I ought to approach the Lord's Table in my present state. May God help me to decide for the best. Called on Mr R. & had talked with him. I longed for him to pray for me & with me, but I had not the courage to ask him.

Saturday, 30 June 1866

Walked down to Sutton & saw Cull. He told me Bal had left & was going to Sandhurst.[279] How my conscience reproached me! I have never been to see him nor have I written to him. And this is frien[d]ship! I heard with deep pain that lately he has been much under A.'s control. Poor dear fellow he is so easily led. May God raise him up some true friend. I must write to him. Met Bee on my way home.

Sunday, 1 July 1866

How merciful is my God! How manifold are his loving-kindnesses! Felt so peaceful in the morning. My boys behaved very well & were very attentive. God seemed to be with us. Dear Mr R. stopped as he went up the School & said to me 'How are your boys getting on? you will do them some good some day.' May the Lord help me. Was enabled to join in the service with more heartiness than usual, but as if to humble me & shew how wholly I am dependent on the Holy Spirit for every good thought or desire, a bad tune to a beautiful hymn put me out a great deal. Alas, alas black indeed must be my heart, when such a trifle can so thoroughly disturb me. In the evening stayed Sacrament. It was so calm & peaceful. God was I pray & trust near me, for I felt happy & tranquil. Praise be to his own Holy name for ever & for ever. Amen.

Monday, 2 July 1866

Visited the School in the afternoon & took the First class.[280] The subject was a curious one 'On Herbs'. I felt rather lost. The effect of limiting my reading. Packed up. Felt very irritated, unreasonably so, at finding my filterer, small telescope & bradawl gone & the random of my gun broken, the author of such misdeeds being unknown. Alas! how little Xtian patience & forbearance do I shew. And yet but yesterday I knelt & received the symbols of my Saviour's death

277 Hebrews v. 12.

278 Zechariah iv. 10.

279 The Royal Military College, Sandhurst. Perhaps Ballenden failed the entrance examination, for he does not appear in the Sandhurst Cadet Registers.

280 Green Lanes School.

& passion & stedfastly purposed to lead a new life. How the flesh lusteth contrary to the Spirit.[281] Vincent Holbeche dropped in to tea & left about 10 p.m.

Tuesday, 3 July 1866

Left home with my Father, Mother, Miriam & Hodgson at 7.45. Started from Birmm. Station at 9.10 reached Gloucester at 11.15. As we had an hour to spare we left my Father with his Paper in the Waiting Room, & went to the Cathedral. It was well worth seeing. The Lady Chapel especially was most beautiful, so light & elegant. In the plain Communion Table I cd recognize Dean Law.[282] Saw the tomb of Edward the 2nd. Left Gloucester at 12.45. Our route to Chepstow lay through a beautiful country, well wooded & dotted with fine spires. Soon after leaving Chepstow we came in sight of the Severn. Then we hurried through the great copper-mining district of South Wales, a scene almost worse than the Black Country. The scenery afterwards changed again & we were whirled through an agricultural district with hills clothed with woods on all sides. We reached Milford about 40 minutes behind time, crossed the Haven in a small steamer, took the omnibus for the Station & arrived there too late – the train had not waited. We were doomed to stay an hour, at a miserable edifice, as large as three bathing machines, & called in irony 'a Station'. At last the train did come & we reached Tenby at 10 p.m. very tired & very thankful that our long journey had been accomplished at least in safety if not with speed & comfort.

Wednesday, 4 July 1866

Our lodgings at Mr Coleman's Bath House are very comfortable;[283] they face the sea. Bathed with Hodgson. In the evening went a short walk with Miriam along the South Sands, which are magnificent, & round the town. The old wall with its towers is very curious. My Father I am glad to say none the worse for his long journey.

Thursday, 5 July 1866

Tried to work in the morning but did very little. Bathed with Hodgson. I can certainly swim better than I could last year. In the afternoon went with Maggie,[284] Miriam & Hodgson to Hoyle's mouth. It was a long time before we were able to find its whereabouts, & we wandered sadly out of our way. At last after a diligent search, we were successful. It is a large cavern with a lofty & somewhat gothic

281 Galatians v. 17.

282 Henry Law (1797–1884), dean of Gloucester 1862–84.

283 John Coleman (1806–74), Tenby lodging house keeper.

284 Chavasse's cousin, Margaret C. Chavasse (1839–1930), also on holiday in Tenby with her mother, Margaret C. Chavasse (1804–84), widow of Horace Chavasse, vicar of Rushall 1842–61.

entrance. We could only penetrate a few yards in, the darkness was so great. We found four candles left by some beneficent strangers & sadly we bemoaned our shortsightedness in bringing no matches. We uttered our regrets aloud when suddenly to our amazement from the rock that overhung the cliff a lady exclaimed, 'We have left candles behind us, if you wish to explore the cavern.' We made known our want & in another moment down dropped a box of matches. Thus furnished with lights we entered the cave in single file. We penetrated about 60 yds. As a general rule the passage was high enough for us to stand erect, but in places it was so low that we were were [*sic*] obliged to stoop double. At intervals it widened into small rooms. Altogether it was very curious. We wrote our names in the furthest caverns & reached the light in safety again. The poor, it is said, believe the cave to be inhabited by a wild boar. We came back to Tenby at 7.30 & drank tea at Aunt's lodgings.

Friday, 6 July 1866

Went for a ride round by St Issell's to Saundersfoot. The views were beautiful. At Saundersfoot the carriage dropped us down, & we walked about a mile along the shore. It was rather rough & rocky in places, but the ladies managed admirably. I am afraid the exertion rather tired my Father. Maggie & Miriam found several fresh shells &c. We reached home about 6 p.m.. My Father, I am thankful to say, seemed to revive after a cup of tea & became himself again.

Saturday, 7 July 1866

Drank tea at Aunt's lodgings. At 5.30 started for Giltar Point. Maggie & Miriam found some very good shells. It was rather a steep ascent to the top of the cliff, but the view when we were there quite repaid the exertion. We had a glorious expanse of sea & a delightful breeze. We reached Tenby again about 8.30.

Sunday, 8 July 1866

Went to the parish Church. The congregation was large & consisted chiefly of visitors. I am afraid that the majority of residents are Dissenters. What a significant tale does such a fact tell of the neglect & laziness of the Church clergy in former days! Archdeacon Clark, the vicar, preached the Sermon.[285] Our seats are unfortunately behind the pulpit & worse still behind a pillar, consequently we heard but little of his discourse. It was founded on Psalm 51. The singing, I am sorry to say is not congregational. In the evening went alone to Penally Church. Mr Hughes the vicar is a thorough Evangelical.[286] The Church itself is small &

285 George Clark (*c.*1810–74), rector of Tenby 1854–67, archdeacon of St David's 1864–74.

286 John Hughes (1793–1873), vicar of Penally 1819–73.

dark. Although a wet night, the seats were all well filled, the singing was hearty & without an organ & the Sermon earnest, practical, & impressive. The text was 'I can do all things thro Xt which strengtheneth me.'[287] I was glad to see two soldiers there. Got rather wet as I returned, but I by no means regretted my journey. The sermon gave me something to think about.

Monday, 9 July 1866

Walked with Maggie to Gumfreston. Rather lost our way, & went about a mile beyond our destination. When we, at last, had reached the church we found the carriage had arrived. Looked over the church, & at the Spring. The place seemed very badly kept. The tower was very curious. The vicar is an eccentric, but I hope, good old man.[288] Altogether I was disappointed in what I saw. Drove on to St Florence a pretty village about 2 miles beyond Gumfreston. The driver was an exceedingly civil fellow. He told me that one of the horses which were now drawing us, had been driven 160 miles in two days.

Tuesday, 10 July 1866

Walked over to Pembroke Dock & met Maggie, Ada, & Tom at the New Milford Station. They seemed very tired after their long journey. The express was late, but fortunately the Tenby train waited. We reached Bath House about 9 o'clock.

Wednesday, 11 July 1866

Left Bath House at 9 o'clock in a break & 4 horses with Aunt & Maggie for the Stacks Rocks – 20 miles away. Up a long hill commanding some noble views, down again into the valley through the little village of Lamphey with the ruins of its Bishop's Palace through Pembroke down a Hill which seemed almost perpendicular & up another just as steep, through the Park of Stackpole Court, past the Hall & out again into the Road, still on till the High Road was left behind & we Drove along a way made at the summit of a range of cliffs[:] we reached St Govan's Chapel about 12.30. It is situated in a space betwixt two rocks wh seem to have been rent in twain by some volcanic eruption. The descent is very steep, very rough & very romantic. There are steps, but they are much worn. Tradition declares they have defied all attempts to count them. The saint is said to have leapt against the rock when pursued by his enemies.[289] The rock opened, received him & closed again. The fissure is still visible whence it is said he effected his egress.

287 Philippians iv. 13.

288 Gilbert N. Smith (*c.*1796–1877), rector of Gumfreston 1837–77.

289 According to tradition, St Govan, 6th century abbot of Dairinis, spent his last years on this Pembrokeshire headland and was miraculously hidden by the rock from pirates.

Here too are pieces of the bell stone wh when struck emit a sound like a bell[290] & here are thousands of a rare little shell wh Maggie & Miriam carried off by hundreds. Then we drove on past the frightful fissure the Huntsman leap, over wh some daring riders are said to have leapt, past the seething cauldron to the Stacks Rocks. Here we lunched. It was a marvellous sight. Two pillar-shaped rocks covered with birds, constantly flying up & down & raising a curious cry. The driver told us they were Eligugs. The prospect was magnificent. The noble cliff, the glorious sea, breaking on the rocky shore below us, the blue expanse of heaven & the wild forelands stretching on either hand. We came back thro' Pembroke. There the horses were bailed & we looked over the Castle. We reached Tenby about 7. Tired but happy.

Friday, 13 July 1866

Sailed to Lydstep Caverns. They can only be seen at the full of the moon when the tide is very low. The sea was not very rough; no one of our party was actually seasick although several felt squeamish. The Caverns themselves are well worth seeing, but somehow I did not seem to care for them. I do not feel to have any energy. I feel irritable & languid. Our journey home occupied about an hour & a half. The boatmen fished & caught 7, gunnel &c. Aunt Margaret & Maggie left. I am very sorry that they are gone. I write this at 11 o'clock at night. I am in a curious state of mind. I feel depressed, & yet at times I can be cheerful enough. Everything seems dark & gloomy. I know that my heavenly Fatherly [*sic*] has gifted me with innumerable benefits, & yet I cannot feel thankful. Sin is a burden, & yet I cannot mourn for it. Help me Gracious Spirit. Give me the comfort of thyself again. Faith, I need, oh give me Faith adorable Saviour. Blot out my sins & shortcomings by thy most precious blood. Then indeed I shall be happy, – happy in Christ Jesus.

Saturday, 14 July1866

Was much surprised to receive a call from Robert Holbeche. He had rowed down the Wye with a friend whom he had left behind at Carmarthen, & walked down to Tenby. He dined & drank tea with us. After dinner we all went to Hoyle's Mouth. We had some fun on our way home. In trying to get a short cut we got into the middle of a gateless field & consequently had to clamber over walls &c. Bathed after tea, & were shut by the tide in the little cove where we had undressed. Had to climb a steep cliff & finally found ourselves in a potatoe garden. We saw the owner, explained our difficulty, & made everything straight.

290 A silver bell above St Govan's chapel is said to have been stolen by pirates, but their ship was wrecked in a storm, and the bell rescued by angelic hands and entombed in a rock which gives a metallic sound when struck.

Sunday, 15 July 1866

At 9 a.m. went to the Communion at the Church; about 40 communicated. I do not derive that benefit which I ought from the Sacrament. Oh may God make it a more comfortable ordinance to my soul. Alas the fault lies entirely with myself. Oh that I may be permitted to discover what that fault is, by Christ's assisting grace forthwith remedy it. Enjoyed the morning service much. Praise be to my God. My heart seemed so full. How much do I owe to my heavenly Father. Mr Rowley one of the surviving missionaries of the University Mission to Central Africa [preached].[291] His sermon was a powerful one. His text 'what shall a man give in exchange for his soul'.[292] After having sketched rapidly the activity of the money-exchange, & the eagerness displayed in the pursuit of pleasure he shewed how profitless all pleasure & all wealth was to a dying man, picturing very powerfully a scene on a sinking vessel & a death bed. Christ was then our only stay. He described his own Mission, & its failure sent to try the faith of the Church by its Great Head. He strongly reproved the prevailing notion that like a Profit & Loss account, the amount of money spent was to be placed against the number of heathen converted – the price of one soul was not to be estimated. To save souls from Hell was the object of the society. I liked him very much. R. H. came to dinner. Had two hours to myself in the afternoon. In the evening walked to Penally Church. Mr Hughes preached from Rom VI 19. (1) The unprofitableness of sin as taught by experience (2) The folly of sin as taught by grace (3) The joy of the righteous. It was a most earnest telling sermon. 'Conscience' he said 'is the representative of God in the breast of man'. My Father & Mother spoke to Mr & Mrs Hughes after church. Met on our way home a little girl so like ___. I cannot forget her.

Monday, 16 July 1866

'Wave after wave'. The Birmingham Banking Co. stopped.[293] My Father is a large share holder, & the share holders are responsible for the whole amount £1,500,000. It is difficult to realize it. May God be with us. To the winds with the money, provided my beloved Father's health will bear the strain. Lord now fulfil the gracious promise given by thee who cannot lie 'As thy day is, so shall thy

291 Henry Rowley (*c.*1825–1908), deputation for the Society for the Propagation of the Gospel 1865–73, organising secretary for S.P.G. 1873–1900. The Universities' Mission to Central Africa was founded in response to an appeal in 1857 by David Livingstone. The first missionary expedition of 1860–3, of which Rowley was a part, resulted in the deaths of Bishop Charles Mackenzie, Rev. Henry Burrup, Rev. Henry Scudamore and Dr John Dickinson.

292 Matthew xvi. 26 and parallels.

293 The Birmingham Banking Company was founded in 1829 and failed in 1866. It was soon resurrected and in 1889 merged with the Royal Exchange Bank to form the Metropolitan and Birmingham Bank.

strength be'.[294] The future lies with God. He will direct us for the best. Help me, holy Father, to support & comfort those so dear to me. In the afternoon walked over to Saundersfoot with Robert Holbeche & bathed there. And here at the close of this day, I sit writing in my bedroom, & as I look back on my past life, I see the marvellous signs of the Providence of God which has led me safely through so many chequered scenes & brought me to my present position. And can I with such a retrospect dare to suppose that the same loving, Fatherly hand will leave me now? Will he who has borne me through the dark & cloudy day & upheld me when the Sun of prosperity shone brightest, forsake me when the way seems roughest, & the gloom seems deeping tenfold? No, a thousand times No. He is the same yesterday, today & for ever[295] – the great Unchanged, Unchangeable I Am. Blessed be thy name thou Eternal Jehovah. Amen & Amen.

Tuesday, 17 July 1866

Bathed from a machine before breakfast. Walked over to Manorbier Castle with R. H. in the afternoon. I was rather disappointed in the ruins. They are well situated, as regards the sea, & were no doubt strong, but they have little pretentions to architectural beauty. The Church is interesting but was being restored. My Father bears up wonderfully under his heavy loss. He will I am afraid be some £10,000 or £12,000 poorer. He talks about resuming his consultation practice in Birmingham. May God give him strength to ride safely over this great trouble. His loss will not be so large as I expected – perhaps when the whole affair is settled & wound up it may be less.

Wednesday, 18 July 1866

My Mother, Father, Miriam & Hodgson left Tenby for home at 7.45. My Father felt that he ought to be on the spot to see what could be done. Stringer & Hatter are to go, & the whole establishment is to be cut down.[296] We must leave the rest to God. In the evening walked to Waterwinch. The road & glen are certainly very pretty. R. H., Tom & myself bathed, while Maggie sketched the little cottage there, & Ada read. On our journey home got some ferns. Kept constantly thinking about the Bank failure. I must do my utmost, God helping me to retrench. There is some talk of re-establishing the Bank. A meeting of share holders & directors is to be held tomorrow. How much have we to be thankful for. Enough still remains for us to live upon. In how many cases alas! will almost utter ruin be the result of this widespread calamity.

294 Deuteronomy xxxiii. 25.
295 Hebrews xiii. 8.
296 ? Servants in the Chavasse household.

Thursday, 19 July 1866

A very warm day. In the evening went a very pretty walk to Scotsborough House & thence thro' the woods to Knightson & home by the Road. The round proved longer than we expected, but it was so delightfully cool & picturesque.

Saturday, 21 July 1866

Heard from home. The Bank affairs are turning out much better than was at first expected. It is proposed to start a new company. If such a project be carried out the share holders will receive £5 per share, instead of having to pay up £10. Mr Bee was married on Wednesday!![297] The news electrified me. He had kept it such a profound secret. Met with an adventure. As we were bathing as usual from the rocks, I noticed as I came out of the water a man speaking to Bob. He then walked up to me & asked my name & address. I gave it to him, supposing he was on the staff of the newspaper, & was collecting the names of visitors. On asking R. however I found he was the Inspector of Nuisances & had taken down our names for bathing contrary to the statutes, from the shore. Dressing as fast as we could, we were rejoined by Tom, who had carefully secreted himself behind a rock & had escaped notice but who was now vigorous is his exhortations to us 'to duck' the Inspector. We followed the man up the shore & found him engaged in taking down the names of the remaining dozen gentlemen who were hastily dressing. Of course their indignation was great, but the man was good tempered & confessed that the want of proper notices posted up in conspicuous places was a great sign of negligence. The fine he said was £2. He then went & left us to our own reflections. To pay £2 & have our names published in the paper was not a pleasant look out. Some took a gloomy view of things; others were more cheerful & quietly foretold that we shd hear no more of the matter. At 3.30 started with Tom for Carew Castle. It [is] the most pleasant ruin that I have yet seen. I was extremely pleased. On our way back went into the Church wh had been lately repaired &c. Reached Tenby about 9.15. Heard nothing about the Summons.

Sunday, 22 July 1866

Felt calm & happy. God granted me much of his presence in my morning devotion. He seemed so near me. Went to church & was enabled to join in the Prayers from my heart, & yet not half so earnestly or so fervently as I would, for at times my mind sadly wandered, showing how needful it is for me to watch even when I am nearest to my Lord. Dear Lord Jesus thou didst send an indescribable peace over me – a foretaste of heaven. Ah, if I were more attentive to my religious duties, if I strove to look with the eye of faith singly to Jesus, if I were more constant in

297 Thomas Bee married Sarah H. Cook at Sutton Coldfield on 18 July 1866.

prayer would not my heavenly Father vouchsafe to bless me with more of such a happy frame? How much have I to thank God for! What marvellous compassion has he shewn towards me. Notwithstanding all my sins & shortcomings, notwithstanding my hardheartedness, he yet breathes upon me his Blessed Spirit. Praised by his Holy Name. Walked over to Penally in the evening. There was a Sermon for the Mission to Seamen.

Monday, 23 July 1866

Worked most of the day. In the evening gave way to an inexcusable *fit of passion.* How deceitful is my heart. Oh dear Lord do help me to keep it in subjection. Felt unhappy – may God in his infinite mercy pardon me. After tea went bathing with Tom. Walked down to the rocks wh the 'Inspector' mentioned yesterday & undressed there. The bottom was very stony, & T. cut his foot against the jagged corner of a rock. I had to carry him up to Bath House on my back. He bore the pain exceedingly well. It was a nasty gash. R. got no money, & wanted to go home with us. I had to asked [*sic*] Mr C. to lend us £2. I did not like the job at all. I think R. really ought to have asked for himself.

Tuesday, 24 July 1866

Left at 7.45. Thro' the stupidity of a porter one of our boxes was left behind at New Milford Station. I fear I did not bear the vexation as I ought to have done. I am so unreasonably hot. Spoke to the Station Master at Carmarthen about it & again to the Superintendent at Gloucester. Went up to the Cathedral. Mag & myself got in to Service. Mr Evans of Pembroke was one of the Canons in residence.[298] Saw the Crypt & the Cloisters. The latter are very fine. Lord Ellengborough [*sic*] was in the Cathedral at the same time that we were,[299] & the verger's delight at having a live lord to conduct over was ludicrous. We left the City at 4.30. At Worcester we met Aunt & Maggie. Reached B'ham at 6.30. Charlie, Fanny & Miriam were there to meet us. Found my Father wonderfully well. The Bank affairs seem much brighter. Walked down with him after tea to Mr Redman's. He talked to me about the devotion of his sons. L. had offered & pressed him to take the money he had given him when he started in life. C. wished to give up Mt Pleasant & go in to a smaller house. N. in great trouble wrote entreating him to turn into money the mortgage on his works. My Father seemed so affected. Ah, who would not freely sacrifice life itself, were it needful, for such a Father. Oh Lord help me to be a loving, dutiful son.

298 Evan Evans (1813–91), master of Pembroke 1864–91.

299 Edward Law, earl of Ellenborough (1790–1871).

Friday, 27 July 1866

T. V. Holbeche came in the evening. My Mother & Father dined at Charlie's with Ludovic & Fanny. Bank Meetings are being held almost daily. The New Bank seems to promise fair. I hope my Father will not over work himself. There seems to have been gross mismanagement on the part of the directors.

Sunday, 29 July 1866

Mr R. asked me to relinquish my Class to a young man who teaches in Mr Burges's Sunday School,[300] but who at present is living out at Maney. I did so gladly. Not that I have little or no affection for my lads, but simply because I felt that he wd probably have more experience than I have had, & be better qualified to impress & instruct & improve his hearers. I took a class of smaller boys. It was a change, & I felt my own incapacity painfully. How hard it is to clothe the blessed truths of Scripture in such simple & attractive language as to gain the ear & strike the heart of the young. But oh how inexpressibly soothing to feel, that however weak the vessel may be, the great Shepherd himself, in his deep love for his lambs, will be with both the teachers & the taught. In the afternoon wrote out part of Ryle's Sermon from my notes & read Dr Miller's Sermon preached in Exeter Hall 'How can these things be'.[301]

Tuesday, 31 July 1866

The Share List of the New Bank closed. I am thankful to say enough applications have been received to justify the opening of the old Premises. Dined at Mr J. Holbeche's. Gould was there, the son of Mr G. of Wolverhampton.[302] He is curate to Mr Lee[303] & was I believe tutor to Lord Shaftesbury's children.[304] He seemed an exceedingly nice fellow. He told me that some gentlemen at Birmingham supplied Mr Christopher with money to distribute books among the undergraduates. I suspect Mr Lee is one.

Friday, 3 August 1866

Called in at the School & took the first class. The subject they read was a curious one – 'On roots'. I fear I did not make the lesson very interesting.

300 John H. Burges (1826–99), vicar of Bishop Ryder's Church, Birmingham 1857–74, rector of Devizes 1874–99.

301 J. C. Miller, *How can these things be? A sermon* (London, 1857).

302 Baring Baring-Gould (1842–1917), curate of St George's, Edgbaston 1866–8, secretary to C.M.S. 1888–1913; son of Alexander Baring-Gould (1814–99), vicar of St Mark's, Wolverhampton 1846–68, of Christ Church, Winchester 1874–90.

303 George Lea (*c.*1805–83), minister of St George's, Edgbaston 1864–83.

304 Anthony Ashley Cooper, 7th earl of Shaftesbury (1801–85), evangelical philanthropist and social reformer.

Saturday, 4 August 1866

Walked up to Walmley with Maggie. Left her in her district, & went alone to call on Mr Robinson. He was very kind. Mrs R. lent me De Sanctis on 'Popery & Jesuitism' to read.[305] He is a converted Priest.

Sunday, 5 August 1866

Overslept myself. Alas, Alas how often I am guilty of this sin of sloth. I was obliged to cut short my devotions – & Sacrament Sunday too when of all times I seem to need more Communion with God. In spite of all my shortcoming in this respect, God in his infinite mercy was with me in speaking to my Sunday School boys. Mr Lees did not come, so I took my old class. Received the Holy Communion with My Father, Mother & Miriam & Maggie. It was delightfully calm, but alas I did not enjoy that measure of peace & gratitude that I feign would. Oh my Father, if there is any sin that comes betwixt thee & me, in thy infinite mercy shew it to me. Wash me clean, thoroughly clean in my Redeemer's blood. I seem lately to have made but little way. My own utter impotence becomes daily more palpable – of mine own self I can do nothing – arise Almighty Father, endue with strength, enrich me with thy Spirit, for Xt's sake. Grant that 'I may do all things thro' him strengthening me'.[306]

Tuesday, 7 August 1866

Went to Albert Smith. It seemed like old times again. Called at the Reading Room & saw 'the Times'. Reached home about 9.30. Went to bed early feeling thoroughly jaded. Depressed & anxious. How little has Xt been in my thoughts. How soon has the remembrance of his dying love faded from my mind. 'Oh wretched man that I am who shall deliver me from the body of this death. *I thank God thro' Jesus Xt*' our Lord.[307] Blessed, blessed, thrice blessed words.

Wednesday, 8 August 1866

Went to the Walmley Tea Drinking. Rain fell fast while the children were having their tea, but eventually the weather cleared up, & we had a game at football. It was very good fun. After all was over the children were assembled in front of the Hall Door, & the Doxology sung. It was beautifully solemn. The sweet childish voices, rising up high & clear thro' the stillness of the calm summer evening; the air cool & balmy after the recent rain; the sky covered with breaking clouds & the

305 Luigi Desanctis, *Popery and Jesuitism at Rome in the nineteenth century. With remarks on their influence in England* (London, 1852). Desanctis left the Roman Church to become a minister of the Reformed Italian Church at Geneva.

306 Philippians iv. 13.

307 Romans vii. 24–5.

sun just sinking in the west; all combined to render that scene impressive. How it made one's soul long for that time when

Infant voices shall proclaim
The glories of the Saviour's name.[308]

Friday, 10 August 1866

Mrs Webster came to dinner;[309] also Miss Jane & Miss Catherine Holbeche. Warren Smallwood came to stay for a week.[310] Went down to Albert Smith. Felt rather tired. Walked home with the Miss Holbeches. Was very glad to get to bed.

Sunday, 12 August 1866

The Lord's day, but how little grateful did my soul feel for the rest of the Sabbath. Lees came to the Sunday School & took the 1st class. I had one of the lower ones. Alas, alas, it was a great effort to speak to the dear little ones of a Saviour's love. An effort! Oh how wicked, how cold must be my heart. Touch me, Lord, with a live coal from off thy altars. Give me burning zeal, fervid love. Mr R. preached a very beautiful sermon in the morning, on the necessity of recognising God's hand in all our concerns. He asked me this morning, 'Who is greatest in the kingdom of heaven.' I answered 'the least'. I knew to what he referred. But oh – am I humble? Never, never was there a prouder heart, & a more ambitious mind than mine. Make me Father more like Jesus – meek & lowly in spirit. Read part of Bickersteth's Life.[311] What a delightful man he must have been. How comforting to think that he had the very same trials to battle against wh are now besetting my way. He overcame thro' the blood of the Lamb. Is it presumptuous for me to trust my entire cause to the same Jesus?

Monday, 13 August 1866

Changed the books for the men in the Park. I had not been for some time. Mr & Mrs Bartlett came.

Tuesday, 14 August 1866

Went down to Albert Smith, but the boy said he was engaged so that did not have my 'lesson'. Maggie, Miriam & Warren went to Mr Albutt's.

308 'And infant voices shall proclaim Their early blessings on his Name', from Isaac Watts's hymn, 'Jesus shall reign where'er the sun'.

309 ? Frances B. Webster (*c.*1830–1901), wife of Montagu Webster, vicar of St James's, Hill, near Sutton Coldfield 1860–1903.

310 J. Warren Smallwood (1850–1926), merchant.

311 Thomas Birks, *Memoir of the Rev. Edward Bickersteth* (London, 1851).

Wednesday, 15 August 1866

Mr & Mrs Bartlett left. Went a walk with Warren round by Sutton, Langley & Walmley. It has done me much Good. Fanny, who was confined on Sunday, & her little boy going on exceedingly well.[312] Poor thing she had rather a bad time of it: but God be praised she got safely over it, tho' the doctors say she could not have lasted much longer. I felt her safety as indeed an answer to prayer. Oh who would not lay every want & every need before such a merciful Father? Mr Oughton came to dinner.

Thursday, 16 August 1866

Got up at 5 a.m.. Started at 6.15 with Warren & William for Little Aston on a fishing excursion. Did not catch very much, only a few perch & no pike. In fact we never had a run. Nevertheless we had a most enjoyable day. Unfortunately thro' the smallness of our hooks we missed two very nice perch. Returned home about 8 p.m.. The outing has done me so much good. The fresh air, the glorious park, the row on the water, the entire relaxation from work, did wonders for me. 'Praise the Lord oh! my soul & forget not *all* his benefits.'[313]

Sunday, 19 August 1866

Had my new class. God enabled me to speak to them with unwonted freedom. To him be all the praise. My thoughts wandering during the service. Alas how deceitful & desperately wicked is my heart. Mr R. preached a beautiful sermon, on the necessity of acknowledging God's hand in all our troubles. Oh that I had more faith that I recognize a Father's love in all *my* concerns. Gave Stringer a copy of the 'Anxious Inquirer'.[314] May he prove an anxious inquirer indeed & find that for wh he seeks.

Monday, 20 August 1866

Warren Smallwood left us. I am afraid that he must have found his visit very slow.

Tuesday, 21 August 1866

Went to Albert Smith's. The boarders were coming back. The school will not be so full this half. Went to Dr Lakin's at 9 p.m..[315] My heart beat fast, & I felt almost faint when I reached the drawing door. I looked back up the passage to *his* room.

312 Howard S. Chavasse (1866–1938), surgeon, first child of Charles and Frances Chavasse.

313 Psalm ciii. 2.

314 John Angell James, *The anxious inquirer after salvation directed and encouraged* (London, 1835).

315 James H. Lakin (*c.*1824–77), surgeon.

I seemed to remember everything as tho' it was but yesterday. I could not enjoy myself much. We left for home about 11.15.

[2? August 1866]
Mr & Mrs Blake drove over in the afternoon & stayed tea. Miss Ryland & Miss Fanny Holbeche also came up.[316] I had never seen the former before. She is a wonderful old lady – 94. She asked me several questions about Mr Christopher. Heard from poor Poole's Father.

Sunday, 26 August 1866
Late again in bed. This bad habit is growing on me. I must battle against it by God's help. My boys not so good, being holiday time their lessons were very imperfectly learned. Mr R. preached on truth. Felt languid & unwell. Could not settle to any thing. Is my heart getting frozen in sin? Quicken me thou living God. Charlie & Willie Harrold came to tea. The former went to church[:] the latter would not. My Father was consequently obliged to stay away from church with him. Walked home with Miriam, & had some delightful conversation with her. My wicked heart is so cold, proud & reserved that I do not seem to like to unburden myself to any one. But God, in his infinite goodness, enabled me to break through myself, & oh how great was the comfort. How pleasant to find that others have the same doubts & trials & fears & temptations as yourself, & yet that God has mercifully brought them safely through. I often fear that my religion is too exclusive, that I keep too much to myself & do not assist others sufficiently to bear their burdens.

Monday, 27 August 1866
Vincent Holbeche & Johnson came to tea. I saw the latter yesterday. He is in the bank of England, & has been sent down to the Birmingham Branch. He lodges with Mr Felton & goes into town every morning by train. He is just the same as ever – striving I believe & trust to live for Xt. I shd not be surprised if he went out as a missionary eventually. He tells me that he has given up the idea, but God, I think, will revive the desire. His eldest brother is just going out.

Tuesday, 28 August 1866
Mr Turner worse. My Father had to stay with him. He came home at 2 o'clock very depressed, & as I read the paper, & he was having his dinner & telling my Mother how ill Mr T. was, he burst into tears. It quite unnerves me to see my Father distressed. Oh what would I not suffer to ease his mind of his painful load

316 Lucy Riland (1775–1869), a major benefactor of Walmley church. She was daughter of John Riland, vicar of Sutton Coldfield 1790–1822.

of anxiety. Went to Mrs Holbeche's dinner party in his place with my Mother & Miriam.

Wednesday, 29 August 1866

Went to dinner at Penns at 6. T. V. H. came also. Rained very heavily as we walked home. Again had reason bitterly to regret the hastiness & arrogance of my impatient heart. In Willie's room[317] I saw a book edited by Orby Shipley & consisting of a number of Essays on Church subjects. I opened at one by a Lady, & my eye fell on a passage strongly animadverting on Evangelicals in general. It accused them of being utterly devoid of intellect, worldly minded & inconsistent.[318] I foolishly suffered myself to be nettled, & spoke hotly & I fear almost uncharitably. W. gave me the best reproof by remaining perfectly silent. Alas how different was my conduct to that of my Master. When he was reviled he reviled not again. Oh for more of a Christ like spirit. Oh for more gentleness & love & charity.

Thursday, 30 August 1866

Wrote to W. expressing my sorrow for my hastiness. Pride rebelled, but oh glory to God, he enabled me to subdue it. Walked down to Walmley to call on Mr R. but he was out. Heard on Monday from Bertie informing me that Henry had resolved to quit business & to enter the Church as a minister.[319] How wonderful are God's ways! Joyous, joyous news indeed. Another labourer for the dear Master's vineyard, now [?] soldier to fight close under our great Captain's banner. I wrote to both Henry & Bertie. Oh may the Lord bless him in his choice & resolution. He is to read with a Yorkshire clergyman & wishes if possible to matriculate at Oxford.

Friday, 31 August 1866

The last day of the month. Only six weeks more of vacation. How little I seem to have done for God during the 10 that have past. Went down to Albert Smith's & reached home about 9 feeling very tired.

317 William Rawlins.

318 'Evangelicals have much changed. Intellect is found among them no more, and worldliness has sapped their earnestness. Bitter invective has taken the place of hard work, and conventional has succeeded to actual self-denial. A man may live a self-indulgent life, or amass money, without losing caste among them – but he must not enter a theatre. A woman may dress in the height of the fashion, play croquet, and flirt, without any condemnation – if only she does not dance.' From 'The last thirty years in the English church: an autobiography' in *The church and the world: essays on questions of the day*, ed. Orby Shipley (London, 1866), p. 246.

319 Henry C. Squires (1846–1910), m. Wadham 1867, C.M.S. missionary in India 1871–89, rector of St Peter-le-Bailey, Oxford 1889–93, vicar of Holy Trinity, Richmond 1893–1910. In 1878 he married Ada Chavasse.

Saturday, 1 September 1866

Received a very kind note from W. R.. I feel very thankful that I wrote. Went thro' the Park & changed some of the books. I could not find the policemen. Would that I were more bold for Christ. Alas I can scarcely summon up enough courage to speak a word in my Master's name.

Sunday, 2 September 1866

A happy Sabbath indeed. I took a large class of boys at the Sunday School, for on account of the rain Mr Lees did not come. I took the X of St John. I had not prepared it, & I fear that I did not explain & point out its beauty in a sufficiently clear manner. Mr R. preached the Anniversary Sermons. We are entering on the 22nd year.[320] Read during the afternoon & in the evening received the Sacrament. Oh who can tell the rapture of that blessed time. I came to that holy banquet, bowed down with sin, but yet my merciful Lord met me there. Never before did I feel him so near. And I so unworthy too. God's grace is indeed a free gift. My deserts are hell & destruction & yet lo he gives me inexpressible joy & peace. I felt so happy after it was over. My heart seemed so full, when I reached home, & got by myself, words of praise & thanksgiving flowed from my lips. Oh precious Jesus how abundantly hast thou answered my prayer. Oh loving Jesus, now, more than ever I feel that thou lovest me. May I feed on thee by faith. May my soul be stirred up to serve thee better, not in a self righteous spirit, but humbly, prayerfully, trustfully.

Monday, 3 September 1866

Walked down to Walmley to ask Mr R. if he wd have any objection to my going & reading to old Short now & then.[321] He said none whatever. How kind of him. Never can I repay the debt of gratitude I owe to him as my spiritual Father. I can but pray for his welfare. Overtook Maggie & Miriam on my way home & went with them to the mill & stone house.

Wednesday, 5 September 1866

Went & read to old Short. I chose the Pilgrim's Progress. It is a wonderful book, the more I read it, the more I seem to see Bunyan's marvellous insight & experience. The poor old man looked very ill & seemed once or twice to be deeply touched by the simple language of the burdened Christian. Oh that God may apply its words with power to our hearts.

320 St John the Evangelist church, Walmley, was built in 1845.

321 Joseph Short (*c.*1797–1867), shoemaker.

Thursday, 6 September 1866

Walked down to Sutton. Saw Bee & arranged with him about some Latin & Greek in wh he wants help. He still wishes to matriculate at London University & to be ordained. His wife seems a very nice person. Mr & Mrs Blagy came. They are just the same as ever.

Friday, 7 September 1866

Had a dinner party. Everything passed off well. The gas was lighted for the first time. Goddard & his sister came. Mr & Mrs Blagy & my Mother & Father drove over to Lichfield.

Saturday, 8 September 1866

Mr & Mrs B. left. Ground all day. At 6 went to dine at Miss Holbeche's. Had some delightful conversation with Miss Catherine. Ah, when talking to fervent & earnest Xtians how cold seems my heart. It seems to me blacker every day. I think & praised be God for it, that I am seeing daily more plainly, how vain it is to trust to myself for anything. I feel so utterly helpless, so completely steeped in sin. Yes I must look up to Jesus. He is looking down on me. Let me but catch one glimpse of my Lord hanging on the tree, & my sins will indeed fall off my back.

Sunday, 9 September 1866

As T. did not come to the Sunday School, I took his class with my own. His boys did not know a word of their lessons, & from what I could glean *never* attempt to learn them. Surely such a state of things ought not to be allowed to exist. Idle habits are so hard to eradicate. I hardly know what to do. To complain of the negligence of a fellow is invidious & yet it seems the only course open. May God direct me for the best. Read a good deal of Bickersteth's life. Oh to be more like him. How humble & lowly he was. How vile indeed do I appear when compared to him. Solemn thought. What must I appear to the righteous eyes of God? Throw around me, precious Jesus, thy faultless robe of righteousness & cover my nakedness.

Monday, 10 September 1866

Bodington called & stayed talking an hour & a half.[322] My plans were consequently all upset, & I was prevented from going to read to old Short. Felt irritable at the interruption. How slight a thing throws me off my balance.

322 Herbert J. Bodington (1849–1932), m. Queen's 1868, rector of Suffield, Norfolk 1877–92, vicar of Upton Grey, Hants. 1898–1919.

Tuesday, 11 September 1866

Went & read to Short. I really enjoy Bunyan more & more each time I read the Pilgrim Progress. May God bless the book to my soul. Went to Albert Smith as usual.

Wednesday, 12 September 1866

Went to Bee & helped me [*sic*] on with his Virgil as well as I could. Mainey Robinson came to tea. Mamma & Maggie dined out. Played at croquet & chess. M. sat down & had a rubber. I did not play myself, but my conscience reproached me that I did not prevent him. I know Mr R. disapproves of cards, & yet I suffer his son, the son of him to whom I owe what worlds cannot repay, to sit down to whist without a word. And yet I profess to be willing to confess Xt before men.

Saturday, 15 September 1866

Walked into Birmingham. Read at the Library for a couple of hours & was measured for some clothes &c. Walked out again at 3 o'clock. Maggie went with me. She stepped out nobly, but I fear the distance was too long.

[Friday, 14 September 1866]

Fanny's baby baptized. Ludovic performed the ceremony. Maggie was Godmother. Ikey & myself Godfathers.[323] I have taken on myself solemn vows. Oh may the Lord help me to perform them.

Sunday, 16 September 1866

My boys tolerably good. They do not learn their lessons as well as I shd like but I hope they will improve. They are generally attentive. I fear that there is as much or even more need for reform in their teacher. Oh the deadness of my heart! What can exceed it. Mr Robinson preached in the morning on Prayer, & in the evening on the 'baptism' wherewith Xt was baptized for our sakes.

Saturday, 22 September 1866

I have not written my diary for a week, for I have had nothing worth recording. I have gone on as usual. But when I look back on my thoughts, words & deeds during the last six days, what a humiliating spectacle presents itself. My heart has been throughout cold & dead. Instead of looking up to Jesus, I have been contemplating myself. I have suffered my work to occupy an undue portion of my time. My evening prayers have been drowsy, my morning prayers wandering & distracted. Far from enjoying any blessed, soul reviving communion with God, I

323 Fanny Chavasse's brother, Isaac A. Evans (*c.* 1831–1912), farmer.

have suffered myself to be the slave of vain thoughts & imaginations which all tend to magnify self & to lead me from the truth as it is in Jesus. How I have neglected every means of grace! How I have wilfully shut my ears to the Gospel message! How vain glorious have I been! How worldly, slothful, censorious, envious, discontented, irritable, hypocritical yea a 'very painted hypocrite'. And yet I have yearned in my inmost heart to be found nearer to Jesus. I have longed to love Jesus more, to work more earnestly for Jesus. Oh blessed thought that Jesus loves me. *Me*, the vile & specious worm. Me, though I crucify him daily. Me, though I reject him hourly. Oh the surpassing love of Jesus, to love such a one as I am. Oh the wonderful mercy & gentleness of Jesus, to be willing to save so rebellious a child. To him then I must come, just [as] I am. I cast myself at the foot of his cross. I plead nothing but Cavalry, Cavalry [*sic*]. Jesus Master pity me! Thou dost pity me – yes I believe that even now thou art ready to receive me. Bind me to thee sweet Saviour so fast that I may never, never, never be able to break away.

Sunday, 23 September 1866

Got up feeling jaded, but thank God the languor wore off while I was at the Sunday School. In Church I felt drowsy. I fear that I give way to wandering thoughts more than ever. Am I allowing my work to usurp so large a portion of my time & to engross so large a share of my attention, as to materially affect my religious duties? May the Lord help me to keep the world down to its proper level. Oh how hard it is, to take just sufficient interest in the things of the world as to enable one to advance the better the glory of Jesus. How difficult to bestow just so much zeal to worldly concerns as will not draw one away from God. Mr R. preached in the morning on 'prayer', in the evening on the approach of the Second Advent of our Lord. T. V. H. called during the afternoon & so shortened my time for private reading. He went to Church with us.

Thursday, 27 September 1866

My twentieth birthday. I have passed twenty years of my life. And oh how humiliating is the retrospect. How much have I lived for this world, how little for Christ. In what dark colours do my own sin & depravity stand out, & how wonderfully bright seems the long suffering of God. What a merciful Providence has watched off [*sic*] me, guiding my reluctant steps in a way that I knew not, & bringing me, when I least expected & least desired it, to prepare for the holiest & best of earthly professions – the Ministry of God's Word. First the schoolboy at Chesterfield looking forward to Medicine as my future calling with some lingering hope of the army. Then struck down by sickness, brought to the very door of the grave, face to face with the King of Terrors, & made to feel that I dared not die that my religion had hitherto been mere formalism & lip service, specious indeed to the eye of man, lulling even my own soul, but at the proof found to be but a vain thing, a broken reed, a shadowy support. Then a daily pupil at Mr Felton's coming under the Scriptural teaching of Mr R. – still a formalist, the impressions apparently so sincere, & the horror of dying unprepared all gone, melted like summer snow. Then, thro' continued weakness, afflicted with a curvature of the spine, wh once seemed likely to cripple me for life & still requiring watchful care, supposed to be unequal for any great labour & sent for a year to Oxford St.[324] There, what opportunities of doing good were neglected, what wickedness was suffered to remain unrebuked. There too apparently shut out from all hope of entering a profession, my reading hours limited, my work for the most part mechanical, & my future prospects a wealthy merchant[:] who cd have foretold a change of life for me? But just when what faint sparks of religion I had still smouldering in my soul, seemed all but quenched; just when from a mere formalist, I seemed to be sinking a step lower & becoming altogether worldly minded; just when I thought that I had become accustomed & reconciled to my mode of life, & all ambition for seeking another appeared to have gone[:] lo as it were a hand from heaven is put forth & I am snatched from business. My spine was worse, I must rest it as much as possible. Then the eight long months of idleness, lying on a couch & doing little else but read English, months fraught with sorrow & weariness & death, when the Gracious Lord first moved my heart, & thro' the instrumentality of dear Mr R.'s Confirmation lectures drew my wayward will towards him. Then the sudden change for the better in the state of my health, my beloved Father's determination to send me to College, & my own desire to become a physician – the darkness past, the Sun breaking out at last. Then the deepening of my convictions under the preaching of dear Mr R., & the silent & wonderful influence of the yet unseen E..[325] Then the gradual & mysterious desire, faint at first, & scarcely perceptibly but gathering strength daily to prepare by God's help for the Ministry. Then the laborious struggle with Albert Smith to prepare for College & to recover lost ground; the hopes of gaining a Scholarship, & the scattering of those hopes, the longing to become a great scholar, & the loving Wisdom wh forbad that longing to be gratified. And lastly the commencement of my University career & the untold privileges & mercies of my first year at College. Oh as I look back what can I do but wonder at the marvellous signs of God's hand. Is he not visible even in my sorrows? Has he not, as I humbly trust he has, made the death of my precious E. the means of loosening my affections from the things of this world? Who am I most Holy Father that I shd have received all this at thy hand? Death & Hell wd have been my just reward, & lo thou hast

324 No. 63 Oxford Street, Birmingham, one of the business premises of Chavasse's cousin, Horace Chavasse (1834–1917), iron and steel merchant.

325 'Euphrosyne'.

crowned me with innumerable blessings – my cup of bliss seems running over.[326] All the past forgiven for Jesus' sake. Precious Jesus! oh may I from this day forward live more for thee. I need more of God's most Holy Spirit. I seem to see my own appalling sinfulness more clearly each day. I need more light, more knowledge, more faith, more love. I long to walk closer to Jesus, but my own vile heart keeps me back. Oh that I may from henceforth strive to live nearer to him, not conformed to this world but transformed by the renewing of my mind.[327] Another decade lies before me. Boyhood is fast passing away, & Manhood approaching. I see the difficulties, the perils, the responsibilities wh surround my path. To attempt to battle against them in my own strength would be vain & presumptuous. I must put all my confidence in Jesus.

Fanny came down with the baby. Read to old Short in the afternoon.

Saturday, 29 September 1866

My Father & Mother went over to Rushall to spend Sunday. Walked up to Sutton; changed some of the books in the Park. Called on Mrs Sadler. I thought she looked very ill.

Sunday, 30 September 1866

My last Sunday at home. Rained very fast in the morning. I walked to the Sunday School but Miriam very reluctantly stayed at home. As there were few teachers, I took two classes & read with them a chapter that I had not prepared. I did not succeed in interesting them. They were rather noisy, & one or two positively troublesome. Who is to blame? No one but the teacher. How often do I find the hour spent in the Sunday School, the exact reflex of my week-day life. Alas how much have I to bewail my own dullness of heart & indifference. I had these boys as a charge for whom I must one day give an account to the great Lord of the vineyard. Well might he call me an unprofitable servant. But oh! I will fly to Jesus & cling fast to his cross. I must pray more for these poor lads. I must pray more for a loving spirit & for patient forbearance. Blessed thought God's word cannot return unto him void.[328] Went with Miriam to the School in the afternoon. Mr R. preached as usual. Read a large portion of Bickersteth's Life. God enabled me to pour out my whole soul before him in prayer. He brought my sins to my remembrance, & as dear Mr R. said 'when God brings your sins before your face, it is a sign that he has cast them behind his back.' Oh Lord my Strength & my Redeemer.[329]

326 Psalm xxiii. 5.
327 Romans xii. 2.
328 Isaiah lv. 11.
329 Psalm xix. 14.

Monday, 1 October 1866
My Father & Mother came back from Rushall. Went & read to old Short. I think he is fast approaching his end. He seemed very drowsy & unable to concentrate his attention. What a perilous course, to defer coming to Jesus until one's death's bed.

Tuesday, 2 October 1866
Went to the Green Lanes School & took leave of Mr Cramp.[330] Heard the boys read for a quarter of an hour. I do not think it wise putting them down to the 'Articles' & their Scripture Proofs. In the evening went to Albert Smith. I fear I uttered my opinion of the Regius Professor rather too freely.[331] I must strive by God's help to be more guarded with my remarks.

Wednesday, 3 October 1866
Went to Bee in the afternoon. I think he is getting on with his Greek. In the evening Henry & Kitty drove over. We had a large dinner Party.

Thursday, 4 October 1866
Henry & Kitty left. Read to Short for the last time that glorious description of the entry of Christian & Hopeful into Heaven. May the dear Lord move his heart. Called on Mr R. but he was out, then bid Mr Felton goodbye.

Friday, 5 October 1866
Changed the Library books for the last time. Went to Bee for the last time. Went to Albert Smith for the last last time – perhaps for ever. Now that the last day has come I do feel a little depressed. I fear that I only value my great advantages when I am about to lose them. Finished Bickersteth's life. His death was like his life, a glorious example of childlike trust in Jesus. Jesus was to him all things in life, Jesus was his staff & his rod in death. A Saviour indeed – and I can, by God's help, have him for my Saviour too.

Saturday, 6 October 1866
Got up late feeling tired & jaded & troubled with a dull wearing headache which however left me as the morning went on. Packed up my things. My dear Mother, tho' very unwell herself, working like a Galley slave. Oh the depth of a Mother's love. In my morning devotions cold & wanderings [*sic*], but in the middle of the day when my boxes were all ready, some overpowering thoughts of the responsibilities of another Term & my own utter weakness came upon me. God enabled

330 James Cramp (1813–98), first headmaster of Green Lanes boys' school 1840–78.
331 Robert Payne Smith.

me to come to his mercy seat in prayer, & as I raised up to him my cry for help & strength in my Redeemer's name, that exquisite text flashed thro' my mind 'My Beloved is mine, & I am his.'[332] Oh who can tell the exceeding comfort of those few words. My Bible being packed up, I took my Prayer book & opened at the Epistle 'Put on the *whole* armour of God.[333] May these two sweet texts be for my consolation & admonition during the coming term. I commit myself wholly to the care of Jesus. But ah the deceitfulness of my heart. Before I left home, a little trivial remark served to call up all the latent envy which I thought subdued. Oh for more of the mind of Jesus. Started for Worcester at 8.19. Reached Aunt's at 6.30.[334] Found to my horror at the Worcester Station that my carpet bag was not visible. Whether I left it in the Sutton Coldfield train, or whether it never started from Wylde Green (I do not recollect ever seeing it) is doubtful. Omitted to mention that I went down to Walmley in the morning & saw Mr R.. He was so very kind, & prayed so earnestly with me. How can I thank God sufficiently for placing me under such a devoted man. He is indeed to me like a Father. I can view him in no other light. Truly I am rich, with such a dearly loved Father as I have, & such a dear spiritual Father as Mr R..

Sunday, 7 October 1866

Went to St George's church. The incumbent is a very good man,[335] but the congregation was not large, & the service struck me as being very cold. I do not long for a high Ritual; I do not wish for splendid singing & music but I do yearn for congregational singing, for the whole congregation to join in the responses. The sermon was on the strong man armed – Satan, the palace – the human heart, the stronger than he – Jesus Xt.[336] In the afternoon went to the Cathedral. The singing was confined to the choir, the people stood & listened. Alas for my beloved Church. In the evening went again to St George's. Mr Lane the curate preached.[337] I much enjoyed his Sermon. 'I am Jesus whom thou persecutest.'[338]

Monday, 8 October 1866

Walked to Powick, where if all be well Ada is to go to school. The village stands on the crest of the hill. The church yard looks over the valley thro' wh flows the

332 Song of Songs vi. 3.
333 Ephesians vi. 11.
334 Margaret Chavasse.
335 Benjamin Davis (*c.*1809–96), vicar of St George's, Claines, Worcester 1841–73, of Cleeve Prior, Worcs. 1873–94.
336 Luke xi. 21–2.
337 Charles Lane (*c.*1839–99), curate of St George's, Claines, Worcester 1865–9, vicar of Wheelock, Cheshire 1872–99.
338 Acts ix. 5; xxvi. 15.

Teme a tributary of the Severn. There was rather a good epitaph on one of the gravestones

'All you that do my grave pass by,
As you are now, so once was I,
As I am now so you must be,
Therefore prepare to follow me.'[339]

I then went thro' a country thickly studded with apple trees, thro' lanes with hedges covered with blackberries to Bransford & thence to Worcester. Altogether it was a most interesting walk. In the afternoon went to see the present of the Worcester Corporation to the Countess of Dudley, but we just missed it.[340] Carpet bag came.

Tuesday, 9 October 1866

Went to see this exquisite gift again, & found it at the Manufactory. It consists of two diminutive tea cups, a teapot, a sugar basin, a cream jug, & a small tray. It is valued at 200 guineas; to me it seemed worth 5. The painting & ornamentation was however exquisite. Afterwards went over the Porcelain Works. I was very much pleased & interested. No boys are allowed to work under 14 years of age. Every thing is paid for by the piece. I was glad to see some of Cassell's advertisements pinned up in the workshops. In the afternoon went for a walk. My feet were sore, so that I found locomotion painful. Aunt had an evening party.

Wednesday, 10 October 1866

Went to Malvern. Looked over the Abbey Church – a magnificent building. Then drove along the foot of the Hills right round the Range. The views were magnificent, especially those on the Herefordshire side. Returned to Worcester at 5.

Thursday, 11 October 1866

Walked round by Martin Hus[s]in[g]tree & Hin[d]lip. Apples & blackberries & acorns everywhere in abundance. In the afternoon attended the Cathedral service. It seemed so cold & lifeless. Went round the building. King John's Tomb is interesting, & so is a tablet & quaint inscription erected in memory of the wife of

339 This epitaph and variations on it were popular in the eighteenth and nineteenth centuries.

340 In December 1865 the city of Worcester presented the earl and countess of Dudley with a cabaret service in celebration of their recent marriage. The Royal Porcelain Works (now Royal Worcester) made a duplicate set for public display, still held by the Museum of Worcester Porcelain.

Izccak [*sic*] Walton.[341] The work of Restoration is being pushed forward, but the verger seemed to think that it would not be completed for 7 more years.[342] I do delight in a fine church or Cathedral. Lofty roofs, noble pillars, broad aisles, a majestic reach from east to West & grand transepts solemnize & touch my heart. Who can wonder at the Puritan Milton's passionate outburst?[343] Had to read aloud a portion of a most senseless novel. Hic misero miles![344] Heard from Oxford. I was right about the day for return.

Friday, 12 October 1866

Walked over to Kempsey & spent the day with Aunt Charlotte.[345] After dinner she took me round the village & over the Church. A branch of a tree growing into the Church was very curious. The tomb near of 'Edmund Wylde' is said to be an ancestor of my Mother's.[346] Called on the Bournes[347] & saw Bank House where Col. Grant lived.[348] Aunt seemed to be very happy & has a very nice place. Walked into Worcester again at 6 o'clock. Had some sweet thoughts of Jesus as I walked. Oh that I could ever feed on him in my heart by faith.

341 'Here lyeth buryed, soe much as could dye, of ANNE the wife of IZAAK WALTON who was, a woman of remarkeable prudence and, of the Primitive Piety, her great and generall knowledge, being adorn'd with such true Humility, and blest with soe much Christian meekenesse, as made her worthy of a more memorable Monument. She dyed (Alas that she is dead!) the 17th of Aprill 1662 Aged 52. Study to be like her.'

342 Worcester Cathedral was 'restored' and rebuilt between 1857 and 1874 under the direction of architects Abraham Perkins and George Gilbert Scott.

343 From John Milton's 'Il Penseroso' (1645):

'But let my due feet never fail,
To walk the studious Cloysters pale,
And love the high embowed Roof,
With antick Pillars massy proof,
And storied Windows richly dight,
Casting a dimm religious light.
There let the pealing Organ blow,
To the full voic'd Quire below,
In Service high, and Anthems cleer,
As may with sweetness, through mine ear,
Dissolve me into extasies,
And bring all Heav'n before mine eyes.'

344 'This soldier in misery'.

345 Charlotte Chavasse (1799–1886), mother of Sophia Bourne and Albert Chavasse.

346 Edmund Wylde (*c.*1588–1620), sheriff of Worcestershire. A choirboy's confiscated chestnut, thrown behind Wylde's effigy by the sexton, germinated in 1830, grew over ten feet tall and died in the summer of 1895.

347 Sophia Bourne's mother-in-law, Elizabeth Bourne (*c.*1794–1875), lived at Church House, Kempsey, with her four daughters, Marianne (*c.*1824–1907), Caroline (*c.*1826–1910), Emily (*c.*1833–1906) and Mary (b. *c.*1834).

348 Ludovick Grant (1750–1830), army officer with East India Company, father of Catherine M. Grant (1800–42), first wife of Chavasse's father.

Saturday, 13 October 1866

Left Worcester for Oxford at 2.15 & reached my destination about 4.45. Sent my luggage on by omnibus & wrote to Aunt & my Father from the Union. Got to Corpus at 5.35. My new rooms looked beautiful. Praised be God for giving me such a liberal Father. Mrs Baldwin & Charles are no longer scouts of the staircase. Instead of them we have Allen & a new boy named James. When I had unpacked, & put away my books & clothes had some tea with Channing who dropped in. Scarcely had he finished & gone when Churchill, Lock & Scott came in. Dear fellows how my heart bounded to see them. Two of them had some tea. Finally Knox made his appearance, looking I thought unwell; he followed their example. Went to Mr C.'s meeting at 8.45. Eight men were there & Nash & Tonge.[349] We sang those sweet hymns, 'Not all the blood of beasts' & 'How sweet the name of Jesus sounds'.[350] Mr C. spoke to us very earnestly on the responsibilities of another term, exhorting us to cast away all timidity & shyness & speak more lovingly & more boldly for Jesus. Bidding us in conclusion look singly & steadily up to this our great High Priest. And here at the beginning of my second academical year looking forward to the race I have to run, how at the very outset, my heart seems to die within me & my spirit to fail. Oh what can I do in my own strength? Nothing, nothing. Jesus, Master help. All my hope, all my strength is in thee. Thou canst endue me with a lion's might. Thou canst feed me with heavenly food. Thou canst draw me nearer to thee daily. I am thy younger brother – oh mine Elder Brother let me cling to thee. Trusting only in thee, & in thy strength I make the following resolutions

I. To be more instant in prayer – a. For myself b. For my friends c. For everything I undertake.

II. To study more God's Holy Word.

III. To avoid controversy as far as possible.

IV. To be decided myself, but charitable & forbearing towards those who differ from me.

V. To do everything as for Jesus.

VI. To make everything subservient to one gt aim & end – 'the Ministry of God's word'.

VII. To be more sympathizing & zealous for the spiritual welfare of others.

VIII. To be more watchful over my words, deeds & thoughts.

IX. To bring all my joys, doubts, & difficulties to the feet of Jesus.

X. To trust more confidingly in Jesus.

349 Thomas A. Nash (*c.*1833–98), curate of St Aldate's, Oxford 1860–8, vicar of St Philip's, Heigham, Norfolk 1868–77, rector of Lowestoft 1880–9, of Little Wenlock, Shropshire 1889–98.

350 Hymns by Isaac Watts and John Newton respectively.

By God's help I will read over these resolutions weekly. May he give me a double portion of his Spirit, & enable me to perform them. May he hide me under the shadow of his wings, & keep me in safety. I earnestly hope & pray that I desire not honour or wealth or popularity. Let me long only to be useful. Let me yearn for closer communion with, a clearer sight of my dear Redeemer. Like the plague stricken Israelite I would look up with the eye of faith to the cross of Xt for consolation & encouragement, nourishment & strength.

Sunday, 14 October 1866

Got up at 6.30. When dressed & ready for chapel could not unlock my bedroom door. In my exertions to turn the key, I broke the handle. It wanted then but 10 minutes to eight. Fortunately Channing was passing at the time & I sent him for James, who burst the door open. I felt very thankful. Our places in chapel are altered. There are 11 freshmen. Scott & Lock came to breakfast. Saw Albert for a few minutes. He seemed fagged I thought. Went with Lock & Knox to hear Archdeacon Clarke [*sic*].[351] The congregation was not large. Read the first chapter of Bonar's 'God's way of Holiness'. At lunch time Mylne came to see his old rooms & with him Symonds.[352] They commonized with me. After Hall went with Knox to St Aldate's. Dear Mr C. was most earnest, my cold heart needs awakening. Sanctify me sweet Saviour. Knox had some tea on our return. He is not well I am sure. He seems depressed. Went to Tonge's at 9 p.m.. W. introduced some of his theories. How they sicken me. They appear to incumber rather than to aid one's faith. How sweet to turn bewildered from them to the simplicity of trusting in Jesus. I was very silent – too silent. I must read up beforehand. Read with (thank God) much comfort Ps XXIII & the references. Oh the privilege of being a lamb of Xt's.

Monday, 15 October 1866

Albert came to breakfast. He goes down today. I shall very much miss him. Furneaux gave us our first logic lecture. At 4.15 went to the Prayer Meeting. About 10 were present. A discussion arose afterwards respecting altering the time. Finally it was decided to hold the Meeting at 4.30 on Mondays & Wednesdays. Streeten came in to tea. Do not feel well. Cannot work. Feel chilly & queer altogether. Jesus is all my trust.

351 University sermon, preached by Charles C. Clerke (1798–1877), archdeacon of Oxford 1830–77.

352 Arthur G. Symonds (1844–1924), m. Corpus 1863, advisor and secretary to various M.P.s 1875-1918.

Thursday, 18 October 1866

Breakfasted with Streeten. Furneaux gave us back our translations. Mine was very feeble & very inaccurate. I stand low in his estimation, I fancy – it is good for pride. Went a short walk with Knox. Was much startled & deeply moved to hear from Lock that Addis, Hopkins & Garrett of Balliol & Wood of Trinity had gone over to Rome.[353] For the first time in my life the reality of a perversion came home with stunning violence to my heart. I could scarcely believe it. Even now (11.30 p.m.) I do [not] seem to realize the truth. Only yesterday I saw H.'s wan face. Oh what a terrible thought, to leave light for darkness, a reformed for an apostate Church; to brand all their friends & relatives as schismatics & heretics. To join the Roman Church only to be overwhelmed in her certain & fast approaching ruin. Oh if the Histories of their inmost hearts could be known, shd we find that their Bible had been studied with prayer, Jesus approached in calm & childlike faith, & their Heavenly Father earnestly implored for His guiding Spirit? They have gone, & it remains for us whom they have left diligently to examine ourselves, lest we too, tho' now protesting against Roman error, cherish in our hearts the fatal seed, whose fruit will lead us on in their very steps. Ritualism! Ritualism! if a man of clear & logical mind be ensnared by thy splendours, thy gaudy flowers will not satisfy his hungering soul – he will know no rest, until, ere he himself suspects it, he is borne into the full blaze of Roman Ritual & Roman superstition. Oh Jesus, keep me & all dear to me safe from the tempter. Succour thy Church – her foes are numberless, & even her own sons are proving traitors & her destroyers.

Friday, 19 October 1866

Went with Tonge to Mr Linton's Prayer Meeting. Mr L. himself was absent so T. conducted it. Called later in the afternoon on Honey. He told me that Newman was coming to Oxford next week to receive into the Roman Church 'a distinguished member of the University', whom none knows as yet but rumour is busy with many a great man's name. U. declared to Honey his opinion that this was but the beginning of a great movement. Alas it seems to be but the first heavy drops of the thunder shower. No less than 20 undergraduates are said to be contemplating secession. Where will it end? The Head of the Church only knows. The sky is dark & lowering & the Ark is tossed upon high rolling waves. Our eyes must be uplifted to the great Captain of our Salvation. Help us Lord Jesus.

353 William E. Addis (1844–1917), m. Balliol 1861, Roman Catholic priest 1872–88, became a unitarian, lecturer at Manchester College, Oxford 1898–1910, returned to the Church of England, vicar of All Saints, Knightsbridge 1910–17. Gerard Manley Hopkins (1844–89), m. Balliol 1863, Roman Catholic priest and poet. Alfred W. Garrett (1844–1929), m. Balliol 1863, Indian education service in Bengal 1868–84, emigrated to Tasmania. Alexander Wood (1845–1912), m. Trinity 1863.

Saturday, 20 October 1866

Called on the Halls. Felt languid & could not get thro' much work. Next week, by God's help I must really buckle to. Went to Christopher's Meeting. No less than 38 men were present. How comforting. θεῷ δόξα.[354] Mr C. was most earnest. My own heart reproached me sadly. I had persuaded no one to come. Oh Jesus I am a barren tree, pour into my branches quickening life. Dear Mr C. spoke on Ph III 4 'Rejoice in the Lord'. A positive command. He pointed out the increased usefulness which lay before a man by his being a rejoicing Xtian. He referred to depression, bidding us look singly up to Jesus. It was not *the strength* of our faith which saves us; our faith might be very weak but God's strength was made perfect in weakness. That we must not brood over past sins, for we shd never know happiness until we felt that we were washed clean in the Saviour's blood. Our Repentance must not stop at conviction, we must go on to know the Lord, whom to know was life & peace. He exhorted the older men to take a bold stand for Xt, to speak in their Master's behalf. The freshmen, he lovingly advised to choose their friends carefully & to cast in their lot with those who loved the Lord Jesus, but yet to be courteous to all men. Spoke to Bazley after the Meeting about the recent Secessions. He took a gloomy view of affairs. Very many men seem wavering. Oh thou all wise Spirit direct them that seek thy aid. And looking to myself, who love the Church of England so dearly, what an unprofitable servant do I seem to be. While Satan's emissaries are so zealous how lukewarm am I. Enable me gracious Father, firmly & lovingly to bear witness for the truth. I need more light, more faith, more earnestness. Supply my need out of thy exceeding fulness.

Sunday, 21 October 1866

Went to the Sunday School with Tonge.[355] It seemed like home days having a class. I had five little boys, who behaved very well & seem to have been well taught. May God bless them to me, & me to them. Went in the evening to St Aldate's with Childs,[356] & after tea to Tonge's with Horton.

Tuesday, 23 October 1866

Smith & I went to our district. By God's help, I will give up two days in the week to it. Some of the people seemed glad to see me. Others were indifferent & others appeared to think my coming rather a nuisance. What a comforting thought, that not a word spoken for Jesus can be in vain. The Tract distribution Prayer Meeting

354 'Glory to God'.

355 Chavasse began to teach a class at the St Peter-le-Bailey Sunday School.

356 Christopher Childs (1846–1928), m. Corpus 1866, surgeon, lecturer in public health at University College, London.

held in Elsmere's room. About 16 men were present. Moor was there. I was so glad to see him. The Botley district was discussed. Mr B. the clergyman is very chary in giving his consent.[357] The rules of the society require that the clergyman's consent shd be gained. The question is can a forced consent be so regarded. In my own mind I think not. We must act up to the spirit of the rules. It was finally settled that Nash shd see Mr B..

Wednesday, 24 October 1866

Had a short walk with dear Lock & afterwards with Bazley & Ward. We went together to the Prayer Meeting. Seven were present. Felt hot & tired, & did not derive that benefit from it that I might have done. Alas how terribly do I neglect these precious means of grace. Help me, my Saviour. Gave a small wine in the evening. Afterwards called on Diggles [*sic*] at Merton.[358] He is a mathematical scholar, & seemed poor fellow rather lonely. A sad accident happened on the river. Poor Bradley of New was drowned thro' the upsetting of a light four.[359] He was only 19, & elected just 10 days ago to an open exhibition at New. And if it had been me – shd I have been prepared to go? Oh that I may see & feel the uncertainty of life, & plant myself more firmly on the Rock of ages. The mournful news cast a gloom over every one. May it be a warning to many & to me. I feel poorly & jaded. My head aches & I cannot work. Maybe the all wise God will soon send for me. Am I fit to stand at the bar before him? Not in my own righteousness for they are but filthy rags, Jesus is my only, my reiterated plea. B. came to my room in the evening & began to argue about Baptismal Regeneration & the Real Presence. I refused to be drawn into an argument. C. too came & had some tea, & when we were alone, he told me that as yet he had not formed his views, he was very young, he had plenty of time. He thought at present he was Broad Church, he had once been High & so on. I asked him, whether he thought poor Bradley too young to think on religion & what if he had been in his place. He seemed struck & soon afterwards went back to his own room. Oh thou Blessed Spirit turn his heart to love spiritual things.

357 William H. Bliss (1835–1909), vicar of North Hinksey (of which Botley was part) 1866–9, seceded to Church of Rome 1869, archivist, representative of British Public Record Office in Rome.

358 John W. Diggle (1847–1920), m. Merton 1866, vicar of Mossley Hill, Liverpool 1875–97, archdeacon of Westmorland 1896–1902, of Birmingham 1903–4, bishop of Carlisle 1905–20.

359 John H. Bradley (1847–66), m. New 1866.

Saturday, 27 October 1866

Dined with Barker at Brasenose. Afterwards went with Diggle to Mr C.'s meeting. Mr Carus gave us a beautiful address.[360] May God bless his words to my soul, & the souls of those who heard him. Some 120 undergraduates were present.

[Friday, 26 October 1866]

Bontein of Oriel came & lunched with me, & afterwards we went a walk together.[361] I found him a truly humble Xtian. Thank God for another dear friend. We held the same views on all important points, & how much was there for me to learn from his bright faith, his childlike trustfulness, his simple dependence on Jesus. Dined in the evening with Streeten at Queen's & went with him to Chapel. Went to the N. V.. Monnington read on Wycliffe.[362]

Sunday, 28 October 1866

Went to my class. My little boys very good & attentive. In the evening went with Brooks to St Aldate's. Canon Carus preached on 'the necessity for studying the Bible'. I feel it so, but yet do not suffer the feeling to influence me. Teach me Lord to love thy Word more & more.

Monday, 29 October 1866

Charlie Black came to lunch. Afterwards went & left some tracts at a few new houses in my district. Went to the Prayer Meeting. The number of men attending is very small[:] generally not more than ten. Raise up good & faithful men, oh thou Lord of the Harvest. In the evening went to the Bible Meeting.[363]

Tuesday, 30 October 1866

Went with Smith to Hincksey. I think some of my happiest days are those spent in my district. May God make me a blessing. I am indeed but a weak instrument, but in his infinite love he does not despise my weakness.

Thursday, 1 November 1866

Rowed down to Iffley for the first time this term. I felt rather strange with the oars.

360 William Carus (1802–91), fellow of Trinity, Cambridge 1829–51, vicar of Christ Church, Winchester 1860–70.

361 Courthope S. Bontein (*c.* 1847–1902), m. Oriel 1866, joined Plymouth brethren.

362 George J. Monnington (1844–1924), m. Queen's 1863, various curacies; or Thomas P. Monnington (1846–1937), m. Corpus 1866, vicar of Penrith 1888–1905, rural dean of Ulverston 1905–18.

363 Annual meeting of the Oxford auxiliary of the British and Foreign Bible Society.

Friday, 2 November 1866

Went to Linton's Prayer Meeting. Afterwards wrote several letters at the Union. In the evening Coles read an Essay 'on English Catholics & the see of Rome'. The Paper was very nicely written, but singularly destitute of facts. A large number of men were present.

Saturday, 3 November 1866

Went a walk with Knox. In the evening went to the Prayer Meeting. About 36 men were present. How comforting & cheering. Surely our God is a God who heareth prayer. I felt very unhappy that I had not asked more men if they wd accompany me. I had only tried C.. Alas! how selfish is my religion, & how cowardly & fearful is my heart. May the Lord give me strength.

Sunday, 4 November 1866

Received the Sacrament in our college Chapel. My mind felt unsettled & I did not derive that calm comfort from it that I fain would have. Jesus all my confidence is in thee. Went to the Sunday School. My dear little boys very good. Read in my rooms until 2 p.m. then went a short walk with Scott. Amidst much error, he has the germs of truth. This is the first walk I have taken on a Sunday merely for a walk's sake. I felt so languid & listless in trying to read for 6 continuous hours that I went out with him. I think at Oxford the case is somewhat different to home. May God direct me to do what is right, & not suffer me to throw a stumbling block in the way of a weak brother. If I do go out, I must strive to talk on religious subjects. In the evening went to St Aldate's with Knox; afterwards to Tonge.

Monday, 5 November 1866

There was a small battle between town & gown but nothing very serious [:] the Proctors were too active.[364] Gave a small breakfast.

Tuesday, 6 November 1866

My Father & Mother came. I got leave from the Dean for them to have a hot dinner in my rooms.[365] Afterwards took them down to the river. Met Mr Christopher. I was so glad of the opportunity of introducing him. Went to Magdalene College Chapel at 5 p.m.. The singing is superb, but I could not join. Sat & talked in my rooms until 10. My Father & Mother slept at the Clarendon.

364 The annual Bonfire Night disturbances.

365 John M. Wilson (1813–81), fellow of Corpus 1841–69, dean 1856–69, president 1872–81, Whyte's professor of moral philosophy 1846–74.

Wednesday, 7 November 1866

We all breakfasted in my room. After taking a walk along the High, my Father & Mother left at 11.30. I was very sorry to lose them. I so much enjoyed their short trip. How thankful I ought to be for such parents. Lunched with Smith: afterwards went a walk with Shepherd of Wadham.[366] Attended the Prayer Meeting. I took the Chapter & first Prayer. I felt very nervous but the Lord gave me strength & I very much enjoyed the Meeting. θεῷ δόξα.

Thursday, 8 November 1866

Called on Bone of Pembroke & took him to my district.[367] I hope he will be induced to join the O.U.T.D.S.. He knows Thornton of Cambridge the son of Spencer Thornton.[368]

Friday, 9 November 1866

Went to Linton's Prayer Meeting, but was unfortunately late. I did not get away from Conington's lecture until nearly two, but I did not make as much haste as I might have done.

Saturday, 10 November 1866

C.'s Meeting again well attended. I never experienced so wonderful an answer to prayer.

Sunday, 11 November 1866

Went to the Sunday School. My little boys very good. In the afternoon walked round the Parks for an hour with Ward. He broached his views about the Napoleonic Theory. Would that he were not so fanciful. He is so humble & earnest withal. In the evening went with Downer & Bontein to St Aldate's.[369] Mr Christopher preached. Went with Knox to Tonge's. We had a large meeting, & I hope a very profitable one.

366 Clement C.-W. Shepheard (later Shepheard-Walwyn) (*c.* 1848–89), m. Wadham 1866, rector of Sacombe, Herts. 1885–9.

367 William M. Bone (1848–1927), m. Pembroke 1866, rector of Bishop's Fonthill, Wilts 1892–1900, of Swayfield, Lincs. 1906–24.

368 Claude C. Thornton (1844–1921), m. Trinity, Cambridge 1862, vicar of High Cross, Herts. 1881–92, rector of Northwold, Norfolk 1892–1910. George R. Thornton (1845–1905), m. Jesus, Cambridge 1864, vicar of St Barnabas, Kensington 1881–1905.

369 Arthur C. Downer (1847–1943), m. Brasenose 1866, vicar of Ilkley 1878–86, rector of St Cuthbert's, Bedford 1886–97, of Selham, Sussex 1913–20.

Tuesday, 13 November 1866

Went to Hincksey with Smith. It is a work of faith. I begin to fear that many who talk so fairly of religion, do not really feel what they say. Oh Father turn their hearts to thee. Keep me from lip-service. Give me more of the mind of Christ.

Wednesday, 14 November 1866

Went down the river & steered Evans' four. I shall be glad when the race has been rowed. Was just in time for the Prayer Meeting.

Thursday, 15 November 1866

At 8.30 Our heat was rowed. We got the Berkshire side. Crawford's boat took the lead & would probably have won had not a four steered right across their way & obliged them to easy for one stroke. We then got ahead & tho' C. put on a good spurt he could not overtake us & we won by three quarters of a boat's length. Bussell's crew won the second heat, contrary I think to expectation. Hanbury took off in consequence of C. having strained himself & very wisely.[370]

Friday, 16 November 1866

The final heat of the Challenge fours was rowed. The wind was very boisterous & the river very high & rough. Unluckily we got the Oxfordshire side, & had to battle against wind & tide. Bussell's boat lead off & gradually improving its position won with comparative [ease] by a length & a half. The result was a great surprize. We were thought sure of the victory. So for the second time I have won a pint. I am afraid E. was rather disappointed. I think part of the blame must rest with him. He does not excel as a stroke although so good an oarsman. He does not seem to be able to quicken. I am glad it is all over.

Saturday, 17 November 1866

Went to my district alone. Asked Diggle to accompany me but he was engaged. Had a very happy visit. Many of the people seemed so willing to hear, & God gave me strength to speak. In the evening went to the Prayer Meeting with Knox, Downer & Bontein to hear Mr Bardsley.[371] He gave us a most able & earnest address on the Character of our Lord as Priest. Shewing how he was called from among the people, was perfect, & was able to sympathize with us. He drew a powerful picture of the Aaronic priesthood as a type of Xt, & of the essential difference between the Levitical & Christian priest, concluding by impressing upon us the blessedness & incomparableness of the Ministry as a calling. I very much

370 Robert W. Hanbury (1845–1903), m. Corpus 1864, M.P. for Tamworth 1872–8, for North Staffs. 1878–80, for Preston 1885–1903.

371 James Bardsley (1808–86), rector of St Anne's, Manchester 1857–80.

liked him. He is not prepossessing in appearance but he is so earnest & so clear. His address was a most valuable one. Barker wants me to read my Essay on Friday;[372] I do not think that I can get it ready so soon. Felt very cold & listless spiritually. I have enjoyed some sweet moments lately, but I have been so negligent & wandering in my prayers & so careless in my Bible reading leaving it often until I have been so tired as to be scarcely able to keep my eyes open. May God forgive me. I have gone back lately. Oh stay my backward career my Father. In spite of the inestimable privileges I enjoy here, how low is the spiritual state of my soul. How worldly, how ambitious, how dead & indifferent. How little have I done for the Lord & his cause, how occupied I have been with my studies & amusements. Oh for a nearer walk with God that I might never fall away. Oh for faith that I might see through the darkness that seems settling round me. Hide not thy face sweet Jesus. Oh hold thou me up.

Sunday, 18 November 1866

Went to my Sunday School. What a privilege it is to have a class. Hastened up to St Mary's to hear the Bishop of Lincoln.[373] Unfortunately I was rather late & he had got well into his subject. The parts of the Sermons wh I heard were most admirable. He spoke very strongly about Rationalism & Ritualism. Superstition he called the Nemesis of unbelief. Heard Bardsley in the evening.[374] Tupper, Knox & Brookes came to tea.

Monday, 19 November 1866

Julius came to lunch.[375] Did not get to the Grinds in time to run for the 100 yds race. Tried for the quarter of a mile but shut up ignominiously. Saw the Merton's Strangers' race. Went to the Prayer meeting. Wrote to Miriam. Read Bonar's introduction to Brief thoughts on the Gospels.[376] Oh how it comforted me. I see now, praise be God in what lies my listlessness & backsliding. I have not been looking wholly to Jesus. I have been absorbed in contemplating my own vile heart & how can I wonder at the effect such a contemplation produced. 'Only believe', oh how those simple words came home to my heart. They ring in my ears. Oh Jesus how precious dost thou seem when thus viewed. Unspeakably precious. Oh the simplicity of the Gospel! May the Spirit press home to my heart this great truth.

372 At the 'New Vitality'.

373 John Jackson (1811–85), bishop of Lincoln 1853–68, of London 1868–85.

374 Bardsley preached at St Aldate's in aid of the Church Pastoral Aid Society.

375 Churchill Julius (1847–1938), m. Worcester 1866, archdeacon of Ballarat 1883–90, bishop of Christ Church 1890–1925, archbishop of New Zealand 1922–5.

376 *Brief thoughts: I. On the gospel II. On the way of coming to satisfaction as to our state before God III. On holding the beginning of our confidence*, ed. Horatius Bonar (London, 1867).

Wednesday, 21 November 1866

Thomas & Bone came to lunch.[377] Afterwards went for a walk with B. & attended the Prayer Meeting on our return. I again lead. I think some senior man ought to be asked. In the evening went to the workhouse with Barker. He asked me to deliver an address there. I consented supposing I should have to speak to a small congregation of 12 or 13. I found however some 50 people assembled, a regular reading desk, & a pulpit. I felt somewhat dismayed, as I had only jotted down some very short notes. Barker read the prayers, & afterwards I spoke to the people from that precious verse, 'Jesus Xt the same yesterday & today & forever'.[378] I was very disconnected, but God gave me fluency. I clung close to the first words of my text. Oh the blessed privilege of speaking to others of Jesus. Had tea in Bazley's rooms. A man named Johnson was there. Did not get to bed until 1.30. But I did not grudge the time. How could I? May the Lord help me to spend & be spent in his service.

Thursday, 22 November 1866

Went a walk with James Hall to Shotover. He is a very nice fellow.

Friday, 23 November 1866

Went to Linton's, & then with Scott walked round by Godstow. Alas! he is far from the truth, & how little able was I to point out his errors. May the Spirit of Truth lead him into all truth.[379]

Saturday, 24 November 1866

Got up late, & had little time for private devotion. This bad habit has been growing on me lately. I must try to turn out earlier. Felt cold & listless, selfish & censorious. Oh Jesus how longsuffering thou art. Went with Smith & Bontein to Hinksey. At first could not speak to the people, but strength was given me. Blessed be God. Called on some new people & offered to leave a tract but the woman refused. I felt discouraged. Such failures must only excite me to more earnest efforts. Thomas came to tea, & went with Knox & myself to Mr C.'s meeting. About 30 were present. My thoughts were somewhat wandering, & I was not so much refreshed as usual. Alas for my own vile heart. I seem to make new resolutions only to break them, to start afresh only to fall back; to enjoy & feel the inexpressible sweetness of being near Jesus only to relapse into deadness of heart, & to experience the exceeding bitterness of being far off from him. Oh

377 ? Henry D. Thomas (1847–89), m. Wadham 1866, vicar of Longdon, Worcs. 1885–9.

378 Hebrews xiii. 8.

379 John xvi. 13.

the wretchedness of unbelief. Afflicted with bodily weakness & spiritual deadness of heart, how great is my need of the Physician.

Sunday, 25 November 1866

Went to my class. In the afternoon heard the Bishop preach at St Mary Magdalene. Read in the evening until 8.30 & then went to Tonge's. Felt very drowsy & languid all day.

Tuesday, 27 November 1866

Went at 7.30 to Linton's.[380] About 12 men were there. They seemed to think it somewhat slow, but I enjoyed it. I had a good talk with Tonge, & the prayers before supper were peculiarly refreshing. I am in a very low spiritual state. May the dear Lord quicken me with his Spirit. Did not get to bed until 2.15.

Friday, 30 November 1866

The last few days I have done little else than work at my Essay. It was finished last night. I read it in Duggan's room. About 12 men were present. Knox very kindly went with me; it was pleasant to have a dear friend near at hand. I felt very nervous but God my merciful Father helped me through. Praised be his name. Geldart & Grose proved valuable champions, & the conversation which followed tho' desultory was interesting. 'Xtian Symbolism' has proved a very interesting subject, tho' it has cost me much time & trouble.

Saturday, 1 December 1866

Went down the river in the afternoon. Voted at the Union for Sanday as President.[381] He was elected. Mr C.'s Meeting well attended. I never knew him so earnest. He was himself moved to tears, & so were many of the men. He spoke of the infinite love of God, of the precious blood of Xt whereby each one of us cd enter into the Holiest of Holies, & of the necessity for all to be cleansed in that healing fountain. I enjoyed it so much. How trifling & poor did all earthful honours & pursuits seem when compared with Jesus. It is the old sad, sad story with me. I have gone astray from that dear Saviour. Oh when shall I love him so dearly as never to forsake.

380 On Tuesday evenings in term time, Linton hosted small groups of undergraduates at his home.

381 William Sanday (1843–1920), scholar of Corpus 1863–6, fellow of Trinity 1866–73, principal of Bishop Hatfield's Hall, Durham 1876–83, fellow of Exeter 1883–95, Lady Margaret professor of divinity 1895–1919.

Sunday, 2 December 1866

Received the Sacrament in our College Chapel. May God help me henceforward to lead a new life & to devote myself more entirely to his service. Went to the Sunday School. My little boys behaved very well. Little H. had learnt 6 verses of the Gospel instead of two. It seemed as much pleasure for him to say them as for me to hear him. Albert came to lunch & stayed with me during the greater part of the afternoon. He returns to London tomorrow. In the evening went with Knox to St Aldate's. Mr C. preached. There was a collection for the new Schools.[382] Felt very drowsy. Alas how much good do I lose by my deadness & formality. Oh for a heart to praise God, fervently, lovingly & continuously. Downer came to tea & went with Knox & myself to Tonge's. About 15 men were present. I could not attend as I shd like to have done. I get so sleepy after a time.

Monday, 3 December 1866

Lunched with Charlie Black & went for a short walk with him. Attended the Prayer Meeting. Took the second prayer. That half hour of sweet communion with God calmed & soothed me. I am not well in myself, & this makes me feel depressed. At times I become happier, but the Sun seems to hide its face again behind the clouds & all becomes dark. I cannot pray without wandering, & coldness. If I try to read my Bible, it appears as if the Devil came & took the good seed out of [my] heart. I find when I reach the end of the chapter that I scarcely know about what I have been reading. I cannot concentrate my attention upon any thing. More than ever, dear Jesus, do I need thee. Save & help me in my hour of need, let me not fall a prey to the enemy. No, No, *No*. Thou hast given me the desire to love thee. Thou too wilt give me the strength.

Tuesday, 4 December 1866

At 6.30 went with Barker, Downer & Diggle to Coal harbour [*sic*]. We found about 20 people assembled in a little cottage. I took the first address & Barker the second. Downer & Diggle each prayed. It was a very delightful time. The service only lasted an hour. There seemed such reality about it. Oh what an unspeakable privilege, & yet how great a responsibility to speak to my fellows about their immortal souls. Oh may the Lord fit me for so solemn an undertaking, giving me faith, love, humility & teaching me how to speak. May he take from me all sense of self aggrandisement & cause me to see nothing but Xt crucified. D. & D. came to tea afterwards. Went to the Union at 9 p.m. & voted against the Sunday Opening. The motion was thrown out. Felt very tired in the evening. Work has not altogether prospered. However I managed to get nearly 8 hrs. Attended the

382 The new St Aldate's parish schools, opened in January 1866.

business meeting at the Union, & voted against the Sunday question. I am glad to say it was rejected.

Friday, 7 December 1866[383]

Went to Linton's Prayer Meeting & afterwards wrote some letters at the Union. In the Evening Geldart read an Essay in my room on St Paul & St James. It was very good.

Saturday, 8 December 1866

Went to Hincksey for the last time this term with Smith. How quickly has the time gone & how little do I appear to have done. S. has taken his degree. In the evening went to the Prayer Meeting.

Sunday, 9 December 1866

Felt tired & jaded. Went to the Sunday School. Tried to read when I returned, but fell asleep in my chair; was constantly interrupted all day long. In the evening went with Maitland & Bidder to St Aldate's.[384] Mr C. preached. Went to Tonge's as usual.

Monday, 10 December 1866

B. came to Lunch.[385] We went together & called on Mr C.[:] he received us with his usual kindness. Our conversation turned on the real Presence. B. I noticed seemed somewhat uncomfortable. When we left the house my worst fears were realized. I found he held the doctrine strongly. In fact he appeared to have learnt to maintain all the most extreme points. Baptismal Regeneration, Apostolical Succession & Ritualism all seemed to find favour in his eyes. Eight weeks ago he came up to Oxford a professed Evangelical. I feared he was never really spiritually minded & now how sad is the result. A fellow collegian holds him so completely in his power, as to be able to impress anything upon him. I expostulated, argued & besought him to think seriously of the steps he was taking. He replied he had counted the cost, he felt far happier than he had ever felt before, & was convinced he was right. I advised him to take his difficulties to his Father who is a clergyman & to ask him to explain them. But he said his Father had never doubted & therefore cd not enter into his feelings. How feeble & ignorant I felt in speaking to him. It caused me to throw myself more entirely on Jesus & to lift up my heart to him for strength & guidance. Oh how my heart did ache, to see so much

383 Chavasse dates this and the next two entries incorrectly as 6–8 December.

384 Henry J. Bidder (1847–1923), m. Corpus 1866, fellow of St John's 1873–1923, vicar of St Giles', Oxford 1887–1903.

385 The name has been obliterated, probably William Bone.

promise so rudely blasted. May God change his spirit, & shew him his errors. Worked in the evening but did not do much work.

Tuesday, 11 December 1866

Went into collections at 2.30. Furneaux gave me back my Logic & Translation – neither well done. Hicks went thro' the Cicero Paper with me.[386] He cheered me up. Wished all good bye. James H. dropped in to see me. Paid a few small bills. Poor B. ploughed for 'smalls'.[387] Some of the men seemed to regard it as a joke, & were highly amused, but while I pity B. I have some concern for the honour of the college. Left Oxford by the 5.20 train Lock going with me. It was very delightful taking him home. Reached Birmm about 7 but found no boxes of mine. They had never been put in at Oxford, & yet I feel certain I saw them ticketed. I left word with the Station Master. Reached Wylde Green at 8.10. My dear Father had come down to meet us at the Station. Introduced L. to all the family. It was rather a trying ordeal for him. Home again. Praised be God for all his mercies. 'Safe home at last', surrounded by dear familiar faces, drinking in the sound of dearly-loved voices. Oh for that happy time when safely harboured in our Heavenly home we shall dwell never to part.

I began this volume of my diary bowed down with a deep sorrow. I close it still mourning for my dearly loved E. but enabled to look forward with more faith to that blessed time when, if God permit, I shall again see her.

Wednesday, 12 December 1866[388]

Took Lock to Sutton. Shewed him the Town Hall, Reading [Room] & Church. Brought him home thro' the Park. In the afternoon did some work. In the Evening copied some of Tozer's notes.[389]

Thursday, 13 December 1866

Went with Lock over Oscott College.[390] J. Wallis was our guide.[391] Poor fellow. He is a pervert. My heart ached for him when I saw his adoration of the altar in the chapel. He seems so earnest. Alas that Satan shd have blinded his soul so grievously. May the enlightening Spirit shine into his heart & lead him back to the simple truth as it is in Jesus. Called in at the News Room. Maitland & Hollin[g]s

386 Edward L. Hicks (1843–1919), fellow of Corpus 1866–74, rector of Fenny Compton 1873–86, of St Philip's, Salford 1892–1910, bishop of Lincoln 1910–19.

387 Henry Bidder.

388 Here Chavasse begins a new notebook.

389 Henry F. Tozer (1829–1916), fellow of Exeter 1850–68, 1882–1916, classicist and geographer.

390 St Mary's, New Oscott, near Sutton Coldfield, a Roman Catholic seminary opened in 1838.

391 John E. Wallis (1821–88), barrister, editor of the *Tablet* 1856–68, consul at Port Said 1879, judge of international court at Cairo 1882–8.

have both gained firsts.[392] The other three, I feel very sorry for Rawnsley.[393] He has worked so steadily. It is a large first – some 25. Balliol has 8 of these. The second consists of 40 men.

Friday, 14 December 1866

Went to B'ham by the 10.49 train. Took Lock over Mr Cooper's Gun barrel Manufactory & over Gillotts.[394] Shewed him the Town Hall, the Oratory &c.[395] Came home by the 4.20 train. The Law & History class is out. M. is in the 4th class.[396] James Hall has gained his first again. I am very glad for his sake.

Saturday, 15 December 1866

We were to have gone to Lichfield, but rain set in & we deemed it advisable to put off our visit until Monday. Lock consenting to stay an extra day. In the evening went to supper at Charlie's. Came home again about 10.30.

Sunday, 16 December 1866

Lock went with us to the Sunday School & took the class I had during the Long Vacation. As Lees does not attend now, I found my old boys without a teacher, & so took them. Mr Hirsch preached in the morning.[397] I liked his sermon very much although I thought he rather failed to apply his remarks. In the afternoon we had Howard Palmer a nephew of Mrs Rawlins.[398] He preached on the responsibilities of 'a steward'. I shd like Lock to have heard Mr Robinson. Had an hour to myself in the evening. The retrospect of the week was sad & humiliating. Oh my Father, how easily do worldly trifles wean me from thee. Oh for more real vital godliness. Oh for more real communion with my God.

Monday, 17 December 1866

Worked for a couple of hours in the morning. Started for Lichfield at 1 p.m.. Called at the Sutton Reading Room on my way, & found that both Mylne & Willert were in the 1st class in Greats.[399] Poor Brooke only got a third.[400] At

392 Henry de B. Hollings (1846–1915), m. Corpus 1864, fellow 1868–1915, barrister.

393 Bussell, Digby and Rawnsley all received seconds in Moderations.

394 Cooper and Goodman, gun makers; Joseph Gillott and Sons, pen makers.

395 The Birmingham Oratory, opened in 1849 under the leadership of J. H. Newman. It moved to its present position on the Hagley Road in 1852.

396 Charles Morris.

397 Herrmann Hirsch (*c.*1826–1905), curate of St Mark's, Whitechapel 1864–6, rector of St Michael's, Wood Street, London 1880–96.

398 ? James Howard Palmer (1841–1927), master at Bradfield College 1862–9, vicar of East Worldham, Hants. 1897–1919.

399 Louis Mylne; Paul F. Willert (1844–1912), scholar of Corpus 1864–7, fellow of Exeter 1867–94.

400 Samuel R. Brooke (1844–1916), m. Corpus 1862, master at Grantham School 1874–98.

Lichfield we both went into the Free Newsroom & attentively conned the Class List. We then looked over the Museum & afterwards went up to the Cathedral. I enjoyed [*sic*] the glorious pile every time more & more. Lock was very pleased. We reached home again about 5.

Tuesday, 18 December 1866

Lock went home. I accompanied him as far as B'ham & saw him off. I am very sorry he has gone. Alas I have much to reproach myself with as regards him. I have never spoken so openly & faithfully to him on the subject of religion as I ought to have done. May God forgive my cowardice & endue me with more courage. May he indeed bless dear Lock & make him one of his own dear Children for the Redeemer's sake.

Wednesday, 19 December 1866

Mr Robinson preached in Sutton Church on 'Xt as the bridegroom of the Ch[urch]'. It was a beautiful sermon & very comforting. I enjoyed the whole service very much. I sadly need rousing. I do indeed long to love Jesus more & to serve my Heavenly Father better, but I do not take the proper means to accomplish my wishes. I need a more fervent spirit of prayer, & more ardent & childlike faith.

Saturday, 22 December 1866

Called on Mr Robinson. He has very kindly given me 4 sick people to visit. May God enrich him & bless him & reward him. Never can I repay the debt I owe.

Sunday, 23 December 1866

Went to the Sunday School with Miriam. I read the 1st of St John with my boys, but I found that I had not prepared the chapter as carefully as I had imagined. Mr Robinson preached both in the morning & afternoon. Had a quiet evening to myself. Thank God, on looking back at the past week, I can humbly say that I have enjoyed more real communion with him in prayer. Jesus has at times been very near & this too after all my waywardness & sin. Oh who is such a God as our God. Praised be his holy name for ever & ever.

Tuesday, 25 December 1866

Xmas day. A dull misty morning more like November than December. God enabled me to enjoy the morning service & the sermon & also the Communion to wh I stayed with Miriam. But in the afternoon I felt very drowsy. Alas how much I lose by my own negligence. True I feel very unwell & weary, but in worldly concerns I can take sufficient interest. This day especially on wh 'the Word was made flesh'[401] demands the offerings of a full heart, & oh how meagre, how unworthy are all I give. Dear Jesu, they are accepted, I wd believe, for thy dear sake. Give me more of thy mind. Nicholas & Mary with Tom & Kittie & Charlie & Fanny came to dinner. I felt so worn out that I fear I must have been somewhat of a wet blanket. Oh for more of my Lord's loving, sympathising heart. Oh for more grace to fulfill [*sic*] the divine injunction not only 'to weep with them that weep' but 'to rejoice with them that do rejoice'.[402]

Wednesday, 26 December 1866

Went to see Poor Starkey.[403] My heart felt very cold when I went, but the visit thank God did me good.

Friday, 28 December 1866

W. Rawlins & his sister walked down to see my Father. R. has been overworking & is very seedy. Would that I had courage to open my heart to him. In the evening went to a party at Miss Holbeche's. We came home about 11.30. I felt very taciturn & very depressed. This feeling is growing upon me. I am giving way to a morose, unsociable & Pharisiacal [*sic*] spirit wh neither commends the profession I make, nor advances but rather grievously retards the spiritual state of my soul. It must not be. By God's help I must rouse myself. Tho' I am so far inferior to others intellectually & physically, am I therefore to bemoan my lot? No. There is a work, a great work for me to do somewhere, I feel it is so. It is my duty to make the best use of the talents my Father has given me. To qualify myself as far as I can for my future blessed calling. To improve, by divine aid the passing moment, resting well assured that I am just what my Master intended that I shd be, & consequently am exactly fitted in every respect for the work in life he has appointed. Blessed thought that I shd be deemed worthy of working for God. Lord Jesus I am miserably weak & sinful, do thou help me.

Monday, 31 December 1866

The last day of the year. It seems but yesterday since I watched the 'old year out & the New Year in'. But yesterday, & yet it has been a year fraught with much joy & much grief, with many changes & surprises & disappointments, with times of deep happiness & months of deep sorrow. Smiles & tears in what quick succession do they follow each other? But how has it gone with my soul? Am I nearer to my God than I was at the commencement of the year, or have I been drifting from him? Here too the retrospect is dark with shadows of unbelief, & bright with the

401 John i. 14.
402 Romans xii. 15.
403 William Starkey (*c.*1840–67).

glories of heavenly love. On my side ingratitude, rebellion, waywardness, weariness, murmuring & mistrust; on God's side long-sufferance, infinite tenderness, wisdom, mercy & goodness. I have experienced hours of deep depression & darkness, & days of happy trust & unknown joy. Now my heavenly Father & my adorable Saviour have felt so near to me, prayer has been so delightful an exercise, & my Bible so loved & so precious that earth seemed heaven, & my heart overflowed with such blissful happiness, that it seemed a foretaste of the ecstatic joy prepared for them that love God. Now I have felt cast down & miserable, the Lord appeared far off, religious devotions became irksome, God's work distasteful, the world grew more attractive & my soul hard, sensual & proud. Then came the awakening time when my sinfulness stood out before my eyes in its glaring colours, & oh unspeakable mercy the dear Lord was always ready to hear my cry for mercy & pardon & grace. And here at the close of the year I remain a living monument of redeeming love. But in spite of all my backsliding, in spite of all my grievous transgression, in spite of all my shortcomings, I think that I may humbly say that I have advanced, that I am closer to God; his honour is dearer to me; Jesus is more precious to my soul, my own sinfulness more apparent & more hateful to me & I do desire more to impart to others the blessedness of clinging close to Jesus. Oh Jesus mine Elder Brother, how exceeding[ly] loving art thou. Parents & relatives & friends may love with the deepest love, but oh thy love is immeasurably greater than theirs. It was love that parted me from my E., love tender, wise & pitiful which wooed my wandering soul to thee, & taught my aching heart to carry all its grief to Jesus. It was a stunning blow & wrung from me many a bitter tear, but faith looking up with streaming eyes towards heaven, caught the bright ray of love & mercy & saw thro' glistening tears the rainbow of hope smiling thro' the breaking storm. Yes – All is love & God is Love & Xt is love. 'And we are Xt's & Xt is God's.'[404] May the New Year that has commenced while I have been writing these lines be blessed to me & mine. May the Lord give me grace to walk closer to him & to make his glory my great concern. May I be enabled more & more every day 'to account all things but dross that I may win Christ'.[405]

Drank Tea with Mr Robinson. Came home at 10 p.m..

Tuesday, 1 January 1867

A new year of grace. Oh that I may grow in grace throughout it. Went to church in the afternoon with my Father, Miriam, Ada. Mr Robinson delivered an address & gave us as a motto for the coming year St Thomas' words 'My Lord & My

404 1 Corinthians iii. 23.
405 Philippians iii. 8.

God'.[406] In the evening a large family party sat down to dinner. Every one was present except Fanny, Ludovic's wife. Miss Holbeche & Miss Jane dined with us as usual. The ground is covered with snow, & the air feels frosty & bracing. I feel much better than I have felt lately. Blessings seem all around me. Praised be my Heavenly Father for all his mercies.

Thursday, 3 January 1867
Went & read to Brown & Starkey. It is a blessed privilege to be enable[d] in some small degree to minister to others.

Friday, 4 January 1867
Skated for about an hour in the morning on Powell's Pool.[407] Felt seedy & did but little work. A dinner party at home in the evening.

Sunday, 6 January 1867
Maggie & myself started to go to the Sunday School but the snow was so deep that we were obliged to turn back. Went to church in the carriage. Mr R. gave us a very delightful Sermon on 'Idle Words'.

Monday, 7 January 1867
Rain fell & a rapid thaw set in. The snow is melting away very fast.

Wednesday, 9 January 1867
We had a dance at home. I did not join but endeavoured to talk to those who had no partners. I felt very foolish, & uncomfortable, & was far less patient than I ought to have been. Robert Holbeche & his sister came. Grant ran over from Walsall to see my Father, who was with Mrs Jenkins the whole evening. Went to Bee.

Thursday, 10 January 1867
Went a walk with Bob in the morning & worked in the afternoon & evening. Did not feel very bright.

Friday, 11 January 1867
Went to a dinner party at Ashfurlong. Happily we did not stay late but came away at 10.30. Mr C. has just built a large billiard room.[408] Billiards is a game I never had any desire to play. Went to Bee for an hour as usual.

406 John xx. 28.
407 A lake in Sutton Park.
408 Thomas Colmore (*c.*1807–70) of Ashfurlong Hall, solicitor.

Sunday, 13 January 1867

I have determined by God's help to write Sunday by Sunday a short retrospect of my spiritual state throughout the week that I may endeavour to observe more accurately the rise or decline of religion in my soul. May my Heavenly Father make it to me a blessing & an effectual aid. During the week past –

Prayer has at times been a delight, but how often have I felt it a tax & a burden? I have suffered during the last few days of the week my Classics to encroach upon the time I allot to devotion & have in consequence been hurried & assailed by wandering thoughts. At Family Prayers too I have been often inattentive. The wicked habit I had contracted of never attending at all, but of suffering my thoughts to roam at pleasure, is now proving a bitter rod to my soul. Oh may God help me in this need.

My Bible has proved precious occasionally but not always. I have devoted too short a space to its study. I do not find the Prophets so beneficial as the New Testament & I experience much difficulty in bringing my mind to follow the argument. Too often I read merely with a view to criticism, endeavouring to extract arguments for or against some disputed doctrine. But praised be God the comfort that several chapters have afforded me, have effectually convinced me, that it is my own changeable heart that is to blame, & that the amount of profit I derive is determined by the earnestedness [*sic*] of my Prayers for the enlightening Spirit & by my own hungering & thirsting for righteousness.[409]

Towards others. My conduct towards my Parents has not always been strictly respectful, forbearing & loving. I have felt irritable & sometimes spoken irritably, nor have I evinced that tender anxiety & care of them which I am bound to shew. Towards my sisters & others about me, oh how negligent have I been. How little have I helped them on their heavenward course? How silent have I been on spiritual matters? How careless about their souls' health. Wrapt up in myself, I have too often felt contemptuous, Phariasical [*sic*], & selfrighteous. If I have warned them against danger how uncertain & feeble has been the sound? Have I condemned some practice, how censoriously & how proudly have I blamed? Proud, cowardly, irresolute, envious, my evil heart indeed seems black in this respect. How little too have I done for Jesus, & what few acts I have done for self-approbation & complacency, have defiled & polluted. But in spite of all this sin, tho' I have given way to passion, spoken illnatured words, exaggerated more than once, indulged in vain & self exalting thoughts, been sadly worldly & tho' I have to confess with deep sorrow that I have made no progress in experimental religion, Jesus is still very precious to me. I do love him. I do long to serve him. I do yearn to please him & to love him more & more. To him then as to a loving

409 Matthew v. 6.

Friend & an Elder Brother will I go, & pouring into his ever listening & sympathetic ear the long tale of my transgressions, I will implore his forgiveness, beseeching him to fill me with his Spirit, to sanctify by his grace, to cleanse me by his blood, & to give me more faith, more love, more hope & more humility, that so all the fruits of the Spirit may flourish & abound in my soul.

Could not go to the School on account of the snow. Nevertheless we all managed to get to Church. Mr R. gave us a very profitable sermon on 'God's People'.

Monday, 14 January 1867

Walked down & read to Starkey for a little. He appears to be very resigned. How wonderful is the grace of God wh can enable the believer to look on death undismayed.

Wednesday, 16 January 1867

A dinner party at home – all passed off exceedingly well. In the afternoon went down to Bee for an hour. Tom & Hodgson busily skating. I went to Powell's Pool yesterday for an hour, but it was somewhat late, & I was obliged to leave at 5 o'clock.

Friday, 18 January 1867

Went to Bee as usual. In the evening accompanied Miriam, & my Father & Mother to a dinner party at Ashfurlong. Mr Colmore has just built a very nice billiard room over the kitchen. Willie is coming up to Oxford on the 24th to matriculate at Trinity.[410] He is at present reading with Albert Smith. We came home again at 10.30. The frost still continues. The ice must now be some six or seven inches thick. There is a great deal of distress of one sort or another. How thankful I ought to feel for my Holy Father's goodness to me.

Saturday, 19 January 1867

Walked up to Walmley in the afternoon & saw Mrs Hinsley. She has had a great deal of trouble lately of one sort or another. But oh her faith is so buoyant & bright notwithstanding she has so much to contend. What a lesson does her calm submission teach me?

Sunday, 20 January 1867

My last Sunday at home. How soon I shall have returned again to Oxford, & how important are the next two terms. 'The lot is cast into the lap, the *whole* disposing

410 William H. Colmore (1848–1907), m. St John's 1867, vicar of Moseley, Warwicks. 1876–1907.

thereof is the Lord's.'[411] And how has it gone with my soul? Alas! hard & continuous work is beginning to tell upon my spiritual growth. I feel a growing worldliness of soul, a greater interest in the things of time, & a distaste for thoughts of eternity. My prayers appear to become more languid & more wandering & wearisome, & the Light of God's Spirit slowly receding seems now to be far off – oh so far. My Bible little pondered over, has too often been read unprofitably & I experience a growing selfishness, misanthropy & formality. God's work once so delightful has become irksome to me, but oh the deceitfulness of my heart. I have yet been content to look back on my own miserable actions with complaisancy [*sic*] & satisfaction. Far from pondering often on Jesus my thoughts have invariably turned to my approaching Examination which I have at times regarded with hope & confidence, & at others with distrust & dismay. Oh where has been the casting of every care on Xt? Oh where has been the childlike trust in his everlasting love? where the calm assurance that all will be well? Ah I have been looking too much to my own self & too little to Him. Can I believe that he will suffer me to disgrace myself or injure his cause by taking so low a class as to mar my future usefulness. No. No. I will trust my Lord in the sure expectation that he will not forsake me. My soul seems under a cloud now, but at his word there shall be light again. I feel far off now, let him but draw me & I shall be close again. I have let fall the shield of Faith,[412] & my great adversary is triumphing over me but if I but stretch out my hand I shall catch it up again & prove more than conqueror thro' Him that loveth me[413] & gave his life for me. Went to the School both in the morning & afternoon, & also to Church. My boys tolerably good. Some of them are very rude, & their example is bad for the little ones.

Monday, 21 January 1867

Went into town & was measured for some clothes. Called on Sophy at the Bank. Miss Ray engaged to be married.[414]

Wednesday, 23 January 1867

In the evening drank tea with Mr Robinson at Walmley. Maggie, Miriam & Ada went with me. Came home about 10 p.m.. My Mother & Father dined at Miss Holbeche's.

411 Proverbs xvi. 33.

412 Ephesians vi. 16.

413 Romans viii. 37.

414 Elizabeth Ray married Thomas Goode, brush manufacturer, on 20 June 1867 at Edgbaston parish church.

Friday, 25 January 1867

Vincent Holbeche & Fred Robinson came to tea.[415] The latter has not got into Woolwich.[416] He has still another chance. Robert H. & his sister walked down in the middle of the day to call. Tom went to School on Tuesday.

Saturday, 26 January 1867

The end of the Xmas Vacation. How soon it has come! Thoughts of self-reproach rise in my mind. How much I might have done & how little I have done for Jesus. I need, sadly need a more missionary spirit. Left home by the 2.24 train. T. V. H. kindly came to the Snow Hill Station & saw me off. Monnington got into our carriage at Leamington. It was raining hard when we reached Oxford, & it was some little time before the luggage could be got out & sorted. Arrived at Corpus at 5.45. Unpacked & then had some tea. Afterwards went with Knox to the Prayer Meeting. Mr Goodheart gave us a very stirring address. His words came with peculiar force at the beginning of the term. Oh may God keep & bless me throughout this coming year. May I labour solely for him; not for mine own honour, not for mine own gratification, but for the Lord's glory. May I grow each day more like my Master Jesus.

Sunday, 27 January 1867

At the beginning of another term it is indeed needful for me to review the past prayerfully & earnestly, & trusting in the Lord's help to dedicate myself anew to his service. At present I feel utterly miserable. My conscience accuses me of prevarication, which to my mind is no less heinous an offence than lying. I have fallen & in my deep remorse, all for the while seems dark & dreary. The Lord seems to have hidden his face behind a cloud. Words of prayer appear to fall idly from my lips. My thirsting soul yearning, longing to be close again to Jesus, feels desolate, forlorn, agonized. And what must I do? Has God cast me off? Satan would have me think so, but 'the word of the Lord standeth sure'.[417] I will besiege the throne of grace. Implore Jesus to pardon me, & to cleanse me, *and he will*. He cannot cast me out. My deep necessity shews the urgency of the case. Delay is death. I feel that I have not lived close to him of late. I feel that the world has been insensibly gaining an hold upon me. Hard reading has deadened my heart; languor & weariness have been suffered to diminish my times of devotion. But the Lord has not forgotten to be gracious. My own heart condemns; his Spirit is striving even now with me. Oh Jesus beloved Saviour how oft have I grieved thee & thou

415 Frederic R. Robinson (1848–1923), son of Rev. Gilbert Robinson, army officer, emigrated to California and later settled in British Columbia.

416 The Royal Military Academy, Woolwich.

417 Isaiah xl. 8; 1 Peter i. 25.

hast brooked it all. Oh Holy Father, that hast borne so long with me, how longsuffering thou art. Oh Blessed Spirit how oft have I repulsed & turned away from thee, & yet thou hast refused to be quenched. Bear yet with me oh my Father, & draw me to thee. Have mercy on me most precious Jesus & pardon & raise me up. Turn thou all powerful Spirit the wayward current of my heart to thee. Oh glorious Trinity have mercy, let me not fall into the hand of the destroyer. Restore unto me the joy of thy Salvation.[418] 'Having begun the good work, oh carry it on unto the end'.[419] Lord I am oppressed[:] undertake for me. Yes, I must go to Cavalry [*sic*]. My only hope is there.

Went to the Sunday School as usual. In the afternoon walked out for a short distance with Shepheard. We opened our hearts to one another. Praised be God who has given me such friends. In the evening & in the morning heard Mr Goodheart preach at St Aldate's. His sermons were most earnest & useful.

Monday, 28 January 1867

Furneaux commenced lectures as usual. My work was somewhat interrupted by friends dropping in, so that in all I could read for 5½ hrs. I lunched with Barton & Hatch.[420] The latter has just gained the New Fellowship. Afterwards went to the Union & wrote home. At 4.30 attended the Prayer Meeting. About 10 men were present. Bazley took the leading part. A discussion arose afterwards whether our mode of proceedings might not be assimilated to the Cambridge plan. The decision was however put off until the next meeting.

Wednesday, 30 January 1867

A wet day. Read at the Union. At 8 o'clock went for the first time to Barton. My work was not well done. I sometimes feel dispirited, but I may be assured that all will be well. Was much annoyed at forgetting the Prayer Meeting, which I had hoped to attend.

Thursday, 31 January 1867

The last day of the month. I begin to feel more settled now & have got regularly to work. I have so much Composition &c to get through that I have but little time to give to my books. Called on Hodge who has come up to Balliol[421] & then went for a walk with Charlie Black who lunched with me. He goes to Barton as well as myself.

418 Psalm li. 12.

419 Philippians i. 6.

420 Walter M. Hatch (1844–77), m. New 1862, fellow 1867–77, head-warden of St Paul's College, Stoney Stratford 1870–5, philosopher.

421 Edward V. Hodge (1848–1932), m. Balliol 1867, headmaster of Oakham School, Rutland 1879-1902, rector of Lyndon 1909–22.

Friday, 1 February 1867

Went to Mr Linton's meeting. There was a large attendance for the first Friday in term. Afterwards returned to Corpus & went for a walk with Knox.

Saturday, 2 February 1867

I feel very glad that the week is gone. The first few days at college always 'drag their slow length along'.[422] Went to Mr Christopher's meeting. There was a tolerably [good] attendance of men. I look forward to them with great joy, for tho' Mr C. himself does not always give us very carefully prepared addresses, there is something week by week that comforts & strengthens me. I do not work on my return home, so that it seems a peaceful close to a week of hard work & excitement & turmoil.

Sunday, 3 February 1867

A week of hard work has made the rest of a Sabbath most exquisite. Oh the rapturous bliss of Heaven's eternal Sabbath. I find a certain disinclination to review my week's course. The enemy would have me plead as my excuses weariness & languor. But it was while 'they slept' that the tares were sown.[423] I have indeed need of my Lord's injunction to watch, & during the last week I have too often neglected it. I feel that I have from time to time given way to fits of depression & mistrust neglecting to cast all my care upon Jesus. I feel with deep sorrow that I have suffered timidity & indecision to mar my usefulness. Alas how little have I done for Jesus among my own dear friends. It is true that I have held sweet converse with some who do love the Lord, but in how few cases have I gently & lovingly spoken to those who are still far away. Endue me O my God with the boldness of a Paul, the love of a John, the zeal of a Stephen. In this great University how helpless I feel. Have I left my impress as an unflinching soldier of Xt Jesus behind me wherever I have been? Have I striven to adorn his doctrine in all things? In controversy, when dragged into it, have I always spoken without bitterness, nay have I not sometimes brought disputation on, by a zeal wh has not been tempered with forbearance & discretion? Alas my heart indeed condemns me. I have to mourn too a feeling of envy at the far superior attainments of others, & of discontent with mine own. I have often spoken censoriously & rashly, & I have not been always perfectly ready to bear another's burden & so to fulfil the law of Xt.[424] On the score of wandering thoughts in chapel, I have much to humble me. How profitable & comforting those services might be. May my Holy Father

422 'A needless Alexandrine ends the song, That, like a wounded snake, drags its slow length along', from Alexander Pope's *An essay on criticism* (1711).

423 Matthew xiii. 25.

424 Galatians vi. 2.

enabled [*sic*] me to pray heartfeltly the loved prayers of our Church. Nor is the giant Pride subdued. Alas like the fabled hydra, he has far more heads than one & shews himself in many different forms. I was put on the committee of the Prayer Meeting; & Pride would fain puff me up with thoughts of my usefulness & importance, but many little things sufficed to shew me, what a sinful worm I am. That beautiful simile in Deut. of the eagle & her young wh Mr R. took as the text of his sermon a fortnight ago comes home with power now.[425] I need ever to be borne on the Lord's wings. If I essay to fly myself, I inevitably fall. I feel each day my growing need of Jesus. He has loved me, & oh I love him, not with a tenth of the fervour that I would, yet still a love that draws me closer to him & makes my conscience ache when I think I am straying from him.

Therefore this week by God's help I will endeavour 1. To be more Watchful. 2. To be more Pray[er]ful. 3. To fight more resolutely ag[ainst] Pride. 4. To avoid controversy as much as I can. 5. To be more bold for Jesus. 6. To be more ready to sympathize with others. 7. To guard ag[ainst] Wandering thoughts in Chapel. 8. To leave all care of the future to God.

Went to the Sunday Schools in the morning & to St Aldate's & Tonge's in the evening.

Tuesday, 5 February 1867

Went with Downer to Coal Harbour & delivered an address there. We had some delightful conversation on our way. I seem, thank God to realize more fully the immediate justification of the sinner who believes in Jesus.

Wednesday, 6 February 1867

A committee meeting of the Missionary Union.[426] Afterwards went for a short walk with Ward. We stayed to the Prayer Meeting on our return. Poor B. came in during the evening, & told me that he would not join the Tract Distribution Society. He has got hold of very high sacramentarian views – alas I fear he is not really spiritually minded. Oh may God change his heart.

Thursday, 7 February 1867

Went with Smith to Hinksey. Read to old Dingle & Farbrother;[427] left tracts at the other houses. I endeavoured to speak a word to many at the door. Some acquiesced in what I said without appearing to *feel* it, others appeared impatient. I met one man however who seems a true Xtian & a dear lover & diligent reader of his Bible. He is a railway superintendent. Smith told me about an old man

425 Deuteronomy xxxii. 11.

426 The Oxford Missionary Union, relatively inactive during Chavasse's time.

427 Robert Dingle (*c.*1791–1870), smith journeyman.

named Paed who lies dying in my part of the district.[428] I went to see him. He is very old & could scarcely hear or speak. Oh how awful to put off till one's dying hour, coming to Jesus.

Friday, 8 February 1867

Intended to have gone to Linton's meeting, but Hicks kept me so long with composition that I was too late. Went for a walk.

Saturday, 9 February 1867

Went for a short walk with Knox round the Parks. In the evening went to Mr Christopher's meeting[:] there was a large collection of undergraduates. Bishop Smith, Mr Keene a missionary fr[om] the Punjab, Professor Cowell & Mr Bilderbeck of Madras addressed us.[429]

Sunday, 10 February 1867

Prayer is the Xtian's pulse & each day I see more & more clearly my great need of drawing near to my heavenly Father. If my devotions be curtailed or cold how severely do I feel the effect. And on looking over the past week, I can see my spiritual thermometer rising or falling with my spirit of devotion. I desire & long for closer communion in prayer, but too often I allow worldly anxieties to distract my thoughts. Let it then be henceforth my earnest entreaty to be taught to pray, to receive a spirit of prayer, to live in a prayerful mind. But not only have I need to mourn over the coldness of my devotions but also over the listlessness which has frequently characterized the perusal of God's word. I feel that this is mainly due to two causes. 1st to my not setting aside a sufficient portion of time to meditation. 2nd to a want of earnestness in my petitions for the enlightening guidance of God's Spirit. I love my Bible, but alas I feel that I do not always profit by what I read in its sacred pages. Oh that hereafter I may be permitted to drink largely of the pure water of life that springs up so freely from this blessed fountain. My worst enemies this week have been my Indecision, Timidity & Pliability. I need so much a holy boldness. I need an unflinching fortitude, & unshaken firmness. I too often suffer my zeal to carry me away & by me indiscretion I too frequently injure the cause I fain would serve. How hard it is to be charitable, & yet a fearless exposer & reprover of error; how hard, to retain the gentleness of a Xtian in

428 Richard Paed (*c.*1781–1867), paper maker.

429 George Smith (1815–71), bishop of Victoria, Hong Kong 1849–65. William Keene (*c.*1829–95), C.M.S. missionary in India 1854–82, vicar of Gayton, Staffs. 1884–95. Edward B. Cowell (1826–1903), principal of Sanskrit College, Calcutta 1858–64, first professor of Sanskrit at Cambridge 1867–1903. John Bilderbeck (1809–80), C.M.S. missionary in Madras. These men were in Oxford to preach on behalf of C.M.S. and to support the annual meeting of the Oxford Church Missionary Association on Monday, 11 February.

controversy & to be ever animated by single, holy & Xtlike motives. When I look at my own conduct, & at my respon[si]bilities; when I considered what I *might* do for my Lord & what I *am* doing, is not the remembrance & the thought distressing, nay almost overpowering. 'But the promises of the Lord stand sure.' If I wait until I am worthier to come to Jesus, I must wait for ever. Alas would that this heart of mine wh sometimes seems overflowing with joy & peace & love could ever retain that blissful feeling. Languor, coldness, deadness assume their reign too soon, this foretaste of the joy of heaven passes away. Oh for that happy time when it shall remain for ever.

Went in the evening to Carfax & heard Bilderbeck preach. His sermon was not so good as his address of last night. The Church was well filled. Bishop Smith preached at St Aldate's. Tonge went over to Claydon to take Mr Fremantle's duty & so we had no Sunday evening class. About 10 o'clock I had a regular influx of men who stayed fiercely arguing until 11.45. Knox was with me I am thankful to say & we stuck together. When they had gone & all was again quiet, I cd but fling myself upon my knees, & pray for wisdom & meekness for myself & grace & God's enlightening Spirit for them. It was a stormy closing to a calm Sabbath day.

Tuesday, 12 February 1867

Lunched with Bone, & was to have gone with him to call on Mr C.. He had however an engagement & so we did not go. Ward & Elsmere went to Coal Harbour.

Wednesday, 13 February 1867

Lunched with Smith & Diggle & afterwards went to our district. I came across a poor man who lost his leg on the railway a few months ago.[430] He has not much light yet but he seems to long for more. Oh that the Lord may bring him to a knowledge of the truth. Met also a very nice young man who attends Mr Nash's Bible Class. How God has his own people in every place hidden away from the eye of the world.

Friday, 15 February 1867[431]

Went to Mr Linton's prayer Meeting. There was a good attendance. He sent me an invitation to an evening party on Tuesday which I was obliged to decline as I take the address on that day at Coal Harbour. After the Meeting went to the Union, read the Papers & wrote a letter. I fear I am a bad correspondent at present. In the evening went to Barton as usual.

430 Daniel Beard (*c.*1827–73), marine store dealer.

431 Chavasse dates this entry incorrectly as 14 February.

Saturday, 16 February 1867

My third week at College gone! I have not felt well lately & have got thro' but little well [*sic*, work]. The prospect rather discourages me. I see that I must be more systematic & get up earlier, & not trifle away my time. Went with Bontein for a walk. Called & saw poor old Paed again. His mortified leg has burst, he is speechless & somewhat deaf. The wistful look he gave me with his dim eyes, & the convulsive twitching of his mouth showed that he was troubled about his soul. We prayed with him, & surely the dear Lord will have mercy on him. I had some pleasant talk with B.. He is a man of wonderful faith & untiring devotion. How humble he made me feel! He seems to view everyone he comes across as a soul for which he is bound to speak. In the evening went to Mr C.'s Rectory. About 40 were present. Mr C. read Gal I 1-10 & was very earnest in exhorting us to speak lovingly & firmly to those who were in error, or who did not know the truth. May God give me boldness & wisdom. I feel how sadly I come short of what is my duty. I am suffering these precious college days to slip by, & oh how very little have I done for Xt.

Sunday, 17 February 1867

Went to my School. Tonge was there again. Read to myself until 1.30. Then went out with S.. He lost his way & consequently we were out longer than I intended & I was unable to find time to write out, or even properly to look back upon my conduct during the week past. I was [*sic*] not let this occur for the the [*sic*] future. Heard West preach in the evening at Trinity Church.[432] I enjoyed him very much. He preaches so simply, forcibly & with such wonderful graphicness. Attended Tonge's meeting as usual.

Monday, 18 February 1867

Went to my district & saw old Paed. Attended the prayer meeting.

Tuesday, 19 February 1867

Elsmere & Ward went to Coal Harbour & the latter gave the address. Went for a walk with Churchill.

Wednesday, 20 February 1867

Attended the Prayer Meeting. Went for a walk with Lock. I fear he is getting some unsound views. Oh how feeble & unfit I feel to cope with earnest, yet mistaken

432 Joseph West (*c.*1800–76), vicar of Holy Trinity, Oxford 1844–69, rector of Standlake, Oxon. 1869–76.

[opinions]. May God give me strength. My own weakness must lead me to cast myself entirely upon him.

Thursday, 21 February 1867

Worked until 3 p.m.. Then went to my district. Met Nash on my way, & asked his advice about the school.[433] He strongly approved of the plan. Saw poor old Paed. His end is near. He has led a life of sin, & now he is face to face with death. He seems anxious about himself, but as he seldom or never speaks, & hears but imperfectly, it is hard to ascertain his real state. Called on Mrs Bell & made enquiries about the School.[434] The final decision stands over until I have consulted Smith. Saw the poor man who has lost his leg. His name is Daniel Beard. He seems really seeking the Lord. Oh may his affliction prove to him the means of bringing him to his God. Enjoyed my quiet & solitary afternoon very much. Oh how I need an increase of faith & wisdom & love in my dealings with the souls of men. Eternity is the stake. Oh I need to realise more & more that awful truth. Ingham dropped in to tea. The debate at the Union was on 'Monasteries'.[435]

Friday, 22 February 1867

Went for a walk with Churchill. Intended to go to Mr L.'s meeting but was kept by Hicks so long that it was hopeless to arrive at his house in time. C. appeared somewhat surprised at some views I held. Alas! his view of salvation is very indefinite. May God change his heart & direct him.

Saturday, 23 February 1867

Went in the evening to hear Dr Blakeney's address on Ritualism at Mr C.'s Rectory.[436] Lock, Hollin[g]s, Phelps & Bidder went. We were rather disappointed. He was somewhat bitter I thought, at times. Some of his remarks were useful, but I do not think on the whole his address was a good one. The room was very full & I saw men of all shades of opinions present. I had to endure as I walked home a running fire of raillery & argument. Oh that they all knew Jesus.

Sunday, 24 February 1867

An illspent Sunday. A Sunday of much excitement & variety & of little retirement & meditation. Went to the Sunday School. Heard Dr Blakeney's sermon in the morning & stayed to the Sacrament at St Aldate's. In the afternoon went to lunch

433 Chavasse intended to open a Sunday School at New Hinksey.

434 Rachel Bell (*c.*1808–74), seamstress.

435 On whether 'the re-establishment of Monasteries, though with some changes in their constitution, would be beneficial to the country'.

436 Richard P. Blakeney (1820–84), vicar of Christ Church, Claughton, Birkenhead 1852–74, of Bridlington, Yorks. 1874–84.

with Barton. Oh that I had had the courage to refuse his invitation. We went a walk afterwards & did not get back until 4.45. In the evening heard Dr B. again with Lock & Knox. Has this been a sweet Sabbath to me? Alas no. It has rather been a day of restlessness & disquiet. I have felt unwell & now to bodily sickness is added mental grief. How little have I prayed? & of that little, how cold & wandering were my petitions? How little of my Bible have I read, how short the time I have given to its study. I am indeed dissatisfied with myself. How much more then must I have displeased my heavenly Father. Can such a state of things exist? No I must go to Jesus. Oh were he an earthly friend shd I not blush to be ever so grossly injuring him, & ever asking & ever receiving his forgiveness. Alas I make good resolutions apparently only to break them. I pray, as I fancy earnestly for grace against some sin, & scarcely have I risen from my knees & the words passed fr[om] my lips when I fall into the same sin. Decay of inward spirituality tells upon my usefulness. I feel more listless, more timid, more selfrighteous, more passionate, more repining than ever. What then must I do? Have I prayed in vain? Has God forgotten to be gracious? No. No, my prayers have lacked faith; my resolutions have been taken too much in my own strength. Permitted to enjoy much happiness of soul, I have grown careless & proud. The Lord in his infinite love wd have me see mine own utter helplessness. Ah & how plainly I do see it & so after having vainly striven to run in my own strength, I am freed at last again to cast myself in my Saviour's arms, & to let him bear me. I must go to him in the spirit of a little child, & he will indeed [?] bear me up & support me.

In the evening heard Blakeney preach on Confession at St Aldate's.[437] The Church was crowded. Lock went.

Monday, 25 February 1867

Continued collecting for the Irish Society.[438] It is hard work but the cause is good. At 3 p.m. went alone to my district; arranged with Mrs Bell about the School. Poor old Paed is dead. Oh that the dear Lord may have snatched him like a brand from the burning.[439] Prayed with his poor, sorrowing widow, whom I believe to be a true Xtian.[440] An unusually large gathering at the Prayer Meeting; some 11 or 12 men were present. Went to see B..[441] He is in great trouble. The vicar of Sutton has written to the Provost complaining of B.'s preaching in the parish.[442]

437 Blakeney preached in the morning on 'The Bible as to absolution' and in the evening on 'The Church of England as to absolution and confession'.

438 The Society for Irish Church Missions.

439 Amos iv. 11.

440 Lydia Paed (*c.*1808–72), servant at paper mill.

441 Courthope Bontein, who with Arthur Downer, Henry Bazely and Charles Ward, began evangelistic meetings in Sutton Courtenay in a barn lent by a farmer.

442 R. J. Howard Rice (*c.*1828–1901), vicar of Sutton Courtenay 1856–1901.

The Provost called for B., reprimanded him, & forbade him to preach anywhere on any pretext. A hard sentence indeed. 'But the Lord may come' expostulated the fearless B. 'before I am ordained & precious souls are perishing.' 'I will take the responsibility Sir', was the stern rejoinder. To make matters worse the Provost has written to his father who a highly honourable man is yet not spiritually minded, & blames poor B.. B. is hesitating whether or not to take his name off the books.[443] He regards preaching as his gift. I strongly advised him to do no such thing. He is at liberty during 28 weeks in the year & he can preach then. During the 24 he is at Oxford there are other paths of usefulness lying open. Oh may the Spirit of God direct him.

Tuesday, 26 February 1867

Went in the evening to Coal Harbour. Elsmere gave the address. The attendance was smaller than usual. I have not made it sufficiently a matter of prayer. Elsmere gave me an account of poor dear Poole's last days on earth. Wrote to B..

Thursday, 28 February 1867

Called on Mrs Bell & made all the arrangements about the school. She was most kind & met my views in every way. Finished my collection yesterday for the Irish Society. I cd only scrape together £2.

Saturday, 2 March 1867

Wrote to Miriam, her birthday is tomorrow. Bone came to lunch & we went together & called upon Mr C.. I was rather amused to find Ba. there.[444] He reddened rather when he saw us enter the room. Poor B. seems to be going to still further lengths. How different are his present views to those which he held 4 months ago. In the evening went to Mr C.'s meeting. There was a good attendance. The time has been changed to 8.30. I am sorry. The extra quarter of an hour was useful.

Sunday, 3 March 1867

Communion Sunday. I enjoyed it very much in our quiet chapel, although I think that I shd have derived more benefit, had I spent more time in self-examination. By God's help I must not allow my work to interfere with duties so important.

At 2 o'clock went with Downer & Diggle to New Hinksey to commence our school. I had pictured to myself a room full of young urchins, but when we opened the door, we found one small boy & one girl seated each on a form. Our hearts

443 Bontein soon migrated from Oriel College to Magdalen Hall. Cf. William Tuckwell, *Reminiscences of Oxford* (2nd edn., London, 1907), pp. 187–8.

444 ? Alfred Barton.

sank. But dear Downer with his usual promptitude & decision exclaimed 'we must go out & fetch some more'. Whereupon Diggle & myself started in search of some more scholars. We found five & two more came afterwards & so we began with nine. May the blessing of God descend upon us! May he pour his Spirit upon teachers & upon taught! We have begun in a spirit of prayer, may we so continue & end it.

Tuesday, 5 March 1867

Worked in the afternoon & at 6.30 started for Coal Harbour with ~~Elsmere~~ *myself*. I had to go alone. We had a very pleasant meeting, so calm & so soothing.

Wednesday, 6 March 1867

Went to my district. We have handed half of our houses, Legge St over to Downer & Bontein. I feel very thankful we have such men to help us. I have been very much pleased with a man named Beard who has lost his leg. I think he is seeking Jesus. I sent him Newman Hall's sweet book, 'Come to Jesus!'[445] He appeared to me to be fully aware of his own sinfulness but to be afraid to go [to] the Lord. His affliction has softened his heart. May the good seed take deep root there.

Friday, 8 March 1867

Berry of Magdalen came to Lunch.[446] We went down to the Torpids together. I liked him very much. He is so humble & earnest a Xtian. He went [to] dear Bal lately while abroad in Switzerland. He did not give me a very good account of him. But he is in the Lord's keeping – the God who watches over the fatherless – & we must trust to Him.

Saturday, 9 March 1867

Saturday again. Oh how pleasant to feel the week's work coming to a close & to look forward to the rest of the Sabbath!

Sunday, 10 March 1867

I have not written anything during the last few Sundays & today I must be brief. How [h]as it gone with [my] Soul since I last wrote? I enjoyed at times much happiness. I have felt at other times sad & downcast. I have stumbled, often very grievously, but the Lord has ever raised me up. During the last week, Prayer has been occasionally irksome, but often & once particularly most delightful. Oh that I may enjoy closer communion with God. My Chapel services still are unsatisfac-

445 Newman Hall, *Come to Jesus!* (London, 1848).

446 Digby M. Berry (1848–1922), m. Magdalen 1867, tutor at London College of Divinity 1875–80, minister in Melbourne, Australia 1884–1907, in Johannesburg 1907–22.

tory. Oh I do indeed need quickening in this respect. Wandering thoughts still assail me. I kneel down. For a few moments my attention is centred on the Lord. Suddenly, some trivial circumstance strikes my mind, & forthwith I find my imagination roving far away. I have also to mourn increasing irritability. I suffered a small thing to put me out. Mr C.'s meeting last night was unprofitable merely because I felt angry at Mr C.'s altering the hour, & making rather a long speech after Mr Brock's address.[447] Oh for the gentle, forbearing spirit of my Master! Oh for meekness & charity! I feel keenly moreover, how little I am doing for Jesus among my unconverted friends. I am either so 'moderate' that their views coincide with mine or state my convictions so dogmatically that I anger & prejudice them. Oh for wisdom, for discretion, for *tact*. I need courage. Naturally timid & retiring, I shrink with fear from opposition. It must not be. As a soldier of the Cross I must be willing to suffer reproach for his name. The Bible must be my armoury. From it I must cull weapons of defence & attack. I must beware lest the fear of man bring a snare. And in my inmost [heart] How needful it is to be ever watchful. Selfrighteousness is an insidious foe. Pride, is lurking in covert, shewing himself from time to time in a thousand different ways. Sloth at times presses me hard & Satan, ever wakeful turns my languor & weariedness against me. But my trust must be in my Lord. My motto for this year is '*My* Lord & *my* God'. I do indeed at times feel Jesus inexpressibly precious. But the Devil wd have me think at other times 'that I have no lot or part in him' – then how sweet & comforting are the promises of Holy Writ.

In the afternoon went with Downer, Berry & Diggle to the school at Hinksey. We had 24 children. I could have laughed outright with joy & thankfulness. θεῷ δόξα. We all got on famously. Downer took the big boys, Berry the next size, Diggle the girls, & I myself the little ones. Oh that God may graciously bless the teachers & the taught. Heard Mr Dalton preach at St Aldate's in the evening.[448] Intended to have gone to Tonge's afterwards but felt so tired that I went at once to bed.

447 Isaac Brock (1828–1911), minister of Chapel of Ease, Islington 1865–8, principal of Huron College, London, Ontario 1868–73, president of King's College, Windsor, Nova Scotia 1885–8, rector of Kentville 1893–1900.

448 William Dalton (1805–80), vicar of St Philip's, Wolverhampton 1859–80. Dalton and Brock were on deputation from the London Society for Promoting Christianity Amongst the Jews, whose Oxford auxiliary held its annual meeting on Monday, 11 March.

Tuesday, 12 March 1867

We kept our place in the Torpids. Went with Goodier to Coal-harbour.[449] I gave the address. The meeting was very refreshing to a poor book-worn student. Classics deaden the soul. Thank God for these sweet oases.

Saturday, 16 March 1867

Nothing very remarkable has occurred since I last wrote. I have been so pressed for time that I have no leisure to make any entries. I only feel inexpressibly thankful for the rest of tomorrow. How I love that word 'Sabbath' – it has such a sound of peace about it. Went to Mr C.['s] meeting as usual; we had a good attendance.

Sunday, 17 March 1867

We went to our Sunday School. No less than 35 children were present. It was a blessed sight. The Lord's hand is so manifestly with us. We knelt down on our return & offered up our thanks & praises to Him who has so marvellously prospered us.

Monday, 18 March 1867 – Saturday, 23 March 1867

The Scholarship Examination has being gone on [*sic*] during this week. There are 57 candidates. Bodington came to try, not expecting to get it. He stayed with me the greater part of the time. The result was made known at 1.30 on Saturday: the scholars elected are Illingworth, Ormerod, Skrine, Little & Abbott.[450] Downer went in for practice. It is said to have been an uncommonly good year. Bodington returned to Birm. on the Saturday. He will probably come up for Brasenose. Bidder has gained a scholarship at University much to every one's surprise. Bazley asked me to act as librarian to the Missionary Union. I consented with some hesitation. I do not exactly know what duties are required. Went to Mr C.'s prayer meeting, & so closed another week of hard work.

449 Joseph H. Goodier (1846–1920), m. Brasenose 1866, curate of St Peter-le-Bailey, Oxford 1870–2, vicar of Holy Trinity, Ripon, 1877–1905, of Dacre 1905–20.

450 John R. Illingworth (1848–1915), fellow of Jesus 1872–84, rector of Longworth, Berks. 1883–1915. Joseph A. Ormerod (1848–1925), fellow of Jesus 1871–5, registrar of Royal College of Physicians 1909–25, consulting physician to St Bartholomew's Hospital. John H. Skrine (1848–1923), fellow of Merton 1871–9, master at Uppingham School 1873–87, warden of Glenalmond 1888–1902, vicar of St Peter-in-the-East, Oxford 1908–23. William Little (1848–1922), fellow of Corpus 1871–1922, lexicographer. Henry N. Abbot (1848–1929), solicitor.

Sunday, 24 March 1867

The last Sunday in Term. How solemn to look back on the past eight weeks! How humiliating to the creature! How exalting to the Saviour. Surely I ought to love much for I have much forgiven.[451] I have indeed come painfully short of all my good resolutions. I have done little for Jesus considering my great opportunities. I have spoken little for Jesus considering the wide field open to me. My motives, how selfish have they been! My actions how tainted with sin. Oh with me there is nothing but vileness. I must look up to Christ Jesus. His perfect robe of righteousness will hide my nakedness. I stay up during the coming Vacation. Time will consequently be given me for reflection & self-examination. My most formidable foes are Pride, Timidity, Self-righteousness, Envy, a lack of that Charity which speaketh no evil & Worldliness. Desperately does the flesh at times resist the Spirit. Having then hitherto made good resolutions only to break them, can I make fresh ones? Yes I *must*, trusting, simply trusting the Lord to help me & He will [help] me. I must pray more for his Holy Spirit. I must pray for Faith, Courage, Humility, Charity, Contentedness, Love, a mind more like the mind of Jesus, a will more subject to the will of God.

Rodgers went with us to the School[452] instead of Diggle who went down on Thursday immediately after the Junior.[453] I like R. very much. We had about 30 children: the room was uncomfortably full. Mrs Bell kindly allowed us to have a form in her little hall & this gave us more space. Berry dropped in, in the evening & we had a nice long talk. How sweet it is to have such dear friends. Friendship is a precious gift of God!

Monday, 25 March 1867

Collections commenced. We had a Logic Paper. I did not acquit myself well. I felt jaded. Went to my district in the afternoon. I feel that I love the place more & more.

Tuesday, 26 March 1867

Hicks gave me back my Logic paper. I had done better than I had expected. Attended, yesterday, the last prayer meeting in the term. Ward took it. His subject was 'Sorrowing yet always rejoicing'.[454] In the evening went to Coal Harbour with Elsmere. This was our last visit this term. I took the address. I am afraid E. is getting somewhat tinctured with error. May God preserve him.

451 Luke vii. 47.

452 Robert H. Rodgers (1846–79), m. Brasenose 1865, curate of Holy Trinity, Oxford 1870–2, tutor at London College of Divinity 1873–5.

453 Examination for the junior mathematical scholarship.

454 2 Corinthians vi. 10.

Poor Mary has lost her baby.[455] The blow is a severe one. May he who has seen good to chastise her, mercifully bind up the wounds he has given in his infinite love. A large number of the men went down. I intend all being well to stay up the whole of the Vacation. I went with Collyer to the President & he gave us permission provided the other Fellows made no objection. Many of the men who are in the Schools in June are likewise staying some until Good Friday, others not so long. We are to dine in Hall.

Wednesday, 27 March 1867

More men went down. No chapel & no lectures. I cannot quite understand my novel position.

Sunday, 31 March 1867

Went as usual to my School at St Peter's, & accompanied them to Church. Mr Linton gave us a very good useful Sermon. In the afternoon went to Hincksey. Rogers & Stewart kindly helped me & all passed off very well. The children were very obedient. After Hall went to Linton's Church. Ford went with me. Had tea with Tonge & a long talk with him afterwards. How much these conversations with advanced Xtians aid & encourage. Thank God for this great privilege.

Monday, 1 April 1867

Channing went down. I went a walk with Ingham in the afternoon. He told me some curious facts about Spiritualism. If it be what he said it is, may the great Captain shield & strengthen his Church. Wrote to Ada who is confirmed tomorrow.

Tuesday, 2 April 1867

Called on Nash & had some pleasant conversation with him. Went to my district. Saw Mrs Herbert who seemed in great trouble about temporal matters & afterwards old Farbrother who was very depressed about his spiritual state. God be praised. He wept very bitterly. I cd but point him to Jesus & bid him pray & pray & pray. I prayed & read to him. Many years ago, he told me, when he was at Oriel[456] an undergraduate there placed a tract in his hand. One sentence of this tract to the effect that if we were even murderers & came to Jesus, Jesus would never cast us out, had sunk very deep into his mind. It was, he said, his only hope. How little did that man know, what that little tract would do – surely it is a lesson

455 Harry N. Chavasse, son of Nicholas and Mary Chavasse, died on 21 March 1867, aged 6 weeks.

456 As a servant.

to tract distributors not to faint or falter if they do not see the fruit of their labours. The work is God's & he will prosper it in his own good time.

Saturday, 6 April 1867

Nothing has happened during the last few days that is worthy of chronicling. I have been hard at work at my Sophocles & have made, I am thankful to say considerable progress. I had a very enjoyable walk with Rogers. The Vacation has given me the opportunity of knowing him better, & a further acquaintance shews what a sterling fellow he is. Rhodes who claims to have been at school with me at Chesterfield came to lunch at the beginning of the week.[457] He was in one of the lower classes & I certainly did not remember him. Left off work rather earlier than usual, but not as early as I ought to have done.

Sunday, 7 April 1867

Attended Linton's church after the Sunday School. I enjoy his sermons so much. I feel that under God's blessing they give me much to think about. In the afternoon Rogers & Stewart went with me to Hincksey. We had a very pleasant school. I have surely great cause to thank God. In the evening went to Linton's Church. Ingham & Lock with me.

Saturday, 13 April 1867

I have really had nothing to record during the past week. I have worked very hard. I called on Smart of Jesus.[458] He came to lunch with me & I went to breakfast with him. He seems a nice fellow. Not I fear *quite* decided as yet. He went with me one day to my district. I hope he will consent in time to join the Tract distribution Society[:] at present he is unwilling. Henry Squires came up last week to matriculate at Wadham. He is much changed: living now, I trust for Jesus. How delightful having him up here.

Sunday, 14 April 1867

How difficult a task it is to read one's own heart – how impossible is thorough self-examination without the aid of the Spirit. In looking back on the past week or rather three weeks, the Tempter brings all that I have striven to do for God into bold relief, but casts a cloud over my many many shortcomings. But that which appears so fair & beautiful, when honestly examined is found to hide a mass of deformity. How base the motives for the best of deeds. What sin appears mingled with all that which I would fain to do for Jesus. What pride, selfrighteousness &

457 William Rhodes (*c.* 1848–84), pupil at Chesterfield Grammar School, m. Oriel 1867, barrister and clergyman.

458 Edward R. Smart (1847– *c.* 1889), m. Jesus 1865, minister in Trinidad and Tobago from 1877.

vanity, what love of & thirsting for applause, what envy & bitterness, what timidity & worldly conformity, what unfaithfulness to man & oh still more what faithlessness to God, what evil thoughts lurking in the heart, & rising when I would most of all be pondering on Heavenly things. God has enabled me to pray from time to time, but the Tempter wd strive to make me trust in my prayers, & yet at other times I have felt cold & dead & been a prey to wandering thoughts. I feel that I have of late been reading my Bible in a too critical spirit, & not sufficiently meditated upon it. And oh what a crowd of sins of omission rush thro' my mind. Opportunities neglected or only partially used, ejaculatory prayer too often omitted. Friends suffered to live away from Xt & not shewn how to come to him. Precious Jesus, these are but a few. Thou knowest all my misdeeds. My prayer is that of the publican of old, 'God be merciful to me a sinner'.[459] This week, by God's grace I will pray continually for 1. Humility 2. Faith 3. Love 4. Boldness 5. A Single Eye 6. A purer heart 6. [*sic*] A Spirit of Prayer 7. A teachable mind 8. An increase of God's spirit. It is passion week too, oh that I may dwell daily on the exceeding great love of my Lord & Saviour. Went to Hincksey as usual. The only help I could get was Lock. The afternoon was wet, & the room crammed. We had nearly 40 children. The school was very disorderly. I had a class of 25 consisting of big & little girls & small boys. It was rather discouraging work, for the children were very noisy & very inattentive. And yet tho' I felt cast down, I am very glad of it. I was beginning to pride myself upon my success as a teacher but my Father has given Pride a fall. I thought to shew off to Lock an orderly school & instead I had to display to him a perfect rabble. But God doeth all things well[460] & praise be his Holy Name.

Tuesday, 16 April 1867

Collyer came back from the Boat race.[461]

Thursday, 18 April 1867

Only four of us left in Corpus. Churchill, Jacobson, Collyer & myself. We are a very happy family. Knocked off work feeling very tired.

Friday, 19 April 1867

Good Friday. Attended Linton's church morning & Evening, & very much enjoyed the services & the sermons. Felt very, very tired but thank God very peaceful. How could I be otherwise when I remembered that 'Jesus died for *Me*.' Good Friday is not an *awful* day to me. It is rather a day which fills my heart with

459 Luke xviii. 13.
460 Mark vii. 37.
461 Oxford beat Cambridge in the annual boat race on Saturday, 13 April.

love to my Father & my Redeemer. I do not care to dwell so much upon the 'awfulness' of very God & very Man dying upon the Cross, as upon his wondrous love which carried him thro' such scenes of suffering & caused him to die blessing his murderers with his dying breath. Ah yes, there is food here for the soul, & the Man Christ Jesus becomes more of a reality, more of a stay, more far more beloved, when viewed by me, a poor wretched sinner, in this light.

Sunday, 21 April 1867

Easter Sunday. There is a sound of triumph in the words & when I heard the Easter hymn at Linton's in the morning, the whole glories of the resurrection seemed to burst upon me. 'Christ the Lord is risen today.'[462] How exultant is the note! How one's heart shd bound with joy & gratitude. May the thought of my risen Saviour oftentimes cheer & invigorate when immersed in the deadening grind for Moderations. Stayed to the Lord's table & enjoyed a most comfortable Sacrament. Churchill & Collyer came to Hincksey with me & the School went on very nicely. I am very thankful to them for their kind aid. Oh that they were both really in Jesus.

Friday, 26 April 1867

The last week of the Vacation has passed. The time has flown very quickly, & I am now face to face with the dreaded term which brings Moderations in its train. Moderations is an ugly monster. Seen at a distance he looks indistinct & hazy, wrapped in mist & cloud, but still unpleasant. A nearer acquaintance serves to dispel the mist & bring out all his frightful proportions. Thank God I have an arm to rest upon. Thank God that Xt is with me. Went & dined with Linton. Afterwards had a most enjoyable walk with Linton & Tonge. Almost all the men came back. I got thro' but little work. Henry Squires successfully matriculated at Wadham.

Summer Term 1867

I have not written a line in my diary throughout the whole term. But as the six or seven weeks have been fraught with many most important & interesting events, & as taken as a whole it has been the most blessed & one of the happiest terms that I ever passed at Oxford, I feel that to record none of its history would be to leave a great & almost irremediable gap in my diary. I will therefore give a short epitome of what has taken place. My dates I fear will not always be very correct.

And first as to my work. I ground very hard up to June 2nd, & succeeded by that time, in finishing all my books. The last few days before the examination, I did

462 Hymn by Charles Wesley.

not work more than an average of 4 or 6 hrs. I felt very glad when Moderations was really come for the long continued & incessant work was very deadening.

At the instance of Bazeley, Ward, Bontein & Downer, Mr Christopher organized a series of addresses to be delivered in the Town Hall. Lord Radstock who has been greatly blessed at Weston, & who was at this time doing a good work at Brighton, was asked to come down for the first.[463] At the outset, he declined, but finally when Bazley went to him & pointed out how wide a field of usefulness was opened, he consented. He delivered three addresses on three consecutive nights.[464] The Town Hall was crowded each time, & Lord R. was so struck with the evident thirst of the people after the Gospel that he expressed his readiness to deliver another address on the Thursday in the following week. Before each meeting, a prayer meeting was held, & God's blessing invoked on the work. I was unable to attend the address on the Thursday as I went with Goodier to Coal Harbour. On the Friday morning Ward came into my room & told me that I. had called upon Lord Radstock & told him that his address had been the means of removing all doubts from his mind.[465] He had accompanied me in the previous week to the preliminary Prayer meeting & had afterwards stayed the whole meeting out. I cannot tell how thankful I felt to God. I have always had so great & admiring a love for him, & of late had felt so earnest a desire to pray for his welfare. It was God's own work! Praised be his Holy Name. I went a walk with I. the same afternoon. Oh may God abundantly bless, keep & strengthen him. Lord R.'s visit has been abundantly blessed, if dear I.'s conversion be the only fruit. By Lord Radstock's advice a daily prayer meeting was started with the especial object of beseeching God's blessing on the weekly Addresses.[466] Downer offered his rooms, as B. N. College is central. Those meetings proved a source of rich blessing to those who attended them as I can testify. About twelve generally met together. The calm, earnest, harmonious spirit that breathed throughout them, & the feeling that God was very near rendered them seasons of the most exquisite refreshment. From the very bottom of my heart, I have cause to thank my Heavenly Father. The address on the following Friday was delivered by Stevenson Blackwood.[467] The Hall was again crowded. As an address, Mr B.'s was much more powerful than any we had heard from Lord R.. Many of the people were much moved. God grant that the impressions made may not easily pass away. Dear

463 Granville A. W. Waldegrave, 3rd Baron Radstock (1833–1913), evangelist.

464 Wednesday, 1 May – Friday, 3 May 1867.

465 ? Robert Ingham.

466 This was the origin of the Daily Prayer Meeting, which superseded the twice-weekly prayer meeting. Arthur Downer credits Charles Ward with the proposal, 'Evangelical religion', pp. 687–8.

467 Stevenson Arthur Blackwood (1832–93), clerk in the Treasury 1852–74, secretary to Post Office 1880–93, founder of Civil Service Prayer Union.

L. & C. [came] & both felt very deeply. I spoke & prayed with L.. He said to me so sadly, 'Ah I have so many impression[s] but they all come to nothing'. Oh God may these impressions be deepened by that blessed Spirit into convictions. Haslam came down the next week.[468] He gave addresses in the Town Hall on the Friday & Saturday. Preached twice for Christopher on the Sunday. Gave another address in the schoolroom on Monday, & took a special service in St Aldate's Church on the Tuesday. I must confess that I did not like him as well as the others. He is evidently a very excitable man, tho' undoubtedly most earnest & unwearying in spreading the Gospel. But I did not like his way of praying. I thought he lacked reverence. Tho' I fully hold that our love to God as our Father ought to aim at becoming that perfect love which casteth out fear,[469] yet I think that that love ought to be tinctured with a certain degree of awe, for we are I think bound to bear in mind that 'God is a Spirit'.[470]

I have to thank [God] also for blessing our labours at Hincksey. Last term Smith, Diggle & myself were the only visitors. Smith has now gone down, but the village has been split up into several districts. Downer & Sever take one, Ward a second, Ingham a third, Diggle a fourth, & myself the fifth. A weekly address has also been started. I called on Hartshorne the curate in charge during the Vacation & obtained his consent both for a cottage lecture & for the Sunday School.[471] Our chief difficulty was in obtaining a suitable room. The only one of any size belonged to two worthy women who keep a daily school, but who are Plymouth Brethren. I called, but was unsuccessful. They strove hard to drag me into a controversy but happily I steered clear of it. Afterwards Bazley & Bontein called, & their solicitations won the day. I am very thankful to say, that tho' the average attendance has not exceeded more than ten or a dozen, yet the people speak very gratefully of the addresses. I hope under God's blessing that the numbers will increase next term. Ward took upon himself the responsibility of providing men to take the meeting, but after the Long I must do so. As yet I have only spoken there once. Our School too, thank God, is thriving. We have now an average attendance of 50 children. We have been obliged to engage another room at Mrs Herbert's. Eight of us now go every Sunday. Knox, Downer, Sever, Diggle & Berry go to Mrs Bell's; Rogers, Ingham & myself to Mrs Herbert's. And oh how much I have to praise God for all his mercies to me in my district visiting! How often have I experienced the truth of the promise that in watering others we shall

468 William Haslam (1817–1905), 'the parson converted by his own sermon', rector of Buckenham, Norfolk 1863–71, minister of Curzon Chapel, Mayfair 1872–8.

469 I John iv. 18.

470 John iv. 24.

471 John A. Hartshorne (1840–1917), curate of South Hinksey 1865–9, vicar of Bledington, Oxon. 1871–1914.

be ourselves watered.[472] I have gone to Hincksey feeling dull & dead from long reading, & the very effort to speak to others of the love of Jesus, has warmed my own heart. Poor old Farbrother is I grieve to say still in the same desponding state – tho' perhaps, thank God, a little better. I do not look upon his case as hopeless. Far from it, I humbly believe that God will in his own good time, give him joy & peace in believing.[473] Goodey I earnestly trust is resting on Jesus only.[474] His faith is still, maybe, very weak, but he has found thro' God's infinite mercy where to look for salvation. It has been also a great delight to me to have dear Ingham in the same village. I have generally now someone to walk to & fro with me, & no more solitary walks. Is not my cup overflowing with mercies. The addresses at Coal Harbour have still been kept up. The attendance has been about the average. We have usually had about seven. Goodier has gone regularly with me this term, & taken the address in turn. On account of Mods I have only found time to speak twice. May God bless our efforts there. Addresses have also been started at Cowley, St Clements & at Ferry Hincksey on Sunday afternoon. Bazley & Downer carry on the meetings at Sutton Courtenay every Monday Evening. They have hired a barn, which is generally densely crowded & as many as 400 people are usually present. I have been seriously debating with myself, how far it is right to give addresses in a parish without the clergyman's permission, & tho' I freely grant that there are very many serious & important reasons why we shd act independently of a minister who is either too indolent to look after his people, or who is inculcating erroneous doctrine, & who would not if asked give leave, yet I think as members of the Church of England we are bound to bow to those whom God has been pleased to put in office, & instead of acting in the teeth of that authority, to implore the God who ordereth the hearts of all men, to open a path whereby the Gospel light can be let in upon these poor dark villages, & move the clergy either to give permission or to bestir themselves, & taught by God's Blessed Spirit to teach those set under them.

Bertie Squires came down from Cambridge & spent a few days with Henry at Oxford in the earlier part of the term. The work of God's Spirit is very manifest in him. He has become so gentle, & forbearing. Thank God he taught me a lesson. He came on the Saturday, & I dined with them at Wadham in the Evening. Both of them went to Christopher's Meeting at 8.45 & afterwards had tea in my rooms. On Sunday evening instead of going to Tonge's I went to Henry's lodgings, & we had a very delightful talk. On the Monday both Bertie & Henry came to breakfast with me.

472 Proverbs xi. 25.
473 Romans xv. 13.
474 William Goodey (*c.* 1810–91), butcher.

At the close of the Vacation Mr Robinson wrote & asked me to called [*sic*] on a godson of his named Wetherall who was coming up to B. N. C.[475] He is not I fear a very decided man, tho' with very good intentions.

No change occurred in college except that Bidder went to University, & at the close of the term a freshman named Surtees came up.[476]

Such is a brief account of the first five or six weeks of the term, untill [*sic*] Moderations began. Fourteen men are in from Corpus & eight[y] six from the whole University.

Our boat kept its place on the river. We are still second.

Thursday, 6 June 1867

I did little or no work – 2 hours at the outside. In the evening went with Goodier to Coal Harbour & gave the last address & took leave of the people. I felt tired when I came home, & so went to bed early. I feel that I have done my best for Mods. I have committed the issue to God.

Friday, 7 June 1867

Got up at 6.30 & so had some little time to myself before chapel. Prayer calms the mind, & I really felt quite collected. The Examination began at 9.30. I found it very comforting to take a text or two of Scripture & repeat them over to myself as I went along the streets & up the stairs of the Ashmolean. God put some very appropriate ones into my mind. We had Logic in the morning, which I did fairly, & Latin Prose in the afternoon. It was a hard piece & mine was somewhat stiff & stilted. Went a short stroll with Knox before Hall & afterwards stayed out until 7 p.m.. Then ground at Homer & Demosthenes till 10.30 – then to bed. One day gone, thank God.

Saturday, 8 June 1867

Homer & Demosthenes in the morning from 9.30 to 12.30. Divinity in the afternoon from 1.30 to 4.30. Worked in the evening. At 8.30 went with Ingham & Knox to hear an address in the Clarendon Assembly Room from Col. Rowlandson.[477] The attendance was very small. The colonel was very earnest, & urged every one of us to ask ourselves why we shd not go. Men are not to be had. Is it not therefore my duty to offer myself? At present, I think there are one or two reasons to prevent me but I will make the subject a matter of prayer. May God teach me whether or no he wd have me to go.

475 Henry E. Wetherall (1849–1905), m. Brasenose 1867, chaplain at Valparaiso, Chile 1883–1903.

476 Anthony Surtees (1847–71), m. Corpus 1867.

477 Michael J. Rowlandson (*c.*1805–94), army office in Madras, a leading member of C.M.S.

Sunday, 9 June 1867

A very calm delightful Sabbath. Had my Sunday classes as usual, & very much enjoyed teaching. It was so different, & seemed so 'restful' sitting in the quiet schoolroom on that peaceful Sabbath day, after all the feverish excitement & turmoil of the Schools. Wished Tonge goodbye. Went early to bed.

Monday, 10 June 1867

Work again. Virgil & Cicero in the morning, & Greek prose in the afternoon. I felt all the better for the Sunday's rest. I generally take a stroll between the papers, which I find invigorating.

Tuesday, 11 June 1867

Sophocles & Aristophanes in the morning, & Greek Verse in the afternoon. Four days of the Examination now past. I begin to feel rather fagged.

Wednesday, 12 June 1867

Tacitus & Juvenal in the morning. Latin Verse in the afternoon. I hoped to score in the latter but my Hexameters were by no means good. I felt so done up. How comforting a few Bible words may be. My eye caught this sentence at lunch time, 'He restoreth my soul'.[478] I feel that God is helping me thro'.

Thursday, 13 June 1867

Critical Paper in the morning[:] about 6 of the questions came out of Tozer's Note book. We had no Xaste paper. I was very glad. All is over now thank God.

Friday, 14 June 1867

I could scarcely comprehend my novel position of having no work to do. I felt very tired. Went to Hincksey & saw some of my people. In the evening attended a meeting at the Town Hall. An address was given by Capt. Fishbourne.[479] Whilst he was speaking the men from the Harrow dinner wh was going on below finding that something was going on, rushed upstairs to see what it was. Those inside held the door, so that they could not get in. When they heard what sort of address was being given they at once went down, though a few, who were rather farther gone than their companions, persisted in entering the Hall & were finally ushered downstairs by a policeman, greatly to their indignation. The people who composed the audience were very much alarmed at this contretemps, but happily they were quieted.

478 Psalm xxiii. 3.

479 Edmund G. Fishbourne (1811–87), naval officer, co-founder of Naval Prayer Union.

Saturday, 15 June 1867

The Bishop of Victoria gave a lecture 'on work in China' in the Hall of Magdalen Hall.[480] He was very interesting.

Sunday, 16 June 1867

My last Sunday at Oxford. Wished my boys at St Peter's & Hincksey good-bye. Heard the Bishop of Victoria at St Aldate's. Ingham & Knox came to tea afterwards & unfortunately C. came in & of course began at once to argue. I was very sorry for I hoped to have a quiet Sunday Evening talk.

Monday, 17 June 1867

Spent the greater part of my time at Hincksey. Called at Mr Linton's & Mrs Hall. In the Evening heard addresses at Mr Christopher's from Lord Radstock & Lord Adelbert Cecil.[481] Went to bed feeling very tired & somewhat sad. I do not like leaving Hincksey & its people. The place has wound itself round my heart. May the Good Shepherd look down with compassion on this poor pastorless village.

Tuesday, 18 June 1867

Went with Churchill to the Schools feeling very nervous yet very much upborne by that precious verse which came in the Psalms of the day, 'He shall give his angels charge over thee to keep thee in all thy ways.'[482] My viva voce lasted for about forty minutes. Got my Testamur. Heard of the riots in Birmingham on account of Murphy.[483] Telegraphed to know if it was safe to cross the town. Received an answer that it was. Left Oxford at 5.15. Met Charlie at B'ham. Reached home safely at 8.20. The town was somewhat full & there appeared to be an uneasy feeling among the people; a line composed of policemen & soldiers placed alternately drawn across the top of the Bull Ring, & none suffered to pass except on business. Park St has been gutted. Thank God that I am at home again. Twenty weeks is a long time to be away, but oh how the hand of my Heavenly Father has brought me safely thro' every trial & difficulty.

Monday, 1 July 1867

The class list is out & I have a third. God has done it & God is love. I went down to the Reading room with Hodgson & Bee. Opened the Times & the first thing I

480 Charles R. Alford (1816–98), bishop of Victoria, Hong Kong 1867–72, emigrated to Canada 1877.

481 Adelbert P. Cecil (1841–89), son of marquess of Exeter, evangelist, joined Plymouth brethren.

482 Psalm xci. 11.

483 William Murphy (1823–72), anti-catholic orator. A protestant mob, incensed by his rhetoric, wrecked Birmingham's Irish quarter in June 1867, requiring hundreds of soldiers, policemen and special constables to restore order.

saw was my own name. The blow was stunning. I seemed bewildered, laid down the paper & went up to see Albert Smith. Came down to the Town Hall again & scanned with aching heart the List. Phelps, Ford & myself are in the third. And I have always so despised thirds! I told them at home, went up into my own room, knelt down & told it all to God. Then hot, scalding tears burst from my eyes like rain. But I remembered that Jesus wept & I knew then that it was no sin to weep. Thank God I could look up & say 'Thy will be done'. My rebellious [heart] does murmur & repine, yet I can feel that all is for the best. Oh for the faith of him of old who could say, 'Tho' he slay me yet will I trust in him.'[484] And is it for this that I have toiled so long & hard, for this that I have sacrificed all pleasure & worked resolutely on for 3 years & more? Yes for this a result pregnant with blessing, a result foreordained, a result sent for some wise purpose. Another tie that bound me to earth has been parted[:] oh for grace to give myself up entirely to the Lord's service. Pride shudders at the thought of the disgrace brought on my college & my name, at the remembrance of what will be the world's opinion & the world's contemptuous judgment. But had I a prophetic vision & could I pierce the veil that hides the future shd I not see that this event is but one link in that mysterious & wonderful chain of providential circumstances which have brought me from the counting house & have set my feet in a path that I knew not? While then the flesh shrinks, shudders & writhes in agony beneath the blow, oh may my faith look up, & even tho' it be with tearful eyes echo…[485]

Tuesday, 2 July 1867

Went down to Walmley & saw Mr Robinson[:] he was very kind & sympathizing. He knelt down & prayed with me. One thought in his prayer struck me very forcibly, that God, had it been his will could have endowed me with talents sufficient to carry off the highest honours. He has given me sufficient to take a third, I cannot doubt but that there is a cause.

Tuesday, 2 July 1867 – Friday, 26 July 1867

I have not written my diary for a long time. I have been in a sort of lethargy – a reaction after intense work, coupled with the thought of my failure – but I thank God that I can trust him. I can believe that all is well. Even now I feel that by his blessing, my disappointment may benefit me in many ways.

1. In keeping me humble. I had been praying for humility. I seemed to be becoming self-righteous & conceited. But Giant Pride is alas very buoyant &

484 Job xiii. 15.
485 Here Chavasse breaks off, perhaps interrupted in mid-sentence.

not easily crushed – like old Prejudice at Mansoul I fear his leg is only broken – with Bunyan I can say, 'wd that it had been his neck.'[486]

2. In depriving me of one of my earthly 'idols'. To take high honours, to win a name for myself, has been my ambition. Instead of all my bright hopes, I have only gained a place I utterly despised – the shock seemed to cast me more on Jesus. I cannot now go forth as a minister of Xt, hoping to effect much by my ability. Jesus, & Jesus only must be my hope, my strength & my fortress.
3. It must lower me in the opinion of others, & the consciousness of such a lowering, must tend to depress me in my own estimation.
4. I cannot doubt that the Law & History course will benefit me more than the Classical Greats, considering the great time I shd have certainly spent on my Greek & Latin Books, had I taken them up, on account of my indifferent knowledge of the languages.[487]

Friends have been very kind & written to comfort me. May the God of all comfort,[488] comfort them in any & in every trouble.

Yet still my repining heart at times, & oh how often, murmurs. I want more perfect submission, that I may even kiss the rod. Thrown much by myself I am apt to brood over the past. How comforting are those words,

'How know I, if thou shouldst me raise
That I shd then raise thee,
Perchance thy glory & my praise
May not so well agree.'[489]

How comforting the thought, that I poor, weak, ignorant, despised sinner, am yet as necessary (yes absolutely necessary) to the body of my Lord & Master as the clever, bold hearted, & noble Xtian.

Friday, 26 July 1867

Started at 3 p.m. for Cambridge. Nothing particular happened until I reached Bedford. There five policemen got into my carriage. One of them used the most abominable language. I prayed that God would give me strength to speak to him. An opportunity arrived. He was left alone with me in the department, & with one young policeman, who appeared to look upon him as a fine pattern to be imitated. I did speak to him. At once, the bold swaggering, reckless demeanour forsook

486 John Bunyan, *The holy war* (1682), an allegory about battle for the town of Mansoul between the armies of Diabolus and Emanuel, son of King Shaddai. In an argument between the townsfolk Mr Prejudice was kicked to the ground, while Mr Anything's leg was broken by an assailant who 'wisht it had been his neck'.

487 Chavasse changed course from Literae Humaniores ('Greats') to Law and Modern History.

488 2 Corinthians i. 3.

489 'How know I, if thou shouldst me raise, That I should then raise thee? Perhaps great places and the praise Do not so well agree', from George Herbert's 'Submission'.

him. He told me that his mother was a widow & a pious woman. He had been rather wild in his earlier days, his relations has cast him out, he had sunk lower & lower until at last he had enlisted in the police court. Poor fellow my heart bled for him. Unkindness had embittered what I feel persuaded was a disposition full of generosity & well intentioned. I could but point them both to the cross of Jesus, & giving them each a tract, I lost sight of them. Oh may the Lord & Giver of Life lead them both to the atoning blood of the precious Saviour. I reached Cambridge at 7 & found Bertie waiting for me at the Station.[490] He had got tea & some chops for me in his rooms, & engaged a bedroom close by his own. It was very kind of him. We talked long together. Having common hopes, common temptations, a common object in view, & a Common Saviour to love, we had much to talk about. We read & prayed together, & I went [to] bed between twelve & one. Thank God for all his mercies.

Saturday, 27 July 1867

Henry came back from Liverpool.[491] He had been summoned there on business. He took me a walk thro' the backs of the Colleges, & along the river's side. We have nothing to equal the calm beauty of the scene at Oxford. When first it burst upon me, it looked like fairyland. The well kept turf & lawns, surrounded by belts of trees, avenues here & there, a background of rich shady foliage, the river with its banks turfed down to the water's edge, & the gray walls of the colleges behind it, all continue to make it an Elysium as far as sight goes. Nor have we at Oxford anything so large as Trinity, or any chapel to equal King's. But having said this, I think Oxford carries off the palm in almost every other particular. The town is very poor & the streets narrow & winding. I met Bodkin in the quad of King's. Afterward we went into the Chapel; it is a most beautiful building. Bertie went to Barnwell in the afternoon. In the evening he took me to the Union. The debating room is better than ours at Oxford, as also the Magazine room, & the view from the outside is much more imposing & compact. But our writing room is incomparably superior to theirs, as also our lavatories. Moreover they have no carpetted reading room. About seven I went with Bertie & called on Willie Rawlins. He has rooms in Neville's Court, high up but very comfortable.

Sunday, 28 July 1867

Felt very unwell. Breakfasted with Willie Rawlins at Trinity. Met Watson, Anderson & Bodkin. Went to Birk's Church with Henry & Fletcher.[492] How solemn it seemed to look on the pulpit from which Simeon, Martyn & Scholefield

490 Bertie Squires.

491 Henry Squires.

492 John P. A. Fletcher (1846–1916), m. Caius 1865, rector of Aston Flamville, Leics. 1883–1916.

had preached,[493] to stand within the walls which Sunday after Sunday had listened to the earnest appeals of such holy men, & where so many eminent Xtians had been born again, or strengthened & built up. The congregation was large. Birks preached 'on the faithfulness of Noah.' Leaning forward over the pulpit he preached for three quarters of an hour with the greatest simplicity & earnestness. He made no attempt at eloquence. He used no notes. He disdained all rhetorical artifices. With marvellous clearness he pointed out the lessons to be taught from the text, & concluded by a searching & practical application. One could not help but listen. With none of the gifts of an orator, he rivets the attention of his audience from first to last. His is indeed a glorious instance of the devotion of unrivalled talents to the service of God. After Church we went to the Prayer Meeting. Some twenty men were there. I liked their manner of conducting it. After the meeting Bertie introduced me to Thornton of Jesus, son of Spencer Thornton of Wendover & cousin of Du Pré of Corpus.[494] He is an unflinching Xtian. At 12.30 I went with Bertie to the Barnwell Sunday School. My class was unruly. Alas, how proud I am – the blow was good for self-conceit. Dined with Henry at his lodgings in Park St. They are small but snug. Went with him & Bertie to hear Perowne's farewell sermon.[495] He has just been presented to a country living. He seems to be a very good man & much beloved. The church was crowded. Thornton came to Bertie's rooms in the evening. I like him exceedingly tho' I shd not think he is a highly gifted man, he is a hard worker & is expected to do fairly in the Tripos.

Monday, 29 July 1867

Dined with Fletcher at Caius. Henry was there also. Afterwards went to the backs & played at croquet. I will put the story of my remaining stay at Cambridge into a continuous narrative. I had a long walk with Thornton round by Granchester, & I enjoyed it much. He took me so far that I was very nearly late for Hall at Trinity. Cobb had kindly asked me to dine with him at the High Table.[496] I had to go in my straw with my face flushed scarlet. Saw Cockburn & his colleague going to call on the Master of Trinity.[497] The former is a very fine looking man …[498]

493 Charles Simeon (1759–1836), vicar of Holy Trinity, Cambridge 1782–1836. Among Simeon's curates were Henry Martyn (1781–1812), missionary in India and Persia, and James Scholefield (1789–1853), regius professor of Greek at Cambridge 1825–53.

494 James Du Pré (1846–82), m. Corpus 1863.

495 Thomas T. Perowne (1824–1913), curate of Holy Sepulchre, Cambridge (the 'Round' church) 1862–7, rector of Stalbridge, Dorset 1867–74, of Redenhall, Norfolk 1874–1913, archdeacon of Norwich 1878–1910.

496 Gerard F. Cobb (1838–1904), fellow of Trinity, Cambridge 1863–93, musical composer.

497 Alexander J. E. Cockburn (1802–80), lord chief justice of queen's bench 1859–80, lord chief justice of England 1875–80. Cockburn and Sir John B. Byles (1801–84) presided over the Cambridgeshire summer assizes which opened on 31 July 1867. Rooms in the Master's Lodge

Sunday, 25 August 1867

It is Sunday afternoon. I feel too weak & weary to go among the excursionists in the Park tract distributing. I will therefore by God's help review the spiritual state of my soul. I bless God that I have indeed great cause for thankfulness, while I have great reason to mourn & grieve. I have obtained thro' the teaching of God's Spirit more knowledge of myself & of the Lord. And what has been the effect of that knowledge? It has taught me to depend more & more entirely on Jesus, & to realize with greater clearness that my salvation is a thing of the past, wrought wholly by Xt, & in no way by myself. How ever can I thank & adore sufficiently the infinite love & compassion of my Heavenly Father? True I knew these blessed truths before but I was not able to realize them so vividly. Oh that the same Holy Spirit will help me to advance still further in this path of knowledge. May I daily know better him, whom to know is life eternal.[499] And is Sin then conquered? Is my heart entirely subjected to God? Am I always filled with joy & peace in believing? Ah no, how very very often can I say with St Paul 'when I wd do good evil is present with me.'[500] Sin conquered! The fight seems getting harder every day. I seem to possess a heart, whose sinfulness becomes more & more manifest, which struggles still at times ag[ainst] God's will & repines beneath his yoke, easy & light tho' it be.[501] Looking at myself what do I see? I see Pride, a terrible foe, insinuating itself into every deed I do. If I labour in some slight degree for Jesus, Pride is hard at me, whispering 'how good, how holy, how devoted.' Nay more, my soul mourns – & I almost weep when I write it, oh that my hard cold heart cd weep, oh that my head were a fountain of tears – mourns with bitter sorrow & agony when I remember of the motives wh prompt any one thing that I do for Jesus. There *is* love for my precious Jesus, but oh how that love is adulterated with the desire of approval from my fellow Xtians & of applause from the world, how great the desire to obtain a reputation for sanctity. Oh heavenly Father, how longsuffering thou art to bear with such a vile wretch as I am! Make me humble, give me a single eye to that service. Pride is at present my great enemy. The Nearer I feel to God, the less am I subject to it. But he is a bold foe & even tries to attack him [*sic*] when nearest to God. Oh what a comforting thought that Jesus felt & conquered this enemy. And shall I a soldier of Xt Jesus, weak & frail tho' I be, shrink from doing battle resolutely with a foe whom the Capt. of my Salvation has vanquished, & whom He will give me strength to vanquish too, if

at Trinity College were traditionally made available to the assize judges.

498 Here Chavasse breaks off. His diary becomes increasingly irregular, with occasional pages left blank to be filled in later, but never ultimately used.

499 John xvii. 3.

500 Romans vii. 21.

501 Matthew xi. 30.

I but ask him? The battle cry of St Paul is in my ears, 'ἀνδριζεσθε'![502] 'The Lord is my banner'[503] – victory then is sure. By God's help I will struggle ag[ainst] Pride more boldly & watch his approaches more jealously.

Sunday, 15 September 1867

It is a dark Sunday afternoon, & threatens to rain. Bertie & myself have therefore determined to stay at home & read quietly instead of distributing tracts in the Park. I am at present in a state of great spiritual drought, I need quickening, purifying, sanctifying. Yet God seems far off, & often very often does my soul seem to cry 'will God absent himself forever.' When I look into my own heart, the spectacle is said [*sic*, sad?]. Tho' I may humbly say that I think my depression is in some measure due to bodily ill health, & to low wearing headaches, wh make me feel very fretful & irritable, yet I feel indeed how true are the words of God, 'the heart is deceitful above all things & desperately wicked who can know it?'[504] Pride, envy, jealousy, anger, peavishness [*sic*], discontent, sullenness, indifference, censoriousness, are ever sweeping over my soul like clouds of shadow over a landscape – at times perhaps I may seem outwardly calm, inwardly none but God can tell how fierce is the struggle. And yet amidst all, thank [God] I can hold Xt Jesus fast. Shorn of every other support, buffetted by foes within & without, I find now the blessing of the glorious Gospel truth that my salvation depends not upon my works, emotions or deservings, but on the finished & perfect sacrifice of my Redeemer. If I loose Xt, he will *never* loose me. I thank God that, thanks humanly speaking to dear Bertie, my Bible has proved more comfortable & precious, but prayer has been difficult. My cold, dead heart has found it so hard to concentrate its attention on Heavenly things; my mid-day devotion has been often hurried over, & once or twice omitted. I have suffered the channel to become choked up, can I wonder if the stream of grace be retarded & diminished. The Lord's work too has proved irksome. I have done it, rather as a duty than a pleasure. On this point, how sad is the retrospect. How much left undone, or only partially done; how seldom have I spoken for Jesus, & even when I have how falteringly. In company sinfully shy, reserved & bashful, how little have I adorned the doctrine of God my Saviour. At home, often silent & depressed, how I have suffered opportunities to slip by, & how little have I striven to aid those who are travelling along the same road. And yet these are not half my sins, & heinous as these are I cannot mourn for them. I hate sin, & the thought of my own transgressions causes me many a pang, but wd that I cd feel what David felt when he cried 'Rivers of water run

502 'Be men of courage'. 1 Corinthians xvi. 13.

503 Exodus xvii. 15.

504 Jeremiah xvii. 9.

down my cheeks because I keep not thy Law.'[505] How sweet it is to turn from the sorrowful sight of my own iniquity & to 'remember the years of the right hand of the most High.'[506] Here is Love & mercy & forbearance & gentleness & purity & forgiveness & Life. Jesus I look to thee. 'Thou didst come to save sinners'[507] & I am a sinner, therefore thou didst come to save me. If I can see or feel nothing else, I can feel *that*.

Monday, 16 September 1867 – Thursday, 26 September 1867

Nothing particular has happened. Henry Whitehouse I am grieved to say is very ill. He has been ailing for some time past. Now the disease has developed itself. My Father seems very anxious about him. Heavenly Father in thy hands are the issues of life & death. If it be possible, if it be thy will give him back to us. Thank God he is very happy in his mind. At first he was very unhappy about his soul, but now everlasting praise be to the Redeemer, every doubt & difficulty has been rolled away & he has been led to see the beauty of the Lord's Christ. Maggie has gone over to Sedgley to help Kittie who is shortly to be confined.[508] May God give them strength, & enable them to trust him in the dark & cloudy day.

The prayer Meeting is going on satisfactorily. The numbers do not increase but I have discovered that Mrs W. is not in high favour with her neighbours.[509] Oh that God may bless & prosper it, & enable me to serve him & promote his glory with a single eye – away, away with self, let Xt be all in all.[510]

I have been out of sorts lately. My Father sent me to Mr Baker.[511] He has ordered me to give up books & go down to the coast. It is a hard blow, for all my plans are upset – but God knows best. My Father has promised to send me down to Ilfracombe. Bertie & Fred Robinson are going also.

Friday, 27 September 1867

Twenty one today. How humiliating is the retrospect. How short the time given to the service of my God, how much to the service of Satan. Twenty one today. I seem to be dreaming. To have lived so long & done so little. How many of God's children have become veteran soldiers of the cross, & acquitted themselves

505 Psalm cxix. 136.
506 Psalm lxxvii. 10.
507 1 Timothy i. 15.
508 Edwin St John Whitehouse, seventh child of Henry and Catherine Whitehouse, was born on 30 October 1867.
509 Mrs Webb.
510 Colossians iii. 11.
511 Alfred Baker (1815–93), Birmingham surgeon who was treating Chavasse's curvature of the spine.

like men for their Master's cause before this age. Help me my Father to devote all to thee.

Saturday, 28 September 1867
I went to bed at 9.30 p.m. but not to sleep. We got up at 1 o'clock & left Wylde Green at 1.45, travelled by the 2.45 mail train to Bristol which we reached at 6 o'clock. Cabbed to the Cumberland Basin & left at 7 a.m.. So far so well. But when the steamer reached Avonmouth, we found that we had to wait until 10. So we breakfasted at an Hotel. The steamer started punctually. I enjoyed the voyage very much. The sea was slightly rough but none of us were ill. We reached Ilfracombe at 5 p.m. & after a little trouble lighted on most comfortable lodgings overlooking the sea.

Sunday, 29 September 1867
Went to St Philip & St James Ch[urch] both in the morning [&] evening. The congregations were large, & the sermons preached by Mr Ashley [Rashdall] of Dawlish very earnest, useful & faithful.[512] In the morning his text was, 'Ye cannot serve God & Mammon';[513] in the evening, 'Behold the Lord cometh.'[514] I suffered myself to be dragged into a long argument – alas how it deadened my heart, even tho' the subject was a religious one.

Monday, 30 September 1867
Walked to Combe Martin by Watermouth. Got caught in the rain. Cd get nothing to eat at Combe. The beer was execrable. Went from thence to Berrynarbor, a pretty village perched on the ridge of a hill with a fine church tower rising up from a belt of trees. We had some bread & cheese to eat.

Tuesday, 1 October 1867
Had a good lunch & started at 1.30 for Morthoe, passing thro' Lee. The Coast scenery was very fine. Lost our way once or twice but finally reached our destination. Had some bread, biscuits & beer at a comfortable little Inn. Afterwards looked over the Ch[urch]. Sauntered to the top of a neighbouring cliff. The view fr[om] the summit was indescribably glorious. Morthoe just visible between the hills on our right. Morthoe rock, or the Mort Stone, black, ominous, rugged rising among the waves in front; behind a valley running inland bare & naked; on our left a vast expanse, the eye roving over Woolacombe Sands a fine reach two miles long to Baggy Pt running far into the sea, & then in the distance

512 John Rashdall (1809–69), vicar of Dawlish 1864–9.
513 Matthew vi. 24.
514 Jude 14.

the long line of Hartland Point looming far away, grand in its indistinctness. So delighted were we that descending the Hill we walked across the Sands & made for Baggy Pt in the hope of reaching its furthermost part, but night came on and we were compelled to desist. We were nine miles fr[om] Ilfracombe & ignorant of the way. Fortunately I had some brandy in my pocket with wh we moistened our lips fr[om] time to time. We passed thro' Pulsborough, & then up the long street of Georgeham, the church just visible on our left, & the ruddy glow fr[om] a blacksmith's shop reminding us unpleasantly of home comforts, up a dark lane on to the bare cliff, & thence a long & weary walk to Ilfracombe, stopping every now & then to knock people up & enquire the way. We reached our lodgings at 9 p.m.. We soon got to bed. Thank God for giving me so much strength.

Wednesday, 2 October 1867
Stayed in. Went up the Capstone hill in the afternoon. The wind was very high & carried away my straw hat.

Thursday, 3 October 1867
Walked to Barnstable. Missed Bittadon Ch[urch] wh we had hoped to see. Dined at the Fortescue Arms. The town is prettily situated, & the Ch[urch] has a leaning spire wh however is not very lofty. It possesses also a good bridge. Beyond, there is nothing to be seen. At 6 p.m. we mounted the coach. None of [us] had great coats & I alone possessed a comforter. The night was bitterly cold, & the monotony of the drive varied by driving showers of hail. The Coachman kindly supplied us with horse clothes & rufs, & we wrapped ourselves up as well as we cd. We found Henry awaiting us at our lodgings.[515] He had come down fr[om] Cambridge.

Friday, 4 October 1867
Started by the 9.20 coach for Braunton. The road was very beautiful. Walked from that village to Saunton, & thence to Braunton Burrows, up the cliffs from wh we had a splendid view, down the other side to Croy &c, where we intended to have dined, but cd get nothing to eat beyond biscuits & some dubious bread & butter. Then thro' Pulboro' & across the Woolacombe Sands to Morthoe. Here we dined on eggs & bacon. Afterwards started for home. In hopes of finding a short cut I led the trustful Bertie across some fields about a mile & a half out of our way. Fresh Henry got back to Ilfracombe long before us. Received a letter fr[om] home.

515 Henry Squires.

Thank God, Henry is better;[516] the abscess has burst favourably & no immediate danger is to be feared. May God, if it be His will, spare him to us.

Saturday, 5 October 1867

Sent our luggage by Coach & started to walk to Lynton. Oh the glory of that walk. The road was fresh to us after Combe Martin. It led up a very steep hill, fr[om] the summit of [which] we had a most magnificent view. The sea lay on our right, a beautiful valley well wooded, & enclosed with hills which locked one the other, some clothed with trees, others bare & heather clad with gorges running up between. Combe Martin lying in the centre of the valley, its ch[urch] tower rising up, its grey stone set off by its bower of green foliage, & these glorious hills looking calmly down – no words can describe the scene.

Friday, 18 October 1867

I stand on the threshold of another term of another academical year. Tomorrow I stand again, if God spare me among old friends, tomorrow I enter afresh on all the trials & joys, responsibilities & advantages of an Oxford life. I go back a third class man. Lord glorify thyself in my weakness. And what have I done for Xt during the Vacation? – how little, miserably little, compared with my high proposals. The retrospect in humiliating; my heart shudders at the thought of my negligence. Yet God be praised, I have been enabled to do something. Never did I ponder on a coming term with a greater realization of my own helplessness. God is indeed shewing me myself. A senior man, now, how vast the responsibility. The prayer meeting, Missionary Union, Tract Distribution Society, District, Cottage Lectures, Sunday Schools, friends to be counselled, friends to be won for Jesus, friends to be warned & entreated, the large influx of new men – all combine to form an overpowering picture. Who is sufficient for these things?[517] Am I? What am I? Shy, bashful to a painful degree, easily silenced, cowardly, reserved (alas for my reserve), unsymphathizing [*sic*], cold, selfish, such am I. Yet Xt will work in me & by me. Scorned of men, I shall not be cast aside as useless by Him. But oh how I need his grace. Longing to pray, I yet cannot pray long together, for I cannot concentrate my thoughts. Longing to grow in holiness, I seem viler & viler. Longing to become openhearted, loving, symphathetic [*sic*], I seem to be more reserved, exclusive, selfish every day. I can weep at times for my unchristian feelings. I yearn for the mind of Jesus, for the humility, love & earnestness of Jesus. Thank God I have at present no doubts as [to] my acceptance with my Lord. I bewail rather my slothfulness in growing in grace. Truly I can say, '*My flesh & my heart faileth*' – yet praised be the Lord I can add, '*but God is the*

516 Henry Whitehouse.

517 2 Corinthians ii. 16.

strength of my heart & my portion for ever.'[518] This shall be my motto for the ensuing term: 'When I am weak then am I strong',[519] strong in a heaven-sent strength, strong in the remembrance that Xt Jesus works in me, strong in the numberless promises given to the weak & fainting, strong because God is *my* God, Jesus *my* Jesus, Heaven *my* Home. Thus armed & with such a hope 'I will fear no evil.'[520]

Called on Mr Robinson & afterwards on Fanny. Went to see old Busby but he was still away.[521] In the evening held the last prayer meeting at Webb's cottage.

Saturday, 19 October 1867

Again in Oxford. I can scarcely realize it. I left home at 10.30. My heart was very heavy. My thoughts wandered away to Sedgley. I never feel how dearly I love my Father, Mother & Sisters until called to part from them. Oh how exceedingly comfortable is the knowledge that they are in Jesus. He will keep his own. Had an opportunity, for wh God be praised, of speaking to a woman in the train. She seemed inclined to listen, & I gave her a tract. I reached Oxford at 2. Sent my luggage on by omnibus, & went to the Union, wrote home & to those who help me at Hincksey. At Corpus I found that one of my wine bottles had broken in the tea box. Fortunately nothing was hurt: a shirt was well saturated, but the b[oo]ks had escaped. Walked down to Hincksey. Called on Mrs Bell & Mrs Herbert. I was very pleased to find that the school had been kept up during the Vacation. Mr Nash had very kindly found teachers. At 8.30 went to Mr Christopher's Meeting[:] there was a large attendance. Mr C. said to me good humouredly as I went out 'Come, you must not wear a gloomy face.' I did not know that I looked sad, but never did I return to Oxford with a heavier heart. Yet all my friends are most kind. They give my hand a warm squeeze out of symphathy [*sic*]. May God bless them all, & make me a blessing to them. He is my trust. We have only seven freshmen this term.

Sunday, 20 October 1867

Lock breakfasted with me. He has changed his rooms. Heard Dr Miller preach in the morning at the University Ch[urch]. His subject was 'glorifying God'. He was very earnest, & his sermon most useful for the first Sunday in term. Oh that I may be enabled to glorify him more during my remaining time at Oxford & throughout my life. Went to our School in the afternoon. We had a good attendance. Mr Nash

518 Psalm lxxiii. 26.
519 2 Corinthians xii. 10.
520 Psalm xxiii. 4.
521 William Busby (*c.*1787–1873), labourer.

kindly sent some men from his Bible Class who carried it on for us during the Vacation.

Michaelmas Term 1867

I have been so very busy during the Term that I have not been able to write my diary. I must therefore adopt the same plan I pursued for the last summer term & give a short resume of the principal events wh have occurred.

And first with regard to my *Law & History work*. I kept ground steadily throughout the term, at a daily average of 6 hrs. I like the course of reading very much. The first three weeks of term I wasted, simply because I did not know how to work, & commenced several methods of analysing before I lighted on one wh satisfied me. However I cannot think that the time was altogether lost. I shall certainly remember that portion of my work all the better fr[om] having gone over it so many times. Newman's Lectures are admirable.[522] We are reading Gibbon & Milman with him at present.[523] He gives us two Essays to write weekly. I also attended Stubb's Lectures on Constitutional History.[524] He reads so very fast that I find some difficulty in gathering on paper the pith of his remarks. I hope to improve by practice. Towards the end of the term when Newman was examining in the Schools, Green took his Gibbon Lecture, but after attending two or three of them, I gave him up – he taught us nothing.[525] Altogether during the term I read & analysed ¾ of my Milman & rather less than ⅓ of Gibbon, took essays to Newman & attended the first course of Stubb's Lectures besides reading parts of other books bearing on the subjects I had in hand. I hope, by God's blessing, for my Father's sake to do better in the Final Schools than in Mods.[526] The lot is cast into the lap; it is comforting to know that the whole disposing of it is the Lord's.

In College work. I feel, on reflection that I have not acted wisely this term. I have neglected my Corpus friends for out college friends, & in college work for more direct pastoral work at Hincksey. Naturally shy & diffident, a cowardly soldier of the Lord who bought me, I have too often shirked the more difficult (to me) task of personal appeals to men. I have shut myself up too much; I have neglected lawful means of gaining any little influence in college such as by steering

522 William L. Newman (1834–1923), fellow of Balliol 1854–1923, reader in ancient history 1868–70.

523 Edward Gibbon (1737–94), historian, author of *The history of the decline and fall of the Roman empire* (1776–88). Henry H. Milman (1791–1868), dean of St Paul's 1849–68, author of *The history of christianity* (1840) and *History of Latin christianity* (1854–5). Milman's edition of Gibbon's *Decline and fall* was the standard until the 1890s.

524 William Stubbs (1825–1901), regius professor of modern history 1866–84, bishop of Chester 1884–8, of Oxford 1888–1901.

525 Thomas Hill Green (1836–82), fellow of Balliol 1860–78, Whyte professor of moral philosophy 1878–82.

526 Chavasse was in the first class in Finals, December 1869.

a four, or speaking at the debating Society &c. Alas when I look back on the high resolves I made of working for Xt among the freshmen, & on the very very little I really did for Him, my heart ache[s] & I can groan for remorse. I thank God, nevertheless for what I have been enabled to do. I was enabled one afternoon to speak to dear C. – but oh how feebly, & I have striven to know all the freshmen – there were but seven. We have also started a Sunday Evening Bible Reading. May the Eternal Spirit bless it. I thank God too that dear Ingham & Knox & Russell & myself seem to be drawn much closer together. I love them all like brothers, & that notwithstanding my usual reserve we have been able to speak to one another & cheer each other on. I see however that by God's gracious help, it is my bounden duty to make more sacrifices & to endeavour more earnestly to get at men who are not in Xt. May my Heavenly Father forgive my gross remissness during this term. If spared to another I will strive to throw aside my feeling of awkwardness & reticence, will associate more with my fellows, & become all things to all men, if by chance God may use me to win some of them.[527]

Town Hall Meetings. These have gone on as during last Term. There was a break of two or three weeks in November on account of the Bread Riots. Lord Radstock came down twice. The second time prevented fr[om] having the Town Hall he gave a short & earnest address to about 20 undergraduates at 40 Pembroke St.[528] The following morning Christopher gave a public breakfast at the King's Arms. Lord Radstock there spoke most earnestly to us. About 60 men were present. Stephenson Blackwood, who tho' very weary, gave a beautiful address on Salvation & Service. Haslam, Capt. Trotter & Earl Cavan also came down.[529] Capt. Trotter I liked very much. By God's blessing his addresses were very profitable to me. He spoke at the Saturday Evening meeting, & on Sunday Evening after Church at Bontein's rooms. I attended all these meetings with Ingham. Whether I can do so next term without neglecting my work, is a question for prayer & reflection.

Prayer Meetings. The daily Prayer Meeting has been removed to 40 Pembroke St. The attendance has not been so satisfactory as last term. The daily average has been about 10. No regular order has been introduced & the prayers are spontaneous. I hold my own opinion strongly on the wisdom of such a procedure, & I expressed it but was overruled. Several freshmen I am glad to say attend very regularly. Mr Christopher's Saturday Evening meeting has largely increased in numbers, the average being 36. Once or twice the room was filled to overflowing. Mr Linton's Missionary Prayer Meeting has maintained its average

527 I Corinthians ix. 22.

528 St Aldate's rectory.

529 John Trotter (1808–70) of Dyrham Park, Herts., founder of Army Prayer Union. Frederick J. W. Lambart, 8th earl of Cavan (1815–87), evangelical peer.

numbers. He read a very interesting letter to us from Sharp who holds Robert Noble's place at Masulipatam.[530] He is a most delightful man. Nothing whatever has been with the Missionary Union this term. As librarian I ought to have made a catalogue of the b[oo]ks. I must do so, if my life be spared next term.

I still have a class at St Peter-le-Bailey Sunday School, not the same that I had before the Long, but three delightful lads. Tonge has gone to Sparkbrook Ch[urch] & Girdlestone Linton's new curate has not yet been ordained. James Hall very kindly promised to take the Class for me during the Vac – there is something going on in his mind; may God bring him to the truth. Our School at Hincksey is I am thankful to say thriving. We have between 70 & 80 children on the books & 10 men teaching every Sunday. We have had some little trouble in finding room for all. Mrs Herbert could not accommodate us after the third Sunday in the term, & a new cottage with a very nice room we were oblige[d] to give up, as the husband objected. However we engaged two other rooms: one at Weaver's,[531] the second at Mrs Janaway's.[532] Dear kind Mrs Bell still lends us her kitchen. I very much wish we cd have all the children together. Closely packed as we are, it is difficult to keep the lads quiet. The girls behave well in their room. Burgon sent for me in the middle of the Term & made every enquiry about the School & village, giving me at the same time a lecture on Apostolical Confession.[533] He is a High Churchman but who can help but love him? He promised to lay the case before the Bishop. We heard nothing further about the matter. With regard to the district itself, Ingham & myself have worked our part. I fear that I did not visit each of my houses very frequently, as both Ward's & Diggle's districts were thrown on my hands – the former has gone down, the latter threw up his on account of his work. Goodey, praised be God, has been enabled to see the truth. Hartshorne administered the Sacrament to him in the course of the Term. Of the spiritual state of another sick man who subsequently recovered, a railway porter laid by with inflammation of the lungs, I cannot speak positively. I fear I did not address him pointedly enough. May God forgive all these my shortcomings. The greater the light & the opportunity, the greater the sin of neglect. An old man named Rolls, confined to his bed thro' old age, was made the means of humbling me. I was asked to see him & when I called on the Sunday afternoon after School, I plunged in medias res. He in a towering rage ordered me out of the room & I had great difficulty in soothing him. I thank God for the rebuff. The next time I

530 Robert T. Noble (1809–65), founder with Henry W. Fox of the C.M.S. Telegu mission and in 1842 of Noble College, Masulipatam. He was replaced by John Sharp (1838–1917), principal of Noble College 1865–70, 1872–8, secretary to Bible Society 1880–1900.

531 Robert Weaver (*c.*1810–81), carpenter.

532 Mildred Janaway (*c.*1820–1900), seamstress.

533 John W. Burgon (1813–88), fellow of Oriel 1846–76, vicar of St Mary's, Oxford 1863–76, dean of Chichester 1876–88.

went to work more carefully & entered into conversation with him on secular subjects. He was then free from pain & pleasant enough until I asked if I shd read to him a chapter from the Bible, when he flatly refused – he knew his Bible he said – alas, then he does not act up to his knowledge. The third time he was equally obdurate, but I left a copy of 'Come to Jesus'. I had to come down & I did not see him again. The Cottage Lecture has been continued, & the attendance has increased slightly. Oh, our God, all these means are for thy glory. Glorify thyself by these weak instruments. The Cottage Lecture at Coal Harbour was dropped after the first Thursday. It will probably be revived next term & held in a different house.

I have had the privilege of making many new friends. Some, I am happy to say are decided Xtians, others are wavering, some few are without God in the world.[534] One great privilege, for which I have to thank God, was a breakfast given by Freeman in Wadham at the end of Term.[535] He came up for a few days to see how things were progressing. He spoke to us of the advisability of entering into College affairs & endeavouring to gain influence thereby. I was very thankful for the hint; I have acted hitherto on a wrong principle. May God help me to do otherwise next term.

The collection for the Bible Society realized £4.5.[536] A sov[ereign] more than last year. The secretary of the Irish Society called & had a long talk. I think the principle on wh their work is conducted, is admirable. I have consented to collect next Term. It is trying for the flesh, but I feel that it is one place or 'the Cross'.

There is one little incident wh occurred during the Term wh I record, that I may see whether after Xtian experience confirm me in the opinion I expressed. A freshman named D. was brought to Xt mainly thro' B.'s instrumentality.[537] The same night both attended the Prayer Meeting. When they entered I was alone in the room. B. whispered to D., who came up & said hurriedly 'I have found Xt this afternoon'. I spoke a few words to him, & at this instant several other men came in. After the meeting, B. beckoned to us to wait for a few moments & motioned D. forward adding 'speak up'. Conjecturing what was coming I made for the door, but I heard D. repeat the same words he had previously used to me, before I cd get out of the room. I wrote to B. when I got back to college & told me [*sic*] what were my feelings on the subject, & how strongly I disapproved of such a course.

534 Ephesians ii. 12.

535 Frederick Freeman (b. *c.* 1841), m. Wadham 1861.

536 Chavasse was responsible for collecting donations to the British and Foreign Bible Society from members of Corpus.

537 Bontein's witness led to the conversion on 7 November 1867 of George B. Durrant (1848–1931), m. Oriel 1867, C.M.S. missionary in India 1876–98, foreign secretary of C.M.S. 1898–1913. Durrant was soon recruited for Chavasse's Sunday School at New Hinksey.

He answered me very nicely, but firmly maintaining the right of acting as he had done. Ingham & several of the others agreed with me. I am inclined to think that I acted unwisely in leaving the room, but I am very glad that I wrote to B..

Truly I can say at the end of this term, that mercy has followed me throughout. My Heavenly Father has strengthened me, & given me the aid I needed. I returned to Oxford with fear & trembling. I leave it with thankfulness for past blessings. Oh that the remembrance of what God has done to me & for me may cause me to devote myself, body, soul & spirit wholly to his service.

Tuesday, 31 December 1867

Thank God, that in spite of rolling years & countless changes 'Jesus Christ is the same yesterday & today & forever'.[538] The year which opened with a family gathering has brought many sorrows in its train & closed with a separation. Many dear friends have been gathered to their rest & among them one who when 1867 commenced promised to live as long as any of us. Dear Henry has gone[539] – but how glorious the closing scene, how inexpressibly comforting the assurance that to him to die was gain.[540] Brought on his sick bed to grasp, to lay hold of the Lord Jesus Christ, & to rest all his hope on him alone, he fell asleep in Jesus. And hope rapidly traversing the interval dwells with joy on the promise that those wh sleep in Jesus will God bring with him.[541]

Looking back on the past year how much have I individually to be thankful for. I have indeed suffered the greatest blow, that has yet befallen me, & had all my hopes for Mods blighted, & the expectations of my friends marred. But fr[om] the depth of my heart I thank my Almighty Father for the chastening. Hard as the disappointment was to bear, & in my own strength I cd not have borne it, I yet can feel that one of my most prized *idols* has been snatched from me. In the pride of my heart I thought to do great things, & for my pride he has sent me hungry away. He doeth all things well.[542] Whatever work he may have for me to do, must be done by strength given me from above. He has taught me to see my own weakness & ignorance.

Friday, 24 January 1868

Returned to Oxford; left home with H[enr]y at 2.24.[543] Met Bodington at Aston. Henry lost his hatbox, & stayed behind to recover it. B. & myself went on by the 3.10 train. Allen had got my room ready for me. Lock & Little had come up. Went

538 Hebrews xiii. 8.
539 Henry Whitehouse died on 17 December 1867.
540 Philippians i. 21.
541 1 Thessalonians iv. 14.
542 Mark vii. 37.
543 Henry Squires.

to see H. in the evening at Wadham. His hatbox had been left in the cab. My motto for this term is, 'The Lord is faithful who will stablish & keep you fr[om] evil.'[544] I feel my responsibility. May God help me to work for his glory more *in college* than I have hitherto done. I am very weak, very cowardly, very ignorant, but He can & He will supply all my need[s].[545]

Saturday, 25 January 1868
Worked part of the morning. In the afternoon went to Hincksey, made all arrangements about the school & saw Good[e]y. In the evening went to Mr C.'s meeting. There was a good attendance. Mr Goodhart gave us a most useful address 'on the work of the Spirit'.

Sunday, 26 January 1868
To Linton's School in the morning. Girdlestone there. He seems a very nice fellow. At 11.30 went to the Prayer meeting in Barker's room. Henry lunched with me & went to Hincksey School. All the teachers have come up but Ingham. Our boys noisy. I must pray more for them. H. took my class & I took Ingham's. They seemed interested in the story of Bartimeus – how full of instruction it is. Rhodes went with me to St Aldate's in the evening. Mr Goodhart preached fr[om] 'I believed, therefore have I spoken'.[546] By God's help I will speak to Rhodes. Had our usual Bible Gathering in the evening. Next Sunday I must try to get more time to myself – it is necessary for my soul's health that I shd.

Monday, 27 January 1868
Called on Dendy & Colmore.[547] Wrote home. Went to the Prayer Meeting. 13 there. Did not get up till 7.15. How hard it is to eradicate a bad habit. By the grace of God I will conquer this indolence.

Tuesday, 28 January 1868
Lectures began; went to Dendy & Newman. Found Phipson with the former. Went to Hincksey in the afternoon. Since my return to Oxford I have felt as if a veil were drawn across my heart. Oh thou Eternal Spirit help me in my need. Let me look on thee & be lightened. Wrote to Bob. God helped me in the Letter. Glory be to his Holy Name. I have a g[rea]t deal of work to do. I must economize my time.

544 2 Thessalonians iii. 3.
545 Philippians iv. 19.
546 Psalm cxvi. 10.
547 Arthur Dendy (1841–1900), m. Balliol 1860, fellow of University 1873–1900.

4

J. C. RYLE: 'FIRST WORDS'. AN OPENING ADDRESS DELIVERED AT THE FIRST LIVERPOOL DIOCESAN CONFERENCE, 1881

Edited by
Martin Wellings

Introduction

Few Victorian bishops and fewer leading Victorian evangelicals are household names among twenty-first century christians, but J. C. Ryle (1816–1900), from 1880 first anglican bishop of Liverpool and a prominent evangelical for much of the second half of the nineteenth century, is an exception in both categories.[1] Several of his expository and devotional writings are still in print and he enjoys an enduring reputation as an articulate exponent and defender of a traditional evangelical interpretation of the gospel. Twentieth-century conservative evangelicals, especially those in the Reformed tradition like Martyn Lloyd-Jones and J. I. Packer, held Ryle in high esteem as an advocate of the 'old paths' at a time when biblical criticism and increasing pluralism in theology seemed to be changing the face of English evangelicalism, when anglo-catholicism was becoming the dominant school in the Church of England, and when all denominations were struggling to engage effectively in mission to urban society. In Packer's opinion, Ryle was 'one of the greatest of Victorian evangelicals', not least because 'in an age of giddy religious Athenianism no new idea had ever passed either his lips or his pen.'[2] This impression of Ryle as the icon of unbending traditionalism can be reinforced by an appeal to contemporary observers, including Ryle's son Herbert, a leading Old Testament scholar, who ceased to serve as his father's examining chaplain in 1887 because their views on the acceptability of biblical criticism had diverged too widely. Herbert wrote from Liverpool, 'I write in a land where antagonistic German criticism has not obtained much foothold, even in the bookshelves.'[3] It would seem that Ryle's *nom de plume*, 'An Old Soldier', familiar in the correspondence columns of the evangelical press, was well chosen.

This picture of Ryle needs to be qualified in two respects. First, the varied agenda of Ryle's admirers – and of his critics – both contemporary and more recent, must be recognized. To contemporaries within his own school of thought, Ryle was the standard-bearer of evangelical doctrine, ecclesiology and missionary strategy, whereas for liberal and high church controversialists he could serve as an Aunt Sally, the epitome of dogmatic, pugnacious and barren evangelicalism, particularly in the context of his involvement as bishop in the prosecution of James Bell Cox for the use of illegal ritual at St Margaret's, Princes Road. Thus an article in the *Spectator* in August 1888 lampooning Ryle's opposition to the recent

1 The principal biographies of J.C. Ryle are: Marcus L. Loane, *John Charles Ryle 1816-1900. A short biography* (London, 1953); *J. C. Ryle. A self-portrait*, ed. Peter Toon (Swengel, Pa., 1975); Peter Toon and Michael Smout, *John Charles Ryle. Evangelical bishop* (Cambridge, 1976); and Ian D. Farley, *J. C. Ryle. First bishop of Liverpool* (Carlisle, 2000). A brief biography by the present writer will appear in the *Oxford D.N.B.* (Oxford, 2004).

2 J.I. Packer, 'Preface', in J. C. Ryle, *Holiness* (Welwyn, 1979), pp. viii, ix.

3 Maurice H. Fitzgerald, *A memoir of Herbert Edward Ryle* (London, 1928), pp. 131–2.

Lambeth conference encyclical began: 'The bishop of Liverpool hates popery; but what a Pope he would make!', while the Bell Cox prosecution generated vitriolic press comments and coloured subsequent assessments of Ryle's episcopate.[4] For later generations of conservative evangelicals, however, engaged in their own conflict with liberalism, Ryle offered an example of traditionalism and an arsenal for polemic.

The second qualification concerns Ryle's flexibility and pragmatism. Although undoubtedly conservative in doctrine, Ryle was innovative in missionary strategy and enough of a realist to adapt to changing circumstances in the Church of England. Both features were evident in the text of his first address to the newly formed Liverpool diocesan conference, delivered in November 1881. As will be seen below, Ryle's attitude to diocesan conferences evolved in the years before his appointment as bishop of Liverpool. The text offered here illustrates an evangelical adaptation to contemporary realities, as well as an illustration of Ryle's missionary priorities and skill as a communicator. Before turning to the text, however, '*First words*' must be set in the contexts of Ryle's life and career, of Victorian evangelicalism and of the development of diocesan assemblies in the nineteenth-century Church of England.

John Charles Ryle was born on 10 May 1816 at Park House, Macclesfield into an affluent and well-connected local family. His grandfather, John Ryle (d. 1808) was an industrialist who made his fortune in the silk trade; John's son, also John, became a banker and served as mayor of Macclesfield and M.P. for the borough from 1832 to 1837. The younger John Ryle married Susanna Hurt, daughter of Charles Hurt of Wirksworth and granddaughter of Sir Richard Arkwright, so the Ryles were linked to the industrial plutocracy of early nineteenth-century England. The older generation of the family had Wesleyan methodist sympathies, but these were later replaced by an unenthusiastic conformity to the Church of England.[5]

After preliminary schooling with the Rev. John Jackson at Over, J. C. Ryle proceeded to Eton in 1828 and thence to Christ Church, Oxford, in 1834. His academic record was distinguished: he was Fell exhibitioner (1835) and Craven scholar (1836), gaining a first class in literae humaniores in 1837 and graduating B.A. the following year. His academic prowess was matched by sporting achievement, and he captained the university cricket XI. Although invited to apply for a fellowship at Oxford, Ryle chose instead to return to Macclesfield and to begin preparations for a career in business and politics. Foundations were laid with

4 *Spectator* (London), 25 Aug. 1888, p. 1152; Farley, *Ryle*, ch. 6.

5 *Ryle*, ed. Toon, pp. 4, 6; Toon and Smout, *Ryle*, pp. 8, 11; *Record* (London), 27 Oct. 1899, p. 1054.

employment in the family bank, service as an officer in the yeomanry and appointment as a J.P.[6]

Ryle's autobiography offers few indications that he was much affected by the theological ferment in Oxford in the mid-1830s. Although he noted the pastoral influence of Edward Denison and Walter Hamilton at St Peter's-in-the-East, and although his younger brother Frederick later served as curate to Samuel Wilberforce at Alverstoke, there is no evidence that Ryle was ever attracted to tractarianism. His sympathies lay rather with the evangelicals: his sister Susan and curate cousin Harry Arkwright turned to evangelical christianity in this period, and in 1837–8 Ryle read a series of evangelical classics, including Wilberforce's *Practical view*, Angell James's *Christian professor*, Scott's *Reply to Bishop Tomline*, Newton's *Cardiphonia*, Milner's *Church history* and Bickersteth's *Christian student*. Tradition attributed his conversion to the experience of hearing Ephesians ii read aloud in an Oxford church. During a brief period reading law in London, Ryle attended the proprietory chapel in Bedford Row, then under the ministry of Baptist Noel.[7]

Ryle's life changed decisively in June 1841, when his father's bank collapsed. The family estates and income were swept away, and with them any hopes of a political career.[8] Ryle decided to take holy orders, recording later that 'I became a clergyman because I felt shut up to do it, and saw no other course of life open to me.'[9] Within a matter of months he was ordained deacon by Bishop C. R. Sumner of Winchester, serving as curate of Exbury, Hampshire, from 1841 to 1843, before preferment by Sumner to the rectory of St Thomas's, Winchester. His five months at St Thomas's 'filled [the] church to suffocation and turned the parish upside-down'.[10] Plans were laid to restore and enlarge the church, but by the time this was agreed Ryle had accepted the lord chancellor's presentation to the living of Helmingham in Suffolk, where he remained for seventeen years. In 1861 Bishop J. T. Pelham of Norwich offered Ryle the vicarage of Stradbroke. Difficulties with John Tollemache, M.P., the leading landowner in Helmingham, encouraged Ryle to accept this move and to begin a nineteen-year incumbency at Stradbroke. Further preferment followed, as Ryle was appointed rural dean of Hoxne in 1870 and an honorary canon of Norwich two years later. In 1880 Ryle accepted nomination to the deanery of Salisbury, but while still dean-designate he

6 *Ryle*, ed. Toon, pp. 12, 16, 29–34; Toon and Smout, *Ryle*, pp. 12–22, 29.

7 *Ryle*, ed. Toon, pp. 38–40; Toon and Smout, *Ryle*, pp. 26, 29, 36. The conversion story is told in W. H. Griffith Thomas, *The work of the ministry* (London, n.d.), p. 185. For Baptist Noel, see Grayson Carter, *Anglican Evangelicals. Protestant secessions from the via media, c. 1800-1850* (Oxford, 2001), ch. 8.

8 *Ryle*, ed. Toon, p. 51.

9 *Ibid.*, p. 59.

10 *Ibid.*, p. 67.

was offered and accepted the new see of Liverpool, thus entering a radically different sphere of life and work. He retired from Liverpool in March 1900 and died in June of the same year.[11]

The thirty-six years' incumbency in Suffolk saw Ryle make his mark on the wider ecclesiastical world as preacher, author and evangelical leader. His first impact beyond his own parish came as a writer of tracts.[12] From *Seeking the Lord early* in 1845 to *Justified! A word for 1895* in 1894 Ryle produced some two hundred titles which sold twelve million copies during his lifetime.[13] Multiple editions and recycled material swelled the volume of publications. Some tracts were directly evangelistic, like *Are you forgiven?* (1849) and *Shall you be saved?* (1852). Others, like *Do you pray?* (1852) and the collection later gathered into the volume *Holiness* (1877), addressed aspects of the devotional life. There were tracts on sabbath observance, on biblical inspiration, on church defence and church reform. Contemporary controversies over disestablishment, over the doctrines and practices of anglican ritualism and over the higher criticism of the Bible drew comment from Ryle's pen. His position was consistent: urging, expounding and defending a conservative evangelical interpretation of christianity, centred on the cross, affirming the need for conversion, emphasising holy living and underpinned by reliance on an infallible and authoritative Bible. Ryle's theology was shaped by the English reformers, the puritans and the leaders of the eighteenth-century revival. It was mildly calvinist in emphasis and firmly loyal to the protestant Reformed religion as by law established. Ryle disagreed with Wesleyan perfectionism, was dubious about Keswick and 'holiness by faith', stood firm against disestablishing dissenters and resisted Gladstone's policy on the Irish Church, excoriated the new school of biblical criticism as rationalistic infidelity and denounced ritualism as treason to the Church of England. The titles of his fourth and fifth charges as bishop of Liverpool spoke for his general theological outlook: 'Hold fast' and 'Stand firm', calling for fidelity to the 'old paths' in a changing social and ecclesiastical landscape. As recent biographers have shown, however, doctrinal conservatism was accompanied by a readiness to innovate in church organization and evangelization, and by a strong streak of pragmatism. In particular, Ian Farley has suggested that the controversy over the disestablishment of the Church of Ireland provoked Ryle to rethink his political and ecclesiastical outlook in significant ways. According to Farley, Gladstone's Irish policy raised for Ryle the spectre of English disestablishment and a revival of Roman catholicism. His response was a strategy for the renewal and strengthening of the national church, comprising a quest for evangelical unity, a new commitment to co-

11 Wellings, *Oxford DNB*.

12 Farley, *Ryle*, pp. 244–9, lists Ryle's publications in chronological order.

13 *Ibid.*, p. 2.

operation between different schools of thought in the Church of England and advocacy of church reform.[14] It is possible to interpret Ryle's priorities in terms of the traditional emphases of mainstream Simeonite evangelicalism without necessarily endorsing Farley's interpretation of the seismic effects of Irish disestablishment, but the point is well made that Ryle's conservatism was creative and constructive, not merely reactionary.[15]

The gifts of communication honed in the writing and rewriting of tracts were also evident in Ryle's preaching. Standing six feet three and a half inches tall, he possessed a commanding presence, and he was a lucid and compelling speaker. According to his son Herbert, he set his face against florid prose and pretentious oratory, making his motto 'Sacrifice style'. Clarity of expression matched precision of thought: 'If you yourself are in a fog, depend upon it you will leave your people in darkness.'[16] He soon moved beyond Helmingham. Family contacts gave him an entrée into evangelical networks: his first wife, Matilda Plumptre, was the daughter of J. P. Plumptre, M.P., member of the committee of the Church Pastoral Aid Society and an early supporter of the Evangelical Alliance. The Tollemaches too had a circle of evangelical friends including Archbishop J. B. Sumner, Bishop H. M. Villiers and the evangelical banker Robert Bevan.[17] Ryle became a sought-after preacher in metropolitan pulpits, and in 1862 was awarded the accolade of an invitation to preach the anniversary sermon for the Church Missionary Society at St Bride's, Fleet Street, the blue riband of the evangelical pulpit. Eugene Stock recalled the sermon as 'one of those perfectly plain, terse, incisive addresses with which the whole Church of England has since become so familiar'.[18]

Known as a writer and a preacher, Ryle took an increasingly prominent part in the national deliberations of the evangelical school. He became involved in the cat's cradle of societies which gave institutional expression to evangelical activism: in the C.M.S., the Islington Clerical Meeting, the Colonial and Continental Church Society, the C.P.A.S., the London City Mission and the London Society for Promoting Christianity amongst the Jews. He was also an early supporter of the Church Association, founded in 1865 to co-ordinate

14 Farley, *Ryle*, pp. 43, 44.

15 For the evangelical school and its place in the wider evangelical movement see Ian Bradley, *The call to seriousness. The evangelical impact on the Victorians* (London, 1976); Boyd Hilton, *The age of atonement. The influence of evangelicalism on social and economic thought 1785–1865* (Oxford, 1988); D. W. Bebbington, *Evangelicalism in modern Britain. A history from the 1730s to the 1980s* (London, 1989); G.R. Balleine, *A history of the evangelical party in the Church of England* (London, 1933); Kenneth Hylson-Smith, *Evangelicals in the Church of England 1734–1984* (Edinburgh, 1988).

16 Recollection of Herbert Ryle, *Record*, 26 Oct. 1916, p. 840.

17 *Ryle*, ed. Toon, pp. 71, 73.

18 Eugene Stock, *The history of the Church Missionary Society* (3 vols., London, 1899), II, 342.

evangelical reactions to the development of ritualism in the Church of England.[19] The Association's aggressive protestantism inevitably alienated high churchmen and exasperated the episcopate, but its encouragement of lawsuits against ritualists proved controversial even among evangelicals. The policy of prosecution was criticized as counter-productive and unspiritual. Ryle defended the Association, calling it 'a society for the relief of perplexed bishops' because it sought to clarify the law with regard to ecclesiastical ritual. As a bishop himself, however, he withdrew from the Association after 1880, and perhaps saw ritual prosecutions in a different light in consequence of his experience of the Bell Cox case, which occupied seven years of his episcopate, earned him considerable press and public criticism and tarnished his later reputation.[20]

In the 1860s Ryle was one of a group of evangelicals who urged engagement with the wider life of the Church of England. This group, including Edward Garbett and Edward Hoare, was regarded with suspicion and dubbed 'Neo-Evangelical' by the ultra-conservatives.[21] The cautiously constructive approach to contemporary church reform epitomized by the group and exemplified by their participation in church congresses and diocesan structures prompts a consideration of the background to diocesan conferences and to the reception of this development by the evangelical school.

Until recently the history of the creation of diocesan synods and conferences in the Victorian church has been written as an appendix to the story of the campaign for the revival of convocation, linking the movement to concerns about liberal theology, church defence and tensions between church and state, and ascribing the chief initiative in the process to high churchmen. The emphasis of this historiography has, however, been questioned by Arthur Burns in his study of the diocesan revival in the Church of England in the first two-thirds of the nineteenth century. Burns argues persuasively that the exploration of synods and conferences had a long pedigree in the Church of England, that it attracted interest and support from a cross-section of theological opinion, and that its motivation was primarily positive, rather than defensive or polemical. The campaign for diocesan assemblies, beginning in the 1830s and gathering momentum through the 1850s and

19 The ritual controversy formed a significant part of the backdrop to mid-nineteenth-century church politics, as evidenced by the number of pieces of legislation mentioned in the text of *'First words'* bearing on the issue (see notes to the text). Ritualism is discussed below in the context of the development of diocesan conferences. For a recent study of the phenomenon see Nigel Yates, *Anglican ritualism in Victorian Britain 1830–1910* (Oxford, 1999) and for an interpretation of the effects on the evangelical school see M. Wellings, *Evangelicals embattled* (Carlisle, 2003), esp. chs 2 and 3.

20 Anne Bentley, 'The transformation of the Evangelical party in the Church of England in the later nineteenth century', Ph.D. dissertation, University of Durham, 1971, p. 134; Farley, *Ryle*, ch. 6.

21 Stock, *C.M.S.*, III, 9.

1860s, was driven by concern for pastoral efficiency as the church sought to improve structures of consultation, to strengthen diocesan identity, to address pressing issues of clergy discipline and to check the development of partisan societies.[22]

The point about exploration is important. No blueprint existed for a diocesan assembly, beyond the research of antiquarians into medieval precedents. Various plans were canvassed by pamphleteers in the 1830s, and Bishop Phillpotts offered a practical example by convening a representative clerical synod at Exeter in 1851.[23] Rumours that other bishops might follow suit were not substantiated, although further schemes were put forward in convocation debates from the late 1850s. When bishops began to summon assemblies from the middle of the next decade, models varied from diocese to diocese, and patterns evolved in the light of experience. The first assemblies were gathered in the diocese of Ely by Bishop Harold Browne, who called an informal meeting of cathedral clergy, archdeacons, rural deans and proctors in convocation in 1864. A more formal conference the following year met for two days, and on the second day lay representatives elected by the ruri-decanal chapters joined the clergy. In 1868 the scheme evolved further into a series of archdeaconry meetings open to all clergy and churchwardens, prominent lay people invited by the bishop and up to four lay representatives chosen by each parish. Browne wanted to avoid the clerical exclusiveness, juridical pretensions and potential illegalities inherent in summoning a 'synod', so he spoke instead of a 'diocesan conference', emphasized practical schemes for strengthening diocesan organisation and vetoed debate on controversial topics.[24]

While Harold Browne was developing regional conferences in the diocese of Ely, a determined attempt to create a full synod was launched in the diocese of Lichfield by George Augustus Selwyn. Selwyn, a strong high churchman and energetic missionary bishop in New Zealand from 1841 to 1869, was nominated to the see of Lichfield at the end of 1867. On the basis of his experience in New Zealand, Selwyn had urged the value of diocesan synods in an address to the Wolverhampton church congress, and, inheriting a plan for a consultative assembly from his predecessor, he set to work to convene a synod in summer 1868. Selwyn envisaged annual meetings in each archdeaconry, attended by the clergy and by two lay representatives from each parish. The diocesan synod would meet triennially, and would be composed of clerical and lay representatives elected by

22 Arthur Burns, *The diocesan revival in the Church of England c.1800–1870* (Oxford, 1999), ch. 9. Compare the older interpretation in M.A. Crowther, *Church embattled. Religious controversy in mid-Victorian England* (Newton Abbot, 1970), ch. 8, and Owen Chadwick, *The Victorian church* (2 vols., London, 1966–70), II, 359–60.

23 Burns, *Diocesan revival*, pp. 223–33.

24 *Ibid.*, pp. 250–2; G. W. Kitchen, *Edward Harold Browne* (London, 1895), pp. 271–9.

the rural deaneries, patrons of livings, members of parliament, school inspectors and diocesan dignitaries. The rural deaneries and archdeaconries supported the scheme, although the earls of Lichfield and Harrowby carried a resolution substituting 'conference' for 'synod'. The two-tier structure of archidiaconal and diocesan meetings soon proved cumbersome and Selwyn dropped the lower tier in favour of an annual diocesan conference which he persisted in calling a 'synod'.[25]

Where Ely and Lichfield led, other dioceses followed, each adopting its own structure, pattern and terminology for its assembly. William Thomson, archbishop of York, introduced informal diocesan conferences in 1869, eventually settling into a scheme of biennial meetings.[26] George Moberly, bishop of Salisbury, began 'to break ground about a Diocesan Synod' towards the end of 1870, setting in train plans for an elected synod of clergy and laity.[27] W. C. Magee held his first diocesan conference in the diocese of Peterborough in June 1871, reporting it to be a 'great success'.[28] Christopher Wordsworth, an advocate of synods in convocation in the mid-1860s, convened an exclusively clerical synod in Lincoln in September 1871. This gathering of the entire clerical body of the diocese was not repeated, however, for from 1872 a representative annual diocesan conference of 250 clergy and 250 laity was held.[29] Among the evangelicals Robert Bickersteth of Ripon called an informal conference in 1870 following his visitation and established an elected structure eight years later, while J.T. Pelham, bishop of Norwich, experimented with collective and elective conferences through the 1870s.[30] By 1881 only three dioceses lacked some form of diocesan assembly: London, where Bishop Jackson believed the diocese to be too unwieldy for such a gathering to succeed, Llandaff, where Bishop Ollivant was too elderly to innovate, and Worcester, where Bishop Philpott regarded conferences as unnecessary.[31] In July 1881 the Central Council of Diocesan Synods and

25 Burns, *Diocesan revival*, pp. 253–6; H. W. Tucker, *Memoir of the life and episcopate of George Augustus Selwyn* (London, 1879), pp. 250–9; G. H. Curteis, *Bishop Selwyn of New Zealand and of Lichfield* (London, 1889), pp. 208–29.

26 H. Kirk-Smith, *William Thomson, archbishop of York. His life and times, 1819–90* (London, 1958), p. 71.

27 C. A. E. Moberly, *Dulce domum. George Moberly, headmaster of Winchester College, 1835-1866; bishop of Salisbury, 1869–1885. His family and friends*, p. 230.

28 John Cotter Macdonnell, *The life and correspondence of William Connor Magee, archbishop of York, bishop of Peterborough* (London, 1896), p. 266.

29 John Henry Overton and Elizabeth Wordsworth, *Christopher Wordsworth, bishop of Lincoln 1807–1885* (London, 1888), pp. 232–7.

30 Montagu Cyril Bickersteth, *A sketch of the life and episcopate of Robert Bickersteth, bishop of Ripon, 1857–1884* (London, 1887), p. 263; J. C. Ryle, *A churchman's duty about diocesan conferences* (London, 1871), p. 6; *Record*, 4 May 1870, n.p.; *Eastern Daily Press* (Norwich), 4 Feb. 1893, p. 3.

31 Chadwick, *Victorian church*, II, 360.

Conferences held its first meeting, provoking a fresh round of controversy about lay representation in the councils of the church.[32]

If diocesan assemblies were increasingly a common feature of church life in the late 1860s and 1870s, considerable variations persisted in their composition and function. Some churchmen hankered after an exclusively clerical synod, while most accepted and valued a mixed assembly of clergy and laity. Some dioceses met in a number of regional centres, whereas most held a single gathering. Some conferences were annual occasions, but others met bi- or triennially. Most had a substantial *ex officio* component among the membership: cathedral clergy, archdeacons, rural deans and proctors, leavened by lay dignitaries and episcopal nominees, but the proportions varied from place to place. Most incorporated clerical and lay representatives elected by the rural deaneries, but some, like the Norwich conference, included the whole body of the diocesan clergy and representatives from each parish. The claims of 'collective' as against 'elective' assemblies remained contentious throughout this period, as did the authority of diocesan conferences to make policy for the diocese and to take decisions binding on the whole diocesan community. These were among the principal issues troubling evangelicals in their responses to this new venture in church organization.

It would be misleading to assume that evangelicals were uniformly hostile to the development of diocesan assemblies. The early advocates of assemblies in the 1830s included evangelicals like John Kempthorne, chaplain to Bishop Henry Ryder.[33] During the 1850s and 1860s the idea of a conference of clergy and laity received very cautious support from C. R. Sumner, bishop of Winchester, and enthusiastic backing from Archdeacon Edward Bickersteth, although other evangelicals, like James Garbett, archdeacon of Chichester, were unconvinced of the merits of the proposals.[34] The Ely experiment, and more especially Selwyn's Lichfield synod, focused evangelical minds and clarified the arguments which then found expression in pamphlets, speeches, resolutions and letters to the evangelical press.

32 *Record*, 12 Sept. 1881; Moberly, *Dulce domum*, pp. 270–1.

33 Burns, *Diocesan revival*, p. 221.

34 C. R. Sumner, *The signs of the times in their relation to the parochial clergy. A charge delivered to the clergy of the diocese of Winchester* (London, 1867), pp. 56–7; Edward Bickersteth, *Diocesan synods in relation to convocation and parliament: a paper, read at the church congress at York, on Thursday October 11, 1866* (London, 1867); Edward Bickersteth, *A charge delivered at his ninth visitation of the archdeaconry of Buckingham, in June 1867* (London, 1867), pp. 29–30; James Garbett, *Diocesan synods and convocation. A charge delivered to the clergy and churchwardens of the archdeaconry of Chichester, on August 3 and 5, 1852* (London, 1852).

Supporters of the assemblies in the 1860s shared the cross-party belief that a synodical revival would promote consultation within dioceses, enhance the pastoral authority of the bishop, strengthen attachment to the church and provide a forum for addressing liturgical irregularities without resort to the courts. Edward Bickersteth argued this case in an address to the York church congress in 1866 and in his visitation charge to the archdeaconry of Buckingham the following year. Others could see benefits in churchmen of different schools meeting for consultation on matters of common interest. Evangelicals in the diocese of Lichfield were divided on Selwyn's plan, but it would seem that, despite vocal opposition, a substantial majority took part in the bishop's scheme. Although suspicious of the word 'synod', with its clericalist implications, Lord Harrowby had no objection to a consultative conference, and following a visit to Sandon Mrs Selwyn wrote that the staunchly evangelical peer was 'a good old man; not of the highest school in the Church, but a great supporter of George and of conferences'.[35] W. F. Wilkinson, evangelical rector of St Werburgh's, Derby, took the same line.[36]

Many arguments were advanced to justify opposition to the assemblies. Some invoked the statutue of praemunire, insisting that synods were illegal unless explicitly authorized by the crown. Others emphasized the practical difficulties of gathering a truly representative diocesan meeting, or of ensuring that meetings did not degenerate into rowdy polemics. It was suggested that synods might hasten disestablishment by trespassing on the prerogatives of parliament.[37] Some of these arguments seem to have been debating points, or, at best, fears easily allayed once assemblies moved from theory to practice and were seen to take place successfully. The more substantial concerns, whether expressed in scepticism or downright opposition, focused on the composition of the assemblies and their claim to authority. In order to understand the genuine fears of a section of the evangelical school on this matter some attention must be given to the broader ecclesiastical context of the late 1860s and to the consequent anxiety felt by a significant number of evangelicals.

In many respects evangelicalism was a strong and influential current in mid-Victorian society. It was culturally pervasive, with an influence far beyond its professed adherents. It was institutionally powerful, able to sway public and parliamentary opinion behind campaigns for social reform. It was numerically significant within the churches, dissenting, methodist and anglican. It was also diverse and fissiparous, prone to fratricidal conflict and easily tempted into a siege

35 Curteis, *Selwyn*, p. 241.

36 *Record*, 24 Jun. 1868.

37 See, for example, the points made at a Church Association conference in 1868, reported in *Record*, 15 May 1868, and the case advanced in John Campbell Colquhoun, *Shall protestant churchmen take part in convocation and diocesan synods?* (London, 1869).

mentality in which the 'saints' became a righteous but beleaguered remnant defending gospel truth and purity against a hostile world.[38] The evangelical school in the Church of England found its collective identity partly in shared theology, partly in reading church history through the lenses of reformation and revival, and partly in an interlocking network of missionary, philanthropic, clerical and polemical societies, an extra-diocesan structure, underpinned by patronage, which did not always sit comfortably with the aims of the diocesan revival.[39] During Palmerston's premiership (1855–65) evangelical representation on the episcopal bench increased significantly, aided by the influence of Lord Shaftesbury, but this era ended with Palmerston's death in 1865.[40] Thereafter evangelicals consistently complained that they were passed over for preferment, judging that the complexion of the bench increasingly favoured high churchmen and tractarians.[41] At the same time fears about the protestant identity of the Church of England, first raised by the Oxford movement in the 1830s, were exacerbated by the steady development of ritualism. It seemed to anxious evangelicals that the bishops were unable or unwilling to take resolute action to check this trend, and the Church Association, formed in 1865, stepped into the breach by initiating or supporting high-profile legal proceedings against ritualists.[42] Evangelicals in this period, therefore, already pessimistic about the state of the church, were becoming suspicious of episcopal intentions and wary of measures which might increase the bishop's power or challenge the autonomy of patrons and incumbents.[43] Synods, moreover, had ominous associations in the eyes of many evangelicals. Setting aside medieval and 'popish' connotations, recent history was not encouraging. The Exeter synod of 1851 was summoned by the combative Bishop Henry Phillpotts in the context of the Gorham controversy, an episode which shook the confidence of anglican evangelicals over their place in the Church of England.[44] Bishop Gray of Cape Town had claimed synodical authority to condemn and depose Bishop

38 For the background to Victorian evangelicalism, see Bradley, *Call to seriousness*; Hilton, *Age of atonement*; Bebbington, *Evangelicalism in modern Britain*.

39 General histories of the evangelical school in the Church of England are provided by Balleine, *History of the evangelical party in the Church of England*, and Hylson-Smith, *Evangelicals in the Church of England 1734–1984*. Evangelical societies are treated by Kathleen Heasman in *Evangelicals in action* (London, 1962). Much useful background information on the period may also be found in Stock's *C.M.S.*

40 Hylson-Smith, *Evangelicals*, pp. 158–9; Nigel Scotland, *'Good and proper men.' Lord Palmerston and the bench of bishops* (Cambridge, 2000).

41 Chadwick, *Victorian church*, II, 336–7; *Rock* (London), 22 Mar. 1889, p. 9. Yates, *Anglican ritualism*, pp. 173–6, categorizes episcopal appointments but such descriptions are by no means exact.

42 *Ibid.*, pp. 216–19.

43 Burns, *Diocesan revival*, p. 254.

44 Carter, *Anglican evangelicals*, ch. 8.

Colenso in 1863. E. B. Pusey and other leading high churchmen had argued for similar action against *Essays and reviews* in 1860.[45] A significant body of evangelical opinion saw in the campaign for diocesan assemblies a high church initiative to strengthen bishops and dioceses at the expense of incumbents and voluntary societies. It was claimed that synods and their standing committees would produce a diocesan machine dominated by clerical cliques of episcopal nominees and partisan representatives. A trenchant leading article in the *Record* in August 1871, prompted by Moberly's Salisbury synod, spoke of 'the ever-lengthening chain which is fast binding on the neck of the Church of England the autocratic government of the Bishops under the name of Diocesan Synods.'[46] Evangelicals of this stamp urged that diocesan assemblies should be collective rather than elective, so that every incumbent could take direct part. There should be full lay participation, to include ordinary churchpeople and not just magnates and dignitaries selected by the bishop. Synodical pretensions should be firmly resisted: meetings should engage in consultation, but not take decisions, and certainly not claim legal or moral authority over the diocesan clergy and community. If these conditions were not fulfilled, it was argued, evangelicals should decline to attend and so deprive the assemblies of any pretence of representative legitimacy.

J. C. Ryle was a prominent spokesman in the debate on diocesan assemblies in the late 1860s and early 1870s. In May 1868 the spring conference of the Church Association debated the question, 'Is action through diocesan synods legal and advisable, and what steps ought to be taken by the friends of Protestant truth with respect to this question?' This meeting, held as Selwyn was preparing for the first Lichfield diocesan conference, declined to reach a resolution on the subject, but most of the speeches reported in the *Record* were hostile to the initiative. Ryle voiced practical objections, arguing that a collective assembly would be too large for effective discussion, particularly in a diocese like Norwich with over a thousand clergy, whereas an elected body would exclude evangelicals and divide the church into warring parties.[47] Writing to J. C. Macdonnell in June 1871 about the plans for his first diocesan conference in Peterborough, Bishop Magee reported that 'I had to encounter a most determined attempt of the ultra-Evangelicals, at the instigation of John Ryle, to break it up, almost before its coming into existence.'[48] There are no further details of this incident in Magee's

45 Peter Hinchliff, *John William Colenso* (London, 1964), ch. 5; Chadwick, *Victorian church*, II, 83–4.

46 *Record*, 18 Aug. 1871.

47 *Ibid.*, 15 May 1868.

48 Macdonnell, *Magee*, p. 266.

biography, and the assertion that Ryle was active in attempting to sabotage the Peterborough conference must be qualified in the light of his pamphlet *A churchman's duty about diocesan conferences*, published in summer 1871 but based on an address given to the Home Counties Clerical and Lay Association in May 1870. *A churchman's duty* began from the premiss that 'Diocesan Conferences are a great fact. Whether they will ever do as much good as their promoters expect, may be very doubtful: but they are a fact.'[49] From this pragmatic if unenthusiastic admission, Ryle argued that diocesan conferences might be useful institutions provided they were constituted on a collective rather than an elective basis and 'confine[d] ... to their proper work' of 'consultation, deliberation, expression of opinion, discussion, comparison of views, – and not action.'[50] Ryle's pattern for the structure of a diocesan conference was the plan adopted by Bishop Pelham in autumn 1870 of convening meetings of all incumbents, churchwardens and parochial representatives in five centres across his vast diocese of Norwich. His model for the business of the conference was that of the annual church congress, where the emphasis was on meeting and discussion and where resolutions were strictly prohibited. Given a collective constitution and avoidance of pretensions to authority and governance, Ryle was willing to urge evangelicals to take a full part in the conferences. Even with an elective constitution, evangelicals should participate, for

> to abstain from all public meetings in which we cannot have our own way, to retire from any assembly of Churchmen where we are likely to meet with any contradiction, to be incessantly finding fault with things around us, but never trying to amend them, all this may seem right to some minds. It admits of grave inquiry whether it is not selfishness, laziness, and cowardice, disguised under other names.[51]

Ryle described conferences as valuable opportunities of doing good, maintaining an evangelical witness and diminishing party feeling in the church by promoting personal acquaintance across the theological divide. His pamphlet and the Norwich model were commended by the *Record* and cited by opponents of Moberly's Salisbury synod as a viable and preferable alternative to the bishop's plans, and at the 1874 Brighton church congress Ryle spoke in a discussion on 'Diocesan Synods', advocating the Norwich pattern.[52]

Pelham's collective conferences, however, proved too unwieldy, and in 1879 the diocese of Norwich moved to an elective diocesan conference. This prompted another pamphlet from Ryle, *Our diocesan conference. What good is it likely to*

49 Ryle, *A churchman's duty*, p. 3.

50 *Ibid.*, p. 11.

51 *Ibid.*, p. 14.

52 *Record*, 8 Sept. 1871; *ibid.*, 12 Oct. 1874.

do? And what dangers must it try to avoid? (1879). Ryle admitted his earlier preference for a collective conference, conceding that 'I was mistaken. It was weighed in the balances and found wanting.'[53] He identified four advantages likely to accrue from the conference: an increase of unity among churchmen in East Anglia, as clergy and laity, members of different social classes and schools of thought gathered; an increase of strength through better organization; the collection of information about the diocese and its social problems; and an opportunity to elicit opinions on church questions currently before parliament or convocation. He noted two dangers: that the conference might concentrate on oratory and neglect business, and that it might try to dictate to the diocese on open questions.

A churchman's duty of 1871 said little about the benefits of a diocesan conference. It hardly advanced beyond a rather grudging recognition that conferences were 'a great fact' and concentrated on arguing the case for a collective rather than an elective constitution. Faced with the collapse of the Norwich collective conference, *Our diocesan conference* left constitutions on one side and focussed on the positive aspects of the conference. Both pamphlets highlighted dangers, agreeing on the risk of a conference making unwarranted claims to authority. There was disagreement though about what might be expected of a conference. In 1871 Ryle advocated discussion and feared activity: 'the moment a Diocesan Conference attempts to do anything it is almost sure to do mischief.' Eight years later his concern was empty words: 'Mere talk … will not keep us alive… [W]e must aim at doing business.'[54] When Ryle came to address the newly formed diocesan conference in Liverpool in November 1881, therefore, he brought to his task more than a decade of reflexion on the principles underpinning the assemblies, some experience of their practical operation and hazards, an awareness of evangelical apprehensions and a ready supply of well-rehearsed arguments and finely-honed phrases.

As an experienced tract writer and preacher Ryle was adept at reworking material for new occasions. *'First words'* of 1881, the inaugural address to his own diocesan conference, owed a clear and substantial literary debt to *Our diocesan conference* and a smaller though not insignificant debt to *A churchman's duty*. The 'great fact' of the existence of diocesan conferences across the Church of England which began *A churchman's duty* formed the starting-point for Ryle's address as bishop ten years later, while the metaphor of the 'new ship' of the Liverpool conference launched in 1881 had developed from the Norwich 'new

53 J. C. Ryle, *Our diocesan conference. What good is it likely to do? And what dangers must it try to avoid?* (London, 1879), p. 4.

54 Ryle, *A churchman's duty*, p.11; Ryle, *Our diocesan conference*, p. 17.

boat' of 1879. Thereafter *'First words'* comprised four main sections, the first three of which drew heavily on the earlier publications.

Ryle began *'First words'* with a discussion of the utility and desirableness of diocesan conferences. The introductory section, rebuking critics for ignoring the 'great fact' of the existence of conferences in nearly every diocese, used the 1871 material verbatim, editing only in order to extend the list of dioceses with conferences and to expand the free church comparison to include methodists and baptists as well as presbyterians and congregationalists.[55] Ryle then offered five advantages of a diocesan conference. The five points (a-e) of 1881 closely resembled the seven advantages advanced in 1879. Two were omitted: the ability of the conference 'to draw together Churchmen of different ranks of society' and its usefulness in 'the collection of valuable information' about the diocese.[56] The other points appeared in the same order, using the same phrases, images and examples. Very light editing removed specific references to Norwich and East Anglia, brought the parliamentary references up to date, and improved a couple of minor infelicities of style.[57]

The second section of *'First words'*, on the constitution and composition of the conference, reverted to the 1871 text, because the comparatively small size of the Liverpool diocese (200 incumbents and 140 curates in a compact region) enabled Ryle to resurrect his preference for a collective conference and rework and restate in slightly briefer terms the argument in its favour which he had abandoned in 1879 in the face of the practical problems posed by the cumbersome diocese of Norwich. Seven of the nine paragraphs repeated *A churchman's duty* verbatim, in effect editing only to substitute 'Liverpool' for 'Norwich'. The eighth paragraph softened the judgment that an elective system 'often' led to the rejection of the best clergy with the less provocative claim that it did not always result in the choice of 'men of light and leading'.[58] The final paragraph used the compactness of the Liverpool diocese to side-step the objection to the 'enormous size and unwieldiness' of a collective conference and used phrases from 1871 to stigmatize elective conferences as 'narrow, exclusive, aristocratic, and oligarchical'.[59]

55 The Wesleyan methodists admitted lay representatives to their conference in 1878. M. Wellings, 'Making haste slowly: the campaign for lay representation in the Wesleyan conference 1871–8', *Proceedings of the Wesley Historical Society*, LIII (2001), 25–37.

56 Ryle, *Our diocesan conference*, pp. 6, 9.

57 East Anglian references included the system of deanery elections; the 'Burials Bill' of 1879 became the 'Burials Act' in 1881; clumsy repetition of the 'delicate' nature of political debates was removed.

58 A quotation from Burke's *Reflections*: see notes on the text.

59 J. C. Ryle, *'First words.' An opening address delivered at the first Liverpool diocesan conference* (London, 1881), p. 15.

The third section of the address, on the action and operation of diocesan conferences, identified three dangers. The first two, oratory without action and dictating to the diocese, were taken almost verbatim from the 1879 text. The third, challenging party spirit and the tendency to stand aloof from uncongenial company, was copied from the conclusion to *A churchman's duty*. Only in the fourth section of '*First words*' did Ryle directly address the specific context of the Liverpool diocese and bring forward material not available in his earlier publications.

Turning from the literary history to the substance of the address, '*First words*' gave Ryle an obvious opportunity to clarify his position on diocesan assemblies at the outset of his episcopate. As has already been seen, this part of the address, comprising three of the four main sections of the text, drew heavily on previously published material and introduced little that was new, beyond topical references and minor stylistic amendments. It is worth pausing, however, to consider the main plank of Ryle's argument and to note that his principal points were pragmatic rather than ideological. The address opened with the somewhat grudging observation of 1871, that diocesan conferences were 'a great fact' and should be accepted as such. They might not justify the high hopes and expectations entertained of them, but to ignore them would be 'childish and unwise'. Furthermore, for Liverpool to neglect to institute a conference would place it 'behind the times'. More positively, Ryle set out five benefits of a diocesan conference. Three emphasized promoting unity in the diocese: breaking down clerical individualism, bringing together clergy and laity and fostering contact between people of different schools of thought. A fourth spoke of improving diocesan organization, and a fifth of consultation on issues of public interest. Strengthening the church, therefore, formed the main purpose of the conference.[60]

In making the case for diocesan assemblies Ryle deliberately dismissed arguments from precedent or tradition. This came out most clearly in his comparison of collective and elective constitutions, where he refused to 'waste time' debating the 'novelty' of elective conferences as against 'the ancient Diocesan Synod' and concentrated instead on objections which were 'purely practical'. Those eager to discuss precedent had to be satisfied with a glancing reference to Hook's *Church dictionary*.[61] This vigorous pragmatism set Ryle apart from many of the proponents of diocesan reform in the mid-nineteenth century. Arthur Burns has shown that, far from being driven solely by an alleged Blomfieldian utilitarianism, the cause of reform relied extensively on historical legitimation, and that while this was an approach particularly associated with

60 *Ibid.*, pp. 5–13.

61 *Ibid.*, p. 14.

orthodox high churchmen, it was supported by liberal and evangelical churchmen too.[62] Some evangelical advocates of reform in the 1860s, like Edward Bickersteth, endorsed and used the appeal to precedent;[63] Ryle consistently did not, and it may be asked why. It might be suggested that precedent tended to favour clerical synods, with their undertones of exclusivity and authority, rather than discursive assemblies composed of clergy and laity, although the 'ancient Diocesan Synod' in the *Church dictionary* included lay parochial representatives. Ryle's general approach to church history, moreover, placed spiritual edification above antiquarian research, emphasized the reformation and the eighteenth-century revival, and had little time for the patristic and medieval periods. 'When a man makes an idol of Fathers and Councils, and disparages the theology of the Reformation, we may be sure there is a screw loose in his theology,' was Ryle's damning dismissal of William Laud's patristic scholarship.[64] More significant, perhaps, Ryle's preferred medium was the tract, not the learned treatise, and the audience he sought to woo was 'the middle classes' – 'farmers, tradesmen and intelligent artisans'[65] – not an academic or clerical élite. He addressed practical and pithy advice to the lay general reader, and did not seek to engage or to persuade the erudite. For Ryle's constituency, the group he saw as the backbone of the Church of England, antiquarianism was an unnecessary and uncongenial waste of time.

If *'First words'* allowed Ryle to set out his position on diocesan conferences, it also gave him scope to comment on contemporary political and ecclesiastical issues. Although he was renowned for trenchant views on most subjects, political questions without a direct ecclesiastical dimension were left severely alone. Ryle was well aware, however, of 'public measures ... affecting the status of the whole Church of England' coming before parliament and convocation; indeed, one of his stated advantages of a diocesan conference was the opportunity to canvass opinion on such matters, and Ryle urged the creation of a 'parliamentary committee of vigilance' to facilitate more effective consultation.[66] Ryle trod carefully around this 'very delicate subject',[67] recognizing the danger of diocesan conferences wasting time on 'wordy debates about "burning" questions',[68] and

62 R. Arthur Burns, '"Standing in the old ways": historical legitimation of church reform in the Church of England, c. 1825–65', in *The Church retrospective*, ed. R. N. Swanson (*Studies in Church History*, xxxiii, 1997), pp. 407–22. I am grateful to Dr Mark Smith for this reference.

63 Bickersteth, *Diocesan synods*, pp. 1–9.

64 J. C. Ryle, *Facts and men: being pages from English church history between 1553 and 1683 with a preface for the times* (London, 1882), p. 222.

65 Ryle, *'First words'*, p. 15.

66 *Ibid.*, pp. 10, 27.

67 *Ibid.*, p. 10.

68 *Ibid.*, p. 17.

'First words' gave examples of recent or proposed legislation without expressing an opinion on the specific issues at stake. The exception to this cautiously apolitical approach was the question of disestablishment: hardly contentious in addressing a diocesan audience. Here Ryle sounded a clear call to arms, redeploying his favourite military metaphors from 1879: 'there is a battle to be fought about this question one day; and if we mean to win that battle we must be organized, trained, disciplined, drilled, and prepared to act together, each in our own place.' The rather vague timing of the 'day of battle' may reflect the waning of parliamentary and popular support for the Liberation Society's campaign for disestablishment as the 1870s drew to a close. Arguably, then, Ryle was reheating rhetoric more applicable to the 1860s than the 1880s, but the spectre of disestablishment remained real and could, moreover, serve a useful purpose to underline the need for unity within the Church of England.[69]

When he turned his attention to internal church politics, Ryle spoke more freely and more firmly than he did in addressing 'delicate' parliamentary matters. Here his context and background need to be kept clearly in mind. Ryle brought to Liverpool a reputation as a pugnacious evangelical, closely identified with the Church Association. In the church congresses of the 1870s he had also made his mark as an advocate of drastic reforms to convocation, to the episcopate and to diocesan and cathedral administration, all driven by the need to make the Church of England more effective in mission and to safeguard its position as a truly national church. His appointment as bishop installed him in a new, populous and impoverished diocese, where mission was an obvious priority and where significant sections of the population were alienated from the Church of England or from christianity in general, and in a city lacking a cathedral but possessing an unenviable reputation for sectarian conflict.[70] *'First words'* indicated how Ryle intended to balance the roles of evangelical and evangelist and offered reassurance to those who feared the appointment of a partisan bishop.

First, Ryle deliberately distanced himself from evangelical insularity and from divisive party loyalties. He had been derided as a 'neo-evangelical' in the 1860s for attending church congresses; here he hit out at the 'fanatics' who despised diocesan machinery as unspiritual, the 'narrow-minded' who refused to mix with any but their own friends and the latter-day Goliaths 'ready to quarrel with everything which is not hammered on their own anvil'.[71] Ryle was careful to speak

69 *Ibid.*, p. 10; D. W. Bebbington, *The nonconformist conscience. Chapel and politics 1870–1914* (London, 1982), ch. 2. Compare Farley's analysis of the decisive impact of Irish disestablishment on Ryle: *Ryle*, pp. 43–4 and n. 14 above.

70 For which see P. J. Waller, *Democracy and sectarianism. A political and social history of Liverpool, 1868–1939* (Liverpool, 1981).

71 Ryle, *'First words'*, pp. 5, 19, 20.

positively of 'schools of thought', acknowledging that '[h]uman nature is so strangely compounded that I believe there will be High and Low and Broad schools in the Church of England as long as the world stands.' '[P]arty-spirit', however, he deplored, citing it as a major practical objection to elective diocesan conferences.[72] Significantly, Ryle took pains to avoid designating evangelicals as a 'party' in the Church, and he reassured churchmen of other 'schools' that he fully acknowledged their place within the pale of the establishment.

Second, Ryle's reform agenda also emerged in the address, although in guarded language. He referred briefly to the unrepresentative character of the unreformed convocations, to the drawbacks of 'huge undivided dioceses' and to the tendency of diocesan conferences to waste time on 'ecclesiastical fireworks' and 'vague, wordy speeches'. These were well-worn themes in his speaking and writing through the 1870s, particularly in his *Church reform papers* of 1870 and in a controversial speech to the 1872 church congress advocating the amalgamation of the Canterbury and York convocations, greater representation of the parochial clergy, full lay participation and an end to discussion in 'houses'. Ryle had also urged a great expansion in the episcopate, with dioceses organized on a county basis. *'First words'* alluded tactfully to these issues, suggesting that the diocesan conference – properly constituted and efficiently run – would ensure that prelates in parliament and proctors in convocation 'will never vote in ignorance of the mind of the Dioceses'.[73]

Reading between the lines, a clear picture of the Church of England as Ryle envisaged it emerged from the address. His defence of establishment has already been noted, as has his frank recognition of the existence of 'schools of thought' in 'our Church's theological rainbow'. Ryle's vision of the church was firmly episcopal: he contrasted the purely advisory proceedings of the diocesan conference with the recommendations of the bishop, which 'justly demand some respect and attention'. Episcopacy, however, should not be monarchical: Ryle argued that one of the benefits of a conference was that it would 'diminish the autocratic authority of the Bishops', reduce their isolation, and encourage consultation. Significantly, this consultation should include laity as well as clergy, and should not be confined to a select group of grandees. Ryle held that the diocese must 'command the affection of the middle classes' by involving them in the conference and by ensuring that their time was efficiently used in the proper conduct of business. Moreover, by bringing clergy and laity together, the conference would remind the laity that 'they are the Church as well as ourselves'. Ryle assumed that it was the laity who would forget their part in the church, not the clergy who would treat the laity as superfluous. *'First words'* sketched an

72 *Ibid.*, pp. 7, 15.

73 Farley, *Ryle*, pp. 54–8; Ryle, *'First words'*, p. 12.

outline of a church drawing together all social classes, theological schools and ecclesiastical functions in a common enterprise of 'aggression on evil' and 'defence of that which is good'.[74]

This reading is reinforced by an examination of the three metaphors for the church and its mission which predominated in Ryle's address. The most frequently used imagery was military, from the bishop as 'a commissioned officer of the Church' and the diocesan institutions as 'headquarters' to the body of the diocese as 'an effective soldiery' and 'our dear old Reformed Church of England' as 'terrible as an army with banners'.[75] This language reflected Ryle's sense of the church as an institution under attack, and also expressed his concern for effective, co-operative and positive action. A second metaphor, far less developed, was that of the diocese as a machine, once again suggesting efficiency and collaboration.[76] The third metaphor, again used more sparingly, was nautical, a familiar ecclesiastical trope with particular resonance in Liverpool. The conference was 'a new ship' which might 'split on th[e] rock' of pointless speechifying.[77] Given the shared themes of common purpose, varied roles and individuals playing their part within a larger whole – reflecting Ryle's sense of the diocese as an organic unit – it is interesting to note the choice of non-biblical rather than biblical imagery: the Pauline figure of the body might have been employed to good purpose to make the same points.

Like his prose style, Ryle's metaphors were all vigorous and purposeful, reflecting his concern for action. In the final section of *'First words'* he turned his attention to the work of the church in the diocese of Liverpool, sketching plans for future development.

When appointed in 1880 Ryle found a populous and compact diocese with immense social needs. The bulk of the population of the diocese lived in the city of Liverpool itself, in a mixture of affluent suburbs, densely populated townships and a steadily depopulating city centre. Evangelization was seen as the new bishop's first priority, a cause which Ryle was keen to champion.[78] *'First words'* addressed this need in two ways.

First, Ryle emphasized the importance of the diocesan institutions. In addition to inheriting existing institutions at Warrington providing pensions for clergy widows and schooling for the daughters of the clergy, four new structures for the new diocese were launched at a meeting in Liverpool town hall in April 1881: the

74 *Ibid.*, pp. 7, 8, 15, 17, 18.

75 *Ibid.*, pp. 8, 10, 18, 20. Compare Ryle's soubriquet 'An Old Soldier' in letters to the press.

76 *Ibid.*, pp. 8, 12, 13.

77 *Ibid.*, pp. 3, 17. Ryle made extensive use of the nautical metaphor in urging evangelicals distressed by the Lincoln judgment of 1892 not to 'launch the longboat and forsake the ship': *Record*, 12 Aug. 1892, p. 822. Compare Ryle, *Knots untied* (Cambridge, 1977), p. 19.

78 Farley, *Ryle*, pp. 93–4.

Church Building Society, the Benefices' Augmentation Fund, the Church Aid Society and the Board of Education and Schools Society. The *Record* hailed this initiative as an effective riposte to the high church sneer that evangelicals were not capable of organizing a diocese.[79] By November, however, the bishop was complaining to the diocesan conference that the position of the institutions was 'eminently unsatisfactory' and that 'want of funds' was crippling schemes for church extension. Ryle professed incredulity that Liverpool churchmen lacked the means to finance the diocese properly. A correspondence in the *Record* later in the year, however, may offer a partial explanation. An anonymous 'Liverpool Clergyman' expressed distrust of diocesan bodies, because the only qualification for influence was payment of a subscription. Diocesan committees therefore included high and broad churchmen and even ritualists. The correspondent argued that spiritual work should be pursued through explicitly evangelical societies. Ryle's archdeacon, the impeccably evangelical John Bardsley, offered reassurance, as did the *Record* in a leading article, but some evangelicals were clearly still wary of diocesan structures. It did not help Ryle's case that the Rochester Diocesan Society had just given a widely publicized grant of £200 towards the building of a new mission church in the ritualist parish of St Stephen's, Lewisham, in the teeth of evangelical opposition.[80] Tension between a diocesan approach to church organization and the evangelical preference for self-governing societies was not unique to Liverpool, but it presented particular challenges to an evangelical bishop with a long record of support for such societies now seeking to shape the structure of a new diocese and to work with greater theological pluralism.

Second, Ryle called for parochial reorganization in the city centre. His starting point was the census of church attendance conducted by the *Liverpool Daily Post* on two Sundays in October and November 1881. The morning census in October showed an anglican attendance of 22,610 out of a population of 552,425.[81] From this statistic Ryle drew the conclusion that Liverpool needed 'an organized system of aggressive evangelization'.[82] He also called for the demolition of redundant churches near the docks, the amalgamation of parishes and the release of funds for new buildings elsewhere in the city. This programme was not the whole of Ryle's strategy for evangelization. As Ian Farley shows, Ryle advocated both an increase in clergy numbers and the mobilization of the laity as evangelists.[83] The struggle

79 *Record*, 27 Apr. 1881.

80 *Ibid.*, 21 Dec. 1881, 23 Dec. 1881, 28 Dec. 1881. The bishop of Rochester was A. W. Thorold, also an evangelical.

81 *Liverpool Daily Post* (Liverpool), 17 Oct. 1881, p. 5.

82 Ryle, *'First words'*, p. 26.

83 Farley, *Ryle*, pp. 97–101.

to develop and implement this strategy occupied much of his episcopate, but it was foreshadowed in the 1881 address.

At the end of *'First words'* Ryle turned his attention to wider issues. He suggested the creation of 'a small Parliamentary committee of vigilance' to advise the diocese on matters before parliament which might affect the Church of England, instancing three recent attempts at legislation: Edward Stanhope's bill to restrict the sale of advowsons, Albert Grey's bill to set up parochial boards with some jurisdiction over services and Earl Beauchamp's bill to prevent the indefinite imprisonment of clergymen who refused to recognize the authority of the ecclesiastical courts. Stanhope's bill addressed a long-standing abuse which made a tempting target for critics of the Church; Grey's and Beauchamp's took different approaches to the vexed question of ritualism in the Church of England. Grey, a Liberal M.P., argued that an elected board empowered to prevent an incumbent altering the style of worship in a parish 'at his sole will' would avoid escalating conflict and eventual resort to law.[84] Beauchamp's bill was prompted by the Miles Platting case in which the Rev. S. F. Green's refusal to recognize the jurisdiction of the chancery court of York under the Public Worship Regulation Act led to his imprisonment in Lancaster gaol for contumacy. The bill proposed a maximum term of six months' imprisonment for such cases.[85] Ryle made no comment on the bills themselves, nor on the other political matter given as an example of the need for vigilance, the draft education code introduced by A. J. Mundella, vice-president of the committee of council for education.

Finally, Ryle addressed the question of the central council of diocesan conferences. The council held its first meeting in London in July 1881 and proposed that each diocesan conference should send six representatives to the central body. The council might then co-ordinate discussion within the church and represent wider opinion to parliament and convocation. The *Record* dismissed the scheme contemptuously as 'a clique of less than half-a-dozen wire-pullers in London'.[86] Ryle was less forthright, but advised caution, given the low attendance at the July meeting and the confusion over the aims of the central council. It may be noted that some of the anxieties expressed with regard to the central council in 1881 – clerical domination, centralization and a challenge to the authority of parliament – were very similar to those regularly expressed about diocesan conferences in the 1860s. By the middle of the 1880s the central council was

84 *Hansard Parl. Debates* 3rd series, 44 Vict. 1881, vol. cclx, col. 1298 (27 Apr. 1881).

85 *Record*, 10 Aug. 1881. For the Miles Platting case, see Yates, *Anglican ritualism*, pp. 263–5 and James Bentley, *Ritualism and politics in Victorian Britain. The attempt to legislate for belief* (Oxford, 1978), pp. 105–11.

86 *Record*, 12 Sept. 1881.

established, and over the next decade houses of laity were created for the provinces of Canterbury (1886) and York (1892).[87]

'First words' effectively illustrated Ryle's 'terse, vivid, epigrammatic style' as a writer and speaker,[88] demonstrating too his willingness to use old material wholesale in new contexts. Although delivered to a Liverpool audience, much of the address concerned itself with broader church questions, making points that Ryle had made before in other places. Evangelization in the Liverpool context, however, was clearly a major concern, and in this respect *'First words'* identified a theme which would remain prominent throughout Ryle's controversial episcopate.

87 Chadwick, *Victorian church*, II, 364.

88 *The Times* (London), 11 Jun. 1900, p. 9.

J. C. Ryle:
Address to the Liverpool diocesan conference 1881

My Rev. and Lay Brethren,

I believe it is an established custom that the proceedings of a Diocesan Conference should commence with an introductory address from the Bishop. I willingly comply with the custom, as it seems natural and reasonable, and I invite your attention while I try to open our first Liverpool Conference with a few prefatory remarks and 'first words.'[1]

I. About the *utility and desirableness* of Diocesan Conferences I shall not waste your time by saying very much. But, considering that a new ship is launched today, and that the assembly I see before me is probably the beginning of a long series of similar meetings, I think it my duty to make a few general remarks about first principles.

Diocesan Conferences are a great fact. Whether they will ever do as much good as their promoters expect, may be very doubtful; but they are a fact. Whether we like them or not, they exist. Whether we choose to take any part in them or not, they live and move and have a being. They have been held already in every Diocese in England and Wales, except London and Worcester.[2] To ignore them as mere fancies and speculations, is impossible; to turn our backs on them, and refuse to touch them, is childish and unwise. If the Diocese of Liverpool did not have a Conference it would be behind the times.

Where is the man who could undertake to prove that there is anything unreasonable in a Diocesan Conference? Common sense itself seems to dictate that a periodical meeting of the Bishop, clergy, and laity of a Diocese, in order to consider matters of common interest to the Church, is right and wise. Methodists and Baptists, Presbyterians and Congregationalists, have long had such Conferences, and found them useful.[3] Why, then, are we to suppose that they are not

1 Perhaps an allusion to Galatians iv.13: 'how … I preached unto you at the first.'

2 Three dioceses had not held diocesan conferences by 1881, since Llandaff should be added to Ryle's list: Owen Chadwick, *The Victorian church* (2 vols., London, 1966–70), II, 360.

3 The polities of the denominations listed differed considerably: conferences among baptists and congregationalists could not override the sovereignty of the gathered congregation, whereas presbyterian synods and methodist conferences were authoritative bodies. See Albert Peel, *These hundred years, 1831–1931* (London, 1931) for the history of the Congregational Union of England and Wales, established in 1831, and Ernest A. Payne, *The Baptist Union* (London, 1958) for the development of the General Union of Baptists from the early nineteenth century. Synods had been part of the presbyterian polity since the sixteenth century. Although the first methodist conference met in 1744 and conferences were integral to the structure of the various

likely to be useful when taken up by Episcopalians? The mere fact that they tend to diminish the autocratic authority of the Bishops, to lessen the isolation of their present position, and to encourage the practice of Bishops taking counsel with their clergy and laity, is no small recommendation of the institution.

To denounce Diocesan Conferences as wicked and wrong, as the manner of some is, to say the least, is unjust and unfair. Where is the sin of them? Of course they are not Evangelistic institutions. They are not preaching missions or revivals, nor anything else of a directly edifying character. But surely we are not to be told that Christians ought to neglect ecclesiastical machinery and organization altogether! No one can read the Acts and Epistles of the New Testament without seeing a good deal said about the outward framework and good ordering of a Church. Meat and drink are not the only things necessary to make up a banquet. Wise men do not despise plates, and knives, and forks, and tables, and chairs. These things have their uses, though we do not eat them. To affect to despise ecclesiastical machinery because it is only *machinery* is wild work, and unworthy of any but a fanatic.[4]

The advantages and benefits of a Diocesan Conference, in my judgment, are neither few nor small. Let me state briefly what they are.

(a) For one thing, Conferences tend to promote *an increased measure of unity among Churchmen.* How little there is of that unspeakable blessing, we all know only too well. At present, Churchmen are terribly separated and isolated by their different opinions. Our parishes are often like islands in some parts of the Pacific Ocean, almost within sight of one another, but inhabited by distinct tribes, variously coloured and dressed, ruled by ever-quarrelling chiefs, and with a deep sea rolling between. Hundreds of incumbents are continually working away, each for himself, in his own fashion, without much intercourse with his neighbours;

methodist denominations, lay representatives were only admitted to the Wesleyan methodist conference in 1878, for which see Martin Wellings, 'Making haste slowly: the campaign for lay representation in the Wesleyan conference, 1871–8', *Proceedings of the Wesley Historical Society*, LIII (2001), 25-37.

4 This section of Ryle's address was taken from his 1871 pamphlet *A churchman's duty about diocesan conferences*, and therefore was probably not directed against groups in the diocese of Liverpool in particular. Suspicion of 'ecclesiastical machinery' smacks of Brethren critiques of the established churches; for the appeal of such views to an earlier generation of evangelicals, see Grayson Carter, *Anglican evangelicals. Protestant secessions from the via media, c. 1800–1850* (Oxford, 2001), ch. 6, esp. pp. 198–9, with background material in chs 1 and 2. Non-seceding evangelicals might adopt a policy characterized by John Kent as 'internal separation from the institutional church', criticizing involvement in convocation as 'worldly': John Kent, 'Anglican evangelicalism in the west of England, 1858–1900', in *Protestant evangelicalism. Britain, Ireland, Germany and America, c. 1750–c. 1950*, ed. Keith Robbins (Oxford, 1990), pp. 193-4. This attitude, exemplified by Charles Kemble, rector of Bath, who urged an exclusive commitment to 'evangelistic and spiritual' work, contrasted with Ryle's insistence that evangelicals should play a full part in convocation, church congresses and diocesan structures.

each thinking himself right and his neighbour wrong. Episcopalians in theory, we are Independents in practice. Of taking counsel together, and of consequent common, powerful, united action, there is a painful absence in every Diocese. Like one of Walter Scott's characters, every man 'fights for his own hand.'[5] The result of this state of things is not merely a degree of weakness in the Church, wholly disproportioned to our numbers, but something far more serious. The Holy Spirit is grieved, and the blessing of God is withheld. The first step towards amendment in this matter is to bring us together upon neutral ground, and about subjects of common interest. This, I think, our Conference will do.

(b) Furthermore, Conferences tend *to draw together clergy and laity*. This is a consummation greatly to be desired.[6] It will do the clergy good to be brought face to face with their lay brethren, and to know their mind about the position and immediate wants of the Church of England. They are often thinking and talking now about the parsons and their proceedings, far more than we are aware. It will do the laity good to be brought face to face with the clergy, and to realize that they are the Church as well as ourselves; and that we do not want to be 'lords of God's heritage,'[7] but rather desire in all things to act in entire unison with them.

(c) Furthermore, Conferences tend *to draw together Churchmen of various opinions and schools of thought*. At present the clergy keep aloof from one another, read their own newspapers, and support their own favourite Societies, and seldom or never see each other, except at ruri-decanal synods[8] and visitations; and then, I often think, they look at one another with as much curiosity as if they were looking at the last new arrival in the Zoological Gardens. The natural consequence is an immense amount of floating misconstruction and misunderstanding. Far be it from me to say that any Diocesan Conference will put an extinguisher on our divisions, melt down all our differences, and make us like the

5 Although this is not the only literary allusion in the text (see nn. 6 and 26 below), Sir Walter Scott (1771–1832) is the only secular author mentioned by name. Scott's work did much to ameliorate evangelical disapproval of imaginative literature in the first part of the nineteenth century. See Doreen Rosman, *Evangelicals and culture* (London, 1984), pp. 179–80, 185–8, 195. The reference quoted here has not been traced.

6 Compare *Hamlet*, Act 3, scene 1, lines 63–4: ''Tis a consummation devoutly to be wish'd'.

7 I Peter v. 3.

8 The office of rural dean, generally disused in the Church of England since the sixteenth century, was gradually revived from the 1790s. From 1839 ruridecanal chapters brought together the clergy of the rural deanery; and by 1870 chapters had been established in almost every diocese. R. Arthur Burns, '"Standing in the old ways": historical legitimation of church reform in the Church of England, c. 1825–65', in *The Church retrospective*, ed. R. N. Swanson (*Studies in Church History*, xxxiii, 1997), pp. 407–22; Arthur Burns, *The diocesan revival in the Church of England, c. 1800–1870* (Oxford, 1999), ch. 4.

fabled Corinthian brass,[9] a body of one homogeneous consistency. I expect nothing of the kind. The prismatic colours of the Church's theological rainbow will never fade away and vanish in the cloudy atmosphere of this world. Nothing is colourless but perfect light, and the day of perfect light will never arrive until the Lord comes. Human nature is so strangely compounded that I believe there will be High and Low and Broad schools in the Church of England as long as the world stands.[10] But yet there is room for much more approximation; and surely we might lessen the distance that now divides us, and get within hail of one another. I have great faith in the effect of seeing and talking with men under the same roof, and around the same table. It often teaches us that members of other 'schools of thought' have good points about them, and are as loyal Churchmen as ourselves. We discover that they are not quite so bad as we imagined, and had heard them described. If Conferences do nothing else, they promote mutual understanding and mutual respect; and respect is, at any rate, a step towards unity.

(d) Furthermore, Conferences, if well managed, tend *to strengthen the Church of England.* An English Diocese rightly organized possesses in itself the elements of great strength. If all the parts of the machine worked together, it ought to be able to do great things for Christ and the Church. It ought to be strong for aggression on evil, and no less strong for defence of that which is good. Without saying anything offensive, I think I may safely affirm that at present our Dioceses are far less strong than they ought to be. We are weak, though endowed and established.

The plain truth is, that numbers and size alone do not constitute strength. In the late Franco-German war[11] the French found, to their cost, that crowds of 'men with muskets' do not make an army. Discipline, training, and organization are the

9 Corinthian brass, or bronze, was an alloy of gold, silver and copper much prized in the ancient world: see M. C. Howatson, *The Oxford companion to classical literature* (Oxford, 1989), p. 156. According to legend, the alloy was created in the incendiary destruction of Corinth by L. Mummius in 146 B.C.E., described in Pausanius, *Description of Greece*, book vii, section 16; a more prosaic explanation suggests that the Roman sack of the city released a large quantity of hitherto unavailable vessels onto the market.

10 For a mid-nineteenth-century discussion of church parties, their names and definitions, see W. J. Conybeare, 'Church parties', edited with an introduction by Arthur Burns, in *From Cranmer to Davidson: a miscellany*, ed. Stephen Taylor (Church of England Record Society, VII, 1999), pp. 215–385. Ryle's careful distinction between 'school' and 'party' is noted in the introduction to the present text, and may be traced throughout *'First words'*.

11 The Franco-Prussian war of 1870–1 opened with rapid victories for the German forces. After the capitulation of the French at Sedan in September 1870 an attempt was made to raise new armies, mostly composed of ill-equipped and untrained conscripts. According to Michael Howard, *The Franco-Prussian war. The German invasion of France, 1870–1871* (London, 1961), the 'huge and miserable armies' raised by the French had little success against the 'small, disciplined and articulated forces of the Prussians' (citing the American edition of 1969 at pp. 245 and 249; chs 6, 8 and 10 describe the field conflict in detail).

first principles of military success. Men must learn how to act together, to stand together, to move together, to support one another, to fill their own places, and to obey the word of command. These are the secrets of an effective soldiery. These are the reasons why a thousand well-drilled and well-officered men are far more powerful, either for attack or defence, than ten thousand untrained and undisciplined peasants, though each peasant individually may be as strong as Hercules.[12]

Now a Conference tends to organize the Church of England in a Diocese. At any rate, I am slow to believe that clergymen and picked laymen, from any Diocese, can meet, confer, and take counsel together annually without adding great power and vigour to the Church, unless they waste their time most strangely. If, by conferring and conversing together, we can only find out the weak points in our present position, and consider the best remedies, we shall have gained something. – If, by taking counsel, when the Church is attacked, we can secure the adoption of prompt, energetic, and combined measures of defence, we shall have gained something more. – If the clerical and lay representatives composing a Conference can only return every year to their respective parishes, primed and loaded with information about the immediate dangers and duties of the church, and make them the subject of discussion and interest in every part of the Diocese, we shall once more have gained something. Common *feeling*, no doubt, is the first step towards common action; and a common Church feeling, I dare say, we possess. But common feeling, however strong, will never produce useful action without organization. The Spanish Guerrillas, in the Peninsular War, were excellent patriots, very numerous, and actuated by one deep common *feeling*; but if there had not been in the field a small regular British army, the French would never have lost the battle of Vittoria, and been driven across the Pyrenees.[13]

Perhaps I am not so much afraid of Disestablishment as some people are. It will never come if the Church of England is true to her first principles, and does her duty. But we may depend upon it there is a battle to be fought about this question one day; and if we mean to win that battle we must be organized, trained, disciplined, drilled, and prepared to act together, each in our own place. I am greatly mistaken if our Diocesan Conferences do not add immensely to our strength when the day of battle really comes. If the clerical and lay representatives of each Rural Deanery[14] do their duty in their respective districts, they will form

12 In Greek mythology, a hero of superhuman physical strength.

13 Guerrillas: Spanish partisans fighting French occupation after the imposition of Joseph Bonaparte as king of Spain; the decisive battle of Vitoria (or Vittoria) took place in 1813, during the Peninsular War (1808–14).

14 See n. 8 above.

a network of most useful defensive machinery throughout every Diocese, which a word from head quarters can at any moment set in motion if required.

(e) Last, but not least, under the head of advantages, Conferences are likely to do great service *by eliciting the opinions of the Diocese about any public measures* which may be brought forward, either in Parliament or Convocation, affecting the status of the whole Church of England.

This is a very delicate subject; but I know not how to avoid it. No doubt there have been many years, in by-gone times, in which Convocation slept in dignity, and Parliament never touched a Church question. These years, however, are passing away. Convocation has been revived,[15] and has come forth refreshed and vigorous, after its hundred years' slumber, hungry for business, and exhibiting considerable activity, in spite of its fetters and anomalous constitution. In Parliament there is hardly a Session in which measures are not thrust on our notice, affecting very seriously, either for good or evil, the rights and privileges of the Church of England, and the duties, interests, and position of her clergy and her congregations. I need hardly remind you of such Acts as the Public Worship Act,[16] the Shortened Service Act,[17] the Lectionary Act,[18] the Act for the Establishment

15 The two ecclesiastical provinces of the Church of England (Canterbury and York) each had a convocation, composed of two houses. The upper house consisted of the bishops; the lower house of *ex officio* members (deans and archdeacons) and proctors elected by the cathedral chapters and diocesan clergy. Following the 'rage of party' in the early eighteenth century, when tory high churchmen in the lower house used convocation to attack whig bishops and politicians, convocation was prorogued indefinitely in 1717. Pressure for the revival of convocation built up in the 1840s, and the convocations met from 1851 (Canterbury) and 1860 (York). Chadwick, *Victorian church*, II, 361.

16 The Public Worship Regulation Act (1874) (37 and 38 Vict., c. 85): a measure seeking to control ritualism in the Church of England by establishing a new legal framework for prosecuting ritual offences. G. I. T. Machin, *Politics and the churches in Great Britain, 1869 to 1921* (Oxford, 1987), pp. 70–86. High church opposition to the act labelled the measure erastian, because the judge of the new provincial courts was a layman and appeal against his decisions was to the judicial committee of the privy council; the ability of the diocesan bishop to veto prosecutions made the measure ineffective as a remedy for aggrieved protestants. Within a short time the act had turned ritualists into martyrs by gaoling, for contumacy, those who refused to recognize the court. The general background and evolution of ritualism are discussed in Nigel Yates, *Anglican ritualism in Victorian Britain, 1830–1910* (Oxford, 1999) and John Shelton Reed, *Glorious battle. The cultural politics of Victorian anglo-catholicism* (Nashville, 1996), while the implementation of the act is covered in James Bentley, *Ritualism and politics in Victorian Britain. The attempt to legislate for belief* (Oxford, 1978). For the ritual controversy in the later nineteenth century, see Martin Wellings, *Evangelicals embattled* (Carlisle, 2003).

17 The Act of Uniformity Amendment Act (1872) (35 and 36 Vict., c. 35): an uncontroversial act authorizing a shortened form of service in parish churches on weekdays as an alternative to the full liturgy prescribed by the *Book of common prayer*. Chadwick, *Victorian church*, II, 310; R. T. Davidson and W. Benham, *Archibald Campbell Tait, archbishop of Canterbury* (2 vols., London, 1891), II, 109–10.

18 The Prayer Book (Table of Lessons) Act (1871) (34 and 35 Vict., c. 37): another uncontroversial measure, revising the lectionary. Davidson and Benham, *Tait*, II, 102.

of New Bishoprics,[19] and the Burials Act,[20] to say nothing of the Royal Commission on Rubrics,[21] and the Royal Commission, recently appointed, on Ecclesiastical Courts.[22] Of course I am not going to say one word on the merits or demerits of any of these measures, whether passed or not passed, or still only 'on the wheels'. But I am going to remind you, that between an unreformed Convocation on one side, and a reformed House of Commons on the other side, the voice of the clergy and the congregations of the Dioceses of England is hardly heard at all, and can only find an utterance in the form of annual contributions to that huge magazine of waste paper, Parliamentary petitions.

Now I take leave to think that, in the absence of a reformed Convocation, which is probably a very distant thing, well-organized Diocesan Conferences may become an admirable machinery for supplying an expression of opinion, both to Parliament and Convocation, about any Church questions which may arise. The voice of the clergymen and laymen, for example, who compose our Liverpool Conference, may be fairly taken to be the voice of this Diocese; and, at any rate, we shall be able to let Parliament and Convocation know what we think, whether we are attended to or not. The Bishops in the House of Lords, and our County and Borough Members in the House of Commons, – the Bishops, Deans, Archdeacons and Proctors in the Canterbury and York Convocations,[23] in whatever way they may please to vote on Church questions, will never vote in ignorance of the mind of the Dioceses from which they come, so long as Diocesan

19 Three acts were passed to create new bishoprics between 1875 and 1878: St Albans (38 and 39 Vict., c. 34), Truro (39 and 40 Vict., c. 54) and Liverpool, Wakefield, Southwell and Newcastle-on-Tyne (41 and 42 Vict., c. 68). These followed a long campaign for diocesan extension stretching back to the 1830s and reflecting concern that the diocesan map bore little resemblance to the distribution of population. Burns, *Diocesan revival*, ch. 8. Ryle was a strong advocate of diocesan extension.

20 The Burial Laws Amendment Act (1880) (43 and 44 Vict., c. 41), permitting nonconformist funerals in parish churchyards. Machin, *Politics and the churches*, pp. 130–3. This was the last of the historic nonconformist grievances to be addressed. See Timothy Larsen, *Friends of religious equality. Nonconformist politics in mid-Victorian England* (Woodbridge, 1999), pp. 53–7.

21 A royal commission sat from 1867 to 1870 to inquire into 'the varying interpretations put upon the rubrics, orders, and directions for regulating the course and conduct of public worship, the administration of the sacraments, and the other services contained in the Book of Common Prayer'. Increasing diversity of practice highlighted by ritualism was one reason for appointing the commission (see n. 16 above); another was discomfort with the rubric requiring the recitation of the Athanasian creed. Davidson and Benham, *Tait*, I, 409–13; II, 127–8.

22 A commission appointed on 16 May 1881 'to inquire into the constitution and working of the ecclesiastical courts'. *Record* (London), 18 May 1881. Archbishop Tait hoped that a reform of the ecclesiastical courts might produce a system commanding general acceptance and that this would diminish the controversy over ritualism. Davidson and Benham, *Tait*, II, 451–2. Machin, *Politics and the churches*, pp. 127–8, notes that the commission failed to agree on its recommendations and that none of its proposals reached the statute book.

23 See n. 15 above on the composition of the convocations.

Conferences exist. The clergy, at all events, will have the melancholy satisfaction of expressing their opinions in an organized and dignified manner. At present, many of them feel that practically they have no opportunity of discussing ecclesiastical measures which may be before Parliament. They are treated like children: they have to shut their eyes and open their mouths and eat whatever the House of Commons may please to send them. It is not in human nature to like this state of things. The clergy have their opinions, and they justly want to make them known. A well-managed Diocesan Conference supplies them with machinery by which their voice can be heard.

II. About the *constitution and composition of a Diocesan Conference* I think it necessary to say a few words. I do so the more readily, because the constitution we have provisionally adopted here differs considerably from that of most Dioceses in England and Wales. I wish to show that we have not adopted it without good reasons.

Speaking generally, there are only two ways in which a Diocesan Conference can be formed. It must either be a collective body or an elective body. Let me explain briefly what I mean by these terms.

An *elective* Diocesan Conference is formed by each rural deanery, or hundred, or district in a county, electing several clergymen and two or three laymen, to act as its representatives. These clerical and lay representatives, together with the Bishop and certain *ex-officio* clerical and lay members, compose the Diocesan Conference. This, I believe, is the constitution of the great majority of the Conferences in England and Wales.

A *collective* Diocesan Conference consists of all the Incumbents, or all the licensed clergy in a Diocese, together with one or two lay representatives from each parish, chosen by the *bonâ fide* Churchmen of the parish.[24] These clergymen and laymen, together with the Bishop and certain *ex-officio* and nominated clerical and lay members, compose the Conference. This is the constitution of the Conference which we are holding this day.

It will be evident at a glance to any reflecting person, that there is a wide difference between these two kinds of Conference. Which constitution is the best? Which is most likely to excite the interest, and receive the sympathy and co-operation of most English Churchmen? I shall offer a few remarks on this point.

24 The definition of '*bonâ fide* Churchmen' proved controversial as the Church of England developed national representative bodies at the end of the nineteenth and beginning of the twentieth centuries: should the electorate consist of the baptized, the confirmed, or the communicants? Compare n. 53 below, where a proposal to create elected parochial boards made no distinction between churchmen and nonconformists.

I say, then, that an *elective* Conference appears to be open to several very grave objections. I will not waste time by saying that it is a novelty, and quite unlike the ancient Diocesan Synods, which always included the whole of the clergy, and sometimes as many as seven laymen from each parish. (See Hook's Church Dictionary: article Synods).[25] The objections I have to state are purely practical.

(a) An *elective* Conference is unlikely to attach to itself the general feeling of the Diocese. At least three-fourths of the parishes will have no place or voice in its proceedings. A collective Conference, on the contrary, secures to each parish a connecting link of interest. When a parish knows that its own clerical and lay representatives are present at the Conference, it will care for the Conference proceedings.

(b) An *elective* Conference is very likely to increase party-spirit and division in a Diocese. The election of two or three representative men in each rural deanery, is pretty sure to divide the already divided clergy into two or three distinct parties. The best men, 'the men of light and leading,'[26] will not always be elected. The minority will always feel that its own opinions are not represented in the Conference, and will regard its proceedings with indifference.[27] A collective Conference excludes no clergyman, and enables every phase of opinion to have a place and a voice in the assembly.

The only objection I can see to a *collective* Conference is its enormous size and unwieldiness. This objection is certainly very grave, and in some huge undivided Dioceses it seems insuperable at present.[28] One thing, however, is clear to my mind. An elective Conference is likely to be wanting in the broad, liberal, popular, and democratic element which the spirit of the times imperatively demands. It is behind the age. It has an unhappy tendency to become narrow, exclusive, aristocratic, and oligarchical.[29] As such, it will never arrest the attention

25 *A church dictionary*, edited by Walter Farquhar Hook (1798–1875), vicar of Leeds and later dean of Chichester, was first published in 1842. Hook, a prominent high churchman, produced thirteen editions of the *Dictionary*; the fourteenth edition (London, 1887) was prepared by his son and son-in-law, Walter Hook and W. R. W. Stephens. The article on 'Synods' may be found in the eleventh edition (1871) at p. 741.

26 Edmund Burke, *Reflections on the revolution in France* (London, 1790; repr. Harmondsworth, 1982), p. 200.

27 Evangelicals regularly complained of under-representation in elective assemblies. See John Campbell Colquhoun, *Shall protestant churchmen take part in convocation and diocesan synods?* (London, 1869), pp. 9, 20. The case for abstention from Selwyn's Lichfield synod included the claim that evangelicals would be outnumbered and overruled. See, for example, *Record*, 17 Jul. 1868: J. N. Worford to editor.

28 Reflecting Ryle's experience in the diocese of Norwich. See the introduction.

29 This phrase, taken from Ryle's 1871 pamphlet, was quoted verbatim by Talbot Greaves in declining to attend Bishop Moberly's Salisbury synod in 1871. *Record*, 17 Nov. 1871.

or command the affection of the middle classes, of the farmers, tradesmen, and intelligent artisans. Whatever be the weight of the objection, however, it will not apply to the Diocese of Liverpool. With only 200 Incumbents and 140 Curates, I do not see that we could have adopted an elective constitution in our Diocese without making our clerical representatives a ridiculously small body. By the force of circumstances we seem compelled to adopt the Primitive system, and exclude no licensed clergyman. We meet as a Collective Conference, and I am glad of it.

III. The last general point to which I wish to invite your attention is *the action and operation of Diocesan Conferences*. This is a point of grave importance, and one about which many mistakes are made. Too much, I believe, is expected from these Conferences, and too much is sometimes attempted. I make, therefore, no excuse for offering two practical observations.

(a) For one thing, I trust we shall always, in this Diocese, endeavour to be, as far as possible, a business-like, and not a mere speech-making Conference. I am afraid, from all I can hear of proceedings in some quarters, that there is a most unhappy tendency in these Diocesan Conferences to degenerate, and to become nothing more than annual exhibitions of what the Americans call 'ad Buncombe' oratory[30] and ecclesiastical fireworks. There is much cry, but little wool; much talk, but little action; a plethora of saying, but a dearth of doing. The Conference once over, nothing is heard of it for a year. Now, I do hope that we shall not split on this rock. I hope we shall steadily avoid merely speculative subjects, and keep in view practical questions and business. I hope we shall be able to show annual proof that we do not meet together in vain, and can point to useful results. Unless we do so, our attendance will become small by degrees and beautifully less: we shall dwindle away into something like the notorious 'Rump Parliament' of the seventeenth century,[31] and become the laughing-stock of the Diocese. Mere talk, I am satisfied, will not keep us alive. There is enough and too much of talk in the present day. None know that better than the middle class lay representatives of our parishes, whose presence and regular attendance at a Conference it is most important to secure. They like business: they dislike mere talk. Their time is too precious to be wasted in hearing vague, wordy speeches, seeing wind-bags emptied, and looking at fireworks. If we want to live and make our mark, we must aim at doing business. Our annual Session of two days is very short, and we must not waste time in wordy debates about 'burning' questions. Common sense points out that, whatever our private opinions may be, there is no use in holding fierce

30 Empty clap-trap oratory. *OED*.

31 Remainder of the Long Parliament of 1640 after Pride's Purge of 1648 reduced the house of commons to fewer than sixty members.

controversial discussions about matters which we have no time to examine, and no authority to settle.

(b) For another thing, I trust we shall always avoid the faintest shadow of an appearance of dictating, or even seeming to dictate, to the Diocese, about open questions, which the law has left undecided. We have not the slightest power, it must be remembered, to enforce our opinions. We have no legal status. We are a mere voluntary association, called into existence by the circumstances of the age, but utterly destitute of authority. We may call the results of our proceedings 'Acts,' if we please, and make recommendations, and pass resolutions about matters affecting the Diocese. But after all, our Acts, recommendations, and resolutions are mere *brutum fulmen*,[32] and are not binding on any one who does not see matters with our eyes. If, for example, we passed resolutions recommending every clergyman in the Diocese to preach either in a surplice or in a black gown,[33] or every parish to support certain particular religious or missionary societies,[34] I am quite certain we should raise a storm, and set the whole Diocese by the ears. A Bishop's recommendations are one thing: they come from a commissioned officer of the Church, and justly demand some respect and attention. The recommendations of a Diocesan Conference are quite another thing: they simply express the opinion of a body of volunteers. There is ample store of subjects for us to handle of real practical importance, and I earnestly hope that we shall not step out of our province by getting on debatable ground.

The proper work of a Diocesan Conference is consultation, deliberation, expression of opinion by resolutions, gathering of information by committees to report, discussion, comparison of views, – and not action.

The moment a Diocesan Conference attempts to do anything which savours of direction or command, it is almost sure to do mischief. It will array class against class, parish against parish, clergymen against clergymen, deanery against deanery, diocese against diocese, from one end of the land to the other. There is nothing

32 Mere noise (*OED*, from Pliny, *bruta fulmina et vana* [*Nat. Hist.*, II, xliii]).

33 One of the early innovations of the ritualists was preaching in a surplice. Yates, *Anglican ritualism*, pp. 56–8. As the practice spread, deliberate adherence to the black gown in the pulpit became a badge of protestant loyalty, codified in the late 1890s in the rules of the Holdfast Union. *Record*, 23 Mar. 1900, p. 284: E. H. F. Cosens to editor.

34 Adherence to the Additional Curates' Society and the Society for the Propagation of the Gospel might indicate high church sympathies, whereas the Church Missionary Society and Church Pastoral Aid Society attracted the support of evangelicals. See also the introduction for comments on the tension between diocesan institutions and independent societies as rival models of supporting mission. Selwyn had spoken disparagingly in 1868 of the government of the church by party societies 'with lay presidents and irresponsible committees' (*Record*, 22 June 1868) and had promised instead a unified diocesan structure; Ryle spoke to the anxieties of evangelicals, used to working through societies and suspicious of overweening and unfriendly diocesan authority.

that a free Englishman dislikes so much as the very appearance of dictation from those who have no authority to dictate. The more trifling the 'recommendations,' the more likely he is to assert his independence, entrench himself behind his legal rights, and refuse compliance. Give him ideas to think over, if you like, but leave him to work out the ideas for himself.

After all, the success of a Diocesan Conference depends, humanly speaking, on the manner, and temper, and spirit, in which its members come together. If men attend its meetings with no heart in the business, in a careless, trifling frame of mind, unprepared alike to contribute anything or carry anything away, – if they come in their war paint, with their armour on and their bristles up, ready to quarrel with everything which is not hammered on their own anvil, and inwardly saying, like Goliath, 'Give me a man to fight with,'[35] – it would be strange indeed if their Diocesan Conference did not prove a dead failure. But if, on the other hand, we come in the spirit of love, courtesy, forbearance, patience, humility, and prayer, with a single eye to the glory of God, and the extension of His kingdom, – not expecting too much, willing to receive what is wise and true and good, from whatever quarter it may come, prepared to contribute what we can, if it be but a mite, or a lock of goat's hair,[36] – more ready to learn than to teach, swift to hear, slow to speak, prepared to hold out the right hand, and work during the Conference with any one in whom we see '*aliquid Christi*,'[37] – then I firmly believe we shall do good service to the cause of Christ, and the cause of the Church of England. Then the Diocesan Conference will be blessed and be a blessing. It will help to make our dear old Reformed Church of England 'fair as the moon, clear as the sun, and terrible as an army with banners.' (Cant. vi. 10.)[38]

(c) My third and last remark is that we must all watch against the tendency to a narrow-minded, isolated line of action, which so unhappily prevails in many quarters in the Church of England. To abstain from all public meetings in which we cannot have our own way, to retire from any assembly of Churchmen where we are likely to meet with any contradiction, to be incessantly finding fault with things around us, but never trying to amend them, all this may seem right to some minds. It admits of grave inquiry whether it is not selfishness, laziness, and cowardice, disguised under other names.

To come forward boldly on every opportunity, – to speak out decidedly but courteously for Christ's truth, fearing the face of no man, – to 'contend earnestly for the faith'[39] and the real doctrine of the Church of England, even if we stand

35 I Samuel xvii. 10.

36 Mite: Mark xii. 42; lock of goat's hair: perhaps an allusion to I Samuel xix. 13, where 'a pillow of goats' hair' disguises the absence of David.

37 'Somewhat of Christ.'

38 I.e. Song of Songs vi.10.

39 Jude 3.

alone, but to keep our temper at all times, – this, I believe firmly, is the bounden duty of every true Churchman in the present day. It may cost us much self-denial and exertion, – it may be a heavy cross to flesh and blood, – it may entail on us many painful collisions and much vexation of spirit; but it is the line of duty. If a man dislikes the Church of England, let him retire from it and join some other body of Christians. But if he remains in our communion, let him do all he can to strengthen and improve it.

To shut ourselves up in a corner, – to avoid the company of everyone who disagrees with us, – to allow the affairs of the Church to be managed by unsound men, and the helm to be left in untrustworthy hands,[40] – all this may seem to some very spiritual and very right. I cannot agree with them. If we want Diocesan Conferences to be really useful to the Church of England, we must come forward and labour incessantly to make them what they ought to be.

I now turn from the general subject of Diocesan Conferences to certain business matters affecting ourselves, about which I am anxious to take counsel with the clergy and leading laity of the Diocese. They are subjects which appear to me to demand immediate attention, and I want to elicit opinions about them at this Session of our proceedings.

(1) First in order, I wish to say a few words about the *constitution, rules, and regulations of the Liverpool Diocesan Conference*. Our present arrangements, you will understand, are provisional, and drawn up to meet the exigencies of our first meeting. The main subjects of our three sessions we were obliged to adopt and announce, in order to start the train of the first Conference. But are you prepared to receive and adopt our constitution and rules in their totality, or can they be improved? The crux, and knot, and straining point of all constitutions of Conferences is the composition of the Standing, or General Purposes, or Management Committee, for the preparation and arrangement of the business or agenda of each Conference. Some such Committee there must be. An assembly which only meets for two days in a year must study the utmost economy of time, and cannot allow its few hours to be wasted over frivolous or mischievous resolutions. A Committee to receive notices of motions and resolutions, with power to sift, accept or reject, and arrange the order in which they shall be brought forward, appears to me a positive necessity. Without it there can be no order or edification. Without it, I must plainly say I would not sanction the Conference, because I could not conscientiously preside. But such a Management Committee must be one that commands the confidence of the Diocese, and is free from the least suspicion of narrowness and partiality. If in this respect, or in any other, our constitution can be improved, by all means let it be improved. I only

40 One of Ryle's favourite metaphors for the church: see the introduction.

say, let it be thoroughly understood that the time has come when provisional arrangements must cease, and our rules be finally settled.

(2) The second, but far the most important, matter of business I want the Conference to take up is the *financial position of our Diocesan Institutions*. I am obliged to say, with pain, that at present their position is eminently unsatisfactory. They were launched, you will remember, under very favourable circumstances, at a great meeting at the Town Hall.[41] Their machinery, with much pains and honest labour, was carefully prepared and set up. But up to this time, I regret to say, they have not received anything like the pecuniary support they deserve, and might justly expect. The hands of the Committees of those most valuable agencies – the Church Aid,[42] the Church Building,[43] and the Church Education Societies[44] – are just now completely tied. They dare not make more grants, for want of funds.

Now, really, this state of things ought not to be, and certainly ought not to continue. To suppose that there is any want of money for charitable purposes in the West Derby Hundred,[45] and in the City of Liverpool, among churchmen, is simply ridiculous. A very wealthy layman in London, to whom I sent my recent Charges, wrote back to say, that if friends were not forthcoming, he thought my friends in other parts of England would be glad to contribute. I told him, in reply, that I should be perfectly ashamed to be a beggar on behalf of such a place as Liverpool, just as Ezra was ashamed to ask the Persian monarch for a guard, when he travelled from Babylon to Jerusalem. (Ezra viii. 22.) There is plenty of money in Liverpool, I believe, ready to be given for Church purposes, if we only knew how to get at it.

Now I will boldly ask my lay friends here present to help the Bishop of a new Diocese in this very important matter. Is it too much to suggest that a small committee of tried and proved laymen should be formed, who will undertake the onerous task of canvassing and asking for money? I have no faith in letters, and circulars, and pastorals; I believe they only fill the waste-paper basket. I want lay

41 On 22 April 1881. *Record*, 27 Apr. 1881.

42 The Liverpool Diocesan Church Aid Society, established to augment stipends and to support clergy and public worship in poor parishes and districts.

43 The Liverpool Diocesan Church Building Society, established to enlarge existing churches, to acquire sites for new churches and to build or hire mission rooms.

44 The Liverpool Diocesan Board of Education and School Society, responsible for the inspection of schools, making grants to improve schools and the maintenance of teacher-training colleges at Chester and Warrington.

45 The West Derby hundred was the administrative region covering south west Lancashire, including Liverpool, Wigan, Warrington, Prescot and Ormskirk. It stretched from Southport in the north to the Mersey estuary. A map of the hundred may be found in G. W. Oxley, 'The permanent poor in south west Lancashire under the old poor law', in *Liverpool and Merseyside. Essays in the economic and social history of the port and its hinterland*, ed. J. R. Harris (London, 1969), pp. 18–19.

helpers, who will ask men face to face for subscriptions and donations. This is not work that ought to be left to the clergy. The main part of their duty in this matter is to have annual collections in their churches for the Diocesan Institutions, and this duty I call on every Incumbent in the Diocese, without exception, to do. Ministers who are always serving tables, and going about scraping together subscriptions, are not in their right place,[46] and are doing work which ought to be done by the laity, as it is in America and Scotland.

I leave the subject here. I trust we shall have some practical suggestions about it from some of the valued and experienced lay churchmen whom I see to-day. We are really in a critical position, and, unless something is speedily done, our Diocesan Institutions will come to a dead standstill, and our valuable Diocesan Finance Association must be given up. We shall be the laughing-stock of all England. Men will say the Lancashire people were content to launch their Bishopric, and to stop there. They provided no means for enabling the Bishop to carry on the work of the new Diocese more vigorously than it was carried on before. Gentlemen of the laity, I do most sincerely hope that you will devise means by which this scandal may be prevented, and our Diocese may hold up its head before the world. If reason and common sense point out that no man would start the 'City of Rome' or 'Servia' for New York with only three days' coal on board,[47] it seems hardly fair to launch a new Diocese, and then expect a Bishop to work Diocesan machinery effectively without pecuniary support.

(3) The third Diocesan subject to which I wish to invite the attention of the Conference, arises out of the *census of morning Church attendance*, which has lately appeared in the *Liverpool Daily Post*. Into the general question of that census I shall not enter. Whether it be accurate or inaccurate, fair or unfair, – whether an evening census, or a census of the whole day, would not be a better test than one morning, – whether the thin attendance at some Churches is not quite capable of explanation, – whether Liverpool is a bit worse than other places, – all these are points which I am not going to discuss now.[48] What Liverpool wants is

46 Allusion to the response of the apostles when a dispute arose about financial matters in the Jerusalem church: the matter was delegated to other officers, because 'It is not reason that we should leave the word of God, and serve tables.' Acts vi. 2.

47 Steamers of the Inman and Cunard Lines respectively, both on the Liverpool-New York route.

48 The *Liverpool Daily Post* took a census of morning church attendance on 16 Oct. 1881, and the results were published the following day. The census showed a total church attendance of 63,576, 22,610 of whom attended seventy-one Church of England churches, occupying under one third of the available sittings. The newspaper commented that a survey of evening attendance would probably have produced better results for methodist and dissenting congregations. Ryle referred to the census in a sermon on 6 Nov., commenting that more people might attend evening services in a busy seaport and using the disappointing figures to urge the relocation of some buildings and the need for clergy gifted as evangelists and able to conduct 'a simple and hearty service'. The *Daily Post* conducted an evening census later in the month. *Liverpool Daily Post*, 17 Oct. 1881,

an organized system of aggressive evangelization,[49] by ministers working on the line of the London Diocesan Home Mission, and by a staff of voluntary lay helpers, which I believe might easily be organized. But what I do wish to press on the Conference is the positive necessity of pulling down some of our Churches near the Docks, and uniting the parishes to which they belong. The thing has been talked of long enough. The time has come for action. Warehouses, and docks, and offices, and railway stations have eaten up the dwellings of thousands in the last 50 years. Large Churches stand near the Docks with thin congregations, for the simple reason that there are no people to fill the seats. We want an Act of Parliament containing power, with full regard for the rights of patrons, incumbents, and parishioners, to pull down certain Liverpool Churches, and, out of the proceeds, to rebuild them elsewhere. As the thing has been done in London, in the City, so let it be done here.[50] We often say, 'Let us arise and build.'[51] For once let us say, 'Let us arise and pull down.' I hope the Conference will not separate without passing a resolution, requesting the Diocesan Church Building Society to form a small committee of picked men, to take up the subject, to collect information, and to make a report embodying the views they arrive at, and the suggestions they have to make.

(4) The fourth subject to which I wish to direct your attention is the desirableness of appointing a *small Parliamentary committee of vigilance*, to whom we may intrust the care of watching all measures brought into Parliament affecting the Church of England, about which it may be useful to convene a Conference, and express our opinions. There is hardly a Session now in which some bill is not introduced, either into the Upper or Lower Houses, involving momentous consequences to our Church, and demanding serious attention. I will instance three measures which cropped up last Session, and will probably crop up again: viz., Lord Stanhope's Patronage Bill,[52] Mr. Albert Grey's Parochial Boards Bill,[53] and Lord Beauchamp's Contumacious Offenders' Bill.[54] To these let me add

pp. 4–5; 8 Nov. 1881, p. 6; 15 Nov. 1881, pp. 4, 7.

49 On Ryle's commitment to 'aggressive evangelization', see the introduction and references there to Ian D. Farley, *J. C. Ryle. First bishop of Liverpool* (Carlisle, 2000).

50 The Union of Benefices Act (1860) provided a mechanism for the union of contiguous benefices in the metropolis (23 and 24 Vict., c. 142).

51 I Chronicles xxii.19.

52 A bill to limit and regulate the sale of advowsons and to prevent the sale of next presentations to benefices, introduced by the Hon. Edward Stanhope (1840–93), for whom see *DNB*. The traffic in livings alarmed reform-minded anglicans, like Stanhope, and offered a target to critics of the Church of England. Stanhope's bill was presented to the house of commons in two forms in 1881, both of which were withdrawn. Another attempt in 1882 also failed. Machin, *Politics and the churches*, pp. 143–4.

53 The Church Boards Bill (*Hansard*, 3rd series, 44 Vict. 1881, vol. cclx, cols 1297ff), like the Contumacious Offenders' Bill (see n. 54), sought a solution to the ritual controversy. Albert Grey (1851-1917), for whom see *DNB Twentieth Century*, proposed that the annual Easter vestry

Mr. Mundella's Code.[55] I say nothing whatever about the merits or demerits of these three measures, or of the Code. But I do think it would be of great advantage if the Conference would appoint a small committee of men, with eyes very open, and minds wide awake, who would undertake to watch ecclesiastical matters in Parliament, and report to our Standing Committee anything which appeared to demand the special notice of the Diocesan Conference. You can quite understand that something might easily turn up requiring an extraordinary meeting of the whole Conference, which the Bishop and Standing Committee should have power to convene.

(5) The fifth and last business which I feel it my duty to bring before the Conference is a rather difficult one, and requires careful consideration. We must decide whether we will or will not send *delegates to the Central Council of Diocesan Conferences*, which has lately been called into existence.[56] I believe, from what I hear, that many think it is a matter of course that we should send delegates, and that we do approve this Central Council. I am obliged to say plainly, that, to my eyes, our line of duty is by no means so clear as it seems to some, and I am anxious that we should 'do nothing rashly.'[57] Let us think before we commit ourselves.

(a) For one thing, I am struck with the fact that out of thirty Dioceses only fourteen were directly represented at the first meeting, on July 7th, 1881; and among those conspicuous by absence were Canterbury, York, London, Durham, Gloucester, Worcester, Salisbury, Exeter, Peterborough, Llandaff, St. David's, Norwich, Rochester, Oxford, and Hereford. Three or four of these Dioceses may have given in their adhesion since July. But I think a sufficient number stand outside to show the necessity of caution.

meeting could authorize the creation of an elected parochial board with a measure of jurisdiction over ritual. Such a board would be elected by the parishioners (including nonconformists), with the churchwardens as members *ex officio* and the incumbent as chair. Where the measure was in operation, recourse to the Public Worship Regulation Act (see n. 16 above) to settle disputes over ritual would not be permitted. The bill was withdrawn in June 1881.

54 A bill seeking to limit liability to imprisonment for refusal to recognize the jurisdiction of the ecclesiastical courts, introduced by Earl Beauchamp, friend of Canon Liddon and 'the ecclesiastical layman *par excellence*' (Chadwick, *Victorian church*, II, 365). The bill was prompted by the spectacle of ritualist clergymen serving prison sentences for defying the Public Worship Regulation Act (see n. 16 above). Although it passed the house of lords, it was counted out in the house of commons in August 1881. The problem of dealing with contumacious clerics without creating martyrs continued to vex bishops, militant protestants and the legislature: see Wellings, *Evangelicals embattled*, ch. 3.

55 Revised education code, introduced by A. J. Mundella, vice-president of the committee of council for education in Gladstone's 1880 administration.

56 See the introduction for discussion of the creation and aims of the central council.

57 Acts xix. 36.

(b) For another thing, I fail at present to see clearly what this Central Council is intended to do. I ask its advocates, and I get very different answers. Some tell us that it is meant to be an organized representation of Church opinion throughout the land. I believe a large number of Churchmen would deny its claim to be anything of the kind. Many sound Churchmen never touch a Diocesan Conference. Some tell us that it is meant to be a kind of head-centre of all Diocesan Conferences, and to advise, suggest, direct, and guide our provincial proceedings. Well, I think we are quite able to manage our own affairs. 'Italia fara per se.'[58] I am not particularly fond of so much centralization. Some tell me it is meant to provide a machinery by which the laity, who are now excluded from Convocation, may make their opinions on Church matters known. But if this is the object of the Central Council, I do not see what clerical delegates have got to do in it. Nor do I see why York Convocation is not to have an Auxiliary Lay Council as well as Canterbury. Nor is it quite certain that either Canterbury or York Convocation would pay any attention to anything the Council may say.

After all, we must remember that this 'Central Council' is an entirely voluntary institution. It has no legal standing, either by canon, statute, or charter. It has no power to enforce its dicta, and no Churchman is bound to attend to them. If it is weak, it will be ridiculous, and bring the Church into contempt. If it is strong, it will excite the jealousy of two integral parts of the British Constitution. Convocation, with all its defects, will not submit to be dictated to by a voluntary association. The House of Commons has a traditional dislike to anything like an ecclesiastical Parliament, and so long as we are an Established Church, will never tolerate even the semblance of an independent body which appears to interfere with its rights and duties. The House of Commons will never allow that it is not ready to help us, if we can only agree among ourselves. It was a shrewd remark of a nobleman in the South of England,[59] that if we did not mind what we were about, the proposed Council would be the first step to Disestablishment.

Such are my views of the Central Council question. I think it wiser to do as has been done in Canterbury and other Dioceses, to refer the matter to a committee, and to wait. I may be wrong and mistaken in my views. But I can only act according to my light, and what my light is you have heard.

Let me conclude all by apologizing for the length of this Address. But this is the first Conference we have held in this Diocese, and this is the first time I have

58 'Italy will look after itself.' Ascribed to the Piedmontese statesman Count Camillo Cavour (1810–61).

59 A note in the margin of the copy in the Bodleian Library identifies this nobleman as Anthony Ashley Cooper (1801–85), seventh earl of Shaftesbury, the most prominent evangelical layman of the period.

had the honour of presiding, and I must therefore ask you to excuse me, on the plea that I shall never do so again.

I pray that the Liverpool Conference may always have God's blessing on its proceedings, and that the spirit of wisdom, charity, and forbearance may pervade all our deliberations. In a world like this we must all 'think and let think.' Let everyone who speaks say what he thinks, by all means. But let us never forget that no two minds are exactly alike, or can view any subject exactly and precisely in the same light. Even St. Paul, and St. Peter, and St. James, and St. John were four different men, and each had his own idiosyncrasies. But they all agreed in loving one Master, and in spending and being spent for His sake. So may it be with us.

Index

Church of England Record Society

COUNCIL AND OFFICERS FOR THE YEAR 2003–2004

'The object of the Society shall be to advance knowledge of the history of the Church in England, and in particular of the Church of England, from the sixteenth century onwards, by the publication of editions or calendars of primary sources of information.'

Membership of the Church of England Record Society is open to all who are interested in the history of the Church of England. Enquiries should be addressed to the Executive Secretary, Miss Melanie Barber, at the above address.

PUBLICATIONS

1. Visitation Articles and Injunctions of the Early Stuart Church. Volume I. Ed. Kenneth Fincham (1994)
2. The Speculum of Archbishop Thomas Secker: The Diocese of Canterbury 1758–1768. Ed. Jeremy Gregory (1995)
3. The Early Letters of Bishop Richard Hurd 1739–1762. Ed. Sarah Brewer (1995)
4. Brethren in Adversity: Bishop George Bell, the Church of England and the Crisis of German Protestantism 1933–1939. Ed. Andrew Chandler (1997)
5. Visitation Articles and Injunctions of the Early Stuart Church. Volume II. Ed. Kenneth Fincham (1998)
6. The Anglican Canons 1529–1947. Ed. Gerald Bray (1998)
7. From Cranmer to Davidson. A Church of England Miscellany. Ed. Stephen Taylor (1999)
8. Tudor Church Reform. The Henrician Canons of 1534 and the *Reformatio Legum Ecclesiasticarum*. Ed. Gerald Bray (2000)
9. All Saints Sisters of the Poor. An Anglican Sisterhood in the Nineteenth Century. Ed. Susan Mumm (2001)
10. Conferences and Combination Lectures in the Elizabethan Church: Dedham and Bury St Edmunds, 1582–1590. Ed. Patrick Collinson, John Craig and Brett Usher (2003)
11. The Diary of Samuel Rogers, 1634–1638. Ed. Tom Webster and Kenneth Shipps (2004)
12. Evangelicalism in the Church of England c.1790–c.1890. Ed. Mark Smith and Stephen Taylor (2004)

Forthcoming Publications

Letters of the Marian Martyrs. Ed. Tom Freeman

The Parker Certificates. Ed. Ralph Houlbrooke and Helen Parish

The British Delegation and the Synod of Dort. Ed. Anthony Milton

The Unpublished Correspondence of Archbishop Laud. Ed. Kenneth Fincham

The Diary of John Bargrave, 1644–1645. Ed. Michael Brennan, Jas' Elsner and Judith Maltby

The 1669 Return of Nonconformist Conventicles. Ed. David Wykes

The Sermons of John Sharp. Ed. Françoise Deconinck-Brossard

The correspondence of Theophilus Lindsey. Ed. G.M. Ditchfield

The Papers of The Elland Society. Ed. John Walsh and Stephen Taylor

The Diary of an Oxford Parson: The Reverend John Hill, Vice-Principal of St Edmund Hall, Oxford, 1805–1808, 1820–1855. Ed. Grayson Carter

Anglo-Catholic Communicants' Guilds and Societies in the Late Nineteenth Century. Ed. Jeremy Morris

Suggestions for publications should be addressed to Dr Stephen Taylor, General Editor, Church of England Record Society, Department of History, University of Reading, Whiteknights, Reading RG6 2AA.